Soviet-East European Relations

Soviet-East European Relations

Consolidation and Conflict

Robert L. Hutchings

The University of Wisconsin Press

Published by

The University of Wisconsin Press
114 North Murray Street
Madison, Wisconsin 53715

The University of Wisconsin Press, Ltd.
1 Gower Street
London WC1E 6HA, England

Printings 1983, 1987

Printed in the United States of America

Library of Congress Cataloging in Publication Data
Hutchings, Robert L., 1946–
  Soviet-East European relations.
  Bibliography: pp. 289–302.
  Includes index.
  1. Europe, Eastern—Relations—Soviet Union.
2. Soviet Union—Relations—Europe, Eastern.
3. Europe, Eastern—Politics and government—1945–   .
4. Europe, Eastern—Economic conditions—1945–   .
I. Title.
DJK45.S65H87 1983   303.4'8247   83–47761
ISBN 0–299–09310–7
ISBN 0–299–09314–X (pbk.)

To
Jonathan

Contents

Figures

Tables

Preface to the Paperback Edition

Gorbachev and Eastern Europe

The image of a Soviet leader being greeted with genuine enthusiasm on the streets of Prague, as happened in April 1987, or of East Berlin youth shouting "Gorbachev" and "*glasnost*" in protests along the Berlin Wall, as they did two months later, would have been hard to conjure up a few years ago, when this book was first published. Under Mikhail Gorbachev, it was the Soviet leadership that represented a dynamic, fresh approach to the challenges of the day—in stark contrast to the gray gerontocracies in power in Eastern Europe. The winds of change were blowing from Moscow and Leningrad; Budapest had become the citadel of conservatism and caution.

After an initial period of domestic consolidation, Gorbachev launched a series of sweeping reform proposals under the rubrics of *glasnost* ("openness") and *perestroika* ("restructuring"), punctuated by such dramatic gestures as the release from exile of Nobel laureate Andrei Sakharov. In foreign policy, the new image and style of the Gorbachev leadership was followed by a steady stream of arms proposals that kept Western governments in a constantly defensive and reactive posture, particularly after the U.S.–Soviet minisummit in Reykjavik in the fall of 1986. Among West European publics, Gorbachev skillfully played on growing antinuclear and anti-American sentiment by stressing the common interests "we Europeans" share in promoting international peace. Even Britain's Prime Minister Thatcher found Gorbachev "a man I can do business with."

But for all his innovation at home and in relations with the West, Gorbachev's early approaches to Eastern Europe were tentative and conservative. He sought

---

The views expressed here are the author's. They do not necessarily reflect those of the United States Government.

closed ranks and improved coordination in foreign policy, stressed Leninist discipline in party policies, and largely followed the lead of his predecessors in intrabloc affairs. At least initially, changes in style did not yield changes in substance—reflecting, perhaps, the intractability of Eastern Europe's economic and political dilemmas.

The demonstration effect of Soviet internal changes, however, was profoundly unsettling, reminding many East European officials of Khrushchev's de-Stalinization campaign and the subsequent upheavals in Hungary and Poland in October 1956. *Glasnost*, which in the Soviet lexicon meant a carefully regulated ''openness'' designed to attack the Brezhnevite bureaucracy and infuse dynamism into the domestic economy, was viewed with particular alarm. For one thing, *glasnost* in the Hungarian, East German, or Czechoslovak contexts would certainly entail a far deeper process of public examination and would unleash potentially uncontrollable expectations for rapid change. For another, Gorbachev's assault on the mismanagement of the Brezhnev leadership in the Soviet Union could only be construed as a critique of the many Brezhnev era holdovers in Eastern Europe, who sought continuity and stability, not change and self-recrimination. Thus, *glasnost* had few adherents among the East European leaders, but it infused a new dynamic into incipient succession struggles, as various heirs presumptive sought to align themselves with Moscow to support their own ambitions.

In this way, the advent of the Gorbachev leadership in Moscow heightened uncertainties and created new divisions in Eastern Europe. More than that, it heralded the end of an era there and created a mix of hopes and fears that an entirely new era, already begun in the USSR, was about to be ushered in.

Eastern Europe in the 1980s

Poland aside, Eastern Europe in 1987 looked much the same as it did in 1980. Except for Poland's Jaruzelski, who became party first secretary in 1981, the same top party leaders were still in office, with two of them (Bulgaria's Zhivkov and Hungary's Kádár) into their fourth decade in power. Reform ideas were mooted but not implemented, leadership changes were rumored but not realized, and intrabloc relations were held largely in abeyance. But beneath the surface, economic, political, and social deterioration had become more acute, the sense of impending change more pronounced. With continued economic stagnation and imminent succession dilemmas, as well as the advent of an energetic and innovative new Soviet leader, the end of an era was clearly at hand.

Even in Poland, despite the many ups and downs of the internal scene after the imposition of martial law in December 1981, the fundamental impasse remained between the Jaruzelski regime and the population at large. The former had demonstrated its capacity to suppress but not to govern; its policies had succeeded in dividing and disorienting the opposition but not in "normalizing" the internal situation. And neither half-hearted reform attempts nor the good fortune of five successive abundant harvests had arrested the prolonged economic crisis.

As in the late 1970s, the Polish economic decline of the 1980s was but the most extreme variant of a more general pattern affecting all of Eastern Europe. Most obviously, the region-wide financial crisis of the early 1980s brought to an end a period of East-West economic détente. Trade with the West collapsed, new credits dried up, and the Soviet financial "umbrella" proved an illusion. By 1982, all the East European countries save Bulgaria and Czechoslovakia had been compelled to enter into extensive refinancing negotiations with Western creditors. Despite massive rescheduling, Poland's debt continued to escalate, as the Jaruzelski regime failed to repay even the interest on outstanding loans. At the other extreme, Ceauşescu's aversion to IMF (International Monetary Fund) conditionality prompted him to break off negotiations in 1983 and to begin liquidating Romania's foreign debt by draining the domestic economy. Elsewhere, the Hungarians and, outside the bloc, the Yugoslavs managed to avert bankruptcy only through periodic refinancing and short-term loans. Only the GDR (German Democratic Republic) buoyed by generous West German loans, managed to survive the financial squeeze and move toward a modest economic recovery.

Economic relations with the USSR fared little better. The price of Soviet oil deliveries to Eastern Europe reached a new peak in the early 1980s, as the five-year averaging mechanism belatedly reflected the full brunt of the 1978–79 increase in world oil prices. Beset with economic dilemmas of its own, the Soviet leadership cut oil deliveries by 10 percent and heightened pressure on the East Europeans for higher-quality goods in return. Thus, the double economic bind of the late 1970s had grown considerably more acute a decade later.

External economic pressures took a heavy toll on material living standards, with all that implied for political stability in the region. In Romania, shortages of energy supplies and basic foodstuffs reached critical proportions, triggering a series of isolated strikes and demonstrations and raising the prospect of a brushfire of popular unrest. Poland's downward economic spiral transformed the relative prosperity of the early 1970s into a dim memory and further undercut regime efforts toward "normalization." Elsewhere the decline was less catastrophic but still severe, and the dangers of economically-induced political crisis were rising steadily. More immediately, failure to deliver the promised improvements in material living standards—linchpin of the tacit social contract of the 1970s—had undermined political stability and deepened societal withdrawal and alienation. Even Hungary, once the showcase of socialist stability and prosperity, was experiencing a prolonged economic decline that threatened the very essence of Kadarism.

This prolonged period of economic stagnation had affected the East European economies in more fundamental ways. Sharply reduced investments had perpetuated the aging smokestack industries, further undermining East European competitiveness in world markets and contributing to the environmental devastation that had already made some parts of Eastern Europe virtually uninhabitable. And the failure to keep pace with the newly industrialized countries, much less with the advanced industrial democracies, in the scientific-technological revolution had further mortgaged Eastern Europe's economic future. By the mid-1980s, some Hungarian reform economists were arguing that closing the scientific-technological gap was critical to Hungary's national survival. They seemed to mean that literally.

Adding to Eastern Europe's decline in the 1980s was the stagnation and immobility of its aging party leaderships. In 1987, the average age of the six party first secretaries was well over 70, their average tenure in office more than two decades. Only General Jaruzelski, a relative youngster among these gerontocrats, and the GDR's Honecker, still spry at 75, seemed reasonably fit and energetic; the others were all in poor health, presiding over leaderships in manifest decline. In Czechoslovakia, virtually the entire post-1968 leadership remained in power, presided over (but not led) by the increasingly enfeebled Gustáv Husák. These were hardly the men to grapple with the difficult policy dilemmas of the late 1980s.

Political malaise in Eastern Europe had been accentuated by a prolonged period of drift in Moscow, stretching from the latter years of the Brezhnev era through the brief interregna of Yuri Andropov and Konstantin Chernenko. Not only did uncertainties in the Kremlin further complicate succession dilemmas in Eastern Europe; but the absence of clear and decisive Soviet leadership left the East European regimes largely to their own devices in coping with the challenges of the 1980s.

Under these conditions—economic stagnation, political malaise, and diminished Soviet authority—the natural proclivities of the several East European regimes were accentuated. The Prague regime's instinctive conservatism turned into obsessive orthodoxy; Ceauşescu's personality cult became a bizarre self-caricature; the GDR's cultivation of better relations with West Germany began to look like an exclusive inter-German "security partnership." As each regime sought to establish some new *modus vivendi* with a disillusioned populace, or at least some self-proclaimed *raison d'état,* their idiosyncrasies became more pronounced, their ideological affinity more ritualistic.

The process of ideological erosion, already evident to rulers and ruled alike, was greatly accelerated by the crushing of Solidarity and the imposition of martial law in Poland. If Solidarity had exposed the corruption and incompetence of People's Poland, the martial law regime of General Jaruzelski symbolized the coercive power underlying the entire Communist enterprise in Eastern Europe. The liquidation of the Prague Spring, the false promises of "goulash Communism," and then the crushing of the first authentic workers' movement in postwar Eastern Europe: all these had irretrievably undermined the ideological premises of Communist rule.

Within East European societies the processes of economic, political, and ideological degeneration prompted a kind of region-wide existential crisis, a search for alternate value structures and a collective identity. These phenomena, too disparate and abstract to define more precisely, entailed a growing conception of civil society distinct from—and, almost by definition, in opposition to—the ruling political systems. They were variously manifested in a broad-based religious revival, particularly among Catholics; the development of new forms of autonomous social activity, including pacifist and environmental movements; renewed interest among Czech and Hungarian intellectuals in a (highly idealized) "Central European" identity; and, above all, a resurgence of national consciousness throughout Eastern Europe.

In Hungary particularly, there was a tremendous revival of interest in Hungarian history (popularized by, among others, the rock opera *Istvan the King,* growing concern over the plight of Hungarian minorities in Romania and Slovakia, a resurgence of romantic-chauvinistic Populism in Hungarian dissident and writers' circles, and intense discussion of the role of small states in helping overcome the postwar division of Europe. In Bulgaria, the late Lyudmila Zhivkova, daughter of the party first secretary, tapped an unsuspected vein of nationalist sentiment in her glorification of Bulgarian history and culture during her brief tenure as culture minister. Underground publishing houses and independent social groups in Czechoslovakia, Poland, and even Romania similarly reflected this growing national resurgence.

The extent to which these sentiments motivated official policy is more difficult to pin down. Certainly there was a great deal of cooptation and manipulation: the Jaruzelski regime's appropriation of national symbols, Ceauşescu's extravagant self-glorification as the embodiment of Romania's historical achievements, and the Honecker regime's expropriation of Martin Luther, Frederick the Great, and others as "objectively progressive" precursors of the East German state. In other cases, official policy played on chauvinistic, exclusivist nationalism, as in Bulgaria's brutal assimilation campaign against its Turkish minority, Romanian reprisals against the Hungarian minority in Transylvania, and an ugly resurgence of anti-Semitism in Poland, Romania, and elsewhere. But even this sham nationalism reflected a new effort on the part of the East European regimes to tap the national theme as an agent of political legitimacy at the time of economic and political decline.

More worrying from Moscow's perspective was the growing tendency toward national self-assertiveness among its allies, particularly in the aftermath of INF (intermediate-range nuclear force) deployments in Western Europe in late 1983 and 1984. East European concern over the Soviet walkout from the Geneva disarmament talks and the threatened Soviet counter-deployments of tactical nuclear weapons in Eastern Europe betrayed deeper anxieties over the erosion of European détente. In response, the Kádár regime undertook a diplomatic offensive to shore up relations with Western governments, Ceauşescu refused to join the Soviet-led boycott of the 1984 summer Olympic games, and the East Germans expressed their determination to "limit the damage" to inter-German relations and announced that Honecker would visit West Germany in the fall of 1984. In the period leading up to Honecker's planned visit, these grievances gave rise to an unprecedented, semipublic display of Warsaw Pact disunity, with the Soviets and Czechoslovaks calling for a tougher line and closed ranks and the Hungarians, East Germans, and Romanians pressing for improved East-West relations and affirming the special role of small states in promoting détente. And while Honecker eventually succumbed to strong Soviet pressure in agreeing to postpone the visit, his open defiance up to the last moment revealed the depth of the dispute.

Beneath the immediate issues of contention was the more fundamental conflict over the extent to which the East European junior allies should be able to pursue their own interests in relations with the West. Thus various East European exponents of the "role of small states" presented what amounted to a repudiation of the Brezhnev Doctrine, asserting the primacy of the national interests of the East European states over their international obligations to the entire "socialist community." For most of the East European regimes, the preservation of European détente was no longer negotiable; it had become an essential ingredient of economic and political stability. More than that, it corresponded to rising pressures from below for national self-expression and self-assertion and, ultimately, for overcoming the Yalta division by affirming the "Europeanness" of the East European states.

Prompted also by continued economic and political erosion, these expressions of national self-assertiveness reflected a new attempt by the East European regimes to build some sort of *modus vivendi* with their growingly restive populations. Unlike the upheavals of 1956, 1968, and 1980–81, their efforts did not involve a frontal assault on Soviet primacy in the region but were aimed rather at achieving greater scope for diversity in the interest of political stability. And Moscow, having so recently faced in Poland a popular revolt of unprecedented dimensions, was now confronted with a new and more subtle set of challenges led by the East European regimes themselves.

The Gorbachev Phenomenon

Such was the East European situation that confronted Mikhail Gorbachev when he assumed power in early 1985. It is difficult to know just how he perceived Eastern Europe and how his perceptions differed from those of his predecessors, but it is evident that the assessment was an extension of his internal agenda in the USSR.

Clearly, Gorbachev proceeded from certain fundamental preconceptions: that economic failures had undermined Soviet power and prestige, that the scientific and technological revolution threatened to leave the socialist system behind and consign it to second-rank global status, and that radical restructuring was required to modernize the domestic economy and revitalize Soviet power. This latter aim demanded a carefully regulated campaign of *glasnost,* or openness, to overcome bureaucratic resistance and breathe new life into society at large. Externally, it required an easing of East-West tension, abatement of the debilitating arms race with the United States, and curtailment of some of Moscow's costly adventures in the Third World.

Gorbachev was also reacting against an ideological worldview in which Soviet interests were seen through the prism of rigid bipolar confrontation with the United States. This orientation, personified in such figures as Mikhail Suslov, Andrei Gromyko, and lesser lights like Boris Ponomarev, gave way to a more pragmatic pursuit of Soviet regional interests under Gorbachev's new foreign policy team headed by Eduard Shevardnadze, Alexander Yakovlev, and Anatoly Dobrynin. In relations with Western Europe and China particularly, Gorbachev saw new opportunities for improving the Soviet position through a more activist and innovative foreign policy.

As to Eastern Europe, Gorbachev probably did not have a fully developed conception of its problems and certainly lacked a clear and coherent plan of action. He viewed with obvious disdain the hidebound leaderships in Sofia and Prague, which epitomized the corruption, inefficiency, and dogmatism of Brezhnev's latter years. Improved economic performance was also a high priority—to transform Eastern Europe from a drain on Soviet resources to an asset in the Soviet modernization drive, as well as to diminish Western economic leverage in the region. And given his ambitious foreign policy program, Gorbachev also required greater discipline and coordination among the East Europeans. This, then, was Gorbachev's early agenda: to assure innovative party leaderships, improved economic performance, and closed ranks behind Soviet foreign policy initiatives. But how to go about it?

Gorbachev's first task was to reassert Soviet authority over Warsaw Pact foreign policy and end the ad-libbing that had characterized East European initiatives toward the West in the early 1980s. This he achieved through a series of Warsaw Pact summits—six in his first year—and the adoption of something approaching a conciliar system, whereby East European leaders were briefed before and after major Soviet policy initiatives. Evidently a compromise was struck in which the East Germans, Hungarians, and others were put on notice that future East European initiatives were to be carefully coordinated with Moscow but were also assured of a more forthcoming Soviet approach toward the West that would allow them greater room for maneuver.

This new Soviet approach was not long in coming, as Gorbachev returned his negotiators to the arms talks in Geneva and mounted a diplomatic offensive toward improved relations with the United States, Western Europe, China, and even Israel. These efforts also involved a much more active role for the East Europeans. Jaruzelski and Honecker paid early visits to China aimed at restoring normal inter-state and inter-Party relations, and several East European governments began exploring the prospects for normalizing relations with Israel.

Such deployment of the East Europeans in support of Soviet objectives was not without its risks. Most obviously, these initiatives threatened to evolve into separate East European interests in regions formerly off limits to them. And the abrupt and unexplained change of heart concerning two former ideological foes—especially China, whose policies had become more heretical than ever—must have shaken the foundations of party orthodoxy in Eastern Europe. (One can only imagine the labored justifications at Party gatherings in Prague or Sofia.) Indeed, Chinese overtures toward Eastern Europe seemed designed, in part, to sow discord in the Soviet camp.

In light of these dangers, it should not be surprising that Gorbachev laid great stress on coordination and discipline within Warsaw Pact councils. The renewal of the Pact itself was instructive. With its original term (twenty years plus an automatic ten-year extension) due to expire in May 1985, the Romanians and others had dropped hints that they favored certain changes to the text—a watering down of mutual defense obligations and more precise provisions for the Pact's eventual dissolution—and that they wanted only a ten-year renewal. In the event, the Pact was renewed for another twenty years without a single change; and Gorbachev, then only two months on the job, had achieved an impressive show of authority. Ceaușescu's acquiescence, by contrast, demonstrated his narrowing room for maneuver: not only had economic pressures forced him to turn increasingly to Soviet markets, but Soviet overtures toward China and Israel—two external pillars of Romania's independent-minded line—had undermined his maverick status within the Pact.

Another case in point concerned East German party leader Erich Honecker's plans to attend the West Berlin ceremonies commemorating Berlin's 750th anniversary in the spring of 1987. As in 1984, Honecker saw the visit to the "other" Germany as a symbol of his own diplomatic status and of the GDR's coming of age. Unlike the open polemics that surrounded Honecker's planned visit to West Germany in the fall of 1984, however, Soviet–East German differences were quietly resolved in the spring of 1987, with Honecker declining the West Berlin invitation but leaving open the possibility of a visit to West Germany later in the year.

The second major item on Gorbachev's agenda was to harness the East European economies to the Soviet modernization drive. Having run up large trade deficits with Moscow in the 1970s, the East Europeans were put on notice that the USSR expected more and better goods in return for Soviet energy deliveries. The heavily indebted Hungarians, Romanians, and Poles were enjoined to reduce their economic dependence on the West; the Bulgarian and Czechoslovak regimes were instructed to revive their stagnant economies and upgrade performance. And all were pressed to join the Soviet-led "Comprehensive Program for Scientific-Technical Cooperation through the year 2000"— "CEMA 2000," for short—through joint ventures and coordinated production in key high technology sectors. These measures seemed to herald a new era of economic imperialism—or perhaps a Gorbachev Corollary to the Brezhnev Doctrine, whereby the economic interests of the East European states were to be subordinated to the interests of the entire "socialist community" (as defined in Moscow).

The actual conduct of Soviet–East European economic relations in Gorbachev's first two years revealed less change than the early rhetoric seemed to promise. Trade figures for 1986 showed undiminished imbalances in Eastern Europe's favor; the Poles in particular continued to run up enormous deficits. Domestically, for all the lip service paid to "restructuring," there was scant evidence of any serious move toward economic reform. Survivors of many a prior Soviet campaign, the veteran East European leaders temporized, as yet unpersuaded of the staying power of the new Soviet leader.

The East Europeans were particularly wary of being drawn into Soviet-sponsored joint ventures in high technology areas, and resistance was evident in the elaboration of the CEMA 2000 program. Owing to its unique access to Western technology via "inner-German" trade, the GDR was the key East European participant; and the East Germans were as determined to protect their position as the Soviets were to exploit it. Elsewhere, the Hungarians, Romanians, and others were similarly reluctant to jeopardize their own carefully cultivated trade relations with the West in support of Gorbachev's domestic agenda. These differences came to a head in early November 1986, when the East European party leaders were summoned abruptly to Moscow—just two weeks after their prime ministers, meeting in Bucharest, had failed to reach agreement on the next stage of scientific-technological collaboration. Gorbachev's stratagem helped push forward the CEMA 2000 program, and it certainly demonstrated his dynamic, activist personal style; but it also revealed the determined obstructionism of the entrenched and cautious East European party leaders.

These frustrations pointed to Gorbachev's more basic dilemma: how to impart some of his own dynamism to Eastern Europe without first engineering a wholesale shake-up of the ossified party leaderships in Prague, Sofia, and elsewhere. Indeed, Gorbachev's early assaults on economic mismanagement, along with calculated snubs of several allied leaders, suggested that he was bent on securing the removal of Zhivkov, Husák, and perhaps Honecker from their top party posts in Bulgaria, Czechoslovakia, and the GDR. If such was his intent, Gorbachev apparently learned that it would be no easy task to unseat allied leaders enjoying solid support within their own bureaucracies. (Gorbachev's inability to secure the early ouster of Vladimir Shcherbitsky from his own politburo may have been instructive.)

Thus Gorbachev appeared to entertain second thoughts about imminent leadership successions in Eastern Europe. Given the longevity of most of the top party leaders, any direct Soviet manipulation of a succession struggle would entail great risks, particularly if it meant reaching down to the second levels of the party bureaucracies for a hand-picked successor. Even if Gorbachev were to identify among these cadres reasonable facsimiles of himself, they would probably lack the bureaucratic support needed to consolidate their rule. Such a surprise selection would provoke serious instability within the top leadership and generate dangerously high public pressure for rapid change. Conversely, to intervene only to choose from among the three or four most senior party officials, themselves creatures of the existing establishment, would hardly seem worth the attendant disruptions. To influence the succession processes indirectly and less abruptly would seem Moscow's safer course.

Gorbachev must also have figured that most of the East European leaders did not have long to go anyway and that he would be faced soon enough with the task of managing several successions, perhaps simultaneously. In most cases, this would involve not just the replacement of the top party leader but the overhaul of his entire politburo; the Soviet task was to assure that preferred, or at least acceptable, successors were named and that stability was preserved in the process. The Hungarian pre-succession of June 1987 seemed to fit that general pattern of gradualism, with Károly Grosz, one of the younger and more dynamic figures in the Hungarian leadership, taking over as prime minister, and Károly Németh, Kádár's lackluster party deputy, moving up to the honorific post of state president—thus clearing the path for the eventual successor to Kádár himself. (György Lázár, moved from the premiership to assume Németh's party post, had made his career as an economist in the state bureaucracy and hence did not appear a serious candidate to succeed Kádár.)

Whatever his motivations, Gorbachev's initial assaults on the party leaderships in Bulgaria, Czechoslovakia, and East Germany gave way to less direct efforts to shake up the ruling establishments by projecting reformist ideas and the example of his own domestic innovations. (Ceauşescu posed a different sort of problem, in that his firm grip over the Romanian leadership made it less amenable to Soviet influence.) These efforts also aimed at shifting the internal party debates in those countries toward the preferred Gorbachev agenda, and in so doing to alter the context (and perhaps accelerate the pace) of pre-succession maneuvering.

Even without direct Soviet calls for reform in Eastern Europe, the demonstration effect of Gorbachev's domestic departures proved profoundly unsettling. The very existence of a reform-minded Soviet leader, coupled with his critique of Brezhnev era mismanagement, served to undermine the authority and cohesion of the more orthodox East European regimes. More than that, the winds of change blowing from Moscow gave fresh impetus to reform sentiment and awakened popular hopes and expectations, as did Gorbachev's highly charged visits to several East European capitals.

Nowhere were these trends more evident than in Czechoslovakia, where political life became interesting again for the first time since the Prague Spring of 1968. The human rights group Charter 77 wrote to Gorbachev welcoming his reformist ideas; from abroad, Zdeněk Mlynář, advisor to Dubček during the Prague Spring, reminisced about his law school classmate Mikhail Gorbachev and proclaimed his policies a vindication of the Czechoslovak reform movement. There were even rumors that Dubček himself had corresponded with Gorbachev. And in February 1987, the long-anticipated trial of leaders of the dissident "Jazz Section" (of the Czech Musicians' Association) ended in a partial victory for the defendants: the sentences handed down were much lighter than expected, and the presiding judge felt constrained to embrace the spirit of *glasnost* by praising the Jazz Section's artistic contributions.

The seeming vindication of reformist and even dissident ideas sent shock waves through the Czechoslovak party leadership, precariously balanced since 1968 between a hard-line faction led by chief ideologist Vasil Bilak and a moderate reformist grouping around Prime Minister Lubomir Strougal. So great did the pressures become that Bilak issued a sharp attack in February 1987 against those who were attempting to use the Soviet reform debate to import "antisocialist" ideas into Czechoslovakia. Although Bilak stopped short of directly condemning the Soviet reform program, his message was clearly that such ideas had no place in Czechoslovakia. It amounted to a repudiation of Soviet authority and a direct challenge to Gorbachev himself.

Thus Gorbachev's planned visit to Prague in April 1987 emerged as a major test case of his East European policy. Several basic issues were in question. To what extent were the East European regimes obliged to emulate Soviet practices? How much diversity would Moscow permit in Eastern Europe? What were the limits of Soviet tolerance?

In practice, Gorbachev had already permitted a surprising degree of diversity and experimentation in Eastern Europe. General Jaruzelski, evidently with Soviet blessings, had consolidated a rather unorthodox form of party-military co-rule, moved toward granting the Catholic Church new legal status, and, most dramatically, released all Solidarity activists imprisoned since the imposition of martial law. In Hungary, dissident intellectuals and establishment reformists were mooting ever more radical proposals for political as well as economic reform. Yet, at the antireform end of the East European political spectrum, guardians of orthodoxy in Bulgaria, Czechoslovakia, and East Germany were resisting any move toward domestic change. These wide variations of approach raised another, more fundamental question concerning Soviet–East European relations: how many roads to socialism?

That these questions provoked controversy in the Kremlin is suggested by the last-minute postponement of Gorbachev's visit to Prague. (The ostensible reason for the delay, Gorbachev's sudden head cold, gave rise to the latest version of an old saw: "When Gorbachev sneezes, does Husák catch cold?") One can only assume that veteran East European hands in Moscow counselled Gorbachev that his policies threatened to undermine the stability of a reliable, albeit inefficient, allied state.

When he arrived in Prague a few days behind schedule, Gorbachev tried to perform a balancing act. Denying that the Soviet party claimed a "monopoly on truth" or a "special position in the socialist world," he affirmed the right of each party to seek its own solutions in light of specific national conditions. At the same time, though, he reminded the East Europeans that the USSR, the country "in which socialism was built," was pursuing policies that "correspond to the essence of socialism." In short, the East Europeans were free to craft their own approaches but not to ignore the Soviet reform drive. And Gorbachev's criticism of the economic mismanagement of the previous Soviet leadership could only be read as implicit criticism of the Brezhnev era holdovers in Eastern Europe as well. Perhaps more important, the atmospherics of the visit—Gorbachev's dramatic walking tour of Prague and the stark contrast between the dynamic Soviet leader and his Czechoslovak counterparts—left behind a palpable sense of impending change.

For many in Eastern Europe, Gorbachev represented fresh hope for the gradual transformation of their political systems toward greater efficiency, diversity, and openness. Certainly, Gorbachev's domestic innovations had far exceeded anyone's initial expectations; by the beginning of his third year in power, there was little doubt that he was bent on fundamental reform. (His chances of succeeding were of course another matter.) Gorbachev's vision for Eastern Europe was less coherent, but it seemed to sanction diversity and experimentation as the keys to dynamism and ultimately to greater unity. His agenda included a more limited and realistic set of goals than those of his predecessors, but more energetically pursued; and he projected a self-confidence that struck some as self-delusion in his ability to manage the process of change he had unleashed. If controlled diversity was his aim, how much diversity could be tolerated before control was threatened?

The very boldness of Gorbachev's vision dramatized some of the fundamental contradictions of Communist rule in Eastern Europe: how to legitimize systems that are widely regarded as alien, how to embrace nationalist aspirations while maintaining internationalist solidarity, how to open certain segments of political life while leaving others closed, and how to "restructure" the political and economic system without fundamentally altering it. For the Soviet leadership, the task was to make the East European states secure, stable, and free-standing while keeping them fully obedient client states. Squaring that circle has been the dilemma of every Soviet leader since Stalin.

Washington, D.C.   R. L. H.
July 1987

Preface

This book was written while events of the most dramatic sort were unfolding in Poland: the strikes of July and August 1980, the rise of Solidarity and its establishment on a legal footing, the convulsions within the ruling Party leading up to its 9th Congress, the halting efforts to build a dialogue between society at large (with Solidarity as its spokesman and the Church as its intercessor) and a regime too corrupted and enervated to respond, and the dashing of those hopes with the imposition of martial law in December 1981. No one who followed those events at close range could fail to grasp their significance for all of Eastern Europe or fail to appreciate the symbolic and practical impact of a powerful, well-organized workers' movement within (and against) a self-proclaimed workers' state. Mindful of the tremendous importance of the Polish social revolution, I have nonetheless resisted the temptation to rewrite the history of Eastern Europe as a prologue to August 1980. The Polish story will have to be written by others; the topic at hand offers scope enough for the present study.

The book concerns relations between the Soviet Union and its East European allies—Poland, East Germany, Czechoslovakia, Hungary, Romania, and Bulgaria—in the period 1968 to 1980. Part One traces the evolution of those relations, beginning with Khrushchev's efforts to reshape the legacy of the Stalinist interstate system (Chapter 1). In the wake of the 1968 invasion of Czechoslovakia, these efforts began anew, as the Soviet leaders sought to restore unity through a process of "normalization" (Chapter 2) and then, in protracted negotiations with their East European counterparts, to restructure alliance relations on a more flexible foundation (Chapter 3). Part Two explores the key dimensions of Soviet–East European relations in the 1970s: interstate and inter-Party relations at the highest levels (Chapter 4); political and military relations within the Warsaw Pact (Chapter 5); economic relations designed to promote "socialist integration," but operating within the context of severe economic deterioration (Chapter 6); and ideological and cultural affairs (Chapter 7). Despite vigorous Soviet efforts toward consolidation in Eastern Europe, as is argued in the Conclusion, the vision of a stable and secure Pax Sovietica remained in 1980 as elusive as ever, and Eastern Europe was entering what threatened to be a decade of instability.

I have incurred more than the usual number of debts in preparing this study. The first is to the many scholars who preceded me in related investigations and who are gratefully, if inadequately, acknowledged in the notes and bibliography. I should especially like to thank J. F. Brown—boss, mentor, friend— from whom I have drawn and freely usurped many useful insights. I have a particularly heavy obligation to the staff of Radio Free Europe, whose excellent and timely research reports proved invaluable in the early stages of the project and whose knowledge, friendship, and counsel proved more valuable still during its final stages.

Special thanks are due Professor Jan de Weydenthal, who stimulated my initial interest in the field and in this project in particular, and Professors Paul Shoup and Inis Claude, who saw the project through its earlier incarnation as a doctoral thesis. Thanks are also due many others who offered helpful advice along the way: Charles Andras, Jack Armitage, Mel Croan, Kevin Devlin, Lewis Feuer, Cam Hudson, Vladimir Kusin, and Bruce Porter should be specially mentioned. I am grateful to Margaret Rauch for her careful and patient typing of the manuscript and for providing, along with Maria Rerrich and Jim Brown, the most congenial and stimulating working environment one could ask for.

My greatest debts are to those who participated only indirectly in the project but whose support and encouragement made it possible. To my mother and father, I have a lifetime of debts which I can never repay but which I affectionately acknowledge. Although this seems a hopelessly inadequate place for it, let me also thank my wife, Kim, for the countless ways she has given love and support during this project and through so much more. Most of all, I am indebted to my son Jonathan, whose spirit, love, and courage will always be an inspiration. This book is for him—from both of us, with love.

Munich   R. L. H.
December 1982

Soviet-East European Relations

Introduction

Bounded by two dramatic turning points in postwar East European history, the period 1968 to 1980 was a critical era of transition in Soviet–East European relations. Just as Yugoslavia's defiance in 1948, Stalin's death in 1953, the Polish upheaval and Hungarian revolution in 1956, and China's open break with the Soviet camp in the early 1960s had defined earlier phases in the evolution of Soviet–East European relations, the invasion of Czechoslovakia in August 1968 and the advent of organized workers' opposition to Communist rule in Poland in August 1980 provide the boundaries of a period which irrevocably altered the political landscape of Eastern Europe.

At least two additional factors underscore the significance of the period 1968–1980. First, it coincided roughly with the "Brezhnev era" in Eastern Europe, whose full impact did not make itself felt until the crisis and subsequent intervention in Czechoslovakia and whose influence was already on the wane by the time of the portentous events of July and August 1980 in Poland. Second, the period was broadly coterminous with the era of East-West détente, a process set in motion in the late 1960s and formally enshrined at the Helsinki conference of 1975, but gradually eroded in the latter half of the 1970s by a series of reversals in East-West relations. For the Soviet and East European regimes, the process of détente helped legitimize the postwar division of Europe and offered attractive economic benefits, but it also brought with it new destabilizing tendencies in the form of greatly increased human and cultural relations between East and West. For the Brezhnev leadership in the USSR, therefore, the chief task of alliance management in the 1970s was to build and maintain a tight, integrated socialist community in an era of détente and expanded contacts with the West.

In the aftermath of the invasion of Czechoslovakia, the Soviet leaders and their more orthodox East European comrades moved decisively, if not always

1

successfully, to restore "unity and cohesion" in Eastern Europe through a coordinated integrationist program in every sphere of their mutual relations. Conducted under the banner of "socialist internationalism," these efforts were manifested in an ambitious drive toward economic integration, an expansion of the political role of the Warsaw Pact, a coordinated campaign toward ideological regeneration, and a proliferation of interstate and inter-Party contacts at every level. Closely related to these efforts were domestic strategies of economic growth, geared to the rapid development of trade relations with the West and designed to usher in a new era of prosperity and stability in Eastern Europe.

These broad strategies—détente with the West, integrationist efforts in Eastern Europe, and consumerist domestic policies—seemed vindicated for a time. East-West negotiations proceeded steadily, if not always smoothly, toward the thirty-five–nation Conference on Security and Cooperation in Europe in the summer of 1975, and East-West trade expanded rapidly in the early 1970s. Soviet–East European integrationist efforts proceeded apace, as new forums emerged and new agreements were signed to facilitate closer ties in political, military, economic, and ideological relations. Domestically, economic growth rates increased everywhere, and visible improvements in material living standards seemed to have bought a measure of political tranquility and stability.

All this began to change at mid-decade. Soaring energy costs and their attendant disruptions on the global economy had a profound, if belated, impact on the unreformed and inflexible East European economies, and the highly touted integrationist schemes of the early 1970s proved largely irrelevant to the pressing economic dilemmas of the day. Confronted with rapidly rising prices for Soviet oil deliveries and Western finished products but finding it increasingly difficult to find Western markets for East European exports, the East European states managed to defer economic disaster only by running up enormous debts on Western financial markets. By decade's end, economic deterioration was evident everywhere in Eastern Europe: balance of payments problems were acute, debt burdens huge and growing, and economic growth rates sharply down throughout the region.

The détente euphoria of the early 1970s, meanwhile, had given way to a decided chill in East-West relations, particularly after the Soviet invasion and subsequent occupation of Afghanistan. In the latter half of the decade, Soviet and East European diplomacy was geared to preserving what was left of European détente while coping with its ambiguous legacy. Trade with the West had proved to be a double-edged sword, as the East European states found themselves hostage not only to Western lenders but also to the bankruptcy of their economic strategies for the 1970s. Economic deterioration, in turn, fueled social discontent; and the "spirit of Helsinki" had contributed to the rise of small but vocal human rights groups throughout the region. Nowhere were these trends more evident than in Poland, where the combination of disastrous economic policy and relatively benign social climate, *inter alia,* provided fertile ground for the development of organized workers' opposition to Communist rule.

Although developments in Poland quickly acquired a very distinctive life of their own, they also were symptomatic of a more general malady affecting all the countries of Eastern Europe. Severe economic deterioration and mounting social discontent were matched only by the manifest unwillingness or inability of the East European regimes—with the partial exception of the Hungarian—to fashion new policies or develop new political vision to deal with much altered circumstances. Thus, by 1980, the integrationist efforts of a few years earlier were in considerable disarray, and Eastern Europe was entering what threatened to be a decade of instability.

Soviet–East European Relations in Theoretical Perspective

Before turning to the substance of Soviet–East European relations, it may be useful to place them in a certain theoretical perspective and briefly examine some relevant theoretical propositions concerning blocs, alliances, and other international systems. Given the considerable attention paid by Soviet and East European ideologists to "socialist integration," it may also be useful to review the ways theorists in the West and the East have assessed integration processes in Eastern Europe.

The term "Soviet bloc" has fallen out of vogue among analysts of East European affairs, largely on the grounds that it suggests a monolithic and immutable pattern of relations, that it carries with it the rhetorical baggage of the Cold War era, or that it has become muddled by the advent of new Soviet friends and allies beyond Europe. As the term occasionally appears in the present study, it may be in order to note that there is some justification—beyond one writer's acknowledgment that the term is "commendably short and undeniably handy"[1]—for retaining the "bloc" concept in the study of the Soviet–East European alliance system.

Although the term is unquestionably vague, a bloc does have certain generally accepted characteristics which may be gleaned from the theoretical literature on alliances and coalitions. In contrast with an alliance, a bloc is of relatively long duration, is cemented by a common ideology, expresses a congruent foreign policy orientation of its member states, and acts as a single entity in international relations.[2] Since it would be untenable to suggest that Romania, as the most obvious example, totally subordinates its international political activity to a unified "bloc" policy, it should quickly be added that congruence does not imply uniformity and that a bloc need not act as a single entity on all issues at all times.

Beyond these general criteria, three principal characteristics distinguish the Soviet bloc from other alliance systems, regional groupings, or security communities. First, whereas an "alliance" in the traditional understanding of the term is formed primarily to counter an external threat, the Soviet bloc is essentially an inward-looking association of states. In this regard, one Western analyst has termed it an "entangling alliance, . . . the central uses of [which] are internal; to contain, to police, and to maintain stability."[3] Brought on the wings of the Red Army in the aftermath of World War II, the bloc was created not only to provide a buffer zone between the Soviet Motherland and the center of "aggressive imperialism" but to facilitate the remolding of the entire region in the Soviet image.

The task of carrying out this remolding, or "Sovietization," fell on East European leaders installed by the Soviet Union and dependent on Soviet support for their political, even their physical, existence. Although some measure of legitimacy may have accrued to them by virtue of longevity, the East European regimes remain fundamentally lacking in popular support, dependent on their ties with the Soviet Union and the other "fraternal states" for their political security. For these reasons, the East European leaders—even Romania's Ceauşescu—require the continued cohesion of the Soviet bloc for the stability, indeed the very existence, of their regimes.

Closely related to this first characteristic is a second distinguishing feature of the Soviet bloc: its high degree of "vertical integration,"[4] or uniformity of internal structure of its members. As General Secretary Brezhnev tirelessly repeated in characterizing relations among the countries of the "socialist commonwealth": "We have an economic foundation of the same type—the social ownership of the means of production. We have similar state systems. . . . We have a single ideology—Marxism-Leninism. We have common interests in . . . defending the revolutionary gains from the encroachments of the imperialists. We have a single great aim—communism."[5] For regimes claiming to rule on the basis of universally applicable historical imperatives, such considerations can acquire very direct relevance. Deviation from accepted patterns of domestic rule, as the Czechoslovak reformers of 1968 discovered, generates fears of ideological erosion and political "spillover" elsewhere in the region. As the "Brezhnev Doctrine" has made clear, moreover, the socialist regimes consider it not only their right but their "internationalist duty" to intervene in the internal affairs of any allied state to insure that the Communist party's "leading role" is preserved and political stability maintained.

Thus, considerations of regime security in Eastern Europe demand not only the "unity and cohesion" of the alliance but, within limits which are vaguely formulated and subject to change, the uniform development of its member states. Nor can these two requirements be separated, for the preservation of existing patterns of Soviet influence and the pursuit of Soviet-led integrationist policies in political, military, and especially economic affairs demand a certain amount of symmetry, or "vertical integration," in the alliance system.

A final distinguishing characteristic of the Soviet bloc is the degree of hegemonic control exercised by the alliance leader. While it is clear that the East European states can no longer be seen as fully compliant satellite states, neither can they be considered partners in a classical alliance of equals. It is on these grounds that Mackintosh has argued that the Warsaw Pact cannot be considered a true alliance and that Johnson has termed it a "quasi-alliance."[6] Similarly, Zimmerman has termed the Soviet Union the "regional hegemon" of the "hierarchical regional system of Eastern Europe." One of the characteristics of such a system, he argued, is that the regional hegemon acts so as to make clear the boundaries of the system, while the junior members of the system attempt to loosen those boundaries in order to pursue divergent national policy goals.[7]

As the foregoing discussion suggests, one of the difficulties in applying theoretical constructs to the Soviet–East European relationship is that the latter is in many respects *sui generis*. Encumbered by the political and ideological aspirations by which the regimes legitimize their rule and intimately tied to matters of domestic policy, the so-called "socialist commonwealth" embraces virtually every dimension of economic, political, military, ideological, and cultural relations among its member countries. Its collective "behavior" therefore frequently deviates from assumptions derived from alliance theory and, in fact, calls into question the relevance of that theory to an understanding of Soviet–East European relations.

Similar difficulties attend the application of Western integration theories to Eastern Europe. Most analysts of general integration theory have dealt only incidentally with Eastern Europe, and their efforts have suffered from excessive reliance on assumptions derived from integration processes in the European Community. In attempting to transfer these theoretical propositions to Eastern Europe, consequently, Western integration theorists tend to postulate a pluralistic "state of nature" in the "pre-integration" period and then examine possible paths toward some final, "integrated" state. The Soviet bloc, however, was in a sense fully integrated from the very beginning. In the immediate postwar period, the East European states fell under Soviet economic control, and their armed forces were required to adopt Soviet military doctrine, regulations, equipment, and even uniform styles. Soviet authority during this early period was unchallenged on matters of foreign policy, ideology, and the tasks of "socialist construction" in the region. Inevitably, as the East European states gained power and influence and began to assert themselves on issues affecting their mutual relations, the hierarchical system imposed under Stalin was transformed into a more collectivist, participatory pattern of relations. Neither integration nor disintegration, this transformation involved a more subtle process of mutual adjustment, a process which Western integration theories are ill-equipped to explain.

The specific difficulties attending application of various integration theories, chiefly economic, to Eastern Europe have been ably reviewed by Andrzej Korbonski and Roger Kanet and need not be reiterated here.[8] It can be said, however, that the liabilities inherent in applying theories derived from the West European experience, as well as what Michael Gehlen has termed the "contrivances" of Soviet and East European leaders to promote an "artificial" integration,[9] have proved severe obstacles to any systematic analysis of the process of integration in Eastern Europe.

Indeed, Gehlen's arguments touch on what may be the most serious difficulty in analyzing integration in Eastern Europe: namely, that spontaneous, voluntary integrative activity among free and independent states is excluded by the very nature of the system. Efforts toward integration in the region have been almost entirely "contrivances" designed to preserve or extend Soviet influence in Eastern Europe, and independent East European initiatives have been regularly subsumed within broader integrative schemes susceptible to Soviet control. Given the disparity in size and power of the participants, the logical outcome of Soviet-style integration could only be the eventual assimilation of the East European states into a Soviet-dominated confederation, a state of affairs to which not even the most orthodox East European leaders could willingly submit. Conversely, the Soviet leaders are unwilling to countenance "genuine" integration—that is, integration among free and equal partners—for fear of losing their grip on important levers of control in the region. Underlying the entire process, moreover, is coercion, for it is Soviet military power, or the threat of its application, which provides the ultimate guarantee of regime security in Eastern Europe, establishes the scope of domestic innovation in the region, and dictates the limits of change in Soviet–East European relations.

All this is not to say that nothing has changed in Soviet–East European relations; indeed, a fundamental feature of their evolution, particularly since 1968, has been the restructuring and partial pluralization of relations between the Soviet Union and its East European allies. Nor is it to suggest that the concept of integration is irrelevant to our purpose, for Soviet alliance management in the 1970s very clearly involved an ambitious integrationist policy designed to replace the dysfunctional control devices of the past with an intricate web of multilateral forums and organizations acceptable to the East Europeans yet amenable to Soviet control.

In Soviet theoretical literature, "socialist integration" is seen as both a means and an end. As a means, it is seen as a process designed to upgrade the domestic economies, enhance military efficiency and security, promote alliance unity, and serve a variety of lesser goals; as an end, it is held to be the eventual economic, military, political, cultural, and territorial union of the countries of the "socialist commonwealth." According to Soviet theorists, this union, or "merger" (*sliianie*), will follow a lengthy period of "drawing together" (*sblizhenie*), a process which will proceed in accordance not only with the anticipated "withering away" of national boundaries on a global scale, but with the more specific process of unification followed in the multinational Soviet state. On the basis of Lenin's "principles of relations between peoples within multinational Russia," for example, it is argued that "the merging of socialist nations to form a 'single world cooperative' is the ultimate aim of socialist economic integration."[10] In the context of Lenin's urging for a "voluntary union of nations," another Soviet analyst saw the Warsaw Pact as the instrument for the "creation of a multi-faceted military-political union"[11] of the member countries. Cultural integration, too, is seen as a merger of the various national cultures into a "new culture," which will be, in terms commonly associated with Stalin's policy toward the national minorities in the USSR, "socialist in content and national in form."[12]

There is a great deal of ritualism in all this, of course, attributable to the internationalist imperatives of the doctrine to which the Soviet leaders subscribe; and it would be fruitless to exert much effort contemplating the prospects for or possible dimensions of a socialist megastate embracing all of Eastern Europe. In practical terms, efforts toward socialist integration have been aimed at the more limited objectives of foreign policy coordination, political and military consolidation through the Warsaw Pact, expanded economic cooperation, and more extensive ties in ideological and inter-Party affairs. Described more generally by one Soviet commentator as "the creation of thousands of unbreakable bonds,"[13] Soviet-led integrationist efforts have aimed at closer alliance unity through the formation of a system of consultation so pervasive and an interdependence so thorough that independent action on the part of the East Europeans would be severely circumscribed.

"Socialist Internationalism": Theory and Practice

The current stage in Soviet–East European relations is linked in Soviet and East European theoretical literature to "socialist internationalism" and "international relations of a new type," terms which gained currency in the early years of the Khrushchev era.[14] Since 1968, however, the terms have received increased attention, and the putative new forms of interstate relations have been the subject of considerable ideological interpretation and justification.[15]

The fundamental principle governing relations among the socialist states is to be found in "proletarian internationalism," a call to action issued most forcefully in the final line of *The Communist Manifesto*: "Working men of all countries, unite!" It is based on the presumed class solidarity of the international proletariat and is held to govern relations among the socialist and workers' movements and, in its Leninist variant, national liberation movements as well.[16] "Socialist internationalism," in turn, refers to a new, higher stage of proletarian internationalism—that which exists between the socialist states—and was first applied to relations among the so-called "socialist nations" which constitute the multinational Union of Soviet Socialist Republics.[17] Just as proletarian internationalism postulates an inevitable "drawing together" of workers everywhere, socialist internationalism holds that the drawing together of socialist states is an "objective law" derived from the sharpening of the class struggle on an international scale.[18] The nature of this process has been concisely stated by one Soviet theorist:

> Proletarian internationalism constitutes a basic principle of the ideology of Marxism-Leninism and of the policies of the communist parties. . . . In the course of creating and consolidating the multinational Soviet state, building socialism and communism in the USSR and in the process of socialist construction in the fraternal countries, for the first time it became the foundation for the development of *inter-state relations of a new, socialist type*. Under socialism, the social base of proletarian internationalism has immeasurably been extended, and now has become the state policy of socialist countries. . . . Thus, *socialist internationalism* has become the chief principle of relations among the fraternal countries.[19]

Like proletarian internationalism, socialist internationalism is held to be a transitional stage toward the realization of Communism on a global scale, justified as being "the most acceptable and objectively inevitable form of combining national and international interests, of materially preparing for their fusion in [the] future."[20] During this transitional stage, it is argued, relations among the "fraternal countries" will be governed by the principles of mutual assistance, voluntary participation, respect for state sovereignty and independence, complete equality, noninterference in internal affairs, and international solidarity.[21] The essence of socialist internationalism, however, is held to be the dialectical "blending" of national and international interests among the socialist countries: while specific, national interests persist during the current stage of development, a number of "objective tendencies" are said to be at work ensuring the increased convergence of specific interests with the general class interests of the "international proletariat."[22]

Since 1968, the theory and practice of socialist internationalism, particularly as regards the "class understanding" of sovereignty, have undergone a significant transformation. The Brezhnev Doctrine and related theses supporting the notion of "limited sovereignty" will be discussed at some length below and need only be outlined here.[23] By invading Czechoslovakia and subsequently defending the action as an expression of their "internationalist duty" to protect the "historic gains" of socialism, the Soviet Union and its supporters decisively tilted both the theory and the practice of socialist internationalism away from emphasis on the nationally specific interests of socialist states and toward the more general "class" and "internationalist" interests of the entire socialist community.

Just as Rousseau defined freedom as the consequence of bringing one's "particular will" into conformity with the "general will" of society, and just as Hegel sought the dialectical unification of the particular and the universal, socialist states are enjoined to subordinate their specific, national interests to the overarching interests of the socialist community. The Hungarians, who are better acquainted than most with the consequences of clashing interests in the socialist world, have put the matter plainly: "Our point of departure in our international policy is that only that which is good for our friends and allies can be good for us. . . . [We] subordinate our particular interest to the totality of interests when [any] divergence prevails because we are convinced that thus we are acting in the true interests of our people as well."[24]

In contemporary theoretical elaborations, socialist internationalism is still held to embrace the familiar "principles" of relations among the socialist countries: complete equality, mutual benefit, noninterference in internal affairs, and respect for state sovereignty and independence. Now, however, all these "rights" are listed after the cardinal set of "duties" governing socialist international relations: "internationalist solidarity, unity and cohesion on the basis of Marxism-Leninism, comradely mutual assistance and support in the building of socialism and communism."[25] These theoretical constructs reflected in part a very real transformation in Soviet–East European relations after 1968—away from domestic innovation in pursuit of regime viability and toward "unity and cohesion" through a comprehensive integrationist program.[26] Conducted under the rubric of socialist internationalism and manifested in heightened efforts toward economic integration, political and military consolidation in the Warsaw Pact, and multilateral action in the realms of ideology and inter-Party affairs, the "new type" of relations which developed in the period 1968 to 1980 constituted a distinctively new phase in intrabloc relations in Eastern Europe.

Between 1948 and 1968, four general periods, characterized by alternations between unity and diversity in the Soviet–East European relations, can be outlined. The period from 1948 to 1953 was one of almost monolithic unity, in which the newly installed "People's Democracies" followed with few deviations the prescribed Soviet line in foreign and domestic policies. Stalin's death in 1953 ushered in a period of diversity and instability, characteristics which were manifested dramatically in the Hungarian and Polish "Octobers" of 1956. With the consolidation of the Khrushchev regime in 1957, the Soviet leaders initiated a new phase in bloc relations, designed to restore orthodoxy and achieve cohesion through the recently created Warsaw Pact and an invigorated Council for Mutual Economic Assistance (CMEA). Beginning in 1962, however, several developments—the eruption of the Sino-Soviet conflict, the debate over economic reform in the USSR and Eastern Europe, and a new wave of attacks on Stalinism—served to upset the fragile unity of the previous period and introduce a new period of drift and disarray in Eastern Europe.

By the mid-1960s, forces were already at work which would initiate a new drive toward cohesion in Eastern Europe. Not only had the pace of domestic innovation in Eastern Europe begun to exceed limits deemed acceptable by the Soviet leaders and their more orthodox East European comrades, but the development of more extensive relations with the West, accelerated by the 1966 Bucharest proposal for the convening of a pan-European security conference, threatened to introduce new destabilizing tendencies into Soviet–East European relations. Before any piecemeal efforts toward restructuring bloc relations could be attempted, however, the crisis and subsequent intervention in Czechoslovakia in 1968 served to force the hands of bloc leaders and demand the swift implementation of a new drive toward "unity and cohesion" in the region.

Neither a radical break with the past nor merely a perpetuation of its legacy, the integrationist drive undertaken in the wake of the Czechoslovak invasion represented an adaptation of old objectives and patterns of behavior to altered circumstances. Of necessity, this drive involved not simply a reimposition of the rigid control of the Stalin era but an interrelated set of measures designed to restore unity, cohesion, and stability in Eastern Europe. The first and most immediate of these was postinvasion "normalization," a Soviet-led drive to restore firm Party control and pro-Soviet fidelity in Czechoslovakia, strengthen Soviet control throughout Eastern Europe, reassert Soviet primacy in the world Communist movement, and regain the initiative in East-West relations.

Normalization, in turn, evolved into a broader effort to restore Soviet authority in Eastern Europe and arrest the drift and disarray that had characterized Soviet–East European relations in the mid-1960s. For the East Europeans, this effort demanded the reinstitution of domestic orthodoxy and eschewal of officially sanctioned reformism in economic and social policy. The liquidation of the Prague Spring had foreclosed the possibility of fundamental reform from within the system; after 1968 domestic orthodoxy and ideological retrenchment were the orders of the day. (The fact that the Hungarians were able to continue along a cautious reform course must be seen in the context of several exceptional factors: the personal authority of Hungarian Party leader János Kádár, Hungary's domestic stability and unswerving allegiance in foreign policy, and the sense of public self-restraint engendered by the collective national memory of 1956, among others.)

Soviet insistence on domestic orthodoxy in Eastern Europe was paralleled by a certain flexibility at the interstate level, as the Soviet leaders undertook to restructure intrabloc relations by replacing some of the dysfunctional control devices of the past with a more collectivist and participatory, though still Soviet-dominated, pattern of relations. This aim, part of an evolutionary process of system-building which may be traced to the early years of the Khrushchev era, was given new impetus after 1968 in Soviet efforts to create new forums and organizations for multilateral cooperation in ideological and interparty affairs, facilitate economic cooperation through a strengthening of Comecon's infrastructure and rules of procedure, and upgrade the Warsaw Pact as an instrument of foreign policy consultation.

This latter effort was closely related to another prime Soviet objective—the welding of a coordinated Warsaw Pact *Westpolitik* for the 1970s, aimed at maximizing the political and economic benefits of détente while minimizing the potentially destabilizing tendencies inherent in increased human and cultural contacts between East and West. In the early 1970s, Soviet and East European diplomacy was geared toward forging a common Warsaw Pact position in the East-West negotiations which culminated in the 1975 Helsinki conference; in the latter half of the decade, it was aimed at keeping détente alive in the face of growing misgivings in the West over Soviet military capabilities and intentions.

At the beginning of the 1970s, the prospects of greatly expanded trade with the West, as well as the expected impact of the global economic boom of the late 1960s, induced the Soviet and East European regimes to embark on ambitious, import-led economic growth strategies. Trade with the West was seen as the motor of sustained economic progress in Eastern Europe; by employing Western technology and credits, the Soviet and East European leaders hoped to modernize and invigorate the domestic economies without treading the perilous path of systemic reform. The optimism surrounding these strategies, in turn, encouraged the Soviet and East European regimes to adopt explicitly consumerist domestic policies, verging on a new "social contract," which sought to secure political stability and popular acquiescence in return for steady improvements in material living standards.

Thus détente, East-West trade, domestic retrenchment, and consumer-oriented economic policies were interlocking parts of an overall strategy designed to restore unity and cohesion in Eastern Europe after the trauma of Czechoslovakia. These elements were to be held together, moreover, by an intensive, Soviet-led drive toward "socialist integration" through Comecon's "Comprehensive Program" of economic integration, an expansion of the political role of the Warsaw Pact, a coordinated, bloc-wide ideological campaign, and a proliferation of interstate and interparty relations at every level.

These combined measures yielded an impressive consolidation of Soviet–East European relations in the early 1970s, as the Warsaw Pact forged a coordinated Westpolitik to deal with the exigencies of East-West détente, integrationist efforts in Eastern Europe produced renewed unity and cohesion, and domestic orthodoxy *cum* consumerism brought a measure of stability and quiescence. By decade's end, however, efforts toward consolidation had been eroded by new political conflicts: between East and West, over the meaning and achievements of détente; between the Soviet Union and its East European allies, especially with regard to the manifest failure of their economic strategies for the 1970s; and within the East European states, as the fundamental political conflict—between rulers and ruled—awakened in dramatic form to challenge Party rule in Poland and threaten the entire interstate system in Eastern Europe.

PART ONE

The Soviet Bloc in Evolution

1

From Budapest to Prague: The Soviet Bloc, 1956–1968

The tragic Soviet invasion of Hungary in October 1956 and the virtually bloodless but no less traumatic Warsaw Pact invasion of Czechoslovakia in August 1968 provide the dramatic boundaries of the formative period of the Soviet–East European alliance system. Before 1956, an alliance system in the region can scarcely be said to have existed at all, for formal interstate relations were eschewed in favor of direct Soviet control through ''advisors'' to the new People's Democracies and a system of party and police rule thoroughly subordinate to the Soviet Union. Imposed in the chaos of the immediate postwar period on countries which were hardly in a position to resist, the Stalinist interstate system possessed neither the flexibility nor the institutional framework for the construction of a stable pattern of relations within the region. The East European states were, as Khrushchev was later to say, ''involuntary allies'';[1] and without a framework which would permit the accommodation of latent nationalist demands, the system could not long endure.

The history of the Soviet bloc during these formative years thus becomes one of Soviet efforts to reshape the legacy of the Stalinist interstate system in the face of growing pressures in Eastern Europe. Beginning even before the new Khrushchev regime had consolidated its domestic position and extending throughout the period and beyond, these pressures were manifested in East European demands for a measure of national autonomy, greater latitude to pursue ''separate roads to socialism,'' and increased participation in bloc decisionmaking. In the aftermath of the Hungarian and Polish ''Octobers'' of 1956, Khrushchev sought to contain these strains within a more resilient and complex pattern of interstate relations, whose principal agents were to be the recently established Warsaw Treaty Organization and the newly invigorated Council for Mutual Economic Assistance.

15

New external pressures likewise confronted the Soviet and East European leaders in the period. Largely obscured from public view until 1960, the Sino-Soviet conflict soon developed to the point of open enmity and emerged as a new source of dissension in Eastern Europe, as the Albanians seized the opportunity to leave the bloc altogether, and others, most notably the Romanians, exploited the differences between Moscow and Peking to expand their room for independent maneuver. The easing of East-West tensions, particularly after the first stage of West German *Ostpolitik* in 1966–67, introduced another set of potentially divisive tendencies into Soviet–East European relations, as the rigid Cold War confrontation gave way to a much more fluid and unstable situation. Not only did the decline of East-West hostilities cast doubt on the objective need for tight solidarity in Eastern Europe and thus render the task of alliance management more difficult for the Soviet leaders, but it offered the Romanians and others welcome opportunities to develop new, potentially divisive economic and political relations beyond the framework of the Soviet bloc.

The combined impact of these external and intrabloc pressures served to introduce a period of drift and disarray which culminated dramatically in the Prague Spring of 1968. In the wake of the Warsaw Pact invasion of Czechoslovakia, as will be seen in the chapters to follow, the Soviet leaders undertook the difficult process of "normalization"—in relations with the West, in intrabloc affairs, and in Czechoslovakia itself. Once normalization had been achieved on terms acceptable to the Soviet leaders, they supervised the even more difficult effort to restructure bloc relations, ostensibly on the basis of the newly reaffirmed principles of "socialist internationalism." Although the task of dealing with the consequences of the Czechoslovak experiment in "socialism with a human face" would fall on Khrushchev's successors, the crisis and subsequent intervention in Czechoslovakia represented the ultimate failure of his attempts to reshape the legacy of the Stalinist interstate system.

The Stalinist Legacy

Khrushchev inherited an interstate system in Eastern Europe whose surface stability concealed an underlying brittleness and unviability. Notably lacking in this arrangement were formal institutions designed to facilitate relations among its member states. Those institutions that did exist were conceived more to meet immediate needs than to form a basis for the future consolidation of Soviet–East European relations. Cominform (Communist Information Bureau), established in 1947 to forge ideological unity, lapsed into inactivity in the second year of its existence; and the Council for Mutual Economic Assistance (CMEA), founded in 1949 in response to the Marshall Plan, remained a paper organization until the late 1950s. Indeed, the only formal ties of any note in this early period were embodied in the bilateral treaties of "friendship, cooperation, and mutual assistance" signed between 1943 and 1950. (See Table 1.1.)

The *casus foederis* of each of the bilateral treaties was mutual defense against external attack, particularly by a rearmed Germany; and signatories were prohibited from entering into other alliances opposed by either party. In keeping with socialist international law, the treaties codified what were held to be the prevailing principles of socialist interstate relations—sovereignty, equality, and noninterference in internal affairs. While later treaties would include commitments to "socialist integration," this early round of bilateral pacts contained only vague references to the desirability of closer economic cooperation. All were concluded for twenty-year periods and contained clauses for automatic renewal for an additional five years.[2]

A number of other treaties and agreements of lesser significance were concluded during the Stalinist period. Included among these were agreements on commerce and trade, scientific and technical cooperation, radio broadcasting, and training of East Europeans in Soviet institutions. Cultural cooperation agreements among the East European states were signed in the late 1940s, but the USSR did not enter into such agreements until almost a decade later; and it was not until the latter half of the 1950s that basic consular agreements were concluded among the states of the Soviet bloc.[3]

In the Stalinist interstate system, strict adherence to the Soviet line was achieved through a variety of more direct means, including frequent consulta-

Table 1.1

The Bilateral Pact System in Eastern Europe, 1953: Treaties of Friendship, Cooperation, and Mutual Assistance (Month and Year Signed)

	USSR	Bul.	Rom.	Hung.	Czech.	Pol.	GDR[a]
Soviet Union		3/48	2/48	2/48	12/43	4/45	—[b]
Bulgaria	3/48		1/48	7/48	4/48	5/48	8/50
Romania	2/48	1/48		1/48	7/48	1/49	8/50
Hungary	2/48	7/48	1/48		4/49	6/48	6/50
Czechoslovakia	12/43	4/48	7/48	4/49		3/47	6/50
Poland	3/47	5/48	1/49	6/48	3/47		7/50
East Germany[a]	—[b]	8/50	8/50	6/50	6/50	7/50	

[a] All treaties signed with the GDR during this period were called Treaties of "Friendship," rather than of "Friendship, Cooperation, and Mutual Assistance." The GDR's special position is explained by the fact that the remaining treaties were directed against external aggression, particularly by a rearmed German state.

[b] Although an international agreement was signed between the GDR and the Soviet Union on September 20, 1955, it was not until June 12, 1964, that the two parties signed a Treaty of Friendship, Cooperation, and Mutual Assistance.

tion between the Soviet leaders and their East European counterparts, direct participation by Soviet ambassadors and advisors in East European domestic affairs, the implicit threat of the Red Army, and, above all, by the imposition of East European leaders trusted by Stalin. Thus, Stalin himself constituted the most important link in the system. Acclaimed as the successful builder of socialism in the Soviet Union and creator of the socialist interstate system, Stalin embodied the very direct source of legitimacy of the East European leaders and the political systems they supervised. To be "more like Stalin than Stalin himself" was the familiar rule of political longevity during this early period.[4]

The Stalinist pattern of rule, therefore, could not survive its leader, and its immediate legacy was a period of instability in both the USSR and Eastern Europe. Two parallel forces were at work during this transition period: the loss of Stalin himself as a cementing element in the bloc and the belated consequences of the unviability of the system he had constructed. Within months of Stalin's death in March 1953, economic crises in East Germany and Czechoslovakia had precipitated workers' riots in East Berlin, Plzen, and other cities. But the events of 1953 were only preludes to the more serious upheavals to come.

Between 1953 and 1956, developments in Eastern Europe were profoundly influenced by the course of events in the Soviet Union. Not only did the power struggle then raging in the USSR create a vacuum of leadership in the bloc, but it provided the East European leaders with a conflicting set of signals: first they were to implement the economic "new course" and the principle of collective leadership, then they were to sabotage those reforms and restore order, and finally they were to condemn their Stalinist excesses, as Khrushchev had done in his celebrated "secret speech" to the 20th Congress of the Communist Party of the Soviet Union (CPSU) in February 1956.[5]

We will probably never know whether Khrushchev fully appreciated the catastrophic impact his "de-Stalinization" campaign would have on Eastern Europe. Clearly motivated by domestic political imperatives, which demanded a break with the Stalinist past, Khrushchev may also have perceived the need to reshape the legacy of the Stalinist interstate system. According to his own account, he was endeavoring to transform the exploitative pattern of economic relations in the bloc and eliminate the more visible forms of Soviet military and political control in Eastern Europe.[6] As Khrushchev, in his inimitable style, was later to say, "You can't herd people into paradise with threats and then post sentries at the gates."[7]

Whatever its motivations, the de-Stalinization campaign sent shock waves throughout Eastern Europe, where a denunciation of Stalin and his methods could only be interpreted as a repudiation of the many "little Stalins" in power in the bloc. Its more general and lasting effect, however, was to awaken the suppressed forces of reformism and nationalism in Eastern Europe. These forces quickly assumed critical proportions in Hungary, where a bitter struggle between Stalinist and reformist factions in the Party and state leadership, coupled with erratic signals emanating from Moscow, brought about the disintegration of the Communist party and the accession to power of a neutralist government of national reconciliation. The well-known events of October and early November 1956 ended with the liquidation of the new Nagy government by Soviet occupying forces.[8]

When the Soviet army invaded Hungary on October 24 and again on November 4, it did so in clear violation of Articles 1 and 8 of the recently signed Warsaw Treaty, which obliged the signatories to refrain from "the threat or use of force" and to observe the principle of "noninterference in . . . internal affairs."[9] If Khrushchev had hoped that the Warsaw Treaty Organization would serve as an instrument of conflict management in the bloc, his hopes were not realized in 1956. Although the treaty was mentioned as one of several justifications for the Soviet action, the Warsaw Treaty Organization never specifically endorsed the invasion, nor did it respond to Nagy's accusation that the pact had been violated.

In any case, while the events in Hungary can scarcely be said to be representative of developments elsewhere in Eastern Europe, they are instructive in that all the potentially disruptive tendencies at work in the region converged at once. Hungary, which had endured one of the most repressive Stalinist regimes, was particularly ill-prepared in 1956 to sustain erratic tampering with the sources of political authority. Once the previous source of political legitimacy—Stalin himself—had been repudiated, the Hungarian leadership was forced to turn inward to erect a new basis for legitimacy and build a firmer relationship between the rulers and the ruled. That this search took on a decidedly anti-Soviet posture was symptomatic of the forces at work within the bloc.

The same basic forces at work in Hungary revealed themselves in somewhat different form in Poland, and with quite different results. In Poland, as in Hungary, the power struggle in the USSR, culminating with Khrushchev's de-Stalinization campaign, set off a wave of criticism and reevaluation, and nationalist and reformist sentiment began to crystallize around Wladyslaw Gomulka, who had been dismissed from the Party leadership in 1948 for advocating a "Polish road to socialism." The eruption of public violence and the polarization of Stalinist and reformist forces paralleled the course of events in Hungary, but with this crucial difference: the Polish Communist party, although deeply divided, remained intact and retained the critical levers of control in the country. When Soviet leaders arrived uninvited and unannounced in Warsaw on October 16, 1956, therefore, they were persuaded to sanction Gomulka's elevation to the post of Party first secretary with a wide mandate to pursue a separate course toward viability in Poland.[10]

Thus, the "lessons" of October 1956 were ambiguous: the invasion of Hungary had affirmed Soviet determination to preserve the "historic gains of socialism'' by whatever means were necessary, but the Soviet response to events in Poland represented a new willingness to recognize the legitimacy of different approaches to socialist development in Eastern Europe. This new orientation was made clear in a Soviet declaration immediately following the October storm in Poland:

> The process of establishing the new system and implementing far-reaching revolutionary reforms of social relationships was attended by no small number of difficulties, unsolved problems and outright mistakes, which extended also to relations between the socialist countries. . . . The Twentieth Congress declared that full account must be taken of the historical past and specific features of each country.[11]

The break with the past was, on the surface at least, complete. Stalin had been denounced, past mistakes admitted, and the possibility of ''separate roads to socialism'' acknowledged. Elsewhere in Eastern Europe, leaderships responded to pressures for reform through a variety of means. In Bulgaria, the disarray occasioned by implementation of the collective leadership principle precipitated, in part, Chervenkov's ill-fated attempt to pursue his own version of the Chinese ''Great Leap Forward.'' In Romania, Gheorghiu-Dej's efforts to rid himself of the Stalinist legacy led him to embark on the beginning of an independent course in Romanian foreign policy. Finally, in East Germany and Czechoslovakia, the surviving Stalinist leaderships countered tendencies toward domestic reform through largely repressive measures. Nowhere, however, did the patterns of domestic control retain the authoritarian hold exercised before 1956. For the Soviet leadership, then, the task which remained was to replace the discredited Stalinist interstate system with a framework which could restore a measure of cohesion to the alliance system.

Toward a New Cohesion

The cohesion Khrushchev sought was one based on a more complex and resilient pattern of interrelationships among the socialist states. Specifically, he saw the Warsaw Treaty Organization and the Council for Mutual Economic Assistance (CMEA) as the basic elements of a new, more viable alliance system. Two tasks of more immediate concern, however, were to reestablish the ideological foundations of the socialist system, which had been termed ''polycentric'' by Italian Communist party leader Palmiro Togliatti as early as June of 1956,[12] and to settle the issue of the stationing of Soviet troops in Eastern Europe.

With the signing of the Austrian State Treaty on May 15, 1955, the previous justification for the presence of Soviet troops in Hungary and Romania—protection of Soviet supply lines to Austria—had lost its validity; and the continued presence of Soviet troops in East Germany and Poland demanded legal clarification, particularly in light of the events of October 1956. Accordingly, between December 1956 and June 1957 the Soviet Union signed "status of forces" treaties with the four East European allies, agreeing to observe the principle of noninterference in internal affairs.[13] During the same period, the number of Soviet troops in Eastern Europe was substantially reduced, and if Khrushchev's account can be believed, his offer to completely withdraw Soviet forces from Poland and Hungary was refused.[14]

As to the ideological underpinnings of the alliance system, the events of 1956 had raised a number of questions which had not been satisfactorily resolved, including the definition of the "correct" road to socialism, the historical meaning of Stalin and Stalinism, and the position of the Soviet Union in the world socialist system. The problem of elaborating a common position on these and other issues was made more difficult by the official dissolution of Cominform and its organ, *For a Lasting Peace, for a People's Democracy*, in April 1956.[15] In the absence of any institutional framework for the resolution of ideological disputes, the Soviet leaders, then beset by internal opposition from the so-called anti-Party group, began to lobby for a unified bloc position, to be announced at the planned conference of Communist and workers' parties.

Following a series of bilateral and multilateral meetings among top Party leaders, the conference convened in Moscow in November 1957, on the occasion of the fortieth anniversary of the Bolshevik Revolution. Strongly influenced by Mao and the Chinese Communists and signed only after strenuous opposition by the Poles, the Yugoslavs, and others, the conference declaration affirmed the leading role of the Soviet Union, "the first and mightiest" of the socialist countries, but acknowledged the legitimacy of different roads to socialism. Concerning relations among the socialist states, the familiar "five principles" were reiterated, but with an important qualification, one which amounted to an early formulation of the Brezhnev Doctrine. "Mutual aid" (of the kind rendered to the Hungarians?), it was argued, "is part and parcel of these relations, . . . a striking expression of socialist internationalism."[16] Although the term "striking" may have been an infelicitous choice for describing the new forms of relations among the socialist states, the Moscow declaration nevertheless provided at least a general ideological basis for the construction of the new system Khrushchev envisioned.

The Creation of the Warsaw Pact

Founded on May 14, 1955, a day before the signing of the Austrian State Treaty, the Warsaw Treaty Organization (WTO) represented the first institutional expression of the new forms of relations in the alliance system. For the first five years of its existence, the WTO, like the CMEA in its early years, was little more than a shell for the future development of new, more durable ties among its member states. To be sure, the pact itself embodied certain commitments which supplemented the existing series of bilateral treaties. Concluded in response to "the participation of a remilitarized Western Germany and the integration of the latter in the North-Atlantic bloc," the treaty committed the signatories to consultation on issues of mutual interest and to render all necessary assistance "in the event of an armed attack in Europe."[17] Organizationally, however, the Warsaw Pact in its early years did little to add to the military ties already established in the bloc. As one Western analyst has observed, "This early alliance system was far superior to the WTO from the Soviet point of view. It was completely centralized but had no central staff. . . . It was a completely integrated system. All the participating states adopted Soviet regulations and training manuals, armaments, equipment and even styles of uniform."[18]

As has been seen, however, a principal aim of the post-Stalin Soviet leadership was to replace the discredited Stalinist control devices with a new, less obtrusive system for the maintenance of Soviet control in Eastern Europe. With the departure of such direct Soviet military advisors as Konstantin Rokossov-

Table 1.2
Warsaw Pact Activity, 1956–1968

Year	No. of WTO meetings[a]	No. of joint maneuvers
1956	1	0
1957	0	0
1958	1	0
1959	1	0
1960	1	0
1961	3	3
1962	2	5
1963	3	2
1964	0	2
1965	5	3
1966	4	2
1967	1	5
1968	7	2

SOURCES: *The Europa Year Book, 1976* (London: Europa Publications, 1977), p. 280; Andrzej Korbonski, "The Warsaw Pact," *International Conciliation*, no. 573 (May 1969), pp. 20–21; Robin Alison Remington, *The Warsaw Pact* (Cambridge: MIT Press, 1971), pp. xvii–xix.

[a] Includes meetings of the PCC, the Joint Command, and WTO defense ministers, foreign ministers, and military delegations.

sky,[19] it became increasingly obvious that a less visible form of Soviet military control was necessary. Toward that end, the Warsaw Pact provided a formal, multilateral framework for political and military cooperation in the bloc.

Articles 5 and 6 of the Warsaw Treaty established a Joint Command of the armed forces and a Political Consultative Committee, which was empowered "to set up such auxiliary bodies as may prove necessary." The Joint Command, in direct operational control over the units assigned to the WTO,[20] consists of the Warsaw Pact commander-in-chief, always a Soviet officer; his deputies, until 1969 the ministers of defense of the East European countries; and a permanent staff headquartered in Moscow and composed of permanent representatives of the general staffs of the member states.[21] The Political Consultative Committee (PCC) is the highest organ of the Warsaw Pact and serves as its key voice in matters of foreign and intrabloc policy.[22] Although little is known about the actual deliberations of the PCC aside from what may be gleaned from its desultory communiqués, a Soviet naval handbook on international law offered a few details as to its procedures: "The Political Consultative Committee is constituted on the principle of equal representation. Each government has one vote. For the conduct of sessions of the Committee a rotation of the chairmanship among the member countries of the Treaty has been established."[23]

At the January 1956 meeting of the PCC, two additional organs were established: the Permanent Commission for foreign policy recommendations and the Joint Secretariat for the administration of technical services.[24] Although it was decided at the same meeting that the PCC would meet not less than twice a year, it has in fact met far less frequently: between 1956 and 1968, the PCC convened only nine times, rather than the stipulated twenty-six.

Both militarily and politically, the Warsaw Pact amounted to little more than a symbolic presence until the early 1960s. Although some steps were taken toward improving the air defense capabilities of the East European states and toward military integration, particularly in the areas of standardization of arms production and adoption of Soviet organizational forms,[25] it was not until 1961 that any attempt was made to infuse the pact with real political or military content. (See Table 1.2.)

In response to a number of developments—including the cutback in Soviet ground forces and the attendant debate between traditionalists and modernists in the Soviet military hierarchy, the heightened tension in Europe occasioned by the Berlin crisis, and perhaps growing Soviet apprehension regarding the Chinese Communists as well[26]—the Soviet leadership led a drive to upgrade the military effectiveness of WTO. In March 1961 a communiqué of the Political Consultative Committee hinted at measures toward "further strengthening of [WTO] defensive capabilities,"[27] and in October of the same year the first joint Warsaw Pact military maneuvers were held. Additionally, East European armed forces were reequipped with modern T-54 and T-55 tanks, MiG-21 and Su-7 aircraft, and delivery vehicles for nuclear warheads (though the warheads themselves doubtless remained under Soviet control).[28]

The political evolution of the Warsaw Pact was considerably slower. Although meetings were held more frequently after 1961, and although the level of representation at PCC sessions increased steadily,[29] growing assertiveness in Eastern Europe, particularly from Romania, made political cooperation increasingly elusive. In fact, it was not until Brezhnev's 1965 call for the "further perfecting of the Warsaw Treaty Organization"[30] that serious efforts began toward improving political consultation through the WTO, and it was not until 1969 that substantive changes in the organization were made.[31]

Comecon and the "Basic Principles"

Paralleling the development of the Warsaw Pact as an instrument of military and political cohesion has been the evolution of the Council of Mutual Economic Assistance (CMEA) as a mechanism for economic integration in Eastern Europe. Founded in 1949 in response to the Marshall Plan and designed to facilitate the coordination of foreign trade plans,[32] CMEA remained inactive until after Stalin's death, and its charter was not signed until as late as 1959. Beginning in 1954, however, CMEA activity began to increase, as the Council met four times between 1954 and 1956 to discuss problems of coordination and specialization. Interrupted by the October events of 1956, negotiations began once again, as a more conciliatory Soviet leadership sought to replace the exploitative Stalinist system with one somewhat more equitable and more responsive to the increasingly complex problems of coordinating bloc economies.[33]

According to its original charter, the purpose of CMEA was to "assist, through the unification and coordination of the efforts of the member-countries of the Council, in the planned development of the national economies, in the speeding up of economic and technical progress in these countries, [and] in raising the level of industrialization of the countries with less developed industry."[34] The original aims of the organization, then, were quite limited; it was not until the 1970s that "socialist integration" was included among its objectives. Structurally and procedurally, the organization was beset with a number of deficiencies. The Session of the Council, termed its "supreme organ," and the Conference of Representatives, replaced in 1962 by the Executive Committee, both were governed by the stipulation that recommendations and decisions could be adopted "only with the consent of the member-countries concerned." Thus, no country could be compelled by a majority to enter into cooperative ventures against its will. An even more serious procedural limitation was the "universality" principle, which required that all members agree to participate in any new cooperative venture before it could be created.[35]

Beyond these procedural difficulties were more fundamental problems militating against successful economic cooperation in the bloc. In their efforts to develop the industrial substructures deemed necessary for socialist construction, the East European leaders had become committed to economic self-sufficiency and were consequently reluctant to engage in the kind of specialization required for extensive economic cooperation. Additionally, the persistence of centrally controlled pricing, based on the presumed requirements of socialist construction rather than on market rationality, denied the East European leaders any mechanism for trading through mutually recognized currency. Finally, in the absence of a supranational planning body in CMEA, the introduction of uncertain external market forces, even those issuing from trade with the socialist allies, threatened to upset the brittle balance of domestic planning.

Some success was achieved after 1956 in the areas of production specialization and coordination of national economic planning through the newly established standing commissions. As is illustrated in Table 1.3, nine commissions were established in 1956 alone, with new ones added at regular intervals. The prevailing pattern throughout the 1960s and beyond, however, remained bilateral trade of the barter variety, and CMEA showed little promise as an agency for the stimulation of multilateral planning and cooperation.

It was in light of these deficiencies, and partly in response to the growing success of economic integration in Western Europe, that Khrushchev initiated the first serious step toward socialist economic integration. It was an ambitious program indeed. On the problems of specialization, it proposed the "Basic Principles of the International Socialist Division of Labor" (signed June 7, 1962), which in effect would have relegated the less developed East European states to the status of suppliers of raw materials to the more advanced countries. On the question of supranational planning, it sought to replace the Conference of Representatives with an executive committee and invest it with the powers of a "united planning organ."[36] As was made clear in a subsequent article by Chairman Khrushchev, the ultimate (and presumably very long-term) goal of the program was the "building of the socialist world economy into a single entity."[37]

In the face of opposition in Eastern Europe, particularly from Romania, Khrushchev was forced to abandon the more ambitious elements of the plan. From the perspective of the East European leaders, the contemplated "division of labor" was considered incompatible with the domestic and ideological requirement of rapid industrialization. Additionally, the creation of a supranational planning body, even if conceived with the most innocent of motives, could only mean domination by the Soviet Union, if for no other reason than the fact that the gross national product of the USSR amounted to more than twice that of the other CMEA members combined. Thus, arguing against the creation of a "single planning body," the Romanian Workers' Party declared, "the planned management of the national economy is one of the . . . inalienable attributes of the sovereignty of the socialist state.''[38] Similar reservations were expressed by the Hungarians and Poles, and at the Comecon summit in July 1963 the Soviet leaders quietly agreed to shelve the integration scheme.

In the more limited spheres of specialization and participation in joint production ventures, however, CMEA activity increased dramatically after 1962. (See Table 1.4.) In addition to the highly publicized ''Peace'' power grid and ''Friendship'' pipeline, joint ventures were undertaken in railway car production and a number of other functional areas, and an International Bank was established to facilitate multilateral clearing, extend loans and credits, and

Table 1.3
CMEA Standing Commissions Established 1956–1968

Standing commission	Year created
1. Electric Power Industries	1956
2. Machine Building	1956
3. Coal Industry	1956
4. Oil and Gas Industries	1956
5. Ferrous Metallurgy	1956
6. Nonferrous Metallurgy	1956
7. Chemical Industries	1956
8. Agriculture	1956
9. Foreign Trade	1956
10. Construction	1958
11. Transportation	1958
12. Peaceful Uses of Atomic Energy	1960
13. Statistics	1962
14. Standardization	1962
15. Currency and Financial Questions	1962
16. Geology	1963
17. Radio Technology and Electronics	1963
18. Light Industries	1963
19. Food Industries	1963

SOURCES: *The Multilateral Economic Cooperation of Socialist States* (Moscow: Progress Publishers, 1977); *Grunddokumente des RGW* (Berlin: Staatsverlag der DDR, 1978), pp. 322–25.

NOTES: Between 1968 and 1980 three additional standing commissions were created: Post and Telecommunications (1971), Civil Aviation (1975), and Sanitation and Health Problems (1975).

A Forestry Commission, created in 1956, was incorporated into the Agriculture Commission in 1958; a Commission for Coordination of Scientific and Technical Research (1962) was disbanded in 1972 upon the formation of the CMEA Council on Scientific and Technical Cooperation. The Standing Commission on Geology was created in May 1956, disbanded in June 1958, and reconstituted in July 1963.

promote conversion to a transferable ruble in CMEA trade. By the end of 1962, it was argued that of 2,500 kinds of industrial equipment produced in Eastern Europe, only 300 were produced in more than one country.[39]

Despite evidence of increased specialization and coordination, trade among CMEA members (as a percentage of total trade) actually declined during the 1960s. (See Table 1.5.) Several factors may account for this decline. One well known Hungarian economist has discussed the difficulties in the transition from the first phase of CMEA cooperation (1949–54), characterized by the coordination of foreign trade plans, to the second phase (1955–70), which saw the initial efforts to coordinate national production plans. During the second phase, the author argued, "major contradictions" had arisen; "contradictions between the interest of independent countries and the socialist world economy as a whole; interest conflicts between economically advanced and less developed countries; differences in the level of productive forces of the individual countries and in

Table 1.4
CMEA Scientific Institutes, Economic Organizations,
and Commissions, 1956–1968

Organization	Year created
Scientific Institutes	
Joint Nuclear Research Institute	1956
Standardization Institute	1962
Interstate Economic Organizations	
Organization for Railway Cooperation	1956
Central Dispatching Admin. (Mir powergrid)	1962
Joint Railroad Freight Car Pool	1963
Agromash (agricultural machinery)	1964
Intermetal (rolled steel products)	1964
Interpodszypnik (roller bearing industries)	1964
Medunion (medical equipment and facilities)	1967
Interkosmos (research on use of space)	1967
Intergovernmental Commissions	
Commission on Computer Technology	1961
Commission on Water Conservation and Floods	1962
Commission on Welding Problems	1964
Commission on Coordination of Research for Comprehensive Mechanization and Automation	1966

SOURCES: *The Multilateral Economic Cooperation of Socialist States* (Moscow; Progress Publishers, 1977); *Grunddokumente des RGW* (Berlin: Staatsverlag der DDR, 1978), pp. 321–41; Harry Trend, "Comecon's Organizational Structure," RAD Background Report/114 (Eastern Europe), *Radio Free Europe Research,* July 3, 1975.

[the] raw materials available to them."[40] To these factors should be added the excessive centralization of the national economies, which made collaboration among enterprises in different countries virtually impossible, and the continuing problems of pricing and currency convertibility.

Thus, as Table 1.6 reveals, the rate of growth of intra-CMEA trade continued to lag behind the expansion of trade within Western Europe.[41] In the absence of any working consensus on the aims or methods of East European economic integration, the issue was held in abeyance until its cautious revival in 1969.[42]

Table 1.5
CMEA Trade Data, 1956–1968
(in Millions of U.S. Dollars)

Year	Total trade		Trade within CMEA	
	Exports	Imports	Value	% of total exports
1956	8,440	7,800	4,830	57
1957	9,600	9,380	5,940	62
1958	10,110	9,740	6,060	60
1959	11,990	11,690	7,390	62
1960	12,970	12,920	8,080	62
1961	14,120	13,820	8,970	64
1962	15,770	15,280	10,170	64
1963	17,000	16,380	11,030	65
1964	18,400	18,100	11,960	65
1965	19,710	18,990	12,460	63
1966	20,910	19,670	15,540	60
1967	22,820	21,100	13,740	60
1968	24,900	23,000	15,240	61

SOURCES: United Nations, *Statistical Yearbook, 1966* (New York, 1967), Table B; United Nations, *Statistical Yearbook, 1973* (New York, 1974), Table B.

Table 1.6
Increase in Trade among Members of CMEA, EEC, and EFTA, 1951–1965:
Annual Average Rate of Increase of Exports at 1968 Prices

	1951–55	1956–60	1961–65
CMEA (Council for Mutual Economic Assistance)	13.4	11.2	9.0
EEC (European Economic Community)		10.5	15.2
EFTA (European Free Trade Area)		6.2	10.8

SOURCE: *Gospodarska Planowa,* September 1968.

Meanwhile, new and more pressing demands claimed the attention of the Soviet and East European leaders.

Drift and Disarray

The failure of the 1962 economic plan was but one manifestation of disunity in the bloc. At least three sets of factors account for a mounting sense of drift and disarray in Eastern Europe: the evolution of the Sino-Soviet schism and its attendant disruptions in what was then called "the world Communist movement"; divisions in Eastern Europe over improving relations with the West, particularly after West German Chancellor Adenauer's retirement in the fall of 1963; and the second wave of "de-Stalinization," a process given new impetus politically by Khrushchev's second attack on Stalin at the 22nd CPSU Congress in 1961 and economically by the discussion surrounding the Liberman plan for economic reform in the Soviet Union.

The Sino-Soviet Split

Even before the Sino-Soviet dispute had escalated to the point of open enmity, the seeming success of the Chinese experiment presented a challenge to Soviet domination of the international Communist movement and its sphere of influence in Eastern Europe. The Chinese announcement in 1958 that the People's Republic was on the threshold of Communism[43] strengthened the positions of those who argued for "many roads to socialism," and Maoism offered an attractive alternate source of legitimacy for the surviving "little Stalins" in Eastern Europe.

Aside from the special case of Albania, only Bulgaria and Romania, which experimented briefly with their own versions of the "Great Leap Forward" and the Cultural Revolution, actually attempted to employ Maoism as a guide for domestic policy. The indirect impact of the split between China and the Soviet Union, however, has been profound: not only did the glaring manifestation of Communist disunity aggravate existing divisions in the bloc, but Soviet preoccupation with the Chinese challenge provided the East European leaders with increased latitude to pursue independent policies.

The East European country most directly influenced by China was, of course, Albania.[44] Until the mid-1950s, the regime of Enver Hoxha had looked to Moscow as a source of support for its unreservedly Stalinist (and rather bizarre) domestic course and protection against the designs, real or imagined, of neighboring Yugoslavia. All of this began to change under Khrushchev, whose de-Stalinization campaign, to say nothing of persistent efforts to displace Hoxha as Albanian party leader, was viewed with considerable alarm in Tirana.

Soviet-Albanian relations continued to deteriorate during the late 1950s and reached the breaking point in the wake of Soviet moves toward *rapprochement* with Albania's two neighbors, Yugoslavia and Greece. Fearing ideological isolation and geopolitical encirclement, the Albanian leaders saw in Maoist China an attractive, and suitably distant, alternate source of legitimacy and support.[45]

By then thoroughly entangled in the rapidly escalating Sino-Soviet dispute, Soviet-Albanian relations moved swiftly toward a full break. Following the purge of a pro-Khrushchev faction in Albania in 1960, the Soviet Union suspended all economic aid programs and undertook a campaign of vilification against the Albanian leaders, who served, not incidentally, as convenient surrogates for the Chinese Communists. Soviet polemics against Albania reached their peak at the 22nd CPSU Congress in October 1961, but by then a complete break was imminent. By the end of the year, the Soviet ambassador had been recalled from Tirana, and Albania had been excommunicated, in fact if not in form, from CMEA and Warsaw Pact activities.[46]

Clearly, the split with Albania had cost the Soviet Union a useful relationship for employment as a lever against the Yugoslavs and the Chinese, a potential means for establishing naval facilities in the Mediterranean, and a small but not inconsequential link in the broader East-West constellation of forces. In terms of the Soviet Union's more immediate aims in Eastern Europe, however, the impact of the break was slight: an impoverished and remote Stalinist enclave in the Balkans, Albania offered little attraction for the other East European states, and the propensity of its leaders for divisive public criticism of its allies ran counter to Soviet efforts to restore a semblance of unity in Eastern Europe.

Of far greater significance were early signs of independent-mindedness on the part of the Romanian leadership. While the full import of Romania's semi-autonomous foreign policy line would be felt only toward the end of the 1960s, its origins already could be apprehended in the early years of the regime of Gheorghe Gheorghiu-Dej, who had maintained his leadership into the 1950s only by interposing himself between Stalin and the many "Muscovite Communists" in the Romanian leadership. In the aftermath of Stalin's death and the first wave of de-Stalinization in Eastern Europe, Gheorghiu-Dej sought to gird his position by reducing Romania's economic and political dependence on the Soviet Union and cultivating new external contacts beyond the confines of the Soviet bloc, most notably with France, Yugoslavia, and China.[47] As a lever to be employed against Moscow, the Chinese connection proved the most effective.

The Romanians, who are nothing if not skillful diplomats, saw in the emerging Sino-Soviet rift opportunities to exploit the situation to Romanian advantage. In April of 1958, the Romanians gained Chinese endorsement of a joint communiqué calling for the removal of "armed forces stationed on foreign territory" in a context which left little doubt that Soviet troops in Romania were what the signatories had in mind.[48] While the Soviet Union's subsequent withdrawal of its forces from Romania may not have been a direct acquiescence to the joint demands, it is clear that a major motive factor was Soviet desire to preempt Chinese influence in Eastern Europe, particularly in the Balkans, through a gesture of accommodation.[49]

To further circumscribe Chinese "splitting activities" in the region, Khrushchev next undertook a campaign to isolate the Chinese both organizationally and ideologically.[50] Throughout 1963 and 1964 Khrushchev attempted in vain to gather sufficient support in Eastern Europe to convene an international Communist conference at which the Chinese would be denounced and the Soviet Union proclaimed the leader of the international Communist movement. His failure, due in large measure to Romania's assumption of the role of mediator in the Sino-Soviet dispute, was the final blow to his efforts to restore unity to the alliance system.

By 1964, it was clear that Khrushchev's policies had escalated the Sino-Soviet conflict without improving the Soviet position in Eastern Europe. His position already severely weakened by a number of other setbacks, Khrushchev was replaced, ostensibly "for reasons of health,"[51] in October 1964 by the collective leadership of Leonid Brezhnev and Aleksei Kosygin.

Warsaw Pact *Westpolitik*

The new leadership assumed power within a rapidly changing international context. The critical years of the early 1960s, which saw the Berlin crises of 1961–62 and the abortive Soviet attempt to install missile bases in Cuba, had given way to a more conciliatory attitude on both sides of the East-West dividing line. In the West, the process of détente following the 1963 Nuclear Test Ban Treaty was accelerated by the "bridge-building" policies of the Johnson administration and the accession to power of the new, more flexible Erhard government in Bonn. On the eastern side of the conflict, Khrushchev had already embarked on his own bridge-building expeditions with overtures to Gaullist France and exploratory discussions with the new West German government.[52]

The pace of events was fast outstripping the capacity of the new Soviet leadership to deal with them. Poland and Romania had already expressed their interest in joining the General Agreement on Tariffs and Trade (GATT);[53] and several East European states, most notably Romania, had begun to explore the possibility of normalizing relations with West Germany. The need for a new, coordinated policy toward the West was becoming urgent.

By the time of the tenth anniversary of the Warsaw Pact, the outlines of a new Soviet strategy began to appear. Beginning with Kosygin's visit to Peking in February 1965, the Soviet effort was to move cautiously toward easing tensions with the People's Republic. On the European front, Soviet efforts after 1965 were to seize the initiative in European affairs through a two-pronged approach: within Eastern Europe, the Soviet leaders aimed at "further perfecting the Warsaw Treaty Organization" as an instrument of foreign policy coordination; externally, they sought to head off independent East European initiatives toward the West by leading the call for the convocation of a European security conference.

Meeting in January of 1965, the Political Consultative Committee (PCC) of the Warsaw Pact issued a proposal for a "conference of European states to discuss measures for ensuring collective security in Europe."[54] In the face of growing apprehensions in East Germany over the status of the "German question," the Soviet leaders soon made it clear that the starting point for a conference on European security must be "recognition of the now existing European frontiers, including those of the two German states."[55] At the same time, however, the new Romanian leadership, headed by Nicolae Ceauşescu, sought to restructure the emerging East-West dialogue by repeating, in a strongly anti-Soviet context, an earlier call for the liquidation of all military blocs.[56]

Amid these competing demands, the PCC met again in Bucharest in 1966. The chief product of this meeting was the Bucharest Declaration, by far the most specific of the Warsaw Pact proposals. It called for recognition of European boundaries, creation of a new security system in Europe, exclusion of West Germany from access to nuclear weapons, and promotion of economic, scientific, and technical cooperation between East and West.[57] Although the outlines of the Warsaw Pact's *Westpolitik* had been presented, the Warsaw Pact allies were becoming increasingly divided, particularly over the German question, and the need for improved foreign policy coordination was becoming urgent.

Brezhnev's 1965 call for the "further perfecting" of the Warsaw Pact, particularly in the area of "coordination of the foreign policy of socialist countries," met with considerable resistance in Eastern Europe.[58] Although the nature of the Soviet proposal has never been made public, it is clear that some new committee or council which would meet more regularly than the PCC was envisioned. It is also clear that the proposal would have expanded Soviet control through the Warsaw Pact, for in 1966 Romania responded with its own set of counterproposals, including calls for the rotation of the post of commander-in-chief among all pact members and the implementation of joint decisionmaking on nuclear matters.[59] In the face of similar demands from Czechoslovakia,[60] the Soviet effort to restructure the Warsaw Pact was quietly shelved, not to be reintroduced until the time of the 1969 Budapest conference.[61]

In the meantime, the accession to power of the Kiesinger-Brandt coalition in December 1966 and the early initiatives of West Germany's Ostpolitik, including the offer to establish diplomatic relations with the East European states, elevated the German question to a position of immediate concern. The first order of business, particularly from the East German point of view, was to renew and strengthen the bilateral treaties binding the East European states. As is shown in Table 1.7, the Soviet treaties with Czechoslovakia and Poland had been renewed in 1963 and 1965, respectively, and in 1964 the Soviet Union and the GDR had belatedly concluded their first treaty of friendship, cooperation, and mutual assistance.

In 1967, most of the remaining treaties were hastily renewed. In March of that year, treaties were renewed among Czechoslovakia, Poland, and East Germany, the so-called "iron triangle" countries, each of which had still unresolved territorial disputes with West Germany. The language of the three treaties was similar: each proclaimed the inviolability of existing European borders, particularly those of the GDR, and each contained special reference to the threat of West German revanchism.[62] East Germany's special concern over the German question was echoed in the subsequent treaties between the GDR and Hungary and Bulgaria and in the Polish-Bulgarian, Soviet-Bulgarian, and Soviet-Hungarian treaties signed during the course of 1967.

Notably absent in this round of treaty-making was Romania. Ignoring what *Pravda* called the "duty" of socialist countries "to render all possible support to the GDR,"[63] Romania had broken the previously united bloc policy toward West Germany by establishing diplomatic relations with the Federal Republic in February 1967. Relations between Romania and the other bloc members,

Table 1.7

The Bilateral Pact System in Eastern Europe: Treaty Renewals, 1954–1968
(Month and Year Signed)

	USSR	Bul.	Rom.	Hung.	Czech.	Pol.	GDR
Soviet Union		5/67	—	9/67	12/63	4/65	6/64[a]
Bulgaria	5/67		—	—	4/48	4/67	9/67
Romania	—	—		—	8/68[b]	—	—
Hungary	9/67	—	—		6/68	5/68	5/67
Czechoslovakia	12/63	4/68	8/68[b]	6/68		3/67	3/67
Poland	4/65	4/67	—	5/68	3/67		3/67
East Germany	6/64[a]	9/67	—	5/67	3/67	3/67	

NOTE: Treaties of Friendship, Cooperation, and Mutual Assistance. In this second round of treaties, the "friendship" treaties with the GDR were upgraded to treaties of "Friendship, Cooperation, and Mutual Assistance."

[a] This was the first formal bilateral alliance treaty between the USSR and the GDR.

[b] The treaty was signed August 16, 1968, four days before the Warsaw Pact invasion of Czechoslovakia.

particularly East Germany, remained strained, and it was not until 1972 that Romania completed its renewal of the early round of treaties.[64]

The disunity resulting from Romanian policies was undoubtedly high on the agenda at the international Communist conference held, after long delay, at Karlovy Vary in April 1967. Although a measure of consensus was evident in the conference resolution, the achievement was a hollow one, for Romania, having refused even to send a representative to the conference, was not among the signatories. There was little time left to restore unity in Eastern Europe, however, for by 1967 attention was being turned to developments of more immediate concern in Czechoslovakia.

The Prague Spring

Two further legacies of the Khrushchev years were a second de-Stalinization campaign, heralded by revelations at the 22nd CPSU Congress (October 1961) of additional errors associated with the "cult of personality," and a wave of economic reform, or at least discussion thereof, set in motion in 1962 by the opening of a reform debate in the Soviet Union. The combined impact of these trends on Eastern Europe, reminiscent in many ways of the crosscurrents of the mid-1950s, served further to discredit Stalinist methods of rule and strengthen embryonic reformist tendencies, particularly in Hungary and Czechoslovakia.

In most cases, the second de-Stalinization drive was endured without serious repercussions: Poland and Hungary already were dealing, albeit in quite different ways, with the consequences of their national explosions of 1956; in Romania and Bulgaria the pressures were far less great. The East German leaders, clearly exempted from any Soviet-led "thaw" in social policy, had secured Soviet permission to stem the emigration flood by erecting the Berlin Wall and were setting about a belated process of domestic consolidation. In Czechoslovakia, however, the 22nd CPSU Congress was interpreted as a message directed to the Party itself and to its leader, Antonín Novotný, who hitherto had paid little more than lip service to de-Stalinization. Heeding the warning, Novotný undertook cautiously and belatedly to embrace the spirit of the times: a huge statue of Stalin was torn down in Prague, street signs were changed, and a commission was established to review the political trials of the early 1950s and consider rehabilitation of its victims, particularly the "Slovak nationalists" sentenced to long prison terms in 1954.

Meanwhile, an economic recession affecting the entire region had prompted the Soviet leaders to undertake a reappraisal of economic planning and management and the possibilities for its reform. Discussion centered on a reform blueprint presented by Professor Yevsei Liberman for partial decentralization of authority, increased reliance on profitability and incentives, and introduction of market criteria (i.e., supply and demand) in pricing.[65] Although Libermanism never took root in the Soviet Union, except for a half-hearted reform attempt in 1965, it served to strengthen the hands of would-be economic reformers in Eastern Europe. Everywhere "reform" programs were announced, but these generally were confined to a streamlining of the existing systems of command planning. The Hungarians, however, seized the opportunity to open a genuine debate on a "regulated socialist market" economy, and preparations began in 1964 toward implementation of a New Economic Mechanism (NEM), which would have considerable success after its adoption in January 1968.[66]

Coming at a time of severe economic stagnation in Czechoslovakia, where national income actually declined in 1962–63, the winds of economic reform began to reach even the top levels of the Party and state leadership. Influenced by reformist economists led by Selucký and Šik, who denounced the "cult of the plan" as a version of the discredited cult of personality, the Novotný regime moved haltingly in 1963 toward a reorganization of the system of planned management.[67] Even with continuing economic deterioration, however, the regime could not bring itself to endorse "market socialism" fully, and in 1966 the leadership officially accepted the Šik reform package in principle but emasculated it in practice by retaining firm central control over economic decisions ostensibly devolved to the enterprises.

As further evidence of the beginnings of change in Czechoslovak public life, a first series of rehabilitations of victims of the Stalinist political trials was announced, and in October of 1963 Prime Minister Široký and other hard-liners were removed from their posts. These events were closely linked to the issue of Slovak nationalism, which had been smoldering since the adoption of the 1960 federal constitution granting sweeping powers to the central government in Prague. The official review of the fifties' trials, as has been seen, centered around the issue of Slovak nationalism, as did the sacking of Široký, beneficiary and co-instigator of the trials which sent hundreds of alleged "bourgeois nationalists" to prison in 1954, among them the noted poet Ladislav Novomeský and the former president of the Slovak autonomous government, Gustáv Husák. Thus the issues of de-Stalinization, reform, and liberalization all overlapped with the Slovak question, and the Party Central Committee felt obliged in late 1963 to acknowledge the errors of the political trials of the 1950s and, implicitly, the validity of the Slovak national cause.

Beneath the surface of official policy in the mid-1960s an even more profound metamorphosis was taking place, as economic reformists, liberal intellectuals, and supporters of the Slovak national cause joined hands with a growing reformist element within the Party itself. Writers and other members of the critical intelligentsia, traditional bearers of national consciousness, particularly in the Czech lands, became the focal point of a national reawakening, expressed largely through the journals of the Writers' Union, *Literární noviny* (Prague) and

Kultúrny život (Bratislava), and later *Reportér*, the new publication of the Journalists' Union. Thus, when Novotný sought to stem the torrent of new ideas and semiofficial criticism of his policies in September 1967, he moved first against the Writers' Union by expelling several of its members from the Communist party and confiscating the journal *Literární noviny*.[68]

By this time, however, Novotný's party was seething with discontent, and speakers at the Central Committee plenum in October openly criticized Novotný and his methods. A few weeks later, brutal police suppression of student demonstrations served to unite the factions opposed to Novotný's rule, and neither a last-minute appeal to Brezhnev nor an eleventh hour *Putsch* attempt could save him.[69] After some additional wrangling at the top echelons of the Party, a Central Committee plenum on January 4 secured Novotný's resignation as first secretary and replaced him with Alexander Dubček, since 1963 first secretary of the Communist party of Slovakia.

No one knew precisely what to expect of Dubček, whose early childhood in the Soviet Union and later Party training in Moscow suggested orthodoxy but whose tenure in Slovakia had been marked by conciliation and tolerance. For Czechoslovak society at large, including large segments of the Party, however, Novotný's ouster was clearly perceived as a green light for reform. Encouraged by a relaxation of censorship, writers and journalists quickly led a long-suppressed explosion of information through exposés of the past, analyses of the present, and blueprints for the future. Determined to come to terms with the reformist spirit, and indeed imbued with it itself, the new Party leadership formed a committee to draft a Party Action Program which would assess the errors of the past and chart a course for the future.

Yet, what took place in Czechoslovakia in the first eight months of 1968 is not explicable in terms of any set of policies of the Party, still less in terms of the background or predilections of its new leader.[70] The Prague Spring, in a few words, was a belated national explosion of long-harbored democratic inclinations suppressed and internalized over two decades of oppressive rule. No segment of society was left untouched: the non-Communist parties shed their subservient demeanor; journalists accustomed to toeing a rigid line unleashed a torrent of unrestrained reporting; trade unions, youth organizations, and professional associations all sprang to life. The Prague Spring was heady, spontaneous—and probably uncontrollable.

In April, the Party Central Committee approved the Action Program.[71] It affirmed the Party's determination that Czechoslovakia would remain firmly committed to the family of socialist states, fulfill its obligations to the Warsaw Pact and Comecon, and maintain its loyalty to the Soviet Union. On domestic policy, however, it proclaimed a full break with the dogmatism of the past, pledging increased democratization within the Party, separation of Party and state functions, relaxation of censorship and safeguarding of political rights, delimitation of the role of the security police, and expansion of Slovakia's autonomy. The Party declared itself to be but one of many social groups; others were to be accorded new rights and a new role within a pluralistic environment. All this was presented as a new model of democratic socialism, a blueprint for the creation of "socialism with a human face."

By this time, events in Czechoslovakia were being viewed with profound concern elsewhere in Eastern Europe. Assurances of Czechoslovakia's commitment to socialism and the Warsaw Pact notwithstanding, the Soviet and loyalist East European leaders clearly feared that the course of events in Czechoslovakia threatened to shatter its Party's "leading role" and with it some of the vital links in the chain of Soviet control and influence in Eastern Europe, thus endangering political security throughout the region. Beyond this, there was concern over the spillover potential of the Prague Spring: if non-Communist parties could be accorded meaningful political independence in Czechoslovakia, Soviet and East European leaders asked themselves, what would prevent the proliferation of similar demands in East Germany or Poland? If censorship could be abolished in Czechoslovakia, on what theoretical or practical grounds could it be maintained in Bulgaria or the Soviet Union? It was this set of concerns, and not the purported danger of Western-inspired counterrevolution, that prompted the Soviet and East European leaders, less Romania's Ceauşescu, to undertake a concerted effort to liquidate the Czechoslovak reform movement.[72]

With the Dresden summit in March, a meeting that the Romanians characteristically refused to attend, there began a long series of bilateral and multilateral conferences devoted to developments in Czechoslovakia. In early May Dubček and other leaders conferred with the Soviet Presidium in Moscow; two weeks later Soviet Premier Kosygin arrived in Karlovy Vary for a prolonged visit. In July Warsaw Pact leaders, minus Dubček and Ceauşescu, met in Warsaw to issue an ultimatum to the Czechoslovak Party; shortly thereafter a bilateral Soviet-Czechoslovak summit was convened in Čierná nad Tisou; and just a few days later Warsaw Pact leaders (again without Ceauşescu) gathered in Bratislava for a final multilateral summit. Accompanying these sessions were incessant media attacks by the "fraternal" countries warning of "antisocialist forces" or incipient counterrevolution and, more pointedly, a series of Warsaw Pact maneuvers, first along the Czechoslovak border in Poland and later on Czechoslovak territory, followed by a long delay in the withdrawal of Warsaw Pact forces.[73]

Seen in retrospect, there is an air of tragic inevitability surrounding relations between the Czechoslovak leaders and their Warsaw Pact allies in the spring and summer of 1968. If only we could explain to them what we are doing and why we are doing it, the Czechoslovak leaders reasoned, then surely they will understand that our reform policies are no threat to socialism or the integrity of the Warsaw Pact. This perception, or misperception, gave rise to a recurrent pattern in the meetings leading up to the invasion: the Czechoslovak leaders would explain, the allies would accuse, Dubček and his colleagues would justify, tempers would flare, then recede, and the meeting would end in seeming compromise, interpreted in Moscow as a binding ultimatum, in Prague as a renewed vote of confidence. Thus, less than three weeks after the apparent compromise at Bratislava, Soviet troops and small contingents from four Warsaw Pact allies—East Germany, Poland, Hungary, and Bulgaria—invaded Czechoslovakia and arrested Dubček and five other leaders of the reform movement.[74]

End of the Khrushchev Era

Although undertaken nearly four years after his ouster from the Soviet leadership, the invasion of Czechoslovakia marked the decisive end of the Khrushchev era in Eastern Europe. His legacy was mixed. Clearly, the alliance system of the 1960s was a more flexible and sophisticated one than that erected under Stalin: the purely exploitative Stalinist pattern of economic relations had been replaced with an elaborate system of links through CMEA, and the undisguised Soviet hegemony of the past had given way to a more participatory, if still Soviet-dominated, pattern of relations. On the other hand, in his halting efforts to transform domestic Stalinism into long-term domestic viability and stability, Khrushchev had failed to grasp the fundamental bankruptcy of Soviet-style socialism in Eastern Europe. And just as the Stalinist system had proved ill-equipped to handle the strains of 1956, the existing framework of inter-Party and interstate relations had proved insufficient to contain the course of events in Czechoslovakia in 1968.

Although Soviet military power prevailed in August 1968, there was no going back to the rigidly ruled empire of the Stalinist era. As an Albanian commentator had noted in 1965, ''It is obvious that the conductor's baton is becoming less and less effective and the centrifugal forces are increasing.''[75] Divergent tendencies once contained by the sheer magnitude of Soviet power were asserting themselves with increased regularity, and the tasks of Soviet alliance management had assumed new proportions. For its part, the Brezhnev-Kosygin leadership in the USSR had shown few signs of coming to grips with these new realities, and their reign had yet to leave its mark on Soviet-East European relations.

The lessons of Czechoslovakia, however, were clear enough. In the first place, the Prague Spring must have dispelled any complacency the Soviet leaders still harbored about the potential merits of Khrushchev-style (much less Dubček-style) domestic innovation. Except in those cases where reform proceeded so gradually as to be almost imperceptible, as in Hungary, domestic orthodoxy was to be the order of the day. Second, in light of the Soviet Union's far more extensive global ambitions, the application of brute force had proved considerably more costly than had been the case in 1956. The task after 1968, therefore, would be to create a system of interstate and inter-Party links so pervasive that recourse to the ultimate unifying force—the Red Army—would be obviated. Finally, the complexity of recent challenges to Soviet rule in Eastern Europe—Romania's semi-autonomous foreign policy line as well as the Prague Spring—contributed to a growing awareness that the tasks of alliance management required a rather more creative application of Soviet power and authority than in the past. Thus, when the Soviet leaders began to seek ways to consolidate their hold over Eastern Europe, the effort would involve not simply a return to the Stalinist past, but the search for a more durable cohesion through a comprehensive integrationist program in every sphere of Soviet–East European relations.

The outlines of such a program could be discerned even before the August events in Czechoslovakia. In military affairs, calls for the "further perfecting" of the Warsaw Pact had acquired new dimensions with the publication of Czechoslovak demands for a restructuring of the pact, particularly those embodied in the celebrated interview granted by Czechoslovak Lieutenant General Vaclav Prchlík.[76] In economic relations, hints of a new campaign toward integration were evident as early as January 1968, when a leading Soviet spokesman on CMEA suggested that economic reforms in Eastern Europe demanded new methods of interstate economic cooperation.[77] As to inter-Party relations, efforts had continued toward the convening of the long-proposed, long-delayed international conference of Communist and workers' parties,[78] and rumors began to circulate that a revived Comintern or Cominform might be in the offing.[79] Before such grandiose designs could be addressed, however, there remained the problem of restoring a measure of unity in Eastern Europe through a bloc-wide effort toward postinvasion "normalization."

2

The Politics of Normalization,
1968–1969

In one way or another, the trauma of Czechoslovakia affected virtually every aspect of domestic, intrabloc, and external policy in Eastern Europe. As the Soviet leaders were soon to discover, the invasion had arrested but had not eliminated disintegrative tendencies in Czechoslovakia, and it had generated a serious backlash on the part of the Romanians, Yugoslavs, Chinese, and the great majority of the nonruling Communist parties in Western Europe. Additionally, the reassertion of Soviet military determination in Eastern Europe had raised questions about Soviet intentions elsewhere in the region, particularly in Romania and Yugoslavia.[1] For these reasons, and despite one Czechoslovak journalist's suggestion that it would be "difficult to normalize something that was always rather abnormal,"[2] the August crisis in Czechoslovakia gave way to a Soviet-led drive toward "normalization" in the bloc.

Of similar concern was the potential damage to Warsaw Pact Westpolitik, so carefully cultivated in the preceding few years. Normalization with the West, as it turned out, was the least difficult of the tasks facing bloc leaders in the aftermath of the invasion. Although interrupted by the events of 1968, East-West negotiations resumed in full force following the conciliatory inaugural address of President Nixon in January 1969. With the accession to power of the new Brandt government in West Germany in October of that year, moreover, new impetus was given to West German Ostpolitik, and East-West negotiations toward a European security conference soon began in earnest.

Thus, normalization within the Soviet bloc was not to preclude better relations with the West, nor was it to mean a return to Stalinist control methods. Banking on the renewed authority which had accrued to them from the decisive action taken in Czechoslovakia and relying on the inherent conservatism of the Bulgarian, Polish, and East German regimes, the Soviet leaders undertook, rather,

40

to restore bloc cohesion through a combination of threats and gestures of conciliation. For the Czechoslovak leaders, "normalization" was to mean restoring the "leading role" of the Communist party and dismantling the embryonic reforms initiated during the Prague Spring; for the remaining East European leaders, it was to mean falling into line even more closely with prescribed (i.e., Soviet) norms of "socialist internationalism." Most intransigent of all was the case of Romania, where the Ceaușescu leadership had sought to secure its position by forging a virtual Romanian-Yugoslav entente and developing closer relations with the Chinese. With an international conference of Communist and workers' parties planned for early 1969, however, the Soviet leaders' first task in normalization was to clarify the ideological meaning and practical implications of the Warsaw Pact invasion of Czechoslovakia.

"Limited Sovereignty": Doctrinal Disputes

The Soviet occupation forces had planned simply to brand the Dubček regime "traitorous" and replace it with a collaborationist regime headed by Alois Indra, the Central Committee secretary for party affairs, and composed of other leading conservatives.[3] On the morning of August 21, a group of Soviet and collaborationist Czechoslovak security officers entered Central Committee headquarters to arrest Dubček and other leaders of the reform movement "in the name of the revolutionary government headed by comrade Indra."[4] Later the same day, Dubček and the others were flown via Poland to Moscow, where Dubček was denounced as "a traitor to the Czechoslovak proletariat and to the cause of international Communism."[5] In Prague, meanwhile, Indra demanded that Czechoslovak President Svoboda recognize him as the head of the new government.

But Soviet hopes for an orderly transition to a regime of pro-Soviet conservatives were soon shattered by the solidarity of Czechoslovak opposition to the occupiers and collaborators. Despite the state of siege then existing in Prague, the National Assembly met in unbroken session from August 21 to August 27, and delegates managed to elude Soviet occupation forces to convene the 14th, "Extraordinary" Congress of the Czechoslovak Communist Party.[6] With the support of every legally constituted Party and state body, President Svoboda refused to recognize any government headed by Indra and demanded to join Dubček in direct negotiations with the Soviet leaders.

In the face of such united resistance, the Soviet leaders had little alternative but to accede to the demands. On August 23, Svoboda and his entourage, composed so as to provide a rough balance between progressives and conservatives, arrived in Moscow, where they were joined by Dubček and the other arrested leaders. The Moscow talks yielded an uneasy compromise: Dubček was to return as Party first secretary, and his regime was to remain largely intact, but the Czechoslovak representatives had been forced to sign a protocol containing fifteen secret "points" for the dismantling of the reforms of the Prague Spring.[7]

Not only did the Soviet failure to install a puppet regime make the prospects for normalization in Czechoslovakia considerably more uncertain, but the acceptance of Dubček's continued leadership rendered untenable the initial justification for the invasion. If Dubček was to return with Soviet blessings to supervise the building of socialism in Czechoslovakia, he could hardly be charged with treason or counterrevolutionary conspiracy. Some more suitable explanation of the invasion was required.

The Brezhnev Doctrine

Although the theoretical justification of the Czechoslovak invasion was later elevated by Western analysts to the status of a "doctrine," there was nothing particularly novel in the notion of "limited sovereignty." The sovereignty of the East European socialist states had been limited from the beginning, and "fraternal assistance"—employed in practice to mean virtually whatever the Soviet leaders wanted it to mean—had always been linked to "socialist internationalism."[8] This theme, as well as the requirement to preserve "the historic gains of socialism," had been reemphasized in the Soviet press even before the Warsaw Pact invasion.[9] Immediately after the invasion, *Pravda* printed an "appeal" by unspecified members of the Czechoslovak government and Communist party Central Committee,[10] and it was on this basis that the Warsaw Pact invading forces first justified their action.[11]

With the return of Dubček to Prague, of course, all references to the "appeal" ceased, and a more elaborate theoretical justification evolved. In a September 11 *Pravda* article, Soviet theoretician Sergei Kovalev presented an analysis of "peaceful counterrevolution" conducted by " 'internal émigrés' closely linked to foreign imperialist forces." This process, Kovalev continued, no less "insidious" than its nonpeaceful counterpart, demanded the "vigilance" of every Communist.[12] In a second, more refined analysis published on September 26, Kovalev asserted that "the weakening of any link in the world socialist system has a direct effect on all the socialist countries." Arguing that the socialist countries had an "internationalist duty" to defend socialism, he went on to justify the "actions taken in Czechoslovakia by the five allied socialist countries" as "actions aimed at defending the fundamental interests of the socialist commonwealth."[13]

All these themes—the existence of "weak links" in the world socialist system, the requirement for defending the "socialist gains," and the demands of "socialist internationalism," "socialist solidarity," and "class support"—

found expression in the speech which gave the Brezhnev Doctrine its name. Addressing the 5th Congress of the Polish United Workers' Party (PUWP) on November 12, 1968, Brezhnev argued:

> Socialist states stand for strict respect for the sovereignty of all countries. We resolutely oppose interference in the affairs of any states and the violation of their sovereignty.
>
> [But] when external and internal forces hostile to socialism try to turn the development of a given socialist country in the direction of the restoration of the capitalist system, when a threat arises to the cause of socialism in that country . . . this is no longer merely a problem for that country's people, but a common problem, the concern of all socialist countries.[14]

Although Brezhnev was later to deny the existence of a theory of limited sovereignty,[15] the clear meaning of the doctrine associated with his name is that the sovereignty of a socialist country is indeed limited—by the overarching commitment to the development of the "socialist commonwealth," by the requirement to defend the "historic gains" of socialism, and by the "internationalist obligations" of socialist countries. As will be seen later, the terms "defending the socialist gains" and the "internationalist duty" of socialist countries have operated as surrogates for the discredited doctrine of "limited sovereignty."[16]

In its ultimate theoretical elaboration, the Brezhnev Doctrine was neither a radical break with past doctrine nor simply an official reaffirmation of the long-standing Soviet determination to preserve its sphere of interest in Eastern Europe. It was, rather, a significant adjustment of doctrine—born of necessity, to be sure—in the direction of socialist solidarity and away from Khrushchev's acceptance of "separate roads to socialism." In this sense, the concept of "socialist internationalism" acquired after the invasion the implicit acceptance of the Brezhnev Doctrine, though it had been used formerly without such a connotation.[17]

It will be useful at this point to pause to consider the role of the Warsaw Pact in the entire episode. As has been seen, in the months preceding the invasion the pact proved useful as a forum for multilateral consultation (though the Dresden, Moscow, Warsaw, and Bratislava meetings were not officially termed WTO meetings) and as a mechanism for exerting pressure on Czechoslovakia in the form of joint military maneuvers on Czechoslovak borders. By early August, however, command of the joint forces had been transferred from Warsaw Pact headquarters to the Soviet High Command, and the invasion itself was conducted as a Soviet military operation under the command of General Pavlovskii, the commander-in-chief of Soviet ground forces.[18] The subsequent theoretical justifications for the invasion, moreover, did not specifically mention the Warsaw Treaty or, aside from oblique references to the threat of West German revanchism, the obligations envisioned therein. Despite these failures of

Warsaw Pact cooperation, or perhaps because of them, the "further perfecting" of the WTO continued to figure prominently in the Soviet conception of a restructured alliance system.

International Communist Reaction

Meanwhile, reactions to the Brezhnev Doctrine and to the invasion itself were swift and varied. In Eastern Europe, the most unqualified support for the Soviet position came from Bulgaria and East Germany. Typically, the series of interpretations by the Bulgarian leaders mirrored those of their Soviet comrades: an initial justification based on the call for assistance from "a group of Czechoslovak Party and state functionaries"[19] was followed by a more elaborate analysis, issued after Brezhnev's speech to the Polish Party Congress, of the "internationalist duty" of "the family of socialist states" to protect "the socialist gains of the Czechoslovak people."[20] The East Germans, who had been the most vocal critics of the Czechoslovak reforms, were if anything even more enthusiastic in their endorsement of the invasion.[21]

In Poland, where the spillover from the Prague Spring was perhaps the greatest, the official response was more uncertain. Party leader Wladyslaw Gomulka, who initially projected an image of sympathetic tolerance toward the Prague reform movement,[22] grew increasingly critical of it in the face of growing domestic pressures for liberalization and the emergence of rifts within the Polish party, particularly from the right-wing Moczar faction.[23] In any case, by the time of Gomulka's speech to the 5th PUWP Congress in November, the official Polish position had become as doctrinaire as that of the Soviet Union, Bulgaria, and East Germany. "The political crisis in Czechoslovakian revisionism," Gomulka argued, threatened to push Czechoslovakia "onto a road of retreat from Marxism-Leninism and proletarian internationalism, to a road of wresting this state from the community of socialist states of the Warsaw Pact." Nor was this all. By acting to preserve the balance of power in Europe, Gomulka continued, the invasion "constituted a preventive move in defense of peace and security in Europe, and thus [was] in the interest of all nations."[24]

Hungary's much more conciliatory posture can be explained by the course of its own internal economic reforms, adopted in January 1968. Obviously, from the perspective of the Kádár regime in Hungary, the more diverse the patterns of development in Eastern Europe, the less heretical would seem its own independent brand of socialism. On the other hand, once the decision to intervene had been taken, the Hungarians came under intense pressure to join, however reluctantly, in the demonstration of socialist solidarity.[25] In the months following the invasion, it is difficult to discern any policy statement which could be said to constitute the official Hungarian interpretation. For his part, Kádár acknowledged some two months after the invasion that Czechoslovakia's "post-January" policies had raised the danger of counterrevolution.[26] Perhaps the most revealing official statement, however, came from Hungarian Prime Minister Jenő Fock, who apologetically declared on a national radio broadcast: "We could not take a popular vote on the events of August 20 [in Czechoslovakia]; this would not have been proper because it was not our affair alone."[27]

The Romanians wasted no time in declaring the invasion "a flagrant violation of the national sovereignty of a fraternal, socialist, free, and independent state."[28] The Romanian view was not surprising, of course, and was in fact entirely consistent with President Ceauşescu's frequently repeated theoretical defense of state sovereignty. According to this view, elaborated well before the 1968 events in Czechoslovakia, the sovereignty of a socialist state cannot be subordinated to class or internationalist interests, nor can the class interests of one country be interpreted by any theorist or group of leaders claiming to speak for the entire socialist community.[29] Under intense pressure from Moscow, the Romanians greatly toned down their criticism of the invasion, but never did they abandon their rejection of the limited sovereignty doctrine.

Among the ruling Communist parties outside the bloc, the most hostile reactions came from the Yugoslavs, the Albanians, and the Chinese. The Yugoslav response largely echoed the Romanian critique of limited sovereignty and of the purported danger of counterrevolution in Czechoslovakia. In March of 1969, however, President Tito issued a more elaborate rejection of the Brezhnev Doctrine:

[In] some East European socialist countries the unacceptable doctrine of a "collective," "integrated," and of an essentially limited sovereignty, is appearing. In the name of a supposedly higher level of relationships between socialist countries this doctrine negates the sovereignty of these states and tries to legalize the right of one or more countries according to their own judgment, and if necessary by military intervention to force their will upon other socialist countries.[30]

The Albanian leaders, offering a plague on both houses, characterized the events of 1968 as a "dogfight between the Soviet and Czechoslovak revisionist renegades and the disintegration of the revisionist cliques."[31] In terms no less vitriolic, an August 23 Peking Review editorial argued the invasion had exposed "the grisly fascist features of the Soviet revisionist renegade clique."[32] Some months later, in his address to the 9th Chinese Party Congress, Lin Piao characterized the Brezhnev Doctrine in this way: "In order to justify its aggression and plunder, the Soviet revisionist renegade clique trumpets the so-called theory of 'limited sovereignty.' . . . What does all this mean? It means that your sovereignty is 'limited,' while his is unlimited."[33]

The remaining Communist parties in power—the Cuban, Mongolian, North Korean, and North Vietnamese—all issued statements in support of the invasion. Of these, the views presented by Fidel Castro were the most interesting. Rejecting the arguments that Czechoslovak sovereignty had not been violated or that the invasion was somehow "legal," Castro admitted "the violation was flagrant" and had "absolutely not one appearance of legality." He went on to support the invasion, nevertheless, on the grounds that Czechoslovakia was "heading toward a revolutionary situation." In such circumstances, Castro concluded, "the right of sovereignty . . . has to give way to the more important interest—the right of the world revolutionary movement and of the people's struggle against imperialism."[34]

Of the nonruling parties in Europe, the great majority, including the powerful French and Italian, opposed the invasion. In a cautiously worded statement, the Central Committee of the French Communist party noted its "disapproval" of the invasion, but at the same time expressed concern over "forces hostile to socialism" in Czechoslovakia and the encouragement given those forces by "leading circles of the revanchist and expansionist state of West Germany."[35] The Politburo of the Italian Communist party reacted much more forcefully, expressing its "strong dissent" and declaring the invasion to have been "unjustified and incompatible with the principles of autonomy and independence of every Communist Party and socialist state."[36]

The reaction of greatest concern to Moscow, of course, was that of the Czechoslovak leadership. On the day of the invasion, the Czechoslovak Party Presidium condemned the action as a breach of international law, and the Ministry of Foreign Affairs sent communiqués to each of the parties to the invasion, submitting that "the five countries have assaulted the independence of Czechoslovakia and violated in an unprecedented manner its territorial integrity."[37] Three days later, in an impassioned address before the United Nations Security Council, Czechoslovak Foreign Minister Jiří Hájek systematically refuted every charge made by the Warsaw Pact occupiers and demanded the immediate withdrawal of foreign troops from Czechoslovak territory.[38] Even after the return of Dubček and the other Czechoslovak leaders from Moscow (on August 27), the Czechoslovak National Assembly declared the occupation an illegal violation of international treaties, including the Warsaw Pact.[39]

Within hours of their return to Prague, the leaders of the reform movement delivered moving speeches explaining the results of the Moscow negotiations and calling on leading Party and state bodies to ratify the Moscow Protocol.[40] Despite suggestions in the Czechoslovak press that to accept Moscow's terms would be "treason,"[41] Dubček retained sufficient support and authority to persuade the Party leadership to accept the inevitable, and the August 31 plenum of the Central Committee agreed to "fulfill the conditions of these negotiations

. . . as a condition of normalization of relations in Czechoslovakia and of relations with the five socialist states of the Warsaw Treaty."[42]

The Reintegration of Czechoslovakia

The terms of the Moscow Protocol were harsh indeed. On matters of foreign policy, the protocol demanded the legalization of the continued presence of Soviet troops until "the threat to socialism in Czechoslovakia . . . has passed," the withdrawal of Czechoslovakia's formal protest to the United Nations Security Council, and the expansion and intensification of economic, military, and foreign political relations between Czechoslovakia and the Soviet Union. In domestic affairs, the protocol obliged the Czechoslovak leaders to "consolidate and defend socialism," restore censorship, "fortify the Party and state apparatus at all levels," and "dismiss from office all those whose continuance in their posts would not promote the imperative task of reinforcing the leading role of the working class and of the Communist Party."[43]

This final stipulation comes closest to defining the essence of "normalization" in Czechoslovakia, for, in addition to its potential for spillover elsewhere in Eastern Europe, the reform movement had threatened to sunder—indeed, had already begun to sunder—the intricate web of interstate and inter-Party contacts on which the cohesion of the Soviet bloc ultimately rests. In what the Soviet press had termed a "witch-hunt" against "loyal, pro-Soviet workers,"[44] the Dubček regime had begun to replace the older generation of cadres. By virtue of training under Soviet tutelage or simply their long service to the Novotný regime, these cadres provided a bulwark of support for Party rule in Czechoslovakia and served as vital links in the complex chain of Soviet influence and control in Eastern Europe. In their place had come new, reform-minded cadres who owed their allegiance not to Soviet tutelage or the inherited traditions of Party rule but to an entirely new conception of "democratic socialism," one which threatened the cohesion of the entire bloc.[45]

Once "loyal" cadres had been reinstated, therefore, the next task of normalization would be to supervise the reintegration of Czechoslovakia into the alliance system. In the course of building a new model of socialism, the Dubček regime had constructed an infrastructure of Party and state rule which by its very nature conflicted with Soviet objectives in Eastern Europe: economic reforms ran counter to Soviet efforts to develop a highly centralized pattern of "socialist integration," the erosion of Leninist discipline in the Czechoslovak military conflicted with the drive toward "combat solidarity" of the Warsaw Pact armies under Soviet leadership, and the experiment in "socialism with a human face" amounted to a direct challenge to the Soviet Union's political and ideological "leading role" in Eastern Europe. Thus, normalization in Czechoslovakia was closely linked to broader Soviet objectives in the region, and it inevitably involved a thorough revamping of the patterns of rule established during the Prague Spring.

Thus defined, normalization in Czechoslovakia may be said to have passed through two general phases.[46] The first, beginning with Dubček's return to Prague and ending with his ouster in April 1969, was one of conflict between continued verbal allegiance to the goals of the Prague Spring on the one hand and, on the other, an ineluctable, if gradual, reversal of the reforms undertaken during that period. The second phase, which stretched from Husák's assumption of Party leadership to his capitulation in the October 1969 Soviet-Czechoslovak declaration, saw the consolidation of the post-Dubček leadership, the beginning of a full-scale purge of the Party leadership, and the almost complete dismantling of the reform movement. Thereafter, postinvasion normalization drew to an uneasy conclusion, and the Czechoslovak leaders set about the far more difficult process of trying to restore some *modus vivendi* with an embittered and disillusioned populace.

Phase One: Normalization with a Human Face

There was an air of unreality surrounding the final eight months of the Dubček regime. Not only did the leaders of the Prague Spring return to supervise the dismantling of reforms they themselves had initiated, but they continued to the very end to subscribe—in word, if not always in deed—to the goals embodied in the Czechoslovak reform movement. Even more paradoxically, it soon became apparent that there was precious little to dismantle, for the experiment in socialism with a human face had been more a national commitment to a democratic brand of socialism than a set of substantive measures which could be rescinded or revised.

To be sure, a number of initial measures were swiftly adopted: Club 231 and KAN were effectively banned,[47] an Office of Press and Information was established to facilitate censorship, and some leading liberals—Šik, Hájek, Kriegel, and others—were dismissed from their posts. On the other hand, the position of progressives and moderates in the top Party organs was actually strengthened, as several leading hard-liners were dropped from the Central Committee. With "normalization" beginning to look more like "polarization," Moscow dispatched Deputy Foreign Minister Kuznetsov to review the situation in Prague.[48]

Evidently dissatisfied with the pace of normalization, the Soviet leaders called Dubček and other leaders to Moscow twice in October. At the first meeting, the Czechoslovak leaders signed a joint communiqué, agreeing to fulfill the terms of the Moscow Protocol and, more specifically, to "step up efforts to raise the leading role of the Communist Party, . . . intensify the struggle against the antisocialist forces, . . . take the necessary measures to place all the mass information media at the service of socialism, [and] reinforce the party and state organs with men firmly adhering to positions of Marxism-Leninism."[49] The second session, held in mid-October, yielded an agreement on the "temporary" stationing of Soviet troops in Czechoslovakia. The crucial second article of this treaty, presented in the form of a passing observation rather than a binding condition of occupation, declared: "The temporary presence of Soviet troops on C.S.R. territory does not violate its sovereignty. Soviet troops are not interfering in the internal affairs of the Czechoslovak Socialist Republic."[50]

During the next few weeks, the political situation continued to polarize. Following Dubček's difficult Independence Day address, in which he reiterated his commitment to the "post-January" policies, student demonstrators massed in Prague's Václavské náměstí (Wenceslas Square) to protest the occupation. Ranged against these forces were the "so-called group of veteran communists," loosely linked with the hard-liners in the Party leadership, whose "wrecking activities" were decried over Prague radio on November 4.[51] External influences only added to the gathering crisis: delegations continued to travel almost daily between Prague and Moscow,[52] and on November 3 the Polish press delivered a ringing denunciation of "antisocialist forces" in Czechoslovakia.[53]

It was in this atmosphere that the November plenum of the Central Committee convened in Prague. The decisions of the plenum, adopted only after Dubček's hurried visit to Brezhnev in Warsaw (where the Soviet leader was attending the 5th PUWP Congress), resulted in a subtle victory for the conservatives. Although Brezhnev's statement of support had vindicated Dubček's position for the moment, the Party Presidium had reinstated three leading conservatives, and, more importantly, Dubček and his followers had been forced into a more centrist position.[54]

A lull following the November storm gave way to a fresh tempest in January. One of the few lasting reforms to have been implemented during the Dubček period was the constitutional amendment transforming the unitary Czechoslovak state into a federation of two socialist republics, the Czech and the Slovak.[55] Beginning on the occasion of the implementation of the amendment on January 1, 1969, and with the apparent support of the Soviet leadership, Slovak Communist party leader Gustáv Husák led a successful drive to replace Josef Smrkovský with a Slovak, Peter Colotka, as president of the National (now Federal) Assembly.

The ouster of Smrkovský, who more than any other figure had emerged as a symbol of liberal reawakening in Czechoslovakia, and the emotional public reaction to it (demonstrated most tragically by the self-immolation of a young Czech student named Jan Palach), revealed what was probably inevitable from the start: that Dubček could never steer a successful middle course between his two opposing constituencies, the Czechoslovak people and the leaders in Moscow. The first phase of the normalization process was fast drawing to a close.

This is not the place to offer a judgment on the record of "the politician with the sad eyes," Alexander Dubček. It can be said, however, that after August he was laboring under impossible conditions and that the inevitability of failure enveloped his efforts to concoct plans which might satisfy the Soviet leaders and at the same time preserve in part the reforms which had been initiated at such a heavy price.[56] To their credit, Dubček and the other Czechoslovak leaders managed to avoid a retreat on the New Economic Mechanism, and new "enterprise councils," modeled partially after Yugoslavia's "workers' self-management," were being formed well into 1969. It was to be up to Husák, Dubček's successor, to perform the final destruction of these elements of the Prague Spring.

The occasion, but hardly the cause, of Dubček's ouster was the spirited public reaction to the victory of the Czechoslovak ice hockey team over the Soviet team in the world championship match in Stockholm. In Prague, where the victory was seen as considerably more than one of a hockey team, mass celebration gave way to several acts of vandalism (some doubtless committed by agents provocateurs) against the Aeroflot office and other Soviet installations. In Moscow, official reaction to the incidents escalated from mild reproach directed against overzealous individuals involved in the vandalism to much more hostile attacks directed against the Czechoslovak leaders themselves, as the Soviet leadership began to recognize an opportunity to rid itself of the troublesome Dubček once and for all.[57] The end finally came on April 17, when a plenary session of the Central Committee of the Czechoslovak Communist Party replaced Dubček as first secretary with another Slovak, Gustáv Husák.[58]

Phase Two: Capitulation and Resovietization

Husák, a participant in the anti-Fascist resistance during the war and victim of the Stalinist purges of the 1950s, when he had been imprisoned as a "bourgeois (Slovak) nationalist," had hardly been a dogmatist in the usual sense of the term; he had helped draft the 1968 Party Action Program, and even after his elevation to the top Party post he continued to proclaim his commitment to most elements of the reform program. Whether from opportunism or genuine opposition to the postinvasion policies of Dubček, however, Husák had become increasingly tied to the conservative wing of the Party. The motives and preferences of one man mattered little, though, for the mood in Czechoslovakia had undergone a decisive shift: national resistance had become, like the guinea pigs of the Vaculík novel, "weak and floppy" in the face of unremitting Soviet pressure;

and even such reform leaders as Svoboda and Černík had come to accept the inevitability, perhaps even the desirability, of normalization.[59]

Husák's mandate was clear enough: he was to step up the process of normalization, restore firm Party rule, and begin the process of "resovietization"—that is, the reestablishment of the patterns of control on which the cohesion of the entire bloc depended. Once those tasks were complete, the way would be clear for Czechoslovakia's economic, military, and political reintegration into the "socialist family of states."

Within a week of Husák's accession to power, there began a series of purges, with conservatives supplanting reformists as editors of national and regional Party papers.[60] Other journals, including the influential *Listy* and *Reportér*, were banned, and normalization soon spread to other mass information media. In the judiciary, social and mass organizations, and lower Party organizations as well, reformists were systematically removed. By June, the purge had spread to the highest levels of the Party, as reformists such as Šik, Kriegel, and the noted Marxist philosopher Karel Kosík were ousted from the Central Committee;[61] and in September, conservatives replaced twenty-nine liberals on the Central Committee, and Dubček himself was dropped from the Presidium.[62]

Using Czechoslovakia's continuing economic difficulties as a convenient pretext, the Husák leadership quickly set about recentralizing the economy. Individual enterprises, which had enjoyed substantial independence since the Prague Spring, were forced to sign binding agreements with central planning authorities to fulfill production quotas, and the embryonic "enterprise councils" were systematically deprived of any real decisionmaking power.[63] By the end of the summer, exclusive economic power had been, for all intents and purposes, returned to the hands of central authorities.

The final breath of the Prague Spring came on the first anniversary of the invasion, as virtually the entire nation observed the "Day of Shame" and thousands of demonstrators clashed with police on the streets of Prague, in what many saw as a deliberately staged show of force by authorities anxious to prove themselves to Moscow. In any case, the immediate response to the disturbances, a harsh executive order "For Strengthening and Defending Public Order," signaled unmistakably a return to the tight control of the Stalinist era. "Resovietization" was all but complete; there remained only the tasks of capitulation and reintegration.

The process of restoring the Party's "leading role" domestically had been paralleled by that of normalizing relations within the bloc. Between April and October 1969, Husák paid formal visits to leaders of each of the invading states and received a continuous stream of military, foreign trade, scientific, ideological, and Party delegations from the Soviet Union and other bloc members.[64]

The economic dimension of bloc relations had acquired particular urgency, for at the 23rd, "Extraordinary" CMEA Council session, the Czechoslovak delegation, headed by Husák just five days after his accession to the top Party post, had expressed a number of reservations concerning the proposed "complex program" of integration.[65] From April on, the Soviet leaders and their surrogates in Prague had lobbied hard for the recentralization of the Czechoslovak economy and the redirection of Czechoslovakia's foreign trade toward CMEA partners.[66] Interrupted by preparations for the June conference of Communist and workers' parties, "economic normalization" resumed with additional external prodding toward the end of the summer.

The success of these efforts was revealed domestically in Husák's speech to the September 25 Central Committee plenary session, in which he presented plans for the further centralization of the economy,[67] and externally in the joint Soviet-Czechoslovak statement of October 29, which established a program for the coordination of Czechoslovak and Soviet national economic plans through 1975 and for long-term cooperation across a wide range of functional economic areas.[68] By late 1969, the Czechoslovak position on CMEA integration had changed from "revisionist" opposition to unquestioning support.[69]

The October communiqué was significant for the additional reason that it marked the complete capitulation of the Husák regime to the doctrine of limited sovereignty. Virtually every particular of the Brezhnev Doctrine found expression in the joint resolution: proceeding from the "class understanding of sovereignty" and the imperatives of "strengthening . . . the socialist gains," the Soviet and Czechoslovak leaders proclaimed the invasion to have been "an act of internationalist solidarity that helped bar the way to antisocialist counterrevolutionary forces." To formalize the capitulation, the two signatories further agreed to commemorate the twenty-fifth anniversary of the postwar "liberation" of Czechoslovakia by signing a new treaty of friendship, cooperation, and mutual aid.[70]

Finally, more than a year after the Warsaw Pact invasion and six months after the installation of the Husák regime, the domestic situation in Czechoslovakia had been "normalized" on terms acceptable to the Soviet leaders. Elsewhere in the bloc and beyond, meanwhile, the invasion of Czechoslovakia had left a similarly bitter legacy.

Alliance Management: The Legacy of Prague

At the same time they were supervising the process of socialist reconstruction in Czechoslovakia, the Soviet leaders had been struggling toward "normalization" in other spheres. With an international conference of Communist and workers' parties scheduled to convene in Moscow in early 1969 and with Soviet authority in the Communist movement severely, perhaps irrevocably, undermined, the Soviet leaders began almost immediately to gather support in Eastern Europe in the hope of using the conference as a forum for the expression of international Communist solidarity. This task, in turn, was made more difficult by growing instability in Eastern Europe, particularly in the Balkans.

Although the Prague Spring did not become the Moscow summer, to borrow Lewis Feuer's phrase,[71] it did engender a spillover effect elsewhere in the region. Aside from Poland, where Moczar's "Partisans" attempted to exploit the political fallout from the Prague Spring, the best-documented case of direct repercussions of the Czechoslovak reform movement was in the Ukraine, where a small but vocal group of nationalist intellectuals sought unsuccessfully to promote their own version of democratic socialism.[72] In the aftermath of the invasion, opposition to the Warsaw Pact action appeared throughout Eastern Europe in the form of letters of protest and public demonstrations; and in Moscow's Red Square a handful of demonstrators led by Pavel Litvinov, grandson of the former foreign minister, assembled to protest the invasion.[73]

These incidents, however isolated or seemingly insignificant, must have caused considerable trepidation among the East European leaders, whose fear of a "rising of the masses" had been amply demonstrated. The events of 1968, then, worked in two directions: on the one hand, the reform movement in Czechoslovakia served to encourage sympathetic activity elsewhere in the bloc, as in the growth of the so-called Democratic Movement in the Soviet Union; and on the other, the implications of precipitous reform as manifested in Czechoslovakia reinforced the determination of the Soviet and East European leaders to retain firm domestic control.

Whatever the underlying motivations, the developments of 1968 gave way to an unmistakable effort to restore domestic orthodoxy in the Soviet bloc. For its part, the Soviet Central Committee warned that events in Czechoslovakia should not lead to expectation of reform or "so-called bourgeois freedoms" in the USSR.[74] After the invasion, the clearest manifestation of domestic hatch-tightening in Eastern Europe was in the gradual reversal of many of the economic reforms initiated in the mid-1960s. In Bulgaria, the economic "reform" announced in January 1969 was in fact a recentralizing counterreform of the market mechanisms which had been cautiously implemented over the preceding three years.[75] A similar process was under way in East Germany, where the SED party organ *Neues Deutschland* summarized the retrenchment of the GDR's "New Economic System" by reviving the old Stalinist formula, "Plan discipline is state discipline."[76] In the Soviet Union, Poland, and Romania as well, where economic reform had been piecemeal at best, centralizers quickly gained the upper hand. Even in Hungary, where the reform momentum initiated in January 1968 continued through 1972 and beyond, Party leaders took steps to insure that economic reformism would not spread to the political sphere.[77]

Under the additional stimulus of growing East-West détente and the attendant

fear of "ideological infection," the bloc-wide effort toward a domestic normalization continued to build over the next few years. Meanwhile, developments of
more immediate import demanded the attention of bloc leaders. Chief among
these was the rapid worsening of Sino-Soviet relations and its implications for
the southern flank of the Soviet bloc.

Balkan *Nervenkrieg*

From the perspective of the Soviet leaders, the firm action against Czechoslovakia had the added advantage of reinforcing the credibility of their threats
elsewhere in Eastern Europe, particularly as against Romania and Yugoslavia.
As has already been seen, that the Romanians and Yugoslavs took these threats
seriously is beyond question. At the same time, however, the events of 1968 had
the opposing, perhaps dialectical, effect of forging a virtual Romanian-
Yugoslav entente against further Soviet encroachment in Eastern Europe. To the
already complex situation was added the growing hostility of the Sino-Soviet
split, soon to explode into military clashes along the Ussuri River, and its
ramifications in the Balkans.

Not surprisingly, the Chinese saw in the aftermath of invasion an opportunity
to exploit the disarray in the Communist world to Chinese advantage. In
Albania, where the leadership had protested the invasion by formally withdraw-
ing from the Warsaw Pact, a visit by a Chinese delegation led to speculation that
plans had been approved for the establishment of a Chinese military base in
Tirana;[78] and in Romania the Chinese connection grew even closer following
China's efforts to reduce Soviet pressure in the Balkans by stepping up anti-
Soviet propaganda and increasing military activity along the Sino-Soviet
border.[79] Most dramatic of all was the reversal of the previously hostile Sino-
Yugoslav relationship, a reversal symbolized in 1969 by the arrival of a Yugoslav trade mission in China and, a year later, by the restoration of full diplomatic
relations.

Relations among the Balkan countries themselves underwent a similar transformation. Romanian-Yugoslav relations became particularly close during this
period, as Ceaușescu and Tito met three times in 1968 to discuss joint measures
for dealing with the Czechoslovak crisis. Even Albania, which at that time
maintained diplomatic relations only with Romania among the East European
countries, joined in the effort toward Balkan solidarity by offering military
assistance to Yugoslavia and Romania in the event of a Soviet attack.[80] At the
obvious urging of the Chinese, Albania continued to move toward rapprochement with Yugoslavia, and in 1971 full diplomatic relations between the two
countries were restored. By 1971, in fact, talk of a "Balkan zone" of solidarity
and cooperation had become such a common theme, particularly in Ceaușescu's

speeches, that the Hungarian press felt obliged to warn of the threat of a Chinese-inspired, anti-Soviet "Tirana-Belgrade-Bucharest axis."[81]

In light of the evolving situation in the Balkans—though it is difficult to distinguish cause from effect here—the Soviet leadership moved to restore influence in the region. In late September 1968, rumors began to circulate that the Soviet Union was planning a major military build-up in the Balkans, and in early October the stationing of two divisions of Soviet airborne troops in Bulgaria—odd man out in the emerging Balkan triangle—was seen as a prelude to the establishment of a permanent Soviet military presence in both Bulgaria and Romania.[82] Although the nature of Soviet military activity in the Balkans, and its underlying motivations, never did become clear, immediate condemnations by the Albanians and Chinese and the arrival in Bucharest of Marshal Yakubovsky, the commander-in-chief of Warsaw Pact forces, lent some initial credence to the reports.[83]

Indeed, there were persuasive military and political motivations for such a move. Most obviously, the Balkan operation would have established a Soviet military presence in the last two Warsaw Pact states without Soviet military contingents and simultaneously would have bolstered the pact's southern flank. Additionally, Soviet doubts concerning the reliability of the East European armed forces, so recently confirmed by the anti-Soviet solidarity of the Czechoslovak army, weighed in favor of stationing troops in the Balkans, and particularly in Romania. Finally, having weathered the reaction to the Czechoslovak invasion, the Soviet leaders might have reasoned that they would find no better opportunity to move against the dissident Romanians.

There were, of course, compelling counterarguments as well. For one thing, the installation of Soviet troops in Bulgaria, which had experienced an attempted coup by a nationalist faction in the army as recently as 1965, could only serve to discredit the pro-Soviet orientation of the Bulgarian leadership. There was also some uncertainty as to the possible reaction of the United States government, which already had warned against Soviet intervention in Romania or Yugoslavia. It was clear, moreover, that the Ceauşescu leadership would consider the installation of Soviet troops on Romanian soil a virtual act of war and would offer considerable, perhaps military, resistance to such an attempt.

In any case, with the eventual withdrawal of Soviet troops from Bulgaria and the abandonment of the plan for a military build-up in the region (if, indeed, such a plan had ever been seriously contemplated), it became apparent that the Soviet adventure in the Balkans had the more limited objective of bringing pressure to bear on the Romanians and Yugoslavs through a show of strength. Soviet pressure continued through the end of 1968, as Yugoslavia became the target of an intensive campaign of vilification in the Soviet press designed to isolate Yugoslavia ideologically and drive a wedge in the emerging Romanian-Yugoslav entente.[84] Similarly, the rapidly escalating *Nervenkrieg* with Ro-

mania, part of the overall Soviet strategy to divide and conquer, was undertaken
to secure Romanian cooperation in Warsaw Pact and CMEA endeavors.

The complex war of nerves in the Balkans continued unabated through 1971,
as the Romanian and Yugoslav leaders sought to counter Soviet ambitions in the
region by cultivating their mutual relations and developing closer ties with
China. For its part, the Ceauşescu leadership managed to resist pressures to
participate in Warsaw Pact maneuvers and continued to pursue an independent
foreign policy line.[85] Under intense Soviet military, economic, and political
pressure, however, Ceauşescu was forced to accede to a number of key proposals, most notably the 1969 Budapest reforms of the Warsaw Pact and the
1971 "Comprehensive Program" for economic cooperation, designed to further
the process of integration in the Soviet bloc.[86]

Moscow's Balkan operation had also been conceived with more immediate
concerns in mind. With dissension in the Communist world approaching critical
proportions, the convening of the long-delayed International Conference of
Communist and Workers' Parties had acquired new urgency, and the Soviet
leadership was bent on isolating its most hostile critics—China, Albania, and
Yugoslavia—and forcing the Romanians into a more cooperative position. The
Soviet strategy bore some immediate results, for with Soviet troops conducting
maneuvers across the border in Bulgaria, the Romanians quickly agreed to
abandon their public criticism of the Czechoslovak invasion and to participate in
the preliminary negotiations for the world Communist conference.[87]

The Moscow Conference and the Quest for Stability

When it finally convened in June of 1969, the Moscow conference was a massive
gathering of representatives of seventy-five Communist and workers' parties
from around the world—the largest inter-Communist conclave since the 1960
Moscow conference of eighty-one parties. It had been proposed as early as 1963,
when Khrushchev was attempting to gather support for the reassertion of Soviet
primacy in the international Communist movement. Quietly shelved after
Khrushchev's ouster, proposals for a conference were again aired in 1966, and a
long series of preliminary talks were held over the next two years.[88] Initially set
for November 1968, the conference was again postponed, as the Soviet leaders
attempted to rally support in the wake of the Czechoslovak invasion.

When negotiations resumed in September and October of 1968, it appeared
that something new might be in the offing: the creation of "permanent organs for
discussing serious, theoretical [issues], at least in the community of socialist
states."[89] This proposal, published in the East German Party organ *Neues
Deutschland,* was widely interpreted in the Western press as a joint Soviet–East
German attempt to establish a new Comintern or Cominform, one presumably

free of the Stalinist excesses associated with the earlier organizations. Reports in the Soviet press were considerably more ambiguous, however, and it appeared that the East Germans had been appointed to float the trial balloon for a proposal which was certain to meet with resistance in the Communist world.

The resistance must have been stiff, for in May 1969 Mikhail Suslov, the ranking ideologist in the Soviet Politburo, acknowledged the existence of "varied conditions which have already ruled out talk of the organization of a united directing center for the Communist movement."[90] Although nothing ever came of proposals for a revived Comintern, they were symbolic of renewed Soviet concern for ideological unity in Eastern Europe, and they presaged the development of other, less grandiose forums for ideological consultation.[91]

Meanwhile, negotiations for the proposed conference continued, as preliminary sessions were held in March and May. Soviet relations with China, Albania, and Yugoslavia were by this time critically strained: bloc leaders, with the exception of Ceauşescu, boycotted the Yugoslav Party Congress in March, and that same month clashes erupted on the Sino-Soviet border. Though achieved at heavy cost, the Soviet effort to isolate the USSR's most hostile critics succeeded, for neither China, Albania, nor Yugoslavia was represented at the Moscow conference.[92] The second half of the Kremlin's conference strategy —to secure Romanian participation—also succeeded, and a Romanian delegation duly arrived in Moscow for the conference opening on June 5.

If the Soviet leaders had entertained any hopes that the conference would yield a show of unity, however, they were quickly disappointed. Dissension began on the second day, when Ceauşescu interrupted the first speaker, a Paraguayan who had launched an attack on Maoism, to remind the conference that during the preparatory talks it had been agreed that participants would refrain from condemning other parties. The warning went unheeded, however, as Polish Party leader Gomulka soon rose to denounce China for maintaining territorial claims against the Soviet Union. Ultimately, more than two-thirds of the parties condemned the Chinese for hurling "invective and slander" at the Soviet Union and other socialist countries.[93]

The issue of Czechoslovakia, which Moscow had sought to exclude from discussion, was raised by an Australian delegate, who argued that if the Chinese case could be discussed, then surely the Czechoslovak invasion was a proper topic. Acting on Moscow's behalf, Czechoslovak Party leader Husák cautioned against drawing "premature conclusions" and promised a "full analysis" soon, but he stopped short of sanctioning the invasion.[94] The issue had been raised, though, and a number of delegations, including most of the West Europeans but not the Romanians, took the floor to criticize the invasion.

The final draft of the conference resolution was marked by similar dissent; indeed, the text was peppered with admissions of "divergencies," "differences," and "difficulties" in the Communist world.[95] Fifteen months in the drafting and composed, according to Prague television,[96] of some seventy-five amendments, the resolution was as curious a piece of patchwork as one might expect from such diverse authorship. Virtually every assertion concerning relations among the parties was either qualified in the text or subsequently repudiated by one or more parties.[97]

In one dialectical sleight of hand, the resolution asserted that the Communist movement "is not afflicted with the contradictions inherent in capitalism" but has, rather, "divergencies" which "need not disrupt the united front of socialist countries." The contrast with the 1960 conference declaration was glaring. No longer was the Soviet Union the "first and mightiest" of the Communist parties; rather, it was now declared, "All parties have equal rights. At this time when there is no leading center of the international Communist movement, voluntary coordination of the actions of parties in order to carry out the tasks before them acquires increased importance."

The Soviet leaders received precious little in return for their concessions on party equality. Sandwiched between two unrelated paragraphs was a single, veiled reference to the Brezhnev Doctrine: "The defense of socialism is an international duty of Communists." Nevertheless, even the artificial unity of the conference had served some Soviet objectives: the Chinese had been repudiated, the Yugoslavs isolated, and the Romanians contained, at least for the time being. Beyond this, the Moscow conference represented the partial success of Soviet efforts toward inter-Communist normalization, for although their leading role in the Communist world had been seriously weakened, the Soviet leaders had managed to avert the total disintegration of international Communist solidarity.

Thus, with the conclusion of the Moscow conference, the difficult period of postinvasion normalization drew to an end. The restoration of Party control in Czechoslovakia and the dismantling of the reforms of the Prague Spring had prepared the way for Czechoslovakia's reintegration into the bloc, soon to be formalized by the October 1969 Soviet-Czechoslovak declaration. Elsewhere in the region general stability had been restored, and the Romanians had been forced into at least a temporary acquiescence to Soviet initiatives in Eastern Europe.

With these tasks behind them, bloc leaders could once again turn to pressing issues involving their mutual relations. In external affairs, little action had been taken toward promoting their early initiatives for a pan-European security conference. Militarily, the Budapest conference of March 1969 had outlined a number of changes whose nature was only beginning to become apparent. In economic relations, too, aside from a vague statement of principle on economic integration, bloc leaders had been marking time since the Czechoslovak events of 1968. All these concerns were soon to find expression in a coordinated "integrationist program" in Eastern Europe.

3

Alliance Restructuring, 1969–1971

Looking backward, there is always a danger of applying an unwarranted determinacy to courses of action chosen from competing alternatives. This caveat applies with particular force to the topic at hand, for in many respects 1969 was a critical year of decision in Soviet–East European relations. To be sure, a number of initiatives—toward the convening of a European security conference, for example—already had been set in motion; but a corresponding number of contradictory developments had yet to be resolved, and a series of genuine policy alternatives confronted the Soviet and East European leaders. Most prominently, this was the time for the Brezhnev/Kosygin leadership in the USSR to stamp its imprint on Soviet–East European relations; having directed the invasion of Czechoslovakia and the uneasy normalization which followed it, the Soviet leaders now faced the task of building a tight, integrated alliance system in an era of rapidly expanding relations between East and West.

The most dramatic manifestation of evolving East-West détente, of course, was the thaw in U.S.–Soviet relations, particularly after the inauguration of the Moscow-Washington ''hot line'' at the time of the June 1967 Arab-Israeli War and the Glassboro summit meeting of President Johnson and Premier Kosygin. Despite the escalation of American involvement in the Vietnam War, negotiations continued through 1967 toward the signing of a nuclear nonproliferation treaty; and by the time of the opening of the Paris peace talks on Vietnam in May 1968, Soviet leaders declared their readiness to enter into negotiations on the limitation of strategic weapons, including the antiballistic missile (ABM). Motivated perhaps by the rapid deterioration of the Czechoslovak situation and the attendant need to stabilize relations with the West, Soviet leaders continued their cautious détente initiatives, and on July 1, 1968, the Soviet Union along with the United States and fifty-nine other countries signed the long-awaited treaty on nuclear nonproliferation.

Seen in Western Europe, and particularly in France and West Germany, as a *Diktat* of the superpowers, the nonproliferation treaty served to aggravate strains in the Atlantic alliance, already weakened by reactions to American involvement in Southeast Asia and France's military withdrawal from NATO in 1966. Following President de Gaulle's 1966 visit to the USSR, Soviet European policy had centered on cultivating the French connection to further divide NATO. With the gradual cooling of Soviet-French relations, particularly following de Gaulle's swing to the right after the May 1968 riots, and the early Ostpolitik initiatives of the Kiesinger-Brandt government, however, the German question began to occupy center stage in Soviet European policy.[1]

The early Soviet bloc initiatives toward a European security conference, complicated by East Germany's intransigence and Romania's independent exchange of relations with West Germany, have already been discussed.[2] Interrupted by the course of events in Czechoslovakia, Warsaw Pact *Westpolitik* resumed in 1969, as the conference proposal was again floated at the June conference of Communist and workers' parties. By late 1969, however, the situation in Western Europe had become considerably more fluid and uncertain, for in April of that year General de Gaulle had resigned the French presidency, to be replaced by the much less adventurous Georges Pompidou, and in October Willy Brandt, the architect of Ostpolitik, had assumed the chancellorship of the first Social Democratic government in the history of the Federal Republic.[3]

During this same period, as has been seen, Soviet relations with China had taken a dramatic turn for the worse, and Chinese influence in the Balkans had reached threatening proportions. Thus, from the Soviet perspective, not only did the fear of a possible "struggle on two fronts" demand the stabilization of relations with Western Europe, but Chinese "splitting activities" in the Balkans aggravated existing divisive tendencies within the Soviet bloc itself.

As to Eastern Europe, the disruptions of polycentric Communism in the 1960s have already been discussed in some detail, as have the more recent developments in Czechoslovakia and the Balkans. To these should be added a gradual drift toward economic disarray in Eastern Europe. With the failure of the 1962 "Basic Principles" plan for CMEA integration, Eastern Europe had begun to turn increasingly to Western markets: while trade among CMEA members doubled between 1962 and 1972, trade with Western Europe in the same period quadrupled, and trade with the United States and Japan increased eightfold.[4] Although the total volume of trade with the West amounted to less than one-third of CMEA trade even in 1972, the bilateral, unregulated nature of the exchanges and their rapid expansion threatened to upset the pattern of CMEA trade and, ultimately, of East European integration itself. Thus, by the late 1960s the need had become apparent for a coordinated approach to the West on the one hand and a new formula for East European integration on the other.

Directions of Change

Writing in early 1969, one Western analyst suggested that the principal choice for Soviet policy toward Europe was between an offensive strategy, designed to exploit fissures in the Atlantic alliance, and a defensive strategy, which would focus more narrowly on promoting cohesion and integration in Eastern Europe.[5] The offensive strategy, he argued, would involve Soviet acceptance, even encouragement, of fundamental changes in the European order and toleration, at least temporarily, of diversity in the Soviet bloc. The crux of the strategy would be Germany: in return for concessions on German unification, perhaps including liquidation of the East German state, the Soviet leaders would attempt to lure West Germany away from the United States and ultimately to secure the Federal Republic's withdrawal from NATO.

The defensive strategy, by contrast, would take as its point of departure the European status quo and would involve careful regulation and monitoring of East-West contacts, particularly those involving the two German states. Within the bloc, the aim of Soviet leaders would be to "give institutional flesh to their dominance of East Europe" by constructing more formalized procedures for foreign policy coordination, promoting supranational economic planning through CMEA, and perhaps developing institutional forums for the resolution of political-ideological disputes.[6]

Although the offensive option may have been overstated,[7] the central dilemma facing the Soviet leaders in 1969 was correctly posed, for the crucial policy choice was whether to tilt toward an ambitious, and also dangerous, strategy of encouraging favorable change in Europe or toward the more conservative strategy of "defending the socialist gains." Ideally, the Soviet leaders may have wished for the best of both these worlds: to promote changes in Europe which would further divide the NATO countries, while at the same time undertaking measures to strengthen Soviet control in the bloc; to aim toward *status quo plus* in the West, *status quo ante* in the East. With their opportunities for divisive activity in the West circumscribed and difficulties in Eastern Europe still unresolved, however, the Soviet leaders tilted toward the less dangerous course of encouraging stability through a coordinated bloc détente policy and a drive toward cohesion in Eastern Europe.

Beyond these general objectives, the Soviet leaders probably did not have a clear conception of Soviet bloc strategy for the 1970s. Even if they did, it soon became apparent that Soviet authority was no longer what it once was in Eastern

Europe, and developments in the bloc over the next few years reflected a genuine plurality of views and interests. Indeed, for most of the crucial period 1969–1971 the Soviet leaders found themselves in the unfamiliar role of mediator of conflicting interests in Eastern Europe, as they sought to weld a coordinated bloc policy toward the West and supervise a new effort toward socialist integration.

Westpolitik: Controlled Bilateralism

The first half of the Soviet strategy, to establish a coordinated détente policy, began to emerge at the March 1969 Budapest conference of the Warsaw Pact's Political Consultative Committee (PCC). Since the 1967 Karlovy Vary conference, little had been heard from the Warsaw Pact concerning the proposed pan-European security conference. With the process of normalization in Eastern Europe already under way (though the Budapest conference was chaired, ironically, by Alexander Dubček), the Budapest appeal reflected a more serious effort on the part of the Soviet and East European leaders to confront the evolving situation in Europe.

Reiterating the earlier call for a European security conference, the appeal specified the Warsaw Pact's "prerequisites" for such a conference: "The inviolability of existing boundaries in Europe . . . ; recognition of the fact of the existence of the German Democratic Republic and the Federal Republic of Germany; renunciation by the Federal Republic of Germany of its claims to represent all the German people; renunciation [by West Germany] of possession of nuclear weapons in any form."[8] So much for a Soviet offensive strategy involving compromise on the issue of German reunification. Under intense pressure from the East Germans,[9] the Soviet and East European leaders not only had gone a long way toward closing the door to reunification but had insisted on rather precise guarantees of East German sovereignty, including de facto recognition of the GDR.

Although drafted in a multilateral setting, the appeal was obviously an amalgam of various bilateral approaches to West Germany, and the language of the document betrayed a number of conflicts among the Warsaw Pact states as to the nature and purpose of the proposed conference. As Harland Cleveland, former United States representative to the North Atlantic Council, observed, "A close reading of the Budapest appeal suggested a hard-fought compromise: The Soviets got their appeal. . . . The East German and Polish 'Hawks' got the pre-conditions on which they had been insisting; and the Czech and Hungarian 'Doves' managed to delete most of the traditional polemics."[10] He might also have noted that through reference to "respect for independence and sovereignty of states," the Romanians got the formal guarantees for which they had lobbied.

Beyond the surface differences revealed in the Budapest appeal were a number of more fundamental Warsaw Pact conflicts on the issue of European cooperation. The East Germans, because of the GDR's advantageous position as the principal exporter of finished goods in CMEA and because of the leadership's acute fear of ideological "infection," were wary of East-West cooperation in any form. At the other extreme were the Romanians, bent on using the process of détente as a means of loosening the Soviet grip on Eastern Europe. Between these two extreme positions were various shades of support for the emerging bloc détente policy.[11]

Beginning with the May conference of deputy foreign ministers in East Berlin and extending through the end of 1969 and beyond, the aim of bloc leaders, chiefly the Soviets and East Germans, was to subsume bilateral East European initiatives toward the West within a more general, multilateral approach toward détente. As is often the case in Soviet–East European relations, this approach was not genuinely multilateral, for the Soviets—no less than the Romanians, albeit for different reasons—were intent on exploiting their emerging bilateral relationship with the West Germans. For its part, the new Brandt government in the Federal Republic acted swiftly to remove the chief obstacles to East-West *rapprochement* by pledging to sign the nuclear nonproliferation treaty and offering de facto recognition to the GDR.[12]

It was in this rapidly changing European context that the Warsaw Pact foreign ministers met in Prague in October 1969—the same month, it will be remembered, of the joint Soviet-Czechoslovak communiqué formalizing the capitulation of the Husák regime. Noting "with satisfaction the broadly favorable response [in the West] to the proposal for an all-European conference," the Prague declaration set the Warsaw Pact's priorities for the conference: discussion of general topics related to European security, renunciation of "force or threats of force" in European affairs, and negotiations toward "expansion of trade, economic, and scientific and technical ties" between East and West. The signatories went on to propose "bilateral or multilateral consultations between interested states to discuss these points in preparation for an all-European conference."[13]

The tension between bilateralism and multilateralism continued as Soviet and East European party and government leaders met in Moscow in early December, less than a week after the Bonn government had signed the nonproliferation treaty. The text of the Moscow summit reaffirmed the principles on which East-West cooperation should be based—including "noninterference in internal affairs" and recognition of "existing European frontiers as final and unchangeable"—and added, along with warnings of West German "revanchism," the entirely new stipulation "that the interests of peace and security require that all states establish relations of equality with the GDR on the basis of international law."[14]

This final stipulation stopped just short of endorsing the East German position: that *de jure* recognition of the GDR should be a precondition for the convening of a European security conference. More than that, it represented a significant breakthrough in Soviet efforts to weld a coordinated Warsaw Pact policy toward the West, for the handling of the German question achieved a workable balance among the various positions: East German pursuit of *de jure* recognition, West German determination to leave open the possibility of eventual reunification, Soviet commitment to the legitimization of the territorial status quo in Europe, and the various positions of the other Warsaw Pact states, particularly Romania.[15]

From the time of the Moscow summit to the opening of preliminary negotiations for the Conference on Security and Cooperation in Europe (CSCE) in late 1972 and early 1973, bilateral and multilateral negotiations between East and West increased rapidly. The conclusion of the Quadripartite Agreement on Berlin, the first Soviet-American strategic arms limitation agreement, and the signing of treaties between West Germany and the Soviet Union, East Germany, Poland, and Czechoslovakia all served to alter the context of Warsaw Pact Westpolitik. In bloc consultations during the same period, the East Germans continued to lobby for a strong Warsaw Pact position on the German question, and the Romanians continued to resist Soviet efforts to weld a bloc approach toward the West.[16]

The basic framework for Soviet bloc détente diplomacy, however, had been established at the Moscow summit. By seizing the initiative in European affairs, Warsaw Pact leaders had established their preconditions for a European security conference—recognition of existing European boundaries and resolution of the German question in a manner compatible with East German sovereignty—and affirmed their joint determination to monitor and regulate the evolving pattern of East-West relations so as to insure "noninterference in internal affairs." For the East European states, the cardinal principle of détente diplomacy was to be "controlled bilateralism": independent East European initiatives were to be conducted under the umbrella of an overarching bloc policy toward the West and regulated through frequent consultations among bloc leaders.

This, in broad outline, was the Soviet bloc offensive strategy for the early 1970s. The task which remained was to develop a corresponding defensive strategy which would facilitate the building of a tight, integrated socialist community in an era of détente and expanded contacts with the West.

Toward Socialist Integration?

In a sense, the elaboration of a defensive strategy in Eastern Europe was a continuation of the process of normalization already under way. As J. F. Brown put it, "Having begun the process of restoring stability in Eastern Europe after

Czechoslovakia, [the Soviet leaders] were understandably loath to see it cracked by fissures emanating from the West." The essence of Soviet policy toward the bloc after 1968, he argued, was "directed consensus," an enforced unity designed "to promote cohesion through a comprehensive integrationist policy at every level."[17]

The Soviet drive for an integrationist policy was shaped, in part, by a number of specific concerns related to the development of East-West détente. First and most immediate, there was the need to insure "controlled bilateralism" in East-West relations by improving the mechanisms for consultation and coordination in CMEA and the Warsaw Treaty Organization. Second, the prospect of increased contacts with the "class enemies" in the West stimulated renewed concern for ideological unity in Eastern Europe. Third, to counter the potentially disruptive consequences of expanded trade relations with the capitalist West, greater importance was attached to the task of promoting economic integration through CMEA. Finally and most generally, the decline of East-West hostilities and the attendant diminution of the objective reasons for bloc solidarity raised new determination to insure "unity and cohesion" in Soviet–East European relations.

It would be misleading, of course, to view developments in Eastern Europe since 1968 solely as responses to the perceived dangers of détente, for Soviet efforts toward "further perfecting" the Warsaw Treaty Organization and improving economic cooperation in CMEA have in fact been part of an evolutionary process of system-building in Eastern Europe. In Communist theoretical literature, as has been seen, this process is one of "socialist integration" or, as one Soviet theorist characterized it, the creation of "thousands of unbreakable bonds"—economic, military, political, ideological, and cultural—"[linking] the peoples of the new world, facilitating their union."[18]

Clearly, the union of "the peoples of the new world" remained a very long-range objective, if even that. For the nearer term, the Soviet drive for socialist integration had the more limited aim of preventing a recurrence of the events of 1968 by creating within the Soviet bloc an interdependence so thorough and a system of consultation and coordination so pervasive that recourse to direct military coercion would be rendered unnecessary.

In pursuit of this desideratum, two fundamental options were available to the Soviet leaders: to attempt to push through an integrationist program from above by establishing supranational planning organs and investing them with decision-making authority, or to promote integration from below through the more gradual processes of consultation and coordination. The first option, sure to meet with vigorous opposition in Eastern Europe, would require heavy application of direct and indirect Soviet pressure and perhaps, given Romanian intransigence, exclusion of Romania from some aspects of the integration scheme; the second, presumably, would demand a restructuring of the alliance system to provide greater East European access to decisionmaking. The fact that the Soviet leaders ultimately tilted toward the second of these options should not obscure the extent to which the year 1969 was one of serious negotiation over the future of intrabloc relations in Eastern Europe. In fact, in late 1968 and early 1969 indications were strong that the Soviet leaders, with the support of the East Germans and others, were aiming at a bold supranational solution to the problems of socialist integration.

The October 1968 East German proposal for the creation of a new, supranational ideological organization along the lines of Comintern has already been discussed in some detail.[19] It should be noted, however, that the proposal was allowed to remain in the air until the time of the Moscow Conference in June 1969, when the Soviets finally signaled their preference for such "natural" forms of ideological cooperation as "bilateral consultations, regional meetings, and international conferences."[20]

In any case, at the same time as the Comintern proposal, the East Germans floated another trial balloon, this one for the creation of a new, more tightly knit Warsaw Pact subgrouping consisting of the Soviet Union and its four partners in the August invasion and excluding Czechoslovakia and Romania.[21] This proposal, too, was left unrefuted until the March 1969 Budapest conference of the WTO Political Consultative Committee, and rumors persisted that the Soviets were bent on creating a supranational, NATO-style unified command in the Warsaw Pact.[22]

Just two weeks later, in November 1968, in his closing speech to the Polish United Workers' Party (PUWP) Congress, Party leader Wladyslaw Gomulka issued a call for a "strengthening of the complex economic links among Comecon countries" in terms which led to speculation that creation of a supranational plan for economic integration might also be under consideration.[23] Such speculation increased the following month, when a Soviet economist published an article proposing creation of "a new organization of general planning" in CMEA.[24] The specter of supranationalism aroused strong concern in Eastern Europe in the early months of 1969,[25] for although official Soviet statements on the issue remained ambiguous, the possibility of a supranational planning body had not been explicitly ruled out by the time of the opening of the 23rd, "Extraordinary" CMEA Council session in April.

Thus, by early 1969 proposals had been aired for the creation of entirely new, supranational organs for economic, military, and ideological cooperation in the Soviet bloc. It is difficult to assess the degree of Soviet commitment to these proposals. Perhaps, emboldened by their recent assertion of military determination to control events in the bloc and fearful of new tendencies toward disintegration inherent in East-West détente, the Soviet leaders felt the time was ripe to push for a wholesale revamping of the alliance system in Eastern Europe. The idea of excluding Romania from some elements of the integration scheme may have held some appeal, too, for the Romanians had proved particularly adept at upsetting Soviet plans for improving the mechanisms of alliance cohesion.

In light of subsequent developments, however, it seems more likely that the supranationalist proposals had been aired by the Soviets to bring pressure to bear on the East Europeans in preparation for impending negotiations on Warsaw Pact and CMEA restructuring. The parallels with 1956 are apparent: just as Khrushchev had done, the new Soviet leaders attempted, under conditions of international détente and intrabloc dissension, to restructure intra-alliance relations and reassert Soviet authority in the region. Somewhat paradoxically, this effort demanded a rather more creative application of Soviet power and influence; its success required greater sensitivity to the role of the junior allies in intra-alliance deliberations. Nowhere were these considerations more evident than in the negotiations surrounding the reforms of the Warsaw Treaty Organization in 1969.

The Budapest Reforms of the Warsaw Pact

Soviet efforts to restructure the Warsaw Pact date, as has been seen, from Brezhnev's 1965 call for the "further perfecting of the Warsaw Treaty Organization." Although the precise nature of Soviet aims was never revealed, it is clear that consideration was given the creation of some new central organ to facilitate foreign policy coordination and, presumably, expand Soviet control through the Warsaw Pact command structure. Early resistance to the proposal, particularly from Romania and Czechoslovakia, took the form of counterproposals for greater East European input into "collective" decisions and reduction of what was seen as an excessive and misdirected East European defense burden.[26]

The proposal to restructure the pact was again aired at the March 1968 Political Consultative Committee (PCC) meeting in Sofia, and national defense ministers were instructed to draft their blueprints for Warsaw Pact reform. Interrupted by the dramatic turn of events in Czechoslovakia, negotiations resumed in the fall of 1968, as WTO defense ministers met in Moscow in October and WTO chiefs of staff convened, significantly, in Bucharest the following month. Bilateral negotiations continued through early 1969, as Soviet Marshal Yakubovsky, the WTO commander-in-chief, twice visited each East European capital.

By this time the nature of East European grievances had become more clear, for during the heady days of the reform movement, Czechoslovak Lieutenant General Vaclav Prchlík had issued a public critique of the existing Warsaw Pact command structure. The Joint Command, Prchlík argued, "is formed by marshals, generals, and officers of the Soviet army [while] the other member countries have only their representatives in this joint command." "These representatives," he continued, "have so far held no responsibilities nor had a hand in making decisions, but rather have played the role of liaison organs [transmission belts?]." He proposed, therefore, that "necessary qualitative changes" be made to strengthen the role of the PCC, establish regular periods for its convening, and restructure relations "in such a way as to emphasize the real equality of individual members" of the pact so that each "can really assert itself and have its share in the programmatic work of the whole coalition." Far from being the position of the Czechoslovak Communists alone, Prchlík added, it was a view shared "in essence" by the Hungarian and Romanian parties as well.[27]

Clearly, Prchlík's views on the requirements for restructuring the Warsaw Pact did not coincide with those of his Soviet comrades-in-arms.[28] With the "normalization" of the situation in Czechoslovakia, however, and the eventual imprisonment of Prchlík himself,[29] the Czechoslovak attitude toward the Warsaw Pact became far more tractable. As for the Hungarians, the Kádár regime proceeded with customary caution, permitting itself only a retrospective critique, issued in 1970, of previous deficiencies in the pact command structure.[30] Of far greater significance, of course, was Romania's continued opposition to Soviet plans for "further perfecting" the Warsaw Treaty Organization.

The fits and starts of Soviet-Romanian relations within the Warsaw Pact framework, particularly over the issue of Romanian participation in joint military maneuvers, is by now a familiar theme. In 1967, as part of an apparent effort to ease strains in Eastern Europe following Romania's separate exchange of diplomatic relations with West Germany, the Ceauşescu leadership had ended its three-year boycott of pact military exercises by participating in joint naval maneuvers in the Black Sea.[31] Such acquiescence was short-lived, however; in May of the following year the Romanians refused to join Bulgaria and the Soviet Union in Mediterranean naval maneuvers. Soviet embarrassment over Romania's absence must have been acute, for reports of the exercises were suppressed in the Soviet press until August.[32]

By 1969, the question of Romanian participation had acquired particular importance, for the pact had become increasingly divided between the so-called first strategic echelon, or "Northern Tier" countries—East Germany, Poland, and Czechoslovakia—and the "Southern Tier," or Balkan grouping.[33] Of the seventeen Warsaw Pact exercises held between 1965 and 1968, for example, all but one had been conducted by the Northern Tier countries, with the occasional participation of Hungary.[34] Strategically, the north-south division of the pact may have been entirely compatible with Soviet interests; politically, however, it conflicted sharply with Soviet efforts to elevate the Warsaw Pact as a lever of control in Eastern Europe and an instrument for coordinating the evolving bloc détente posture. Thus, by 1969 Romanian participation in pact military maneuvers, even if of a symbolic nature, had come to be closely linked to the broader Soviet integrationist drive in the region.

In the fall of 1968, as has been seen, the Soviet leaders attempted with partial success to still Romania's sharp criticism of the Czechoslovak invasion. During this same period, the Romanians remained under heavy pressure from Moscow to agree to hold large-scale military exercises on Romanian territory.[35] In February 1969, just ten days after Ceauşescu had rejected the idea of Romanian participation in military maneuvers, a Soviet delegation paid a surprise visit to Bucharest, apparently to patch up relations in anticipation of the Budapest conference.[36] Although we can only speculate as to what carrots and sticks were wielded during the negotiations, it is clear that some sort of compromise was reached, for the Romanians agreed to participate in limited WTO staff exercises scheduled for late March and apparently gave their seal of approval to Soviet plans for the forthcoming conference.[37]

On the eve of the conference, there was increased speculation that the Soviet leaders, motivated by their long-standing desire to strengthen the Warsaw Pact and doubts as to the reliability of the East European armed forces, might attempt to push through a plan for the total integration of East European military forces through a supreme WTO command.[38] If such was their aim, the Soviet leaders could have counted on the firm support of the East Germans, whose armed forces were already fully incorporated into the Joint Command, and needed fear little resistance from the Bulgarians. The opposing view, expressed by the Romanians, Czechoslovaks, and Hungarians (and certainly shared by the Poles as well), was that the principle of national control over the various armed forces should be strengthened and that steps should be taken to facilitate East European participation in WTO decisionmaking. Thus, as the delegations assembled for the PCC session in Budapest on March 17, a fairly clear division could be discerned as to the requirements for "further perfecting" the Warsaw Pact.

The Budapest Conference

The conference itself came as something of an anticlimax, for it soon became evident that a compromise had been reached during the bilateral negotiations which preceded it. Chaired by Alexander Dubček less than a month before his ouster, the "blitz conference," as one Yugoslav journalist termed it,[39] was the shortest PCC session on record. The short duration of the meeting, Prague radio explained, was "made possible by the work of the national defense ministers and allied commands in drafting the document . . . and by the intense work of delegations led by deputy ministers of foreign affairs."[40]

No agreement could be reached, however, on one topic the Soviet leaders particularly wanted to include in the conference resolution: the recent clashes along the Sino-Soviet border.[41] According to several sources, the Soviet leaders hoped at a minimum to secure the verbal support of its East European allies and suggest, implicitly at least, that Warsaw Pact troops might be dispatched to the Far East.[42] Originally scheduled to begin at 10:00 A.M., the conference was delayed five hours while the Soviet leaders made a final effort to reach a compromise with the Romanian delegation, headed by Ceauşescu. The Romanians remained adamant: inasmuch as Article 4 of the Warsaw Treaty explicitly limited WTO mutual defense obligations to the European continent, they argued, Sino-Soviet relations were clearly beyond the purview of the Political Consultative Committee.[43]

When the conference finally convened at 3:00 P.M., the Chinese issue was not even mentioned. Lasting barely eighty minutes, rather than the planned eight hours, the session amounted to little more than a reading and signing of the prepared documents. The chief outcome of the meeting, as has been seen, was the "Budapest Appeal" for the convening of an all-European security conference. "Before the document . . . was put into words," however (as Budapest radio noted), "steps had been taken to enhance the Warsaw Pact's defensive military potential."[44] The precise nature of these steps was not initially clear, for the separate communiqué read by Marshal Yakubovsky hinted only vaguely at organizational changes "intended to further perfect the structure and command bodies . . . of the Warsaw Pact."[45]

It was clear from the outset, however, that the organizational reforms came closer to the Romanian than to the Soviet formula for Warsaw Pact restructuring. In press releases during and after the conference, the Romanians, Hungarians, Czechoslovaks, and Poles all claimed to have exerted considerable influence in drafting the reforms,[46] and the available evidence suggests that the reorganization was genuinely a collective effort. In an interview granted upon his return to Prague, Dubček noted that proposals had been adopted "to increase the various socialist countries' participation . . . in the command of the Warsaw Pact,"[47] and his foreign minister, Jan Marko, added that measures had been taken to ease the East European defense burden and facilitate WTO consultation on strategic issues.[48] In Bucharest, a Yugoslav journalist—presumably relaying the opinion of the Romanian leadership—suggested that the "implications" of the changes were the "democratization of mutual relations" in the bloc and a "tacit criticism of the hegemonistic relations and methods which [had been] resuscitated with the thesis on limited sovereignty."[49]

Over the next few months, statements by various Soviet and East European party and military officials provided further details of the organizational reforms.[50] All these pointed to six major changes in the Warsaw Pact: the signing of a new statute on the Joint Armed Forces; the transformation of two organs—the Joint Command and the Joint Staff; and the creation of three entirely new bodies—the Committee of Defense Ministers, the Military Council, and the Committee for Coordination of Military Technology. (See Fig. 3.1.)

The two new organs which attracted the most attention in the West were the Committee of Defense Ministers and the Military Council. The former now serves as the supreme military consultative organ of the Warsaw Pact and consists, as its title suggests, of the ministers of defense of the WTO member countries. As Hungarian Defense Minister Lajos Czinege observed, the CDM is "a new body only in an organizational sense because these ministers have also conferred . . . regularly in the past."[51] Its creation was significant, neverthe-

Figure 3.1
Structure of the Warsaw Treaty Organization, 1969

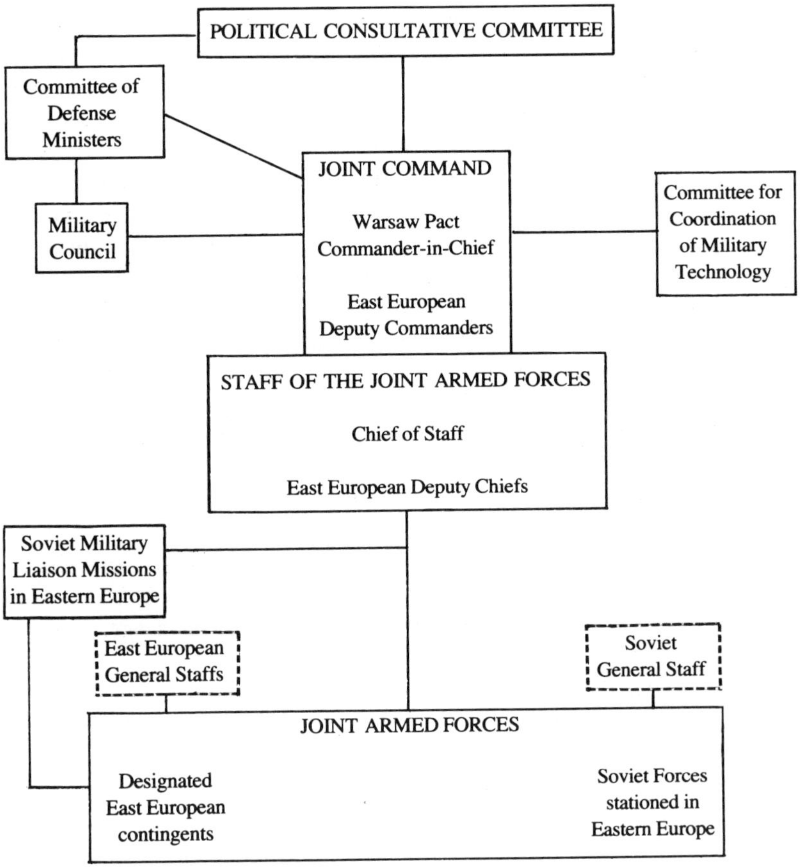

SOURCE: Adapted from Michael Csizmas, *Der Warschauer Pakt* (Bern: Verlag SOI, 1972).

less, in that it elevated the East European defense ministers, who formerly had been subordinate to the Soviet commander-in-chief of the WTO Joint Command, to a status formally coequal to their Soviet counterpart.[52]

Less is known of the Military Council, particularly as to its relationship with the Committee of Defense Ministers, but it now appears that it does not, as Mackintosh suggested, submit decisions for CDM approval.[53] According to General Shtemenko, former WTO chief of staff, the council is a "collective military body with consultative and [recommendatory] functions."[54] Though reportedly dominated by Soviet officials, the council also includes a military representative of lieutenant general or vice admiral rank from each of the other WTO countries, and consequently provides an additional point of access to Warsaw Pact policymaking for the East European countries.[55]

Even less information is available on the Committee for Coordination of Military Technology, which, as its name implies, is charged with coordinating military research and development and "standardizing basic military equipment and weapons systems."[56] Circumstantial evidence suggests, however, that this innovation, too, represented a Soviet concession to the junior allies. In the spring and summer of 1968, Czechoslovak commentators had decried the "economic burdens resulting from our defense policy" and criticized the Warsaw Pact "division of labor," which required the East Europeans to maintain excessively large conventional forces, thereby depriving them of investment funds badly needed for defense modernization.[57] Czechoslovak Foreign Minister Marko's much more favorable appraisal of pact burden-sharing after the Budapest conference, therefore, would seem to indicate that the new committee on military technology was established to ease the East European defense burden by providing for the sharing of technology among pact members, though it undoubtedly had the additional aim of facilitating Soviet supervision over the East European defense establishments.

The organizational changes to the Joint Command and Joint Staff can be summarized briefly. With the formation of the Committee of Defense Ministers, national ministers of defense were removed from the Joint Command and replaced by designated deputy defense ministers from the East European countries. Otherwise, the Joint Command remained basically unchanged,[58] though some of its functions undoubtedly have been usurped by the newly created Military Council and Committee of Defense Ministers. The Joint Staff, which reportedly had convened on an ad hoc basis previously,[59] was in 1969 established as a permanent organ, and East European representation apparently—the qualifier must be employed once again—was upgraded.[60] In addition to performing traditional staff functions, the Joint Staff shares (with the Committee for Coordination of Military Technology) responsibility for standardization and coordination of weapons and equipment and apparently controls the Soviet military liaison missions attached to each of the East European Ministries of Defense.[61] (See Fig. 3.1.)

One organizational "nonchange" should also be mentioned. Despite the long-standing Soviet desire to improve the mechanisms for foreign policy coordination in the Warsaw Pact, no significant changes in that direction were made. The need for such changes was obvious, for the irregular, though increasingly frequent, meetings of foreign ministers and top Party and state officials, both within and without the framework of the Political Consultative Committee, clearly have not played the kind of continuous coordinating role envisioned by the Soviet leaders. Ironically, there already existed an organ, the Permanent Commission on Foreign Policy Questions, which might have played such a role, but there is no evidence that it has ever been so employed or that it entered into the discussions at Budapest.[62]

By the time of the 24th CPSU Congress in 1971, nevertheless, General Secretary Brezhnev could claim, "The period under review [1966–1971]was marked by important successes in *coordinating the foreign policy activity* of the fraternal parties and states. . . . The Warsaw Treaty Organization has been and remains the main center for coordinating the foreign policy activity of the fraternal countries."[63] These "important successes," it seems, can be attributed primarily to the traditional devices of Soviet bilateral diplomacy, the increasingly frequent consultations among pact foreign ministers, and the elevation of the Political Consultative Committee as a forum for the announcement of bloc foreign policy. Organizationally, the only discernible changes in 1969 were the creation of the three new military organs and the consequent exclusion of defense ministers from sessions of the PCC.[64] These changes, in turn, may have facilitated foreign policy coordination by freeing the PCC from purely military concerns and permitting it to focus more fully on foreign policy issues.

These reservations aside, the organizational reforms undertaken at Budapest were the most significant since the formation of the Warsaw Pact. The creation of the new organs gave the WTO a more streamlined structure, similar to NATO's, and provided a more rational functional division among the pact's foreign policy, strategic planning, technological, command, and staff bodies. More significantly, the reforms improved the nominal position of the East European member countries by granting them coequal status on the Committee of Defense Ministers and according them permanent, high-level military representation on the Military Council, the Committee for Coordination of Military Technology, the Joint Command, and the Joint Staff.

Implementing the Reforms: *Kto Kogo?* (Who Did What to Whom?)[65]

In the immediate aftermath of the Budapest conference, three Warsaw Pact joint exercises were conducted, accompanied by ostentatious pronouncements of "fraternal solidarity" among pact members.[66] "Vesna [Spring] 1969" was particularly well publicized, and special attention was paid to the fact that the exercise was commanded by a Polish general.[67] In the ensuing months, meetings of the new "directing bodies" of the Warsaw Pact were held, as the Soviet press noted, in conformity with "the new statute on the joint armed forces and the joint command."[68] Despite this display of apparent unity, it soon became clear that the Budapest meeting had left unresolved a number of disputes over the new command structure. Chief among these was the conflict surrounding the final change undertaken at Budapest, the signing of a "new statute on the Joint Armed Forces."

Although the text of the new statute has never been made public, it is clear that the document is susceptible to various interpretations. In January 1970, an article by General Shtemenko, then WTO chief of staff, generated speculation that the new statute involved a plan for the supranational integration of Warsaw Pact forces.[69] Although a careful reading of the article suggests that Shtemenko added nothing to what was already known about the Warsaw Pact command, it is nevertheless true that certain passages were sufficiently vague to support the more extreme interpretation.

Two passages in particular warrant close attention. Of the unified command, Shtemenko said, "For the collective defense of the socialist cause [the Warsaw Pact member states] have created mighty Joint Armed Forces. Allocated to them from the national armies by the decisions of their governments are formations and units, and also control and rear organs." According to one reading, this passage would seem to suggest that decisions had already been made (at Budapest, presumably) to allocate, on a permanent basis, designated East European units to the Joint Command. The correct reading, as subsequent clarifications confirmed, is that such allocations are temporary and that a decision by the government concerned is required for each and every allocation of troops to the Joint Command. The confusion over this crucial passage issued from the continuing reluctance of Soviet leaders to acknowledge openly that East European contingents are assigned to the Joint Command only on a temporary basis for the conduct of joint exercises (or, presumably, in the event of war).[70]

An even more ambiguous passage concerned the final authority over units assigned to the Joint Command: "The troop contingents allocated by Warsaw Pact member-states for the Joint Armed Forces engage in daily combat and political training according to the plans of the national commands. However, the final decisions on the various issues concerning joint operations . . . are effected *according to the plans of the joint command*" (emphasis added). Under the system which had been followed throughout the 1960s, authority over troops assigned to the WTO remained in the hands of the national minister of defense, who received directives from the WTO commander-in-chief but was responsible to his own Party and government.[71] In this second passage, however, General Shtemenko's clear implication is that once contingents have been assigned to the

Joint Armed Forces, authority over those forces passes from the national commands to the Warsaw Pact Joint Command. Such, at least, was the way the Romanian leaders interpreted the passage, for President Ceauşescu quickly responded: "The only leader of our armed forces is the party, the government and the supreme national command. Only they can give orders and only those orders can be carried out. . . . The idea of yielding a part of the right of command and leadership of the army, however small, by the party and government is inconceivable."[72]

Romania's objections, it seems, had already been registered in Moscow, where a few days earlier Marshal Yakubovsky, WTO commander-in-chief, had sought to clarify the Soviet position in an interview granted to the trade union weekly *Smena*. His remarks are worth quoting at some length, as they represent the clearest description yet given by a Soviet leader of command relationships in the Warsaw Pact:

> The Commander-in-Chief of the Combined Armed Forces acts according to the decisions of the parties and governments which are members of the Warsaw Pact and according to the instructions of the Political Consultative Committee. Through his deputies and the staff of the Combined Armed Forces, in coordination with the Ministers of Defense and where necessary also with the Governments of the Allied countries, he organizes and carries out necessary measures in the interests of increasing the combat readiness of the Combined Armed Forces.[73]

Even this formulation leaves room for doubt, for Yakubovsky failed to specify whether, or in what cases, the "decisions of the parties and governments" can be superseded by "instructions of the Political Consultative Committee."

It is possible to dismiss all the furor over the "new statute" as a consequence of the overzealous remarks of General Shtemenko, himself a notorious Stalinist. Yet it is at least plausible that the "new statute on the Joint Armed Forces and the Joint Command" contains some genuine and significant ambiguities, ambiguities which the Soviet leaders sought to exploit in the aftermath of the Budapest conference.

This latter conclusion is supported by Yakubovsky's continued unwillingness to affirm absolutely the principle of national control over Warsaw Pact forces, and it conforms to the general pattern of Soviet pressure tactics designed to elicit Romanian participation in Warsaw Pact and CMEA activities. The controversy over the new statute was not laid to rest, in fact, until the latter part of 1970—after Romania had participated in its third joint exercise in eighteen months, after the renewal of the Soviet-Romanian Treaty of Friendship, Cooperation, and Mutual Assistance, and after the signing of a five-year Soviet-Romanian trade protocol.[74] Finally, a book published by the USSR Academy of Sciences in 1970 officially acknowledged that forces assigned to the Joint

Armed Forces "are not withdrawn from the jurisdiction of the command of the countries in question."[75]

At the very least, the dispute over the new statute made it clear that the Budapest conference was not the unmitigated victory for the East Europeans that it might have appeared initially. In the first place, some of the reforms were sufficiently vague to permit various interpretations. Second, although formal East European representation was increased in some WTO organs, the organizational changes did little to alter the Soviet Union's carefully preserved dominance in Warsaw Pact deliberations, particularly on strategic and foreign policy matters. Thus, the net impact of the Budapest reforms seems to have been to improve the nominal access of the East European members to the levers of Warsaw Pact decisionmaking, while at the same time increasing Soviet influence in East European military affairs by expanding the spheres of competence of the pact's command bodies. Additionally, as Thomas Wolfe observed, "by drawing Rumania into participation in various joint bodies . . . Moscow could make it more difficult for the Rumanians to maintain independent positions against a presumed majority of Soviet supporters."[76]

In this sense, the Budapest reforms represented a new Soviet interest in a multilateral approach designed to supplement, but not replace, traditional Soviet bilateral pressure tactics in the drive toward alliance cohesion. This pattern was equally evident in the negotiations surrounding the "Comprehensive Program" for economic integration in the Council for Mutual Economic Assistance.

Comecon and the Comprehensive Program

One Western economist, using the analogy of a ship, has described the problems of East European economic integration in this way:

> Neither the helmsman nor several of the crew of the East European boat are willing to unleash this economic integration *from within*. Or in terms of the metaphor, they are unwilling to coordinate the various activities and duties of the crew because none of its members has sufficient authority and power to do so, and the abilities of the captain are doubted and distrusted. Consequently, the ship moves back and forth and ahead by the sheer force of the wind (e.g. the demand for manufactured goods by the USSR from Eastern Europe) and by the resultant of the various forces exerted by the members of the crew. Frustrating attempts to create the conditions for integration *from without* . . . are being introduced.[77]

Economic integration through a supranational planning body, it might seem, would be more in keeping with the modus operandi of the Soviet leaders. As the fate of the 1962 "Basic Principles" plan had shown, however, attempts to create and promote integration "from within"—by strengthening CMEA's infrastructure and rules of procedure—arouse strong opposition in Eastern Europe. After 1969, therefore, CMEA sessions and inter-Party meetings were devoted to the task of reconciling Soviet and East European interests "from without" through the more gradual processes of production specialization and coordination of national economic plans.

CMEA between Plan and Market

Even in 1969 there were lingering suspicions in Eastern Europe that the Soviet leaders might revive the scheme for supranational integration in CMEA. As had been the case in negotiations over Warsaw Pact restructuring, the debate in CMEA soon became one of confrontation between the centralizers and decentralizers in the bloc. The basic conflict was summarized by one Czechoslovak economist:

> One of the conceptions aiming at improving the work of CMEA sees the centre of gravity of those measures in the formation of new CMEA bodies endowed with more extensive rights and obligations; another conception lays emphasis on imparting an objective nature to value instruments and the removal of obstacles hindering the establishment of closer links between the internal markets of member countries [and with] those of third countries.[78]

The conflict, then, was between a plan and a market solution to the problems of CMEA integration, between a solution which would establish central planning bodies in CMEA and invest them with supranational powers and one which would facilitate direct contacts between individual firms and enterprises by removing trade barriers and reforming pricing procedures in Eastern Europe. As one Western analyst has put it, "The 'reformist' managers demand access to enterprises in the 'traditionalist' countries, while the 'traditionalists' call for the coordination of plans and the declaration of firm quotas."[79]

Since Khrushchev's early dream of "building the socialist world economy into a single entity,"[80] Soviet leaders intermittently had broached the question of supranational planning in CMEA—most recently, as has been seen, in a December 1968 article by a Soviet economist. From the Soviet perspective, supranationalism in CMEA would offer obvious advantages: it would help arrest incipient tendencies toward international economic anarchy in Eastern Europe, facilitate the forging of a common CMEA economic policy toward the West, and strengthen Soviet economic control in Eastern Europe.

The opposing conception of CMEA integration was presented most forcefully by the Hungarians, who argued in effect for a loosely knit CMEA free trade area. Alluding favorably to the experiences of the Common Market, for example, an article in the Hungarian press emphasized that the "cardinal question of integration [in CMEA] is the removal of . . . import restrictions and the opening of the internal market to imports from member countries.''[81] The conflict between plan and market in CMEA relations was particularly evident in a CMEA conference held in 1970 on ''the nature and problems of the CMEA market.'' Almost without exception, the Hungarian conferees argued for the freeing of market forces in CMEA trade, particularly through bilateral trade relations, and elimination of impediments to free trade among CMEA members, including those resulting from the excessive centralization of the domestic economic systems.[82] The Hungarian view was disputed by a Bulgarian economist, who emphasized that the CMEA market cannot be ruled by ''spontaneous phenomena'' (i.e., ''economic anarchy''), and a Soviet delegate, who argued for ''the concentration and centralization of production'' in CMEA.[83]

By this time, a division of opinion had begun to emerge in Eastern Europe over the scope and direction of CMEA integration.[84] Closest to the Hungarian position were the Czechoslovaks, who in early 1969 still shared the Hungarian enthusiasm for economic reform but who were rapidly losing their free hand in intra-alliance deliberations,[85] and the Romanians, who had little interest in domestic economic reform but who were quick to embrace any measure opposing Soviet supranationalist designs. The Poles and East Germans occupied a middle ground: both had benefited from their captive markets in Eastern Europe and hence tended toward the status quo in CMEA, but both had indicated some interest in cooperation along market lines among the more advanced East European states.[86] Finally, although Bulgaria's preference for Soviet-style integration was well known, the Bulgarians had become oddly reticent on the subject during this period—suggesting, perhaps, that the Soviet view on integration was itself being reconsidered.

Both the Hungarian and the Soviet views on CMEA cooperation were ''integrative,'' but both were based on assumptions which ultimately would militate against successful economic integration in Eastern Europe. Without denying the existence of some purely economic motives for CMEA cooperation, it can be said that for the Soviet leadership, economic integration was seen as virtually synonymous with expanded Soviet economic control over Eastern Europe.[87] In this sense, the Soviet leaders were loath to permit the mutual opening of internal markets in Eastern Europe and in fact resisted schemes which would encourage intra–East European trade (*sans* the Soviet Union).[88] The Soviet effort, rather, was to promote bilateral trade relations between the USSR and individual East European partners, encourage multilateral cooperation through ventures to which the Soviet Union is an influential party, and establish within the bloc an intricate web of vertical economic links (in the form of various CMEA agencies, commissions, and planning bodies) susceptible to Soviet control.[89] The Hungarians, conversely, proceeding from the assumption that any central planning body would willy-nilly fall under Soviet domination, were unwilling or unable to provide their notion of integration with the required institutional teeth, and favored instead what would have amounted to an East European free trade zone protected by a high tariff wall.[90]

In any case, as a Czechoslovak economist put it, both these plans "represent extremes and cannot be evidently [*sic*] put into practice. . . . only a combination of elements of both schemes can be considered."[91] Faced with these two extreme alternatives—planning through a supranational agency and reliance on uncertain market forces—leaders of the CMEA countries turned by default, as it were, to a third, less ambitious program of integration, one which would involve "voluntary" coordination of national economic plans and creation of new CMEA organs to facilitate cooperation on pressing economic problems. Stated less charitably, in the absence of any discernible consensus among CMEA members, the only alternative available was to make incremental procedural, institutional, and policy changes within the existing CMEA framework.

Lack of agreement on any of the more sweeping proposals for CMEA reform was evident at the 22nd Council session, held in January 1969 on the occasion of CMEA's twentieth anniversary. Decisions on the direction of change in CMEA, it was announced, would be tabled until the upcoming summit meeting (the 23rd, "Extraordinary" CMEA Council session), which finally convened in Moscow in late April.

In the meantime, another development served to complicate the equation of CMEA reform. In March 1969, as has been seen, the Warsaw Pact countries issued the "Budapest Appeal" for the convocation of an all-European security conference. For the CMEA member states, the prospect of expanded trade relations with the West, soon to be included in the Warsaw Pact's agenda for the proposed conference, offered the possibility of employing advanced Western technology and credits to invigorate and modernize the lagging domestic economies in Eastern Europe. At the same time, the expected transformation of East-West trade patterns presented a new set of concerns to CMEA planners. Most obviously, greater attention would have to be paid to the coordination of CMEA foreign trade relations, both bilateral and multilateral, with the capitalist West. Additionally, the task of promoting basic integration of key industries in Eastern Europe acquired greater urgency, not only for the purpose of facilitating the exploitation of the latest in Western technology, but also to counteract the potentially disruptive consequences of expanded trade relations with the West.

All these concerns found expression in an article by Mikhail Lesechko, the USSR's permanent representative to CMEA, written at the time of the Budapest conference. "The Comecon countries are endeavoring to utilize foreign scientific achievements and technological innovations," Lesechko noted, and "are seeking to coordinate their world market activities in order to avoid unjustified parallel expenditure and to obtain all that is best from other countries."[92] In a second article, published just before the CMEA summit meeting, Lesechko excluded the possibility of supranationalism in CMEA, arguing that the implementation of cooperative measures "wholly depends on the wishes of interested Comecon countries and must be founded on their voluntary participation."[93] As will be seen, "voluntarism" and the "interested party" principle were to be the foundation of the Comprehensive Program adopted in July 1971.

The 23rd and 24th CMEA Council Sessions

According to M. V. Senin, a leading Soviet spokesman on CMEA affairs, the 23rd, "Extraordinary" session of the CMEA "marked a new landmark in the development of socialist integration . . . , laying down the aims, content, ways and methods of its further consistent intensification." Socialist economic integration, he continued, is "a process of the drawing closer of these states on the basis of the division . . . of labour guided by the co-ordination of [national economic] plans, joint planning of individual economic branches . . . and other forms of co-operation."[94] Senin's hyperbole aside, the statement of principle adopted at the 23rd session was less ambitious than might have been expected: coordination of national economic plans was to remain the chief vehicle of CMEA cooperation, and the principles of state sovereignty and independence were solemnly reaffirmed.

The vaguely worded summit communiqué included only a general commitment to improving economic cooperation through CMEA, equalizing development levels of the member states, encouraging ties with other states "regardless of social system," and establishing an international investment bank to supplement the existing International Bank for Economic Cooperation. The communiqué further provided for the establishment of direct links among enterprises and reiterated the "interested party" principle in CMEA ventures, but both these provisions were offered without elaboration as to their scope or implications.[95] A more detailed, twenty-five-point protocol was never published, but reports in the Czechoslovak press suggested that the document amounted to a working blueprint for CMEA reform, to be negotiated over the next few years according to a predetermined timetable.[96]

It is clear that the summit communiqué represented a compromise containing, in the words of one Western analyst, "a little something for everybody but reflecting the lowest common denominator on significant issues."[97] The cautious approach to integration must have reassured the Romanians and others apprehensive about Soviet intentions, and the renewed commitment to equalizing development levels offered a concession and an inducement to the Bulgarians and Romanians. Those who had lobbied for changes in the "market" direction—the Hungarians and, to lesser degrees, the Czechoslovaks, Poles, and East Germans—doubtless found some solace in the opening to Western markets and provisions for direct links among individual enterprises. For their part, the Soviet leaders, whose grander designs had been effectively thwarted, were obliged to content themselves with more limited measures toward coordination of national economic plans.

No agreement was to be found, however, on a number of key problems, most notably those surrounding the complex issue of financial reform.[98] Fundamentally, the same two extreme solutions, plan and market, presented themselves to CMEA planners: to establish common prices through a single "plan" applicable to all CMEA members, or to develop comparable pricing systems through the establishment of market reforms in each of the member states. Needless to say, neither option generated serious consideration, much less wide support, within CMEA. Between these extremes were two more realistic options for establishing a CMEA-wide pricing system: one would fix prices by administrative fiat, presumably through the auspices of one or more CMEA organs; the other would establish a systematic link between CMEA prices and those on the world market.[99] Closely related to these considerations were the problems of establishing a rational system of credits and creating a convertible CMEA currency—the latter to be achieved through alignment with Western currencies, employment of the gold standard, or extension of the regionally limited transferable ruble. Decisions on all these vexing problems were simply tabled for further consideration.

Nevertheless, in agreeing to steer a middle course between the Scylla of supranationalism and the Charybdis of market integration, bloc leaders had opened a dialogue on procedural and organizational issues which had frustrated CMEA cooperation from the beginning. Chief among these were the "universality" and "unanimity" principles, which granted each member effective veto power over the creation of any new CMEA body and over its operations once established. Adopted under Stalin at a time when nothing short of universality and unanimity was tolerated in Eastern Europe, these procedural anomalies had been skillfully exploited by the Romanians in the 1960s to prevent the creation of new CMEA organs deemed detrimental to Romanian sovereignty.

In their place, the 23rd CMEA Council session proposed the principles of "interestedness" and "voluntarism." The interestedness, or interested party, principle provided that new CMEA organs or cooperative ventures could be established by any interested CMEA countries, whether or not universal CMEA participation was assured. The principle of voluntarism is somewhat more complex. On the one hand, it guaranteed that no member could be compelled to join new CMEA ventures and that decisions taken by CMEA bodies would be binding only on parties who already had declared their interest. In this sense, voluntarism amounted to a corollary to the interested party principle, in that it prevented tyranny of the majority and preserved the right of any CMEA member to opt out of a given venture at any time. It also meant, however, the erosion of the previous safeguard of unanimity, for decisions on some issues could be taken by interested parties without unanimous consent.[100] (Parties which had declared themselves uninterested would not be bound by such decisions, of course, but neither could they prevent their adoption.)

The Romanian reaction to this turn of events was ambivalent: on the one hand, the Romanians were undoubtedly relieved that the feared drift toward supranationalism had not materialized; on the other, they could not fail to be concerned about the ineluctable erosion of their veto power in CMEA. In any case, Romania's ability to influence the course of events in CMEA had been weakened considerably—by unremitting Soviet economic and political pressure and by the emerging, if still limited, consensus in Eastern Europe on the direction of CMEA reform.[101] Under these conditions, Romanian policy toward CMEA began to shift from aggressive obstructionism to a defensive holding operation designed to prevent extension of the interested party principle to already existing CMEA bodies, such as the permanent commissions, and to preserve the right of voluntarism in CMEA ventures.

Meanwhile, at the 24th CMEA Council session held in May 1970, a formal agreement had been reached on the creation of an International Investment Bank (IIB). According to Article 19 of the bank's Charter, all questions other than those affecting the Charter itself were to be decided "by a qualified majority of not less than three-quarters of the votes."[102] This stipulation marked the first time in CMEA's history that the unanimity rule had been abandoned in favor of majority voting, and it was on these grounds that Romania initially refused to join the IIB. Over the next few months, however, the limits of Romania's maneuverability were quickly exposed. Unwilling to deny itself the use of much-needed investment funds and afraid of finding itself unable to exert influence on decisions of potential importance for all of Eastern Europe, Romania finally joined the IIB in January 1971, twelve days after the bank commenced operations.[103] In other respects, the 24th CMEA session was notable chiefly for its lack of progress in drafting a program for integration. The session did, however, fully reaffirm the commitment to CMEA integration, particularly in the area of plan coordination, and some progress was evident in coordinating the various proposals made by the individual members.[104]

The role of the Soviet Union at this stage of the negotiations is instructive. Apparently satisfied with the general direction of the negotiations and determined to push through even an emasculated integrationist program, the Soviet leaders adopted a role resembling that of honest broker, supervising retreats on difficult issues, such as financial reform and nonquota trade, and gathering support for the less controversial residue of the integration plan.[105]

Between the 24th and 25th CMEA Council sessions, moreover, leadership changes in Poland and East Germany smoothed the way to agreement on an integration program. In December 1970, the replacement of Wladyslaw Gomulka by the more tractable Edward Gierek as Party leader, as well as the circumstances surrounding the leadership crisis, produced a much more receptive Polish attitude toward negotiations in CMEA.[106] In East Germany, too, the new Honecker regime quickly abandoned the reservations of its predecessor concerning the integration plan and announced its readiness to expand economic relations with all CMEA countries, particularly the Soviet Union.[107]

Elsewhere in Eastern Europe, a similar convergence of views was manifest, at least with respect to the minimum objectives of the emerging integration plan. Once the drift of the negotiations had become apparent, the Bulgarians fell firmly in line behind the prescribed Soviet position; and in Czechoslovakia the process of normalization had produced a fully acquiescent foreign policy, particularly on any requirements for "strengthening the bonds" with its allies. The Hungarians, apparently satisfied with the cautious measures under consideration, supported the general program for integration but continued to lobby for the further development of "commodity-money relations," the socialist shibboleth for market reforms.

Even the Romanians, who had almost single-handedly subverted the 1962 "Basic Principles" plan for CMEA integration, found themselves able to do little more than moderate the drive toward closer economic cooperation. Subjected in early 1970 to thinly veiled Soviet economic blackmail, including an apparent threat to withhold shipments of Soviet iron ore to Romania, President Ceaușescu agreed to sign a five-year Soviet-Romanian trade protocol on coordination of national economic plans and renew the long-delayed Soviet-Romanian Treaty of Friendship, Cooperation, and Mutual Assistance.[108] Even as Romanian spokesmen continued to decry "proposals of an integrationist nature bordering on transgression of the independence of socialist states,"[109] Romania was being systematically drawn into new CMEA ventures, including the International Bank, Interkhim, and others. Such acquiescence, revealed again in Romania's participation in the preliminary negotiations toward the drafting of an integration plan, removed the final obstacle to agreement on the Comprehensive Program.

The 25th Session and the Comprehensive Program

Originally scheduled for adoption in 1970 and delayed again in early 1971, CMEA's Comprehensive Program was finally announced at the 25th Council session, held in Bucharest in July 1971. Running some 100 pages, the complicated and occasionally self-contradictory document was published amidst the customary fanfare the following month.[110] The program called for changes which can be discussed under four main categories: the goals and methods of the program, coordination of national economic plans, joint ventures, and procedural rules.[111]

As expected, the Comprehensive Program embodied an odd melange of conflicting aims and cross-purposes, all of which were to be "implemented in accordance with the principles of socialist internationalism." According to Chapter 1, Section 1, the goals of the program are "the drawing closer of [the CMEA] economies and the formation of modern, highly effective national economic structures, of a gradual drawing closer and evening out of their economic development levels, a formation of deep and enduring ties in the basic branches of the economy . . . , an expansion and consolidation of the international market of these countries, and an improvement of commodity-money relations." On the issue of supranationalism, the text is clear and direct: "Socialist economic integration is completely voluntary and does not involve the creation of supra-national bodies; it does not affect questions of internal planning."

Section 2 reiterates the call for an "evening out" of the development levels of the member countries, promising "preferential co-operation terms to industrially less developed countries." This provision, of course, stands in marked contrast to the aim of the 1962 integration plan and amounted to a significant inducement to the Bulgarians and, more importantly, the Romanians. It is also closely related to the functionalist definition of integration, which considers the equalization of differences in relative scarcities a necessary precondition for effective economic integration.[112] Neither the functionalist nor any other useful definition of integration, however, finds coherent expression in the Comprehensive Program, which is notably lacking in clearly defined economic (as opposed to legal or organizational) criteria on such fundamental issues as economic rationality in CMEA trade, price comparability, and labor mobility.

The crux of the Comprehensive Program, rather, is the voluntary coordination of national economic policies, economic plans, and production schedules and the improvement of the legal bases for cooperation. "State monopoly of foreign trade" is fully preserved and serves as the "basis" for further economic cooperation. The forms and methods of such cooperation are elaborated in the lengthy second chapter (Sections 3 through 9) and supported in Chapter 3 (Sections 10 through 14) by detailed goals and timetables for the development of cooperation in specific spheres of the economies.

Section 3 establishes the framework for "mutual consultations on basic questions of economic policy," which are to be conducted bilaterally or multilaterally by "interested countries," which in turn will conclude additional protocols or agreements as necessary. In these and most other economic measures envisioned in the Comprehensive Program, the principles of interestedness and voluntarism are carefully preserved: no member can be forced to participate in a given venture, but no obstructionist member is empowered to frustrate action by the others.

"Co-operation in planning activities, especially the co-ordination of plans," held to be the "main method" of socialist economic integration, is outlined in Section 4, which provides for joint plan forecasting, long-term (five-year) and very long-term (fifteen-to-twenty-year) plan coordination. "The leading role" in this process, it is emphasized, "shall belong to the central planning bodies of the CMEA member-countries." All elements of joint forecasting—the time period and production areas involved, the domestic agencies to be included, and the form of agreement—are to be decided by interested countries through their central planning bodies. Once the joint forecasting is complete, it is again left to the interested countries to determine the necessary protocols, contracts, and agreements to be concluded. In Section 5, the most detailed and coherent section of the program, cooperation in planning among interested countries is extended to research and development of new technology.

The third chief category of interest in the Comprehensive Program concerns the establishment of direct links among domestic organs and the creation of joint economic organizations. Direct links are explicitly permitted, but the language of Section 8 falls far short of the Hungarian formulation discussed earlier. Seen apparently as adjuncts to formal state agreements rather than as direct production agreements, direct links between enterprises of CMEA members are required to be established with "due consideration for systems of planning and management in the given countries"—that is, they are not to impinge on "state monopoly of foreign trade." As to interstate and international economic organizations, it is emphasized that they "shall not be supranational bodies and shall not deal with questions of internal planning."

It is in the discussion of joint economic organizations that the new procedures adopted at the 25th session are presented most clearly: "The lack of interest of any member-country of the organisation in any concrete measure shall not prevent the interested countries from carrying out measures previously agreed by them. Decisions shall not be valid [that is, binding] for countries who have declared that they are disinterested in a given question." The previous unanimity rule is preserved only for "key questions," as defined when any new organization is founded; on all other issues, the principles of interestedness and voluntarism are to be observed. Stated differently, the new procedures effectively prevent a veto by members not interested in a given measure, but they also preclude coercion of a member by an interested majority.[113]

The general provisions for the establishment of joint ventures and for cooperation in planning are incorporated and given practical meaning in Chapter 3, which outlines "main trends and tasks of the development of co-operation" in the chief branches of industry, agriculture, transportation, construction, and water conservation. This lengthy chapter amounts to a synopsis of agreements already reached, a forecast of needs for the near and more distant future, and a timetable for the conclusion of general agreements and more specific cooperative ventures across a wide range of functional areas.

Finally, Chapter 4 (Sections 15 through 17) briefly discusses remaining legal and organizational questions. The "completely voluntary" nature of the program is stressed, as is the interested party principle. Perhaps in anticipation of Romanian maneuvering, it is further provided that each CMEA member "shall be entitled to declare at any moment its wish to participate in a measure of the Comprehensive Programme, in which it for some reason or other had not desired to participate before."

Organizationally, CMEA emerged from the 25th Council session fundamentally unchanged. (See Fig. 3.2.) As before, the "supreme organ" of CMEA is the Council, which normally convenes once each year and consists of heads of state and, on occasion, Party first secretaries of the member countries. Between sessions of the Council, the Executive Committee, composed of permanent

Figure 3.2
Structure of the Council for Mutual Economic Assistance

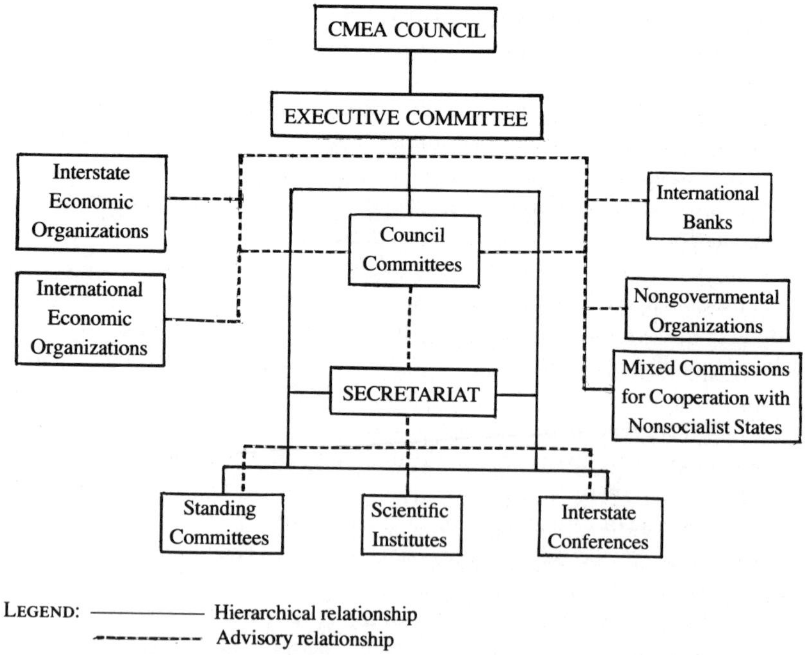

LEGEND: ——————— Hierarchical relationship
            - - - - - - - - - Advisory relationship

SOURCES: *The Multilateral Economic Cooperation of Socialist States* (Moscow: Progress Publishers, 1977), p. 290; *Grunddokumente des RGW* (Berlin: Staatsverlag der DDR, 1978), p. 342; Harry Trend, "Comecon's Organizational Structure," RAD Background Report/114 (Eastern Europe), *Radio Free Europe Research*, July 3, 1975.

representatives of the CMEA countries, oversees the work of the organization. Since it, too, meets relatively infrequently (normally four times a year), CMEA's daily activities are supervised by the permanent Secretariat, which prepares agendas for its superior bodies and coordinates the work of the various subsidiary organs, chiefly the standing commissions and interstate conferences. Each of these bodies, it should be emphasized, possesses only advisory and recommendatory powers; decisionmaking authority rests entirely with the individual countries.[114]

Several new organs should be briefly identified. The most significant of these are the Council committees, all of which were created after 1971 in direct support of the measures embodied in the Comprehensive Program. The Committee on Cooperation in Planning, composed of chairmen of the central planning organs of the CMEA countries, was established in 1972 on the basis of an agreement reached at the 25th session, as was the Committee on Scientific-Technical Cooperation.[115] The work of the latter body is supported by two related organs, the Conference of Representatives of Academies of Science of CMEA Countries (1971) and the International Center for Scientific-Technical Information (1969).[116] In addition to the Council committees, several new standing commissions, interstate conferences, and scientific institutes were also created.[117]

All the above, of course, are purely consultative bodies, empowered only to recommend actions to the various governments or to propose creation of joint cooperative ventures. Of the new production-related organizations, the International Investment Bank has already been discussed. Since 1971, both the IIB and the International Bank for Economic Cooperation (IBEC) have played significant roles in the development of intra-CMEA trade, particularly in multilateral hard currency operations and in financial relations with the capitalist West.[118]

It was in the area of joint production ventures, however, that the Comprehensive Program provided the greatest potential for organizational change. On the basis of the new procedural rules and the agreements codified in Chapter 3 on specific goals and timetables for the creation of new joint ventures, the number of multilateral cooperative ventures increased rapidly after 1971. These have been of three types: large-scale multilateral production ventures, such as the highly touted Orenburg pipeline; interstate economic organizations, designed to promote intergovernmental coordination and specialization in various production fields;[119] and the new international economic organizations, all of which have been created since 1972 to promote specialized cooperation at the enterprise level.[120]

According to official Soviet sources, such cooperative ventures and the other measures envisioned in the Comprehensive Program constituted a "qualitatively new phase" of economic relations in the Soviet bloc. Socialist economic integration, it has been argued, will be a two-stage process: the first, that covered by the Comprehensive Program, will last approximately fifteen to twenty years (three to four planning periods), after which time negotiations would be held to determine the nature of economic relations in the second, presumably final, stage. Needless to say, the possible character of this "final" stage remained hotly disputed: Soviet spokesmen continued to speak of "the future world communist economy, which would be regulated according to a single plan,"[121] while the forecasts of most of the East Europeans, particularly the Romanians and Hungarians, were far less ambitious.

Clearly, the sanguine estimates of Soviet spokesmen do not square with the tangible results of CMEA cooperation. Socialist economic integration, as expressed in the Comprehensive Program, remains at best a blueprint, and a patchwork one at that, for the future development of economic cooperation in CMEA. It is notably lacking in economic criteria or even a clear conception of socialist integration. As a Hungarian analyst noted, "One will not find anywhere in the [Comprehensive Program] a definition of integration, since the program does not attempt to interpret the idea—presumably because the member countries of Comecon take differing views of it and in some cases even contest its existence and practical expression among the socialist countries."[122]

Far from being simply a matter of theoretical imprecision, this lack of clarity on integration as a concept betrayed fundamental differences on several proposals for restructuring intra-CMEA financial procedures. These proposals, given lip service in Sections 6 and 7 of the Comprehensive Program, were closely tied to market integration of the kind favored by the Hungarians and shared to varying degrees by the Poles, Czechoslovaks, and East Germans, but they generated little support from the Bulgarian and Soviet leaders, who continued to favor highly centralized pricing systems in domestic and intrabloc trade. Having failed to reach agreement on such matters as nonquota trade relations, price formation in foreign trade, and development of a convertible currency, the drafters of the Comprehensive Program simply tabled these issues for further negotiations over the next several years.

Despite these deficiencies, the Comprehensive Program amounted to the first significant contribution to the task of improving the framework for multilateral cooperation in CMEA. (Most significant of all, perhaps, was that such elaborate agreement could be reached at all.) The program was particularly important, in the words of one Western economist, for its "recognition that crucial to integration efforts is the effective coordination of investment plans and that such coordination should mean joint planning on a selective basis."[123] Having failed to promote integration "from within" through creation of a supranational planning body, CMEA representatives undertook instead the laborious process of pursuing integration "from without" through the only means on which agreement could be found: voluntary coordination of national economic plans. Such coordination in planning was to proceed through several distinct time frames and at several levels, including that of individual enterprises. Implementation of joint planning was to be facilitated by the new CMEA organs for planning and coordination and by the specific agreements set forth in Chapter 3 of the program.

Additionally, by linking agreements on joint planning to other agreements (on deliveries of raw materials to Eastern Europe, for example), Soviet leaders sought to overcome the potentially limiting stipulation of voluntary participation. Indeed, the new procedural rules, on voluntarism and interestedness, were at once the chief virtues and the chief liabilities of the Comprehensive Program. On the one hand, the new procedures provided a means of overcoming the obstructionism, principally Romanian, which had plagued CMEA in the past; on the other, they made future cooperation dependent on the perceived potential for economic advantage by the East European members (or, failing that, on the ability of the Soviet Union to elicit cooperation through coercion or cajolery).

More generally, the adoption of the Comprehensive Program, like the Warsaw Pact reforms undertaken two years earlier, represented a significant restructuring of relations between the Soviet Union and its East European allies. In 1969, as has been seen, the Soviet leaders apparently entertained some hopes that they might be able to push through a bold supranational scheme for socialist integration in all spheres of intrabloc relations. By 1971, however, such hopes had been almost wholly abandoned in the face of East European resistance, and the integrationist program had taken on a collective character. Neither able to suppress the growing demands of their East European allies nor willing to rely exclusively on bilateral pressure tactics to achieve their ends, the Soviet leaders had come to accept a limited pluralization of intrabloc relations and to permit this process to be reflected, in part, in the institutional mechanisms of CMEA and the Warsaw Pact. This willingness—born of necessity, to be sure—represented a new and somewhat paradoxical Soviet confidence in a multilateral approach to problems of alliance management and, derivatively, in the ability of their more loyal allies, chiefly the Bulgarians, Czechoslovaks, and East Germans, to help ensure that the desired consensus would prevail in multilateral negotiations.

Clearly, as the invasion of Czechoslovakia and the continued presence of some thirty Soviet military divisions in Eastern Europe graphically demonstrate, this line of argument should not be carried too far. Two other factors should be borne in mind. First, the essence of Soviet–East European relations is still to be found in the six bilateral relationships to which the Soviet Union is party, and the highly publicized multilateral conferences of recent years continue to be based on the extensive bilateral negotiations which always precede them. Second, the partial pluralization, or "democratization," of relations within CMEA and the Warsaw Pact is offset by the continued, and carefully preserved, predominance of the Soviet Union in both organizations.

It could further be objected that Soviet interests in multilateralism in relations with Eastern Europe are the product, not of some new-found confidence in the East European allies, but of the familiar Soviet desire to construct new levers of control in Eastern Europe. Actually, these two lines of argument are far from being mutually exclusive, for in their efforts to contain the growing power and influence of their former client states, the Soviet leaders have been forced to rely on their more orthodox East European comrades to promote "unity and cohesion" in the region. Thus, the trend in Soviet bloc relations, not just after 1968 but dating to the mid-1950s, was toward a gradual pluralization of relations within an increasingly elaborate multilateral framework. [124]

In a more immediate sense, the year 1971 marked the end of two decisive years of unparalleled activity in the Soviet bloc. Consider, for example, the developments of just two months, March and April 1969: bloc leaders issued the "Budapest Appeal" for the convening of a pan-European security conference and simultaneously announced the reorganization of the Warsaw Pact command structure, armed clashes erupted along the Sino-Soviet border, Soviet leaders secured the removal of Alexander Dubček from the Czechoslovak leadership, and the 23rd, "Extraordinary" session of the Council for Mutual Economic Assistance announced an agreement in principle on a "comprehensive program" for socialist economic integration. Negotiations over those two years, moreover, were designed to support a complex strategy of pursuing East-West détente while at the same time promoting closer unity within the bloc. Initially Soviet but ultimately collective, this strategy was part of an overall integrationist drive in Eastern Europe, to be implemented over the next few years under the banner of "socialist internationalism."

PART TWO

SOCIALIST INTERNATIONALISM
IN THE 1970s

4

Confronting the Seventies

The Soviet and East European regimes entered the 1970s with a measure of optimism. The disunity brought on by the invasion of Czechoslovakia had given way to a certain "normalization" in Eastern Europe and in relations with the West, where NATO governments were beginning to respond favorably to the Warsaw Pact détente initiatives of the late 1960s. Indeed, East-West relations, particularly trade relations, already were showing signs of improvement, and the belated impact of the global economic boom of the late 1960s had encouraged the East European regimes to embark on ambitious growth strategies expected to usher in a new era of prosperity and stability in the region. In their mutual relations, too, the Soviet and East European regimes had achieved a degree of unity and stability, based on a somewhat more equitable distribution of power and influence, and had embarked on a coordinated integrationist program, conducted under the banner of "socialist internationalism." The various dimensions of this drive—political, military, economic, and ideological—and their mixed results, will be discussed in the chapters to follow.

The optimism of the early 1970s appeared vindicated for a time. East-West relations proceeded steadily, if not always smoothly, toward a Conference on Security and Cooperation in Europe, and East-West trade was expanding rapidly. Within Eastern Europe, economic growth rates increased, in some cases dramatically, material living standards improved visibly, and an impressive domestic stability was evident everywhere.

All this began to change at mid-decade. East-West relations began to founder on misgivings in the West over the evolution of détente and apprehensions over Soviet military capabilities and intentions. Even more important, the global economic recession, triggered by drastic increases in world energy prices, exerted a profound impact on the East European economies, newly sensitized to international economic fluctuations. Economic reversals, in turn, played havoc with the economic growth strategies so loudly proclaimed only a few years earlier and began to threaten the tenuous political stability evident in the first half of the decade. On the ideological front as well, new challenges arose in the international Communist movement, particularly those mounted by the "Eurocommunists" and other autonomist parties in the West, and within Eastern Europe itself, where organized dissident groups in Poland and elsewhere began to challenge some of the fundamental premises of Communist rule.

Thus, by decade's end the key elements of Soviet and East European strategies for the 1970s—détente internationally, economic growth *cum* consumerism domestically, and integrationist efforts in their mutual relations—were in a state of considerable disarray, and the grandiose aims associated with socialist internationalism had been rendered increasingly irrelevant by the pressing domestic and international challenges of the day. The evolution of these challenges, and of Soviet and East European responses to them, was revealed above all at two distinct but authoritative levels: internationally, in the deliberations and resolutions of the frequent summit conferences among the Soviet and East European leaders during the 1970s, and domestically, in Party policies as expressed in the Soviet and East European Party congresses.

Foreign Relations: Soviet–East European Summit Diplomacy

The centerpiece of Soviet and East European diplomacy in the 1970s was the Conference on Security and Cooperation in Europe (CSCE), whose final stage was held in Helsinki in late July and early August 1975. In the first half of the decade, CSCE was a prime foreign policy goal of the Soviet and East European regimes; in the latter half, it was a crowning achievement whose symbolic significance they sought to preserve even while taking steps to undermine some of its practical results. Although the present analysis cannot hope to provide a full treatment of the long, often purely tactical negotiations leading up to Helsinki, still less of the complex issues surrounding the related Mutual and Balanced Force Reduction (MBFR) talks in Vienna, their salient points can be noted briefly.

To begin with, the Soviet and East European leaders entered the 1970s generally agreed on their objectives and priorities in pursuing European détente.[1] The *sine qua non* was recognition of existing European frontiers and, by implication, acceptance of the East European regimes' claims to legitimacy. Beyond this, all sought an expansion of East-West trade and its regulation through formal interstate agreements, and all shared a determination to minimize the potentially destabilizing consequences inherent in expanded human and cultural contacts with the West.[2] Aside from continuing opposition by

Romania's Ceauşescu to his allies' insistence on a bloc-to-bloc approach in East-West consultations,[3] the only real resistance to a common Warsaw Pact Westpolitik had been East German intransigence on the "German question," a hurdle overcome in May 1971 by the replacement of Walter Ulbricht by the more pliant Erich Honecker as East German Party leader.

Similarly, by the beginning of the 1970s both East and West were agreed on the desirability of a pan-European security conference; only its terms remained to be hammered out. Chief among the issues to be resolved were the question of state boundaries in central Europe, the issue of United States participation in the conference, and the scope of the agenda, particularly with regard to mutual force reductions in Europe. By the end of 1971, the question of European frontiers was close to resolution: the Moscow-Bonn nonaggression treaty had been signed, as had the Quadripartite Agreement on Berlin; and treaty negotiations were proceeding rapidly between West Germany and Poland, East Germany, and Czechoslovakia.[4] The other two key issues were resolved in early 1972 by a compromise of sorts: in return for Warsaw Pact agreement to include the United States and Canada in the talks (a foregone conclusion anyway) and minor concessions on the starting point for force reductions talks, NATO abandoned its earlier demand that those talks be an integral part of CSCE and stipulated instead that they be held "either before or in parallel with" the broader security conference.[5]

As agreed, preparatory talks on force reductions and CSCE were held separately in late 1972 and early 1973. When the Conference on Mutual and Balanced Force Reductions (MBFR) officially opened in October 1973, East and West became deadlocked almost immediately, with the West demanding "balanced" force reductions to offset the Warsaw Pact's numerical superiority and the East insisting on "equal" reductions to preserve it. Despite an early NATO concession to drop the word "balanced" from the title of the talks in return for a Warsaw Pact pledge of "undiminished security" for both sides, no amount of semantic acrobatics could overcome the broad gap between the two approaches.[6] It became clear early on that agreement on mutual force reductions could not be timed to coincide with a CSCE resolution, and both sides at Vienna set about the laborious, and largely fruitless, process of attempting to narrow the gap between them and define areas of possible accord.

Meanwhile, the first phase of CSCE, conducted at the foreign minister level, was held in Helsinki from July 3 to July 7, 1973. From the beginning, East and West were divided over their basic preconceptions of European détente—whether it was to be a process of carefully regulated state-to-state relations or a broader process of reconciliation among the peoples of Europe. For their part, the Soviet and East European leaders had reconciled themselves to the fact that there could be no conference without some concessions on expanded human and cultural contacts between East and West, but they sought to limit such contacts under the cover of "noninterference in internal affairs," a stipulation invoked to preserve their ultimate discretionary power over the actual implementation of "freer flow" proposals put forth by Western, neutral, and nonaligned countries. Deliberations on these and other proposals were carried out by specialized committees and subcommittees during CSCE's second stage, which opened in Geneva in September 1973. Originally expected to last only a few months, the session dragged on for nearly two years of wrangling over the content and wording of the CSCE draft resolution. Finally, in late July 1975, heads of state (or their representatives) of thirty-five countries—all of Europe save Albania, plus the United States and Canada—assembled in Helsinki for the formal signing of the CSCE agreement.

Signed on August 1, 1975, the Helsinki Agreement, or "Final Act," amounted not to a set of binding prescriptions but to a series of jointly accepted and inevitably vague objectives.[7] The lengthy document is divided into three sections, or "baskets." The first, "Questions Relating to Security in Europe," consists chiefly of a set of ten principles said to guide relations among the participating states: these included sovereign equality of states, pacific settlement of disputes, inviolability of European frontiers, noninterference in internal affairs, respect for human rights and fundamental freedoms, and equal rights and self-determination of peoples. It also provides for certain "confidence-building" measures, including prior notification of major troop movements and military maneuvers involving more than 25,000 troops. Basket Two, concerning "Cooperation in the Field of Economics, of Science and Technology, and of the Environment," obliges the signatories to encourage expanded trade relations, reduce trade barriers, provide greater economic information, and promote trade in specific spheres of economic activity. Finally, Basket Three, "Cooperation in Humanitarian and Other Fields," calls on participating states to facilitate human contacts through family reunification measures, expanded trade and tourism, and increased contacts among nongovernmental organizations; to provide a freer flow of information and ideas by facilitating distribution of publications and newspapers, encouraging international symposia and meetings, and improving the working conditions of journalists; and to develop cooperation in the fields of culture and education. Any issues arising from these general goals, it is specified in Basket Three's preamble, must be settled by the states concerned under "mutually acceptable conditions." The document concludes with a provision for a follow-up conference to meet two years later for the purposes of reviewing compliance with the agreement and working out new measures toward European security and cooperation.

This final stipulation comes closest to the real meaning of Helsinki, which lay not so much in any set of substantive measures (these were manifestly lacking in the Final Act) as in the evolution of a process, an ongoing search for new avenues of accord, in which the search itself held greater significance than its substantive results. This sense of Helsinki as a process, along with the formal establishment of a set of principles purportedly guiding East-West relations, served to replace some of the psychological barriers dividing the two halves of Europe with something vaguely but palpably perceived as the "spirit of Helsinki." In this sense, Helsinki exerted a far more profound impact in the East than in the West, and the high hopes of the peoples of Eastern Europe that Helsinki would help erode the postwar division of Europe were matched by the growing fears of their regimes over the potentially destablizing tendencies inherent in East-West détente.

Obvious though it may be, one further aspect of the Helsinki process should be mentioned: it marked the diplomatic debut of the East European socialist states as actors, albeit with limited roles, on the international stage. Not only did CSCE and MBFR themselves afford greater scope for East European diploma-

Table 4.1
Soviet–East European Summitry, 1969–1980

			Multilateral conference		
Year	Date	Location	Political Consultative Committee	Other summit meeting	Agenda
1969	Mar. 17	Budapest	X		CSCE, pact affairs
	Dec. 3–4	Moscow		X	Ostpolitik
1970	Aug. 20	Moscow	X		Moscow-Bonn pact
	Dec. 2	E. Berlin	X		CSCE
1971	Aug. 2	Crimea		X	various
1972	Jan. 25–26	Prague	X		CSCE
	July 31	Crimea		X	CSCE, economic affairs
1973	July 30–31	Crimea		X	CSCE, economic affairs
1974	Apr. 17–18	Warsaw	X		CSCE, MBFR talks
	Aug. 3–15	Crimea		X	various
1975	July 31–				
	Aug. 1	Helsinki		X	CSCE
1976	July–Aug.	Crimea		X	various
	Nov. 25–26	Bucharest	X		CSCE, pact affairs
1977	July–Aug.	Crimea		X	various
1978	July–Aug.	Crimea		X	various
	Nov. 22–23	Moscow	X		military détente
1979	July–Aug.	Crimea		X	various
	Oct. 6	E. Berlin		X	GDR 30th anniversary
1980	May 15	Warsaw	X		CSCE, pact 25th anniv.
	July–Aug.	Crimea		X	various
	Dec. 5	Moscow		X	Polish situation

NOTE: CSCE = Conference on Security and Cooperation in Europe; MBFR = Mutual and Balanced Force Reductions.

cy, but the more general process of European détente offered opportunities for separate (if not fully independent) East European diplomatic activity of the sort almost unheard of in the 1950s and 1960s. Because of this trend, as well as the generally shared determination of Soviet and East European leaders carefully to regulate and delimit the process of East-West détente, the tasks of Warsaw Pact foreign policy coordination acquired greater urgency in the 1970s.

Accordingly, top Party and state leaders met frequently throughout the decade in a variety of settings: ad hoc summit meetings, sessions of the Warsaw Pact's Political Consultative Committee, Soviet and East European Party congresses, bilateral meetings between Party leaders, and various other international and inter-Party gatherings. To these should be added the many lower-level meetings on foreign policy matters, most notably those of the Committee of Foreign Ministers, formally incorporated into the Warsaw Pact consultative structure in 1976. The more important of these summit meetings are listed in Table 4.1, as is one entirely new forum created in 1971 for inter-Party consultation: a yearly conference of Party first (or general) secretaries, held in the Crimea in midsummer.

The Crimea Conferences

Although the Crimea conferences were eventually to acquire the status of grand "state of the world" meetings, with particular emphasis on East-West problems, the first of these sessions apparently was called with more limited concerns in mind. Chief among these was a series of unsettling developments in the Balkans and the growing problem of relations with the Chinese.

By 1971, as has been seen, Yugoslavia had opened diplomatic relations with two former ideological enemies, Albania and China, and had moved toward even closer relations with Romania.[8] By June of that year, the Balkan equation was rendered even more complex by two new developments: the highly publicized visit by Romania's President Ceauşescu to China and the dramatic announcement that President Nixon soon would pay an official visit to the Chinese leaders in Peking. From the Soviet perspective, this turn of events must have appeared ominous indeed: not only were the members of the nascent "Tirana-Belgrade-Bucharest axis" proving highly adept at exploiting Sino-Soviet difficulties, but now the specter was arising of some sort of Washington-Peking *rapprochement*, with Romania acting as intermediary.[9]

It was in this atmosphere, and in the wake of Warsaw Pact maneuvers in Hungary,[10] that Soviet and East European Party leaders, minus Ceauşescu, met in the Crimea in early August. The official summary of the conference was unrevealing: it was noted only that the talks yielded "complete unanimity and mutual understanding" (a happy occurrence presumably made possible by

Ceauşescu's absence) on a wide range of issues, including economic integration, the recently held 24th CPSU Congress, initiatives toward a European security conference, and other international topics.[11] It would appear, however, that the matters of most immediate concern were recent trends in China and the Balkans, particularly as they involved Romania, for the conference was followed immediately by a series of sharp attacks on the Romanians in the Soviet and East European media.[12] The Hungarian attack was surprisingly harsh: in addition to reviving the issue of the Hungarian minority in Romanian Transylvania, the Hungarians pointedly criticized the "Tirana-Belgrade-Bucharest line" and warned of the possible emergence of an "anti-Soviet axis, . . . which begins in Peking and ends in the Balkans."[13]

There was an East-West dimension to all this, of course. In anticipation of impending negotiations toward CSCE and the attendant need to present a united Warsaw Pact posture with the West, the Soviet leaders clearly wanted to bring concerted pressure to bear on the recalcitrant Romanians, who were bent on eroding even the appearance of bloc solidarity. Equally important, strictures aimed at the Romanians, Yugoslavs, and Chinese should also be seen in the context of Soviet hopes to convene a European Communist conference which would reassert Soviet primacy in the Communist world at the same time that Helsinki was affirming Soviet coauthorship of European security and cooperation.[14]

Between the first and second Crimea conferences, the Soviet leaders struggled to shore up relations in the Communist world, first with the Romanians and Yugoslavs and later with the Chinese.[15] In August and September 1971, a meeting between Soviet Vice Premier (and permanent representative to CMEA) Mikhail Lesechko and President Ceauşescu and a personal visit by Brezhnev to Marshal Tito in Belgrade were quickly arranged, for the purposes of easing tensions in the Balkans and, more pointedly, repudiating rumors of a possible Soviet intervention in Romania or Yugoslavia.[16] The improvement in Soviet-Yugoslav relations was particularly dramatic: following Tito's visit to Moscow in June 1972, the Soviet leaders announced that generous credits would be extended for Yugoslav industrialization; and in September and November of the following year, leaders of the two countries again exchanged visits.[17]

As to the Chinese, the Soviet leaders continued to pursue a dual policy designed to contain China at the intergovernmental level and isolate the Chinese Communist party ideologically. Thus, while conducting an unremitting ideological campaign against Chinese "adventurism" and "left-wing opportunism" since the 1969 border clashes, the Soviet leaders had opened talks on the redefinition of borders, proposed creation of an Asian collective security system, and offered to sign a treaty on renunciation of force in their mutual relations.[18] Aside from winning Chinese endorsement of a joint trade and credit agreement, the Soviet leaders met with little success in pursuing their so-called "principled line" of normalizing relations with China, and inter-Party polemics continued to escalate. As a *Pravda* editorial explained, in "waging a resolute ideological-political struggle against the great-nation chauvinist principles of Peking and its foreign policy, we are doing everything to defend the interests of the Soviet people [and] the interests of our friends and allies against any encroachment."[19]

One related aim of Soviet overtures to Yugoslavia and condemnations of China, of course, was to prepare the way for the convocation of a pan-European conference of Communist and workers' parties. By endeavoring to bring Yugoslavia back within the "socialist community" and seeking the virtual excommunication of the heretical Chinese, the Soviet leaders evidently were hoping to preempt any European opposition to the CPSU's "leading role" in the Communist movement and, at a minimum, to insure general endorsement of the Soviet foreign policy line.

As for the Romanians, Soviet policies toward China and Yugoslavia had served to erode the principal sources of external support for Ceauşescu's independent-minded line and to encourage a more tractable Romanian posture in East-West and intrabloc affairs. That the Romanians were under intense Soviet pressure to attend the forthcoming (1972) Crimea session is suggested by Ceauşescu's call, issued just two weeks before the conference was to convene, for closer consultation among the parties in order to work out a "better definition of the principles that should govern relations among all socialist countries."[20] Presumably armed with this mandate, Ceauşescu duly arrived in the Soviet Union in late July for the second of the Crimea conferences.

The official communiqué of the 1972 Crimea conference was even more cryptic than usual, noting only that the Party leaders, including Ceauşescu, discussed the "progress of all-round cooperation" and "pressing international issues."[21] These pressing issues included, presumably, the status of East-West negotiations toward a European security conference, for in January 1972 the PCC, meeting in Prague, had reiterated the previous Warsaw Pact call for a speedy convocation of the conference and had clarified its agenda for discussions on European security. Toward that end, the PCC agreed to accept in part the long-standing NATO proposal for talks on mutual force reductions in central Europe. The corresponding NATO compromise, which included agreement to hold MBFR negotiations separate from the broader security conference, removed the last major obstacle to the convocation of the Conference on Security and Cooperation in Europe. After some additional haggling between East and West, representatives of thirty-four participating countries (Monaco was shortly to become the thirty-fifth) assembled in Helsinki in late November 1972 for preliminary discussions toward the convening of CSCE.

By the time of the 1973 Crimea session, the process of East-West negotiation was well under way. Bonn's treaties with the Soviet Union, Poland, East

Germany, and Czechoslovakia had been signed and ratified by all concerned; preliminary discussions on MBFR already had been held; and the first stage of CSCE had closed—just weeks before Soviet bloc Party leaders gathered in the Crimea.[22] With CSCE's second stage scheduled to begin in September, the third of the Crimea conferences promised to be a significant forum for inter-Party consultation and coordination.

Not surprisingly, the communiqué on the Crimea summit focused on East-West relations: the significance of the Warsaw Pact's détente initiatives was emphasized, as was the need for continued foreign policy coordination among pact members. Special attention was paid to the pattern of East-West cooperation in the areas of human and cultural contacts, and it was emphasized that such cooperation "must develop within the framework of strict respect for the sovereignty of every state and noninterference in internal affairs." Far from permitting ideological relaxation, the communiqué noted, the process of détente demands that the socialist states "show constant vigilance" against those who would attempt "to use détente for undermining the positions of socialism."[23] To improve ideological coordination, the Party leaders agreed to convene a conference of all the Central Committee secretaries for ideological affairs and conclude a series of bilateral ideological treaties.[24]

Beneath the surface of this apparent solidarity, obvious conflicts existed, particularly between Romania and the Soviet Union. The "complete mutual understanding and unanimity" phraseology of previous communiqués was replaced in 1973 by the bland observation that "the meeting passed in a friendly and cordial atmosphere." That the Romanians were the chief source of inter-Party discord in the Crimea was revealed in the bilateral meetings which followed the summit: "complete unity of views" was said to have prevailed in all the sessions save that between Brezhnev and Ceaușescu, which was said merely to have taken place in a "friendly atmosphere."[25]

Nevertheless, by 1973 the Crimea summits seemed to have been institutionalized as regular forums for foreign policy coordination, a task which was growing in importance with the evolution of East-West negotiations. The conferences also provided an arena for the resolution of conflicts, involving not only the Romanians (though those conflicts are always the most openly aired) but the other allies as well. In fact, since the year passed without a meeting of the Warsaw Pact's Political Consultative Committee, it appeared that some of the functions of the PCC might have been taken over by the annual conference of Party leaders in the Crimea.

In 1974, however, the Crimea summit was unceremoniously cancelled, as the Party leaders—without Ceaușescu—met instead in a series of bilateral sessions with Brezhnev. By all indications, it was Ceaușescu's outspoken criticism of Soviet proposals at the April 1974 session of the PCC which induced the Soviet leaders to call off the Crimea conference,[26] for in mid-May, following a hasty visit to Brezhnev in Moscow, Bulgarian Communist Party leader Todor Zhivkov met with Ceauşescu in Sofia, presumably to mediate Soviet-Romanian differences. Zhivkov's intercession apparently failed to sway the Romanian leader, however, and Secretary Brezhnev, having already conferred with East Germany's Honecker in June, went to the Crimea for separate meetings with Husák (August 3), Kádár (August 5), and Gierek (August 15).[27]

In 1975 the Soviet leaders again failed to convene a summit conference in the Crimea, perhaps because the usual convening date of the Crimea session would have conflicted with the thirty-five-nation Conference on Security and Cooperation in Europe, which opened in Helsinki in late July. The Party leaders did engage in last-minute consultations on CSCE during a "mini-summit" on the second day of the 11th Congress of the Hungarian Socialist Workers' Party (HSWP) in March, but Ceauşescu, having declined to attend the congress, was not among the participants.[28]

These difficulties in convening summit meetings of the "fraternal parties" revealed a more fundamental dilemma in the Soviet leaders' multilateral approach to the problems of alliance management. As one Western analyst noted at the time, "The Soviets have used periodic conferences, most notably in the Crimea, to ventilate problems and forge unity, two objectives which cannot be realized easily because they are mutually exclusive: ventilating problems weakens unity; and forging unity restricts the ventilation of problems."[29] By 1976 it had become apparent that the Soviet leaders continued to value the symbolic display of unity the Crimea sessions afforded, but not if it meant submitting to the clashing interests which had begun to surface in multilateral gatherings of Party leaders. The Romanians, always wary of institutionalized expressions of alliance solidarity, apparently had given notice that they would countenance nothing more than an informal series of bilateral meetings of Party leaders in the Crimea.

With two burning issues on the inter-Party agenda already behind them—the Helsinki conference and the pan-European conference of Communist and workers' parties—and with the near certainty that the Romanians would boycott a multilateral meeting, as they had the mini-summits at the Hungarian and Polish Party congresses in 1975, the Soviet leaders settled in 1976 for the preferred Romanian format for the Crimea session. Rather than assemble together for a solemn, multilateral parley around the conference table, the East European Party leaders gathered instead for a series of informal meetings between each of them in turn and their Soviet host. For his part, Ceauşescu duly arrived for a "frank and comradely" discussion with Secretary Brezhnev and also took the opportunity to visit Moldavia.

This pattern was repeated every summer after 1976, and the Crimea sessions acquired a ritualistic character quite different from the ambitious summitry of the early 1970s. Every summer in late July or early August, the East European

Party leaders gathered in no particular order for a "vacation" or "short holiday" in the Crimea, met briefly with Brezhnev but seldom with one another, signed terse and vaguely worded communiqués, and returned home, leaving the outside observer not much the wiser as to what transpired. Even the few points of divergence soon became predictable: Ceauşescu normally remained in the Soviet Union only a few hours, the other leaders several days or longer; and Ceauşescu always had a "frank and comradely" talk with Brezhnev, the others having discovered "complete mutual understanding" with their Soviet host.[30]

Clearly, the Crimea sessions remained important forums for regular consultation between the Soviet leader and his East European counterparts, and in some respects the new arrangement offered distinct advantages over the earlier format. The bilateral, informal nature of the meetings presumably facilitated a more open exchange of views and certainly provided greater flexibility of agenda. That much can be gleaned from the official communiqués, which reveal that the topics of discussion, formerly restricted to the major international or intrabloc issues of the day, were broadened to include salient domestic or bilateral problems of concern to the two parties.[31] Whatever their merits, though, the Crimea sessions are no longer the formal, multilateral summits they were first intended to be, and their perfunctory communiqués do not carry the weight of formal policy declarations. For this, the Soviet and East European leaders have returned to familiar forums for foreign policy coordination, most notably the Warsaw Pact's Political Consultative Committee.

Warsaw Pact Summitry after Helsinki

Some four months after the 1976 Crimean round, the Political Consultative Committee convened the first formal Warsaw Pact summit since the August 1975 signing of the Helsinki Agreement.[32] The significance of the session was heralded by the announcement that it would be held in Bucharest, site of the PCC session ten years earlier that had set in motion the Warsaw Pact drive for a European security conference. Determined to maintain the initiative in East-West relations and mindful of the need for careful prior orchestration of multilateral gatherings of this kind, Brezhnev arrived early in Bucharest for three days of private talks with the Romanian leaders. This bilateral preparation apparently yielded a compromise of sorts, for the communiqué issued after the PCC session noted that it had "proceeded in an atmosphere of full mutual understanding," and Romania's Ceauşescu expressed "satisfaction" with its results.[33]

The chief outcome of the PCC session was a lengthy declaration whose title aptly sums up Warsaw Pact Westpolitik in the latter half of the 1970s: "For Fresh Advances in International Détente, For Consolidation of Security and Development of Cooperation in Europe."[34] Anxious to preserve the fruits of détente in the face of growing misgivings in the West and determined to keep the CPSU "peace policy" at the forefront of the East-West dialogue,[35] the Soviet and East European leaders issued in Bucharest the first in a long series of "historic initiatives," all part of a sustained post-Helsinki "peace offensive." Often couched in terms which are patently self-serving or so vague as to be meaningless in practice, these initiatives served nonetheless to exploit growing neutralist sentiment within West European societies and put the West constantly in a reactive and defensive posture, thereby aggravating strains in the Atlantic alliance. Of course, the vagueness of these initiatives was also indicative of growing strains within the Warsaw Pact itself, as the Soviet leaders evidently were compelled to content themselves with formulations acceptable to East European allies increasingly anxious over the fate of European détente.

The 1976 Bucharest Declaration certainly fit this general pattern, urging a revival of the deadlocked MBFR talks in Vienna, calling for the reduction and liquidation of nuclear weapons and the total prohibition of their testing, and declaring readiness to "dissolve the Warsaw Treaty Organization simultaneously with the dissolution of the North Atlantic Treaty Organization." All of these were old proposals, though the last had been consistently reaffirmed only by Romania (and may have been included as part of a Brezhnev-Ceauşescu compromise), but in no case were any concrete measures offered toward their realization. The two new proposals issued at Bucharest fell into the self-serving category: a proposal to forbid new members to NATO or the Warsaw Pact clearly was directed at Spain's planned admission to the Atlantic alliance, and an invitation to all Helsinki signatories to pledge "not to be the first to use nuclear weapons one against the other" struck directly at NATO's deterrent underpinnings, which threatened nuclear response to Soviet conventional attack.

On intrabloc relations, the PCC announced the establishment of two new Warsaw Pact organs: a Joint Secretariat, charged with coordinating alliance affairs between sessions of the PCC, and a Committee of Foreign Ministers, created perhaps in response to Romanian urging and probably intended to take over some of the functions originally meant for the Crimea conferences. The operations and significance of these new bodies will be explored in the chapter to follow.[36]

The most immediate issue facing the Soviet and East European leaders in Bucharest, however, was the CSCE review conference scheduled to open the following June in Belgrade. On this, the PCC reiterated the familiar Warsaw Pact position on European security and cooperation, stressing the economic aspects of East-West relations but condemning "certain forces" who wish to use "Basket Three" human rights provisions as a pretext for interfering in the internal affairs of other states. Then, in a warning which would figure prominently in the Belgrade conference, the PCC declared: "The states participating in the Warsaw Treaty deem it necessary to reaffirm that this is a road without a future and they reject it.''

Soviet and East European leaders did not hold another multilateral meeting before the Belgrade review conference in June of 1977, though Ceauşescu met bilaterally with most of his East European counterparts in the spring and early summer.[37] Rather, final Warsaw Pact coordination devolved to the deputy foreign ministers, who met in East Berlin in late February, and the foreign ministers, who convened in their first formal committee session in late May, just three weeks before the opening of the Belgrade conference. Meeting in Moscow on May 25 and 26, the foreign ministers reaffirmed the Bucharest proposals and warned once again that the Belgrade meeting should "promote greater understanding and trust," that "all its proceedings must be of a constructive character," by which they presumably meant that criticism of the Warsaw Pact's human rights record would be "destructive," tantamount to interference in the internal affairs of the socialist states.[38]

These cautionary words were of little avail, however, for the Belgrade conference quickly degenerated into a welter of charges and countercharges over the human rights provisions of the Helsinki Final Act. Beginning with the preliminary session in June, which was supposed merely to set the agenda for the full conference in October, Western representatives led by chief U.S. delegate Arthur Goldberg presented a detailed catalogue of Soviet and East European human rights violations. The remainder of the three-month session proceeded in a more businesslike but still largely fruitless manner, as Western delegates remained skeptical of the Warsaw Pact's Bucharest initiatives, and the Soviet side refused to budge on American proposals to strengthen the human rights provisions of the Helsinki Agreement. For its part, the Soviet delegation launched a last-minute counteroffensive, but nothing could alter the fundamental fact that the glittering surface of East-West détente, and with it the Soviet "peace policy," had been badly tarnished at Belgrade.[39]

In the aftermath of Belgrade, the Soviet and East European leaders sought to put the best possible light on the proceedings, then quickly forget them and return to the peace offensive. Meeting in Moscow in April 1978, the Warsaw Pact foreign ministers expressed regret that "a number of substantial, constructive proposals" (theirs) had not received favorable attention at Belgrade, but reaffirmed their readiness to continue the process of East-West cooperation. Their understanding of this process was revealed in the stress given in their communiqué to the Warsaw Pact's proposals on military détente and disarmament: the foreign ministers revived the initiatives of the Bucharest summit, urged the formation of a mass movement of "peace-loving forces" in Europe (whose unstated but obvious mission would be to oppose U.S. production and deployment of the neutron bomb, then a topic of considerable transatlantic discord), and appealed without elaboration for "the speediest possible adoption of concrete and effective steps to lessen military confrontation."[40]

By mid-1978, however, the Warsaw Pact peace offensive was in disarray. Already discredited by the exile of Alexander Solzhenitsyn and the revelations at Belgrade, the Soviet Union's professed commitment to the spirit of Helsinki was further belied by a full-fledged campaign against human rights activists in the USSR, manifested most recently by the imprisonment of Yuri Orlov in May and of Aleksandr Ginzburg and Anatoly Shcharansky in July. At about the same time, Western concern over growing Soviet and Cuban involvement in Africa had prompted U.S. National Security Advisor Zbigniew Brzezinski to declare that such activities constituted a breach of the Helsinki Agreement. To this was added mounting concern in the West, particularly in the United States, over Soviet military capabilities and intentions, as outlined in President Carter's major foreign policy addresses at Wake Forest and Annapolis. For its part, NATO had responded with stony silence to Warsaw Pact strictures on military détente and disarmament, and the NATO Council meeting in May had approved a Long-Term Defense Program calling for a 3 percent annual increase in the defense budgets of NATO members.

Even more unsettling in Soviet eyes was the evolution of Chinese foreign policy after Mao. Far from paving the way for any Sino-Soviet reconciliation, the pragmatic orientation of the post-Mao leadership had propelled China toward much closer relations, including limited military cooperation, with Western Europe and the United States. Having already moved swiftly toward full normalization of relations with the People's Republic,[41] the Carter administration dispatched Dr. Brzezinski to Peking (Beijing) in May and shortly thereafter announced the sale of certain types of "nonlethal" military equipment to China, prompting Secretary Brezhnev to accuse the United States, in so many words, of attempting to play the "China card" against the USSR. Ironically, the Brzezinski visit came just days after the departure of Romania's Ceauşescu from Peking, where he had also met with Chinese leaders and also concluded an arms deal, this one for a joint Romanian-Chinese arms production venture.[42] On the European front, Chairman Hua Guofeng paid a highly publicized and successful visit in August to Romania and Yugoslavia—the first such visit ever by a Chinese leader[43]—and in the fall his foreign minister, Huang Hua, toured several West European capitals. As if these were not affronts enough to Soviet sensibilities, on the eve of the November summit meeting of the Political Consultative Committee in Moscow, Chinese forces crossed the border into Vietnam, Moscow's firm ally in Southeast Asia, to conduct a punitive raid in retaliation for Vietnam's invasion of Cambodia (soon to become another Soviet ally).

For all these reasons, the Soviet leaders clearly wanted to use the Moscow summit as a forum for castigating the Chinese, and a Soviet delegation led by

Foreign Minister Andrei Gromyko was dispatched to Bucharest in late October 1978, presumably to lay the groundwork for the PCC session the following month. Given the cordial state of Romanian-Chinese relations, the Soviet leaders may not have expected an outright condemnation of Chinese foreign policy, but they surely demanded a repudiation of the Chinese attack on Vietnam, an ally linked to the USSR by formal treaty.[44]

In the PCC communiqué and declaration issued after the Moscow summit, however, the Chinese were not even mentioned. Rather, the PCC repeated its familiar litany, giving a rather gloomy assessment of the international situation, whose deterioration was attributed to "imperialist and reactionary forces," reaffirming the initiatives of the previous PCC session in Bucharest, and adding a vague eight-point "appeal" for reviving the process of détente. The only really new element in the declaration was a call for a "world conference on disarmament with the participation of all states," but this was not followed up with any concrete proposals.[45] Indeed, the vagueness of the PCC's formal resolutions betrayed mounting Soviet difficulties in achieving the necessary consensus among its East European allies, particularly with regard to Soviet initiatives beyond Europe.

It was only after the close of the summit, however, that outside observers learned why China had been omitted from the communiqué and declaration, and what other disputes had arisen at this, the most stormy Warsaw Pact session since the Prague Spring. The first sign that something was amiss came a day after the summit ended, when the PCC issued a separate "statement" on the Middle East condemning "separate Egyptian-Israeli deals" (i.e., the Camp David accords) and signed by six Warsaw Pact leaders.[46] Conspicuously missing from the list of signatures was that of the seventh participant in the Moscow summit: Nicolae Ceauşescu.

That this was not the only issue of contention at Moscow was made abundantly clear upon Ceauşescu's return to Bucharest, when the Romanian leader unleashed an unprecedented public exposé, albeit in largely veiled terms, of the secret deliberations of a Warsaw Pact summit. In five speeches, two Party resolutions, and several articles in the official press, Ceauşescu divulged the essence of the fratricidal dispute and defended his dissenting position.[47] In addition to rejecting the Soviet position on the Middle East, Ceauşescu refused to endorse a proposal for all Warsaw Pact members to increase their defense expenditures (this in response to the recent decision of the NATO Council) and denounced a Soviet move to strengthen military integration, apparently through a proposed supranational command structure.[48] On the question of China, Ceauşescu apparently rejected a call for rendering some sort of military assistance to Vietnam, or at least for issuing a strong collective warning to the Chinese. (That China was on the agenda is beyond doubt, for several of the East European media added condemnations of China in their summaries of the PCC resolutions.[49]) The Romanian leadership broached the Chinese issue indirectly but unmistakably, declaring Romania's intention to fulfill its alliance commitments but stating that the mutual aid obligations of the Warsaw Treaty were restricted to cases of "imperialist aggression in Europe," adding that Romania sought cooperation not only with members of the Warsaw Pact but also with "other socialist countries."[50]

As in so many cases of highly publicized Romanian divisiveness, one can only speculate as to the extent these grievances were shared (and/or expressed) by the other East European leaders. The issue of defense expenditures, for example, had been raised by Czechoslovak spokesmen in 1968, and it seems likely that all the junior Warsaw Pact allies shared Ceauşescu's concern over rising defense outlays at a time of acute economic deterioration. The idea of aid to Vietnam, too, must have been equally galling to the other East Europeans, who had so recently been asked to countenance Vietnam's admission to CMEA and the specter of development aid that came with it. Finally, despite their readiness to exhort their official media to condemn the Chinese, it may safely be assumed that none of the East Europeans was anxious to render any form of direct assistance to "fraternal" Vietnam. Thus, Ceauşescu's outburst tapped a discontent which was surely not confined to him alone.

In any case, Ceauşescu's public campaign brought Soviet-Romanian relations to their lowest ebb in a decade: Soviet Party leader Brezhnev termed Ceauşescu's methods "demagogic," and the Soviet media launched a counterattack against the Romanian position.[51] Although we may never know what took place behind the scenes in the fall of 1978, the timing and execution of the Romanian exposé suggest that Ceauşescu, having been presented with a virtual *fait accompli* during Gromyko's visit in October but determined to resist, decided in advance to stand fast at the summit and then go public with his grievances, thereby generating international support for his position and, not incidentally, adding some needed luster to his tarnished domestic image.

Having made his case plain, Ceauşescu quickly and tactfully pulled in his reins a bit, sending a delegation led by Central Committee Secretary Dumitru Popescu to an ideological conference in Sofia from December 12 to December 15. Although the Romanian representatives reiterated the Ceauşescu foreign policy line and indeed leveled implicit criticism at the Soviet leadership, they nonetheless submitted themselves to a ringing endorsement of Soviet policy on China, disarmament and defense, and "proletarian internationalism" by the vast majority of the seventy-three parties represented.[52] Soviet-Romanian relations remained strained but less acrimonious through 1979. The Romanians were duly represented at the Budapest meeting of the Warsaw Pact foreign ministers in May, but the bland communiqué issued after the session betrayed continued Romanian (and presumably other East European) resistance to any bold Soviet initiatives.[53] The familiar Warsaw Pact disarmament initiatives were trotted out once more, the only innovation being that the previous proposal for a disarmament conference "of all States" was now limited to the participants at Helsinki, again without elaboration as to its scope or purpose.[54]

By the time of the next Soviet–East European summit, held in East Berlin in October 1979 on the occasion of the GDR's thirtieth anniversary, the Warsaw Pact peace offensive had suffered another series of reversals. The second U.S.–Soviet strategic arms limitation agreement (SALT II), announced with high hopes in May, was foundering on deep suspicions and sharp attacks in the United States, and early indications were that the treaty in its existing form would not gain Senate approval. Additionally, to counter the growing Soviet SS-20 (medium-range nuclear missile) arsenal targeted at Western Europe, NATO was in the final stages of a "Euromissiles" decision which would authorize the construction and deployment in Western Europe of some 572 U.S. medium-range missiles.

Presumably to dissociate himself from Soviet foreign policy failures and avoid another ostentatious display of socialist internationalism, Ceauşescu boycotted the East Berlin summit and attendant festivities. His allies, however, seized the occasion to propose a moratorium on the deployment of new medium-range missiles, suggest negotiations toward their eventual reduction, and announce the unilateral withdrawal of up to 20,000 Soviet troops and 1,000 tanks from East Germany. These themes were picked up again in early December, when the Warsaw Pact foreign ministers, including Romania's Stefan Andrei, met in East Berlin in an unsuccessful last-minute effort to forestall a NATO Euromissiles decision. Without offering any substantive concessions, the foreign ministers reaffirmed their interest in mutual force reductions talks in Vienna, fleshed out their previously vague proposal for a conference on military détente, and declared their readiness to begin negotiations on limiting medium-range missiles in Europe, warning pointedly that a NATO decision to implement the Euromissiles plan would "destroy the basis for negotiations."[55] Having been offered nothing but talk in return for a deferral of the Euromissiles decision, NATO gave formal approval to the plan the following week, but not without encountering second thoughts among several of the junior allies.

Afghanistan and After

Just three weeks later, a new, more serious element of discord was introduced into East-West relations by the Soviet Union's December 27 invasion and subsequent occupation of Afghanistan. World reaction was vehement, from the Soviet perspective unexpectedly so, as statements of condemnation flooded in from governments everywhere, either individually or in collective assembly: the United Nations, states of the Third World, the nonaligned, the Arab states, and the Atlantic alliance all issued sharp rebukes. The United States' reaction was particularly tough, as the Carter administration drew up a list of sanctions and brought pressure to bear on its allies to support them. In Eastern Europe, initial statements of obligatory support (from all but Romania) soon gave way to a palpable sense of unease and concern over the future of European détente. For the Soviet leaders, given the likelihood of a prolonged and bitter occupation of Afghanistan, the key tasks in early 1980 were to put their Warsaw Pact house in order, batten down for harsh but inevitably short-lived Western criticism, and return as quickly as possible to the peace offensive.

In the immediate aftermath of the invasion, the Soviet Union's most faithful East European allies—Bulgaria, Czechoslovakia, and East Germany—quickly joined the Soviet counterattack to Western criticism, laying the blame for the intervention at the feet of the United States, "its imperialist allies," and China, and hailing the "fraternal aid" rendered Afghanistan by the Soviet Union.[56] The Hungarians and Poles offered their perfunctory support, but with manifest reluctance, while the Romanians largely maintained a discreet silence.[57] At the United Nations, however, the Romanian ambassador abstained from the January 14 General Assembly vote, noting during the floor debate that the situation posed a "serious danger to peace and the continuation of the policy of détente" and calling for the withdrawal of all foreign troops from Afghanistan.[58]

With the announcement of various Western sanctions against the Soviet Union—a partial grain embargo, a campaign to boycott the Moscow Olympic games, and others—concerns and misgivings began to grow in Eastern Europe, for here clearly was a case in which Soviet ambitions beyond Europe threatened the entire structure of East-West détente. Privately, semipublicly, or indirectly, the Romanians, Poles, and Hungarians left little doubt that they considered the Soviet action a serious miscalculation which jeopardized their carefully cultivated economic and political relations with the West and which carried with it potentially disruptive domestic consequences.[59] Even the East Germans were at pains to distance themselves from the whole affair by stepping up official contacts with the Bonn government, from which they sought understanding and continued close relations.

For their part, the Soviet leaders moved quickly to restore a façade of solidarity on the Afghanistan issue, and perhaps allay some East European fears as well, by summoning the Warsaw Pact foreign ministers, minus Romania's Andrei, for a series of separate meetings in Moscow, where all signed communiqués stressing "full solidarity" with the new Afghan regime and implicitly endorsing the Soviet invasion.[60] As usual, the Romanians required special handling, and in February Soviet Foreign Minister Andrei Gromyko was dispatched to Bucharest for talks with Ceauşescu. Not surprisingly, the communiqué issued after their session differed markedly from the others, blaming the Afghan situation vaguely on the "accumulation of unsolved international issues'' and decrying ''interference of the imperialist forces in the internal affairs of other states,'' a handy formulation sufficiently imprecise to satisfy both Moscow and Bucharest.[61]

Recriminations over Afghanistan aside, the Soviet and East European leaders were all agreed on the need to revive the spirit of European détente, and the East Europeans were manifestly in a better position than the Soviets to lead the campaign. Thus, East German overtures to Bonn clearly, if indirectly, served Soviet interests as well, and even the independent line of the Romanians was not without its compensations. The key role, however, was assigned to Polish Party leader Edward Gierek, whose personal friendship with West German Chancellor Helmut Schmidt and French President Valéry Giscard d'Estaing made him admirably suited for helping bring East and West together again. At the 8th Polish Party Congress in February 1980, Gierek added a new dimension to the Warsaw Pact proposal for a pan-European disarmament conference by disclosing that Warsaw would be honored to serve as host. Far more important was Gierek's successful role in mediating between Paris and Moscow, and calling on the traditional special relationship between France and Poland, to play host in Warsaw to a French-Soviet summit on May 18 and 19. The first high-level East-West encounter since the invasion of Afghanistan, the Giscard-Brezhnev summit of 1980 served to reverse the growing isolation of the USSR and, more importantly in Soviet thinking, symbolized a return to business as usual in East-West relations.

Meanwhile, another East-West meeting of sorts took place in Belgrade in early May, as world leaders gathered for the funeral of Yugoslav President Josip Broz Tito.[62] Among the most vocal critics of the Soviet invasion of Afghanistan, the Yugoslavs were in an ironic sense among its few beneficiaries, for the long-feared transition to the post-Tito era was allowed to begin at a time when the Soviet Union had its hands full elsewhere, both militarily and diplomatically. The transition was further facilitated by Marshal Tito's prolonged incapacitation, which served to generate unprecedented unity among Yugoslavia's disparate nationalities and gave a much-needed period of trial leadership to the new, seemingly unwieldy collective leadership Tito had designed.[63]

One of the immediate questions raised by Tito's death, of course, was its significance for his close ally Nicolae Ceauşescu. Tito had met Ceauşescu officially no fewer than nineteen times—indeed, Tito's last foreign trip was to Romania in November 1979—and his departure could not but leave Ceauşescu with a certain sense of isolation in the Balkans. As both the Romanian and the Yugoslav media were quick to affirm, however, Romanian-Yugoslav ties were built not only on personal diplomacy but on a shared and enduring commitment to state independence and sovereignty and the principle of noninterference in internal affairs. After the funeral, which was given exhaustive coverage in the Romanian media, Ceauşescu continued to emphasize the unaltered significance of close ties with Yugoslavia and moved to establish personal contacts with its new leaders.[64] Further, having met with many Western and Third World leaders at Belgrade at the time of Tito's funeral, Ceaușescu intimated that he might be prepared to assume some of Tito's international roles, particularly among the nonaligned countries.[65] Finally, to leave no doubt as to the continuity of Romanian foreign policy, Ceaușescu received China's Hua Guofeng and North Korea's Kim Il-Song in Bucharest for brief stopovers on their journeys home from Belgrade.

Less than a week later, Soviet and East European leaders assembled in Warsaw for the Warsaw Pact's twenty-fifth anniversary summit meeting. In terms of recent Warsaw Pact initiatives and their reception in the West, there was seemingly little to celebrate. Under the continued outrage of the prolonged and increasingly bloody Soviet occupation of Afghanistan, the United States had suspended consideration of the SALT II Treaty, NATO had stood fast on the Euromissiles decision, and many of the threatened Western sanctions had become realities. Moreover, the subsequent banishment to Gorky of Dr. Andrei Sakharov, the last figure of world reknown in the Soviet human rights movement, had served to strengthen Western resolve.

On the other hand, misgivings among West European governments, already chafing under what was widely perceived to be a vacillating, inconsistent American foreign policy, had been aggravated by strong U.S. pressure on its allies to join in sanctions against the Soviet Union over Afghanistan and against Iran over the detention of American hostages in the U.S. Embassy in Teheran. As in Eastern Europe, the conviction had grown on the western half of the continent that Europeans were being dragged into superpower disputes in remote lands, that European détente was being threatened by conflicts not of their making. Unlike the East Europeans, of course, the NATO allies were in a position to act on their convictions, and discussion was rife in West European government circles about the "divisibility" of détente and the role Europeans might play in bringing East and West together again.[66] It was to exploit these sentiments, as well as a subterranean neutralist drift in Western Europe, that the Warsaw Pact in early 1980 offered vague inducements on arms talks and made veiled threats regarding the ultimate fate of countries which chose to accept U.S. Euromissiles.[67] Thus, on the eve of the Warsaw summit meeting of the Political Consultative Committee in mid-May, the Afghan invasion and its aftermath had yielded mixed results: sanctions had been imposed against the Soviet Union, but unevenly applied; the Olympic games would be boycotted, but only partially; NATO had approved the Euromissiles plan, but some of its members were wavering; and U.S.–Soviet relations were in a downward spiral, but European détente was salvageable.

Against this background it should not be surprising that the Warsaw Pact issued another long list of proposals, largely devoid of substantive meaning and clearly designed to exploit fissures in the Atlantic alliance.[68] More interesting, perhaps, were thinly concealed conflicts within the Warsaw Pact itself, for the PCC's resolutions betrayed mounting East European anxieties over Afghanistan and its impact on East-West relations. Far from echoing Soviet charges of imperialist aggression in Afghanistan, the PCC called much less stridently for an overall "political settlement" and declared that "Soviet armed forces will begin to be pulled out" as soon as "outside interference" by unnamed other countries ceases.[69] Subterranean disputes between the Soviet Union and its junior allies were further suggested by the fact that the one other proposal extending beyond Europe—a vague and unexplained call for a "top-level meeting of state leaders from all the regions of the world"—was issued in a "statement" separate from the major PCC declaration, perhaps in order to distance the Romanians and others from what they perceived as a transparent publicity ploy.

As usual, the majority of proposals dealt with European security and cooperation, specifically with regard to the Warsaw Pact's peace offensive on military détente and preparations for the next Helsinki review conference, due to open in Madrid in the fall. In addition to endorsing once again the familiar roster of Warsaw Pact initiatives on military détente and disarmament, the PCC devoted considerable attention to the more immediate matter of the Euromissiles. Without mentioning the still-growing Soviet SS-20 arsenal, the PCC declaration affirmed the Warsaw Pact's readiness to enter into negotiations on medium-range missiles but warned that such negotiations could not begin until "NATO withdraws its decision to produce and deploy in Western Europe new kinds of U.S. nuclear missile weapons, or at least holds back its implementation." Intended to sway the European socialist parties and public opinion more generally, this latter formulation was aimed particularly at the Belgians and Dutch, as well as some within Chancellor Schmidt's growingly restive Social Democratic Party, who already were seeking a deferral of the Euromissiles decision, and had the added advantage of allowing the Soviet Union simply to wait and see what developed in NATO. On Madrid, the PCC seconded Polish Party leader Gierek's offer to host a Helsinki-like disarmament conference and made it clear that acceptance of this proposal should be a central concern of the Madrid conference. As to other aspects of the Helsinki review process, the PCC expressed its hope that the Madrid meeting would be held in a "constructive atmosphere," the Warsaw Pact shibboleth for rejecting scrutiny of the human rights provisions of the Helsinki Agreement.

As East and West prepared for Madrid in the summer of 1980, Warsaw Pact diplomacy went into high gear toward achieving a breakthrough—or better, the appearance of a breakthrough—on several military détente initiatives. The last phase of the promised withdrawal of up to 20,000 Soviet troops and 1,000 tanks from East Germany was carried out with great fanfare (and given extensive television coverage in Western Europe).[70] At the same time the Soviet Union proposed a further withdrawal of 20,000 Soviet troops from Eastern Europe in return for a concomitant withdrawal of 13,000 American troops from Western Europe. This latter proposal left East and West still far apart at the MBFR talks, of course, but it had the advantage of breathing some new life into the long-stalled, nearly forgotten mutual force reductions talks in Vienna. On the Euromissiles issue, Brezhnev offered a series of minor concessions to West German Chancellor Schmidt during their Moscow summit meeting in mid-summer (June 30–July 1), and shortly thereafter the United States and the Soviet Union began exploratory discussions on limiting medium-range missiles in Europe.[71]

These few flurries of activity could not disguise the fact that East and West approached Madrid with few of the high hopes and grand expectations that preceded the Helsinki conference five years earlier. U.S.–Soviet relations were at their lowest ebb in years, and East and West were as far apart as ever in their understanding of what Helsinki was all about. The notion that the Helsinki process should facilitate greater cooperation and understanding among the peoples of Europe, and thus promote security and stability on the Continent, had long since foundered on Soviet and East European insistence that human and cultural contacts be carefully regulated on a state-to-state basis. More recently, the Soviet invasion of Afghanistan and campaigns against human rights activists, particularly in the Soviet Union and Czechoslovakia, constituted such obvious affronts to the spirit of Helsinki that many viewed with pessimism the prospects for European security and cooperation.

Yet in the eyes of many, particularly among the peoples of Eastern Europe, the European continent had been altered significantly, and generally for the better, on account of Helsinki. The general recognition of European borders, as well as military "confidence-building" measures, had promoted greater stability, particularly in central Europe; and the notion of Helsinki as a process had contributed to a growing conviction that a whole range of European problems—everything from medium-range missiles to environmental pollution—were the common concern of the entire continent and appropriate topics for consultation and joint action. That the failures of European détente were manifest and manifold should not obscure its lasting, if limited, significance in reducing some of the psychological barriers between the two halves of the continent. Even in the area of human and cultural contacts, some progress had been made in facilitating reunification of families, promoting tourism and cultural exchanges, and easing restrictions on foreign journalists.

For the Soviet and East European regimes, these trends had brought with them consequences not fully appreciated at the time of Helsinki: a freer flow of information and ideas had emerged despite anxious countermeasures in Eastern Europe, and small but influential human rights movements had sprung up everywhere. The most dramatic, if hardly representative, manifestation of these tendencies occurred in Poland, where the Gierek regime's eager pursuit of cordial relations with the West, and the trade and credits they helped secure, exerted a restraining influence on its approach toward domestic dissent. In this relatively benign social climate, the seeds were planted of a genuine Democratic Opposition, which soon took root not only among intellectuals but among peasants and workers as well and which began to acquire political purpose and organization, as in the formation in 1978 of Free Trade Union units in major mining and industrial shipping areas.

On August 1, 1980, five years to the day after the signing of the Helsinki Agreement, preparations were underway at the Gdansk shipyards on Poland's Baltic coast for a strike which would begin the next day, spread and intensify at mid-month, and conclude with the formation of an independent, self-governing trade union at month's end, ushering in the most profound series of developments in the history of Communist rule in Eastern Europe. In some limited sense at least, this, too, may be counted among the fruits of détente.

Imminent developments in Poland, of course, were more directly related to Poland's acute domestic crisis, itself the consequence of rapidly mounting social and economic dilemmas unique to Poland in their severity but present to one degree or another throughout the region. If the external sources of some of these dilemmas were suggested by Soviet and East European summit diplomacy, their more immediate domestic dimensions were revealed, albeit cryptically, in the Soviet and East European Communist party congresses held during the 1970s.

Domestic Affairs: The Party Congresses

Soviet and East European Communist party congresses tend to be dull and unenlightening affairs, notable perhaps for their pomp and pageantry but seldom for their substance. The unexpected occasionally occurs, as at the dramatic, free-wheeling 9th Extraordinary Congress of the Polish Party in July 1981 or the Czechoslovak Party's 14th Extraordinary Congress in August 1968; but these are the exceptions to the generally well-rehearsed, carefully scripted rituals the parties seek to arrange. The Party congresses are significant, nonetheless, in that they represent the confluence of various dimensions of East European political concerns—domestic, intrabloc, inter-Party, and external—as expressed in the most authoritative Party resolutions. For analytical and comparative purposes, moreover, they provide convenient benchmarks for assessing policy changes or longer-term trends in Soviet and East European approaches to the challenges of the times.

Attention naturally centers on congresses of the Communist Party of the Soviet Union (CPSU), owing not only to the Soviet Union's intrinsic importance but also to its key role in setting the tone for the "fraternal" parties in foreign, intrabloc, and to a lesser extent domestic policies. As is illustrated in Table 4.2, two CPSU Congresses were held during the period under consideration: the 24th, held in March 1971, and the 25th, convened five years later in February 1976. Each of these was followed immediately by congresses of the three most loyal East European parties—the Bulgarian, Czechoslovak, and East German.

Coexistence and Consumerism: 1971–1975

The 1971 Round: CPSU, BCP, CPČS, SED, PUWP　　Attended by delegations from no fewer than seventy-nine Communist parties, the 24th Congress of the CPSU, held in late March and early April 1971, was the largest inter-Party conclave in more than a decade.[72] The chief resolution of the congress, as expressed in Secretary Brezhnev's report, was the CPSU "peace program," a

Table 4.2
Communist Party Congresses, 1968–1980

Party	1968	1969	1970	1971	1972	1973	1974	1975	1976	1977	1978	1979	1980
					Congress number (month convened)								
CPSU				24th (March)					25th (Feb.)				
BCP				10th (April)					11th (March)				
CPČS	14th[a] (Aug.)			14th[a] (May)					15th (April)				
HSWP			10th (Nov.)					11th (March)					12th (March)
PUWP	5th (Nov.)			6th (Dec.)				7th (Dec.)					8th (Feb.)
RCP		10th (Aug.)					11th (Nov.)				12th (Nov.)		
SED				8th (June)				9th (May)					

NOTE:　CPSU　= Communist Party of the Soviet Union
　　　　BCP　　= Bulgarian Communist Party
　　　　CPČS　= Communist Party of Czechoslovakia
　　　　HSWP　= Hungarian Socialist Workers' Party
　　　　PUWP　= Polish United Workers' Party
　　　　RCP　　= Romanian Communist Party
　　　　SED　　= *Sozialistische Einheitspartei Deutschlands,* Socialist Unity Party of (East) Germany

[a] The 14th "Extraordinary" Congress of the CPČS, which convened in the early hours of the 1968 occupation, was later declared illegal, and the next CPČS Congress became the legal "14th."

policy said to combine "firm rebuffs" to imperialist aggression with a series of constructive measures designed to promote pan-European cooperation and "peaceful coexistence" with all states, "regardless of their social system." Closely related to the détente initiatives of the socialist countries, Brezhnev argued, was the consolidation of their "unity and cohesion" through the improvement of their collective defense and foreign policy coordination in the Warsaw Treaty Organization and the deepening of socialist economic integration in CMEA. Although it was not fully apparent at the time, these two themes—the peace program in East-West relations and a concomitant drive toward strengthened cohesion in intrabloc affairs—were to be the key elements of Soviet and East European foreign policy throughout the 1970s.

The other new departure of the CPSU Congress, increased attention to material living standards, was a response, in part, to the workers' riots which had erupted along Poland's Baltic coast in December 1970 to protest price increases for certain categories of basic foodstuffs. Coming so close on the heels of the crisis and subsequent intervention in Czechoslovakia, as well as the upheaval in Poland itself the same year, the events in Poland in December 1970 must have sent prickles of fear up the spines of the Soviet and East European leaders. If the Prague Spring had persuaded the more orthodox among them that economic reformism was fraught with unacceptable political risks, the more recent developments in Poland had demonstrated the dangers inherent in prolonged suppression of material living standards.

In the face of these opposing dangers—the Scylla of sweeping reform and the Charybdis of economic stagnation—the CPSU Congress made a clear demarcation between economic reform, of which there was no hint, and economic policy, in which priorities were to be shifted marginally in the direction of the consumer. Encouraged by favorable economic forecasts and the prospects of expanded trade with the West, both Brezhnev and Premier Aleksei Kosygin unveiled what amounted to a new economic strategy for the 1970s, which involved importing Western technology to modernize and invigorate an essentially unreformed system of economic planning and management. One byproduct of this strategy, it was hoped, would be expanded production of consumer goods: for the first time in Soviet history, the coming (1971–1975) Five-Year Plan forecast a higher rate of growth for consumer goods than for producers' goods. As if to underscore the Party's aversion to fundamental reform, however, the emphasis on other aspects of domestic policy was all on the need for heightened ideological vigilance and expanded Party control, particularly in the planned management of the Soviet economy.[73]

In Stalin's day, of course, resolutions of the Soviet Party in foreign and domestic policy were held to be "binding upon all countries."[74] Although the work of the 24th CPSU Congress was held out only as an "inspiring example" for other parties,[75] the CPSU platform continued to be viewed, by the Soviet leaders at least, as a model to be emulated by the "fraternal parties." It was in this spirit that Edward Gierek, who had recently supplanted Gomulka as first secretary of the Polish Communist Party (PUWP), promised that the Polish leaders would "closely study the documents of the 24th CPSU Congress" in preparation for the forthcoming 6th PUWP Congress.[76]

It was presumably for this same reason—to allow the Bulgarian leaders time to "closely study" the work of the CPSU Congress—that the Bulgarian Party Congress, whose convening date already had been adjusted to follow directly that of the CPSU, was postponed for ten days. When the 10th BCP Congress finally opened on April 20, Party leader Todor Zhivkov's report predictably stressed complete harmony with the policies of the USSR, "the Red giant standing tall on one-sixth of the earth, strong, peace-loving, [and] fraternally generous."[77] Virtually echoing the main resolutions of the CPSU Congress, Zhivkov emphasized the need for "further elevation of the Party's leading role" and fully embraced the CPSU "peace program" and efforts toward "strengthening the unity and solidarity" of the socialist community. Similarly, the new Party Program approved by the Congress specified that the BCP's "prime responsibility and daily task" is the deepening of "fraternal ties" with the CPSU and friendship with the peoples of the Soviet Union.[78] As at the CPSU Congress, the role of the consumer was given special attention: the Bulgarian party's "basic concern," Zhivkov pledged, was "care for the man" through "fuller satisfaction of the growing material and spiritual needs of the people." Leaving the realm of the spirit aside for a moment, Zhivkov announced in his report on the Sixth Five-Year Plan (1971–1975) an increase in the minimum wage and forecast a 50 percent increase in consumer goods production, promising that special efforts would be made to eliminate shortages in "certain basic merchandise groups."

As the Bulgarians had done before them, the Czechoslovak leaders altered the interval between Party congresses from four to five years so that the congresses of the Communist Party of Czechoslovakia (CPČS) would coincide with those of the CPSU. Inasmuch as the "Extraordinary" 14th Congress of late August 1968 had been declared illegal, the proceedings of the "legal" 14th CPČS Congress were viewed with considerable interest by Czechoslovakia's allies. As expected, General Secretary Gustáv Husák offered a complete capitulation to the 1968 invasion, expressing his "comradely gratitude to all the fraternal parties" for the "rescue" and subsequent "strengthening" of socialism in the ČSSR.[79] To complete the capitulation, the Congress formally approved the Central Committee's notorious "Lessons from the Crisis Development of the Party and Society since the [1966] 13th Party Congress," in which the Prague Spring was branded an antisocialist conspiracy overcome, according to the report, only by the "truly Marxist-Leninist stand" of the Party after the invasion. Finally, sweeping changes in the Central Committee (more than half of its members were replaced) served to strengthen the position of the Husák leadership; with the exception of President Ludvik Svoboda, retained as a symbol of continuity, the remaining leaders of the Prague Spring were swept away, but so too were several hard-line critics of the existing leadership.[80]

On foreign policy matters, Husák's report was as faithful to the CPSU line as Zhivkov's had been, and the Czechoslovak leader noted "with pleasure and satisfaction" that "Czechoslovak-Soviet relations have not only been fully restored but have reached . . . a qualitatively higher level." Domestically, the chief topic of concern was the further consolidation of the Czechoslovak economy, whose performance had confounded predictions of a severe post-1968 deterioration to achieve (with considerable Soviet aid) steady growth over the preceding two years, particularly in the consumer sector. Presumably to demonstrate once again the efficacy of the Party's "normalization" course—and, not incidentally, to encourage a general social drift toward apolitical resignation— retail prices for a whole range of consumer products were reduced to coincide with the Party Congress. Otherwise, the emphasis at the Congress centered on expanded Party control,[81] the second half of the Husák regime's domestic efforts to secure social support, or at least passive acquiescence, in the wake of the trauma of 1968.

Attention in Eastern Europe was next drawn to the 8th Congress of the Socialist Unity Party of Germany (SED), for just weeks before this congress was to open, the SED announced the resignation of Walter Ulbricht as Party leader and his replacement by Erich Honecker, long groomed as heir apparent. Although Ulbricht retained the post of chairman of the State Council and thus remained the nominal head of state, it is clear that the old leader had been quietly shoved aside, *inter alia,* for his intransigence on the "German question."[82] For these reasons, Honecker's conciliatory remarks on European security, particularly the advocacy of "normal relations" with West Germany, must have been viewed with some satisfaction in the Kremlin. Echoing the orthodox lines taken at the Bulgarian and Czechoslovak Party congresses, Honecker's report to the SED Congress noted a "perfect unanimity" between the SED and CPSU on "all questions" involving their mutual relations and added a revealing reference to the importance of the Warsaw Pact for "*domestic* and foreign policy."[83]

Domestically, attention at the SED Congress naturally centered on economic policy, for at the December 1970 Central Committee plenum the New Economic System (NES)[84] had been abandoned in favor of a recentralization of economic planning. Although the worsening of the economic situation in the late 1960s already had generated second thoughts about the GDR's economic reform course, to say nothing of Ulbricht's continued tenure, it is clear that the labor unrest in Poland at about the same time contributed to growing concerns in the SED leadership over the political dangers of further experimentation in the economic sphere and the urgent need to insure adequate supplies of consumer

goods. Consequently, the economic strategy outlined at the 8th Congress forecast a cutback in investments, deceleration of scientific-technical progress,
curtailment of ambitious reformism, and immediate and continuous increases in
material living standards. As at the Bulgarian and Czechoslovak Party congresses, the SED further resolved to strengthen Party control in all areas of public life
and supervise a campaign toward ideological regeneration and orthodoxy in
educational and cultural policy.[85]

Six months later the 6th Polish United Workers' Party (PUWP) Congress
convened in Warsaw, where Wladyslaw Gomulka had been ousted as Party
leader following the December 1970 workers' revolt in Gdansk and other coastal
cities. Almost immediately, Gomulka's successor, Edward Gierek, had sought
to restore social peace by rescinding the price increases that had provoked the
strikes and demonstrations and by paying highly effective personal visits to
Gdansk and Szczecin, where he reassured workers that the Party leadership was
attuned to their needs. Within the higher echelons of the Party, Gierek had
helped secure the removal of most of the holdovers from the Gomulka era,
gradually replacing them with trusted supporters, many of them from Gierek's
former fiefdom in Poland's Silesian coal-mining region.

Needless to say, events of the preceding year dominated the 6th PUWP
Congress.[86] Having drawn "the essential lessons and conclusions from the
December events," Gierek acknowledged the Party's errors of the recent and
more distant past (including the 1956-1959 period) and pledged new efforts on
behalf of workers, above all "a tangible improvement of [their] material and
cultural conditions."[87] This pledge was made more explicit in the Party guidelines presented to the Congress, which defined the basic aim of the Party's
socioeconomic policy as "a constant increase in consumption and a continuous
improvement in the living, social and cultural conditions of the population."[88]
These objectives, as well as the more precise targets outlined later in the
Congress in the areas of housing construction, wages and consumption, and
social services, ostensibly were to be achieved through a new, consumer-
oriented economic strategy, improved modernization and rationalization of
economic planning, and greatly increased foreign trade and importation of
technology.

Gierek was less interesting on foreign policy. Owing perhaps to the tenuity of
his own position, Gierek aligned himself fully with the CPSU, averring that
cooperation with the Soviet Union is the "supreme principle of our national
policy." Having profited from what he termed the "extremely rich creative
achievements" of the 24th CPSU Congress, Gierek went on to underscore his
party's commitment to "the strengthening of the unity of the socialist community" through socialist economic integration, expanded ideological ties, and the
further development of military-political cooperation in the Warsaw Pact. On
foreign policy issues beyond the Warsaw Pact, Gierek leveled the requisite

broadside at the "divisive course" of the Chinese Communists and lent his full support to the CPSU "peace program."

In sum, the 1971 round of Party congresses yielded near unanimity on the major international, intrabloc, and domestic issues of the day. The two parties out of step, chronologically and otherwise, with this display of proletarian solidarity were the Romanian and Hungarian.

The 10th and 11th RCP and HSWP Congresses   It has become something of a commonplace that the Hungarians have been able to pursue innovative domestic policies without Soviet interference partly because of their solicitous conformity to Soviet foreign policy positions and, conversely, that Romania's domestic orthodoxy made it more difficult for the Soviet leaders to contain the independent foreign policy initiatives of the Ceauşescu leadership. Although developments of the early 1970s did little to refute the general validity of these intuitive judgments, the differences between the 10th and 11th Hungarian Socialist Workers' Party (HSWP) congresses, and between the 10th and 11th Romanian Communist Party (RCP) congresses, reveal the extent to which these general orientations had been buffeted by a much altered international situation.

In 1969, Romanian Party leader Nicolae Ceauşescu was at the height of his domestic prestige and popularity. His courageous defense of Romanian sovereignty in the wake of the invasion of Czechoslovakia, his active pursuit of East-West détente, and his repeated assertion of independence within the socialist community had struck a responsive chord at home and won him considerable support beyond the confines of the Warsaw Pact. Accordingly, his report to the 10th RCP Congress was bold and assertive, even strident. Giving "special appreciation" to relations with China but noting that cooperation with the Soviet Union was only "one of the cornerstones" of Romanian policy, Ceauşescu alluded—in a strongly anti-Soviet context—to the "subjective causes" of conflicts among the socialist countries. Reiterating his earlier call for "the abolition of military blocs," Ceauşescu concluded:

> By the world socialist system, we understand not a bloc in which the states are fused into a whole, giving up their national sovereignty, but the assertion of socialism as an international force . . . in several independent states, which develop independently and organize the relations between themselves on the new principles of Marxism-Leninism and proletarian internationalism.[89]

By 1974, however, Ceauşescu's position had been circumscribed on several fronts: his initiatives toward East-West détente had been largely preempted by a Soviet-led drive toward a pan-European security conference; his intrabloc obstinacy had come under strong Soviet pressure as a result, *inter alia,* of his boycott of the summer Crimea conference; and domestically, his efforts to institutionalize his personal rule had generated growing dissatisfaction within the Romanian Party. All these developments were reflected in the much less confident tone of Ceauşescu's report to the 11th Party Congress in November. Although quick to note Romania's contributions to the progress of East-West détente, Ceauşescu was manifestly at a loss as to how to regain the initiative in East-West relations. He expressed his "great joy" in the "ascending relations" with China, but he now gave equal recognition to improved relations with the Soviet Union, Romania's "major partner in international exchanges and economic cooperation." As to intrabloc relations, Ceauşescu repeated the familiar call for the dissolution of military blocs, but this time with a significant addendum: "The political aspect of the Warsaw Pact must be strengthened even more."[90]

The Romanians had previously lobbied for an improved framework for political consultation in WTO, but never before had this aim been elevated to the status of a prime goal of Romanian policy. This subtle change reflected a partial reorientation of Romanian policy in the early 1970s: as relations with the West began to diminish as a source of leverage in Romanian-Soviet relations, the Romanians were forced increasingly to work from within the Soviet-East European alliance system—through bilateral relations, especially with the Soviet Union, and multilateral cooperation in the Warsaw Pact and CMEA—to preserve the basic contours of its independent-minded policy line.[91]

Meanwhile, similar retrenchment was evident in the Hungarian Party's pursuit of innovative domestic policies. The mood of the 10th HSWP Congress in November 1970 reflected the substantial success achieved under Hungary's innovative New Economic Mechanism (NEM), introduced in January 1968. Noting with satisfaction the overfulfillment of the 1966–1970 economic plan and the overall improvement in living standards over the same period, Party First Secretary János Kádár stressed the continuing importance of economic decentralization and improved "commodity-money" (i.e., market) relations. Far from echoing the CPSU call for expanded Party control, Kádár's report took the opposite view, warning against "dogmatists" who, "in the name of defense of the dictatorship of the proletariat, regard the development of socialist democracy with anxiety."[92]

By the time of the 11th HSWP Congress in March 1975, the buoyant optimism surrounding the NEM had disappeared. Economic difficulties of the preceding few years, particularly those resulting from the precipitous increase in Soviet oil prices,[93] had led to a period of retrenchment and partial recentralization in the economic sphere, trends signaled in March 1974 by the removal of Rezső Nyers, architect of the NEM, from his position as Central Committee secretary for economic affairs. As to the Congress itself, the self-critical remarks of Premier Jenő Fock, who had been closely linked with the creation and implementation of the NEM, presaged not only his resignation two months later but continued economic retrenchment in Hungary. This same theme was expanded on by Károly Németh, Nyers's successor in the Central Committee, who argued that "control over plan implementation and observance of economic discipline must be made more effective on every level."[94] For his part, Kádár stressed continuity with past policies, particularly the so-called "social contract," but noted, somewhat paradoxically, that "substantial decentralization of decision-making authority necessitates even more intensive central direction and control."[95]

In his foreign policy report to the Congress, Kádár dutifully followed the Soviet line on every issue, noting "with satisfaction" that there were "no clouds in the skies of Hungaro-Soviet friendship."[96] Foreign Minister Frigyes Puja's report struck a decidedly more independent note, particularly with regard to bilateral economic relations with the West and Hungary's pursuit of most-favored-nation treatment from the United States and the Common Market countries.[97] Given the perceived inability of the NEM to deliver the promised improvement in material living standards, it is not surprising that the Hungarian leaders began to look to the West for partial solutions to their economic difficulties. The foreign minister's remarks are significant, nevertheless, in that they reveal an evolutionary pattern of foreign policy behavior in Hungary, a pattern in which obsequious verbal allegiance to the Soviet line has been paralleled by a muted but increasingly active foreign policy, particularly in the realm of foreign economic relations.[98]

The 7th PUWP Congress   Economic issues and the question of trade with the West also dominated the 7th Polish Party Congress, held nine months later, in December 1975. The congress opened in an atmosphere of apprehension and foreboding, for although Poland had just completed the most prosperous period in its postwar history, signs of an economic reversal were already on the horizon. The precipitous rise in world energy prices had begun to make inroads into Polish economic stability, as had the Gierek regime's imprudent strategy of using massive Western credits to subsidize the growingly inefficient agricultural sector or to finance showcase industrial projects, as in the case of the Ursus tractor factory near Warsaw. These difficulties, in turn, had begun to take a heavy toll on the credibility and authority of Gierek's leadership, notwithstanding Brezhnev's claim (on the second day of the Congress) that the Polish Party remained "cohesive and confident in its strength."[99]

In his opening speech to the Congress, Party leader Edward Gierek aligned himself fully with the CPSU "peace policy," spoke warmly of the results of the Helsinki conference and the ever-improving ties with countries of the socialist community, and launched the customary attack on the "splitting, chauvinistic policy of the Chinese Maoist leadership." The greater part of his address, and that of Prime Minister Jaroszewicz and other speakers, however, was devoted to the state of the Polish economy. Both Gierek and Jaroszewicz (in his report on the 1976–1980 Five-Year Plan) alluded to the favorable results of the regime's foreign trade and investment policies and pledged to continue with the Polish economic strategy. Of the perenially problematic agricultural sector, both lent their support to the collectivized farms and "agricultural circles" (both of which had become thoroughly discredited in the eyes of most Polish farmers and consumers), hardly mentioning the private farms, which account for more than 80 percent of Poland's agricultural output. Problems of increased prices for fuels, energy sources, and raw materials, blamed on "the inflationary rise of prices on capitalist markets," were noted without elaboration.

Indeed, the only remedy proferred for Poland's economic ills was accelerated modernization and technological development of Polish industry, this to be achieved through what Jaroszewicz coyly termed an "active credit policy." The prime minister acknowledged, however, that "certain amounts" of Western credit assistance had been spent for grain imports to supplement domestic production and referred to the sensitive issue of food prices, which lay at the nexus of the government's agricultural, foreign trade, and development policies. On this issue, Jaroszewicz warned obliquely of the need to "review the structure of consumption" of basic foodstuffs, by which he presumably meant to raise prices so as to stimulate production and reduce consumption.[100]

Gierek broached the subject equally gingerly, pledging "a real further increase of the population's financial incomes" but disclosing that a decision in principle had been taken on the "necessity of certain price rises." The full import of these desultory references, and the full revelation of tenuity of the Polish regime's authority, would come the following June, when the official announcement of drastic price increases for certain categories of foodstuffs sparked protests and work stoppages throughout the country. Within twenty-four hours, the Gierek leadership would be obliged to beat a hasty and humiliating retreat on the issue, suffering a setback from which the regime never fully recovered.

Stability and Stagnation: 1976–1980

The 1976 Round: CPSU, BCP, CPČS, SED   In the meantime, another round of the CPSU and the loyalist Party congresses—the BCP, CPČS, and SED—took place. In contrast to the 1971 round, which broke new ground in at least two areas—the peace policy and officially sanctioned consumerism—the 1976 series was generally devoid of new policies or fresh initiatives. With the Helsinki conference over and intrabloc relations relatively quiescent, the chief task of the Party congresses was to chronicle recent successes and project an aura of stability and continuity. The one disquieting note at all the congresses was the deteriorating economic outlook, which bore adversely on the commitment of the early 1970s to further increases in material living standards throughout the region.

As expected, the 25th CPSU Congress, held between February 24 and March 3, 1976, proclaimed the full vindication of the peace policy put forth at the 24th Congress. "Before our very eyes," General Secretary Brezhnev observed in his opening speech, "the world is changing for the better." West Germany's treaties with the Soviet Union, the GDR, Poland, and Czechoslovakia; the Quadripartite Agreement on Berlin; SALT; general recognition of the inviolability of European frontiers; the Helsinki conference—all these were cited as evidence of the "lasting significance" of the line adopted at the preceding congress. Special attention was given the achievements of Soviet integrationist policies in Eastern Europe and the growing "unity and cohesion" of the socialist community: "the drawing together [sblizhenie] of the socialist countries," Brezhnev averred, "is now operating quite definitely as an objective process." On other international topics, the familiar litany of attacks on the West (still in the throes of "the crisis of capitalism") and China were offered, as were renewed statements of support for revolutionary struggles in the Third World, notably in Angola and Southeast Asia.[101]

The single international issue of real interest at the Congress was the inter-Party clash over preparations for the long-delayed conference of European Communist parties. Representatives of the powerful Italian and French parties were quick to stake out independent positions, particularly with regard to the Soviet interpretation of "dictatorship of the proletariat" and "proletarian internationalism," terms which had been struck from the Eurocommunist lexicon. For his part, Brezhnev acknowledged that there could be differences of views among parties on certain issues, but warned there could be "no question of compromise on matters of principle and reconciliation with views and actions contrary to Communist ideology."[102]

On domestic affairs, economic performance and discussion of the Tenth Five-Year Plan (1976–1980) were the chief topics of interest.[103] In their reports to the Congress, Brezhnev, Premier Aleksei Kosygin, and others sought to put the best possible light on a rather gloomy economic picture, which forecast a marked slowdown of economic growth in most key areas. Particularly hard-hit was the consumer sector: whereas the Ninth Five-Year Plan had promised (but not delivered) a higher rate of growth for Group B (consumer) goods than for Group A (producers') goods, the Tenth decisively shifted economic priorities back toward the producers and away from the long-suffering Soviet consumer. The only implicit acknowledgement of economic failures came with the removal from the Politburo, and later from his post of minister of agriculture as well, of Dimitrii Polyansky, clearly a scapegoat for the disastrous performance of Soviet agriculture.[104] Otherwise, the most interesting aspect of personnel changes was the inclusion in the new Central Committee of a large number of representatives of the mass media—this presumably to strengthen ideological vigilance in anticipation of Western insistence on implementation of Helsinki's "Basket Three" provisions on human and cultural contacts.

The foreign policy aspects of the other three Party congresses held in 1976—the Bulgarian, Czechoslovak, and East German (SED)—can be dealt with briefly. These parties are solid Moscow loyalists, and in none of their Party congresses is there to be found the slightest deviation from the CPSU foreign policy line. Indeed, in preparations for their congresses, Party leaders Todor Zhivkov, Gustáv Husák, and Erich Honecker went to great lengths to affirm their absolute allegiance to the CPSU, though none so far has matched Zhivkov's 1973 assertion that "Bulgaria and the Soviet Union will act as a single body, breathing with the same lungs and nourished by the same blood stream."[105]

Physiological internationalism aside, there were some points of departure in the three East European Party congresses, most notably concerning the consumer orientation of the domestic economies. In Bulgaria, Zhivkov's opening address to the 11th BCP Congress was unusually balanced in its treatment of the country's economic situation, noting both successes in the past five-year period and chronic shortfalls, particularly those arising from lack of efficiency and modernization of production processes. In contrast to the CPSU Congress, the BCP Congress laid particular emphasis on the consumer: in both Zhivkov's speech, under the rubric "the socialist way of life," and in the Party theses published the preceding January, the centerpiece of the BCP economic strategy was raising the material standard of living of the population. Indeed, so frequently was this pledge restated that Zhivkov felt obliged to explain that this concern "is not a consumerist approach, and it is not intended to result in the *embourgeoisement* of the population."[106]

As in the CPSU Congress, great stress was placed in the BCP Congress and Party theses on the ideological struggle, whose significance was said to increase in proportion to the development of peaceful coexistence between countries with different social systems. The link between ideological vigilance and détente had been made more explicit at the February 1974 Central Committee plenum, which warned: "There is a real possibility that foreign influences will infiltrate . . . and that psychological barriers that are hard to overcome will be erected."[107] Otherwise, as at the CPSU Congress, the Bulgarian Party sought to project an image of stability and continuity, proposing few policy innovations or personnel changes.[108]

Continuity was also the order of the day at the Czechoslovak Party Congress held two weeks later in Prague. Unlike the May 1971 congress, convened with the Party still convulsed by the legacy of the Prague Spring, the 15th CPČS Congress projected an image of harmony and stability, reflected in Husák's relatively conciliatory reference to those purged in the post-1968 "normalization" and his suggestion that some might be readmitted to the Party. Issued as "the opinion of the Central Committee," Husák's statement nonetheless betrayed lingering conflicts just beneath the surface between the unrepentant hard-line *tendence* in the Party leadership (whose most vocal exponent was Vasil Bilak) and the rather more moderate inclinations of Husák himself.[109] Outwardly, however, the only other manifestation of divisions of the present and the not-so-distant past came in the single change to the ruling Presidium: the quiet but poignant removal of Ludvik Svoboda, who had been retained as a symbol of continuity in the post-Dubček ruling elite despite his long illness.[110]

On foreign relations, the only points of interest came in the speeches of the foreign delegates, several of whom lent their support to the speedy convocation of the pan-European Communist conference and stressed their fidelity to "proletarian internationalism," a key bone of contention in the preconference debate. Otherwise, economic issues predominated. Both Husák and federal Premier Lubomir Strougal (in his report on the 1976–1980 Five Year Plan) acclaimed the indisputable economic successes of the preceding five years but warned of the "complex situation" facing the domestic economy, referring especially to the adverse terms of trade forecast and mounting difficulties in obtaining adequate deliveries of fuels, energy sources, and raw materials.[111] To counter these difficulties, they outlined new measures to increase labor productivity and efficiency and announced a forthcoming reform of wholesale prices. Both Husák and Strougal were quick to pledge, however, that prices for "basic necessities" would be held stable and to reaffirm their commitment to raising the material standard of living, keystone of the regime's tenuous "social contract" with a disillusioned population.

Similar concerns preoccupied the SED Congress the following month: "SED policy will center . . . on the main task of further increasing the people's material and cultural living standard," declared Party leader Erich Honecker in his opening remarks. To achieve this goal, he continued, would require "a high rate of development of socialist production, increased effectiveness, scientific-technical progress and growth of labor productivity." Unstated but clearly implied in Honecker's remarks, as indeed in those of the other East European leaders at their Party congresses, was the continued importance of trade with the West in the effort to modernize and invigorate the lagging domestic economy. On terms of trade problems, the full import of Honecker's oblique reference to the "development of the prices of raw materials . . . on the world market" was made clearer elsewhere in the address, where he noted that one-third of all domestic investments would be directed toward development of the "power and raw materials base."[112]

Considerable attention was given in Honecker's speech and that of his foreign minister, Oskar Fischer, to the "qualitatively new international position" of the GDR in the 1970s. Cited first was the GDR's "firm position in the socialist community," solidified by the recent Soviet-GDR Treaty of Friendship, Cooperation and Mutual Assistance and reaffirmed at the 26th CPSU Congress (which Honecker termed a "signpost guiding us into the Communist future"). In addition to acclaiming the widespread international recognition recently accorded the GDR and its admission (in 1973) into the United Nations, Honecker listed among the fruits of détente "recognition under international law of the existence of two sovereign German states independent of one another." At the same time, however, he was quick to assert that the struggle between capitalism and socialism remains "the central axis of international development" and demands heightened ideological vigilance, a caveat underscored at the close of the Congress by the elevation of Erich Mielke, minister for state security, to full Politburo membership.

These proceedings, including the adoption of a new Party statute strengthening Party control over state organs,[113] gave little portent of the "comeback of the reformers" which would take place just a few months later, when Willi Stoph and Guenther Mittag, both of whom had lost their posts in October 1973 (presumably for their roles in implementing the New Economic System), were returned to their respective positions as chairman of the Council of Ministers (premier) and Central Committee secretary in charge of economic policy.[114] While their return to power did not herald a new dawn for the NES under "actually existing socialism," it did usher in another period of economic reform discussion, this one more cautiously aimed at improving efficiency and labor productivity.

In sum, the 1976 Party congresses were notable for their lack of new initiatives, even with regard to the manifest deterioration of the economic outlook throughout the region, and their solicitous conformity to the CPSU line, except in the area of consumer policies. But elsewhere in Eastern Europe in the latter half of the 1970s, the Romanian and Hungarian parties had reasserted their independent-minded lines, in the economic and foreign policy realms, respectively.

The 12th RCP and HSWP Congresses   If the period between the 10th and 11th congresses of the RCP and HSWP had been one of temporary retrenchment—on the foreign policy front in the Romanian case, in economic policy in the Hungarian—the pendulum had swung back by the time of their 12th congresses, held in 1979 and 1980, respectively. This return of the pendulum is attributable not only to the resiliency and resourcefulness of the two Party leaders, Ceauşescu and Kádár, but also to the inertial force of the courses on which they had embarked in the mid-1960s: national self-assertiveness *cum* personality cult by Ceauşescu, economic reformism and social conciliation by Kádár.

The temporary quiescence in Romanian foreign policy in the period immediately leading up to Helsinki soon gave way to the familiar Ceauşescu activism.

Particularly notable were his renewed diplomatic activity in Western Europe and the Middle East, his continued cultivation of relations with China and Yugoslavia, and, more recently, his ostentatious courting of the Eurocommunists. Relations with the Soviet Union, conversely, were at their lowest ebb in years as a result of several recent developments: Chairman Hua Guofeng's visit to Bucharest in August 1978, the publicly aired Romanian-Soviet dispute over military expenditures and other issues at the November 1978 Warsaw Pact Summit, and the August 1979 "gasoline war" ignited by Romania's demand that East European visitors pay in hard currency for gas from Romanian pumps.

It was against this backdrop that the 12th RCP Congress opened in November 1979.[115] In his remarks on foreign policy, Ceauşescu pledged that Romania would continue to fulfill its Warsaw Pact obligations and backed the Berlin inititatives on disarmament; but he asserted also that Romania would actively pursue closer ties, including military cooperation, with "other socialist countries" (meaning China and Yugoslavia) and dusted off his old call for the liquidation of military blocs and their replacement by a new security system in Europe. Equally significant, perhaps, was the conspicuous presence of a Chinese delegation, the first to attend a foreign Party congress in over fifteen years, and of Spanish Communist party leader Santiago Carrillo, whom Ceauşescu received first among the foreign delegates. The Soviet Party, by contrast, was represented by the octogenarian Arvid Pelshe, and the other Warsaw Pact delegations were of a similarly low level.[116]

Ceauşescu's strong endorsement of measures toward European security and détente was carefully balanced by a ringing call for ideological vigilance delivered later in the speech: "The party will fight strongly," he pledged, "against the nationalist-chauvinistic propaganda of reactionary circles abroad, the distortion of reality in our country, and efforts to disorient the working people."[117] On economic issues, little was said of the very serious energy dilemma facing the country, which had swiftly gone from net exporter to net importer of petroleum as a consequence of the ambitious, energy-depleting program of industrial development undertaken by the Ceauşescu leadership.[118] Several calls were issued at the Congress for increased rationalization, modernization, and technological development of production, but there was no follow-up to the economic reform discussion that had been introduced the previous year.

Also lacking in the RCP Congress were the direct pledges to the consumer that had characterized all the other East European Party congresses. Rather, the Romanian population was offered more of the increasingly unpalatable blend of nationalism and personality cult. As to the former, the bold assertion of Romanian sovereignty which had propelled Ceauşescu to considerable domestic prestige in the late 1960s had become a decade later something of a self-parody, seen by large segments of Romanian society as barren of any perceptible domestic benefit. With the diminution of the national theme as an agent of political authority, Ceauşescu had turned increasingly to the cult of personality, or cult of the family, as well as to the systematic removal of potential rivals to power, to preserve his unchallenged leadership.[119] Speaker after speaker at the Party Congress rose to lavish praise on Ceauşescu, one suggesting that his "re-election as head of our party is [as much a] part of our life as the Carpathian Mountains are a part of Romania's geography."[120] These panegyrics gave rise to the one unscripted part of the proceedings: toward the end of the Congress, 84-year-old Constantin Pirvulescu, one of the RCP's founders sixty years before, took the floor to charge Ceauşescu with putting his own interests above those of the country and to challenge the Congress to address honestly the real problems facing Romania. Pirvulescu was quickly hooted down, of course, but his outburst tapped a discontent which was surely not confined to him alone.[121]

The tone of the RCP Congress could hardly contrast more sharply with the efficient, businesslike character of the 12th Congress of the HSWP and the self-effacing remarks of its leader, János Kádár. Yet there are some not readily apparent similarities in the two styles of rule, for both Ceauşescu and Kádár have staked the legitimacy of their regimes on a nationalistic brand of socialism. Ostentatiously proclaimed in Romania, the national theme has been tapped far more subtly in Hungary, where the Kádár regime, banking on the collective national memory of 1956 and the sense of self-restraint it engendered, has sought with considerable success to weld a firmer relationship between rulers and ruled. This "social contract" rests chiefly on the twin pillars of economic prosperity and social leniency, but it rests also on the largely unstated notion that Hungarian socialism is evolving in a different, and generally better, direction than that of its neighbors.[122] Hungarians are proud of their independent brand of socialism and the relatively liberal social climate it affords, and proud, too, that the Hungarian model is held out even by the Soviet leaders as a showcase of socialist stability and prosperity.[123] It was this sense of shared responsibility for the fate of the nation—"socialism . . . for the entire people," Kádár termed it in his opening address—that allowed the HSWP, alone among the "fraternal" parties, to confront the challenges of the 1970s with a degree of candor and ingenuity.

In his opening remarks on foreign policy, Kádár followed the usual pattern of saying what was expected of him by his allies, but little more, and leaving the impression that the Hungarians, like the Japanese, would really rather have no foreign policy at all save that which would serve their foreign trade interests. Kádár was more interesting his his ad-libbed closing speech to the congress. Here, he alluded to the concern of many Hungarians over the deteriorating international situation in the wake of the Soviet intervention in Afghanistan,[124] and expressed his "deep conviction . . . that a new world war will not erupt." He then went on to express succinctly the Party's view of Hungary's place in the contemporary world: "We want to be, and are, trustworthy friends of our friends. And so far as the other side is concerned, we are also fair-dealing, trustworthy, and honest partners, and that is what we will continue to be."[125]

By far the greater part of the Congress, however, was devoted to economic and social issues. Most significant in this regard was the revival of the New Economic Mechanism, or the "reform of the reform," heralded by a set of new economic regulators designed to adapt the NEM to a more difficult international environment.[126] Kádár spoke frankly about economic problems, particularly those resulting from soaring energy costs, but reaffirmed his commitment to the NEM and strongly supported increased independence for individual enterprises. Prime Minister György Lázár's report was equally frank: "We have now reached a difficult stretch of the road," he warned, which can be traversed only if "we break with all that is obsolete."[127] As if to underscore the Party's commitment to a fresh start for the NEM, Ferenc Havasi, Central Committee secretary for economic policy and an advocate of economic reform, was elevated to the Politburo, and three officials regarded as opponents of Kádár's moderate reformist line—Antal Apró, Béla Biszku, and Dezső Nemes—were dismissed from their Politburo positions.[128] Finally, Kádár was at some pains to warn that economic improvement could not be achieved without short-term hardships; in his many references to the material standard of living and the Party's commitment to its further growth, he explained that all that could be realistically promised was the "stabilization of the standard of living and the maintenance of our achievements in such a way as to create conditions for further increases during the [coming] five-year plan."[129]

All in all, and at the risk of some exaggeration, the 12th HSWP Congress presented a picture of a Party beset by economic difficulties but confident in its role in society, prepared to acknowledge errors and shortcomings, and determined to address the problems of the day and seek innovative solutions. All of this stood in marked contrast to the proceedings of the Polish Party Congress held the previous month.

The 8th PUWP Congress   When the Polish Party Congress convened in February 1980, no one could have predicted the cataclysmic developments which would convulse the Party and country just six months later. It was clear to all observers, however, that Poland was in the grip of an acute crisis of leadership, an ever-widening breach between rulers and ruled. The severity of this crisis had become increasingly evident since June 1976, when officially announced food price increases provoked widespread protests and demonstrations. The Polish regime quickly rescinded the increases, but not without suffering a considerable (and as subsequent events proved, an irreversible) loss of credibility and authority. Aside from a timid "new economic maneuver" announced in December 1976, the Gierek regime proved itself unwilling or unable to exercise effective leadership or reverse the country's downward economic spiral, itself the consequence of the regime's disastrous credit, investment, and agricultural policies of the early 1970s.[130]

Another consequence of the events of June 1976 was the growth of an organized and articulate "Democratic Opposition," whose most influential exponent was the Committee of Social Self-Defense (KSS "KOR").[131] Although KOR's initial *raison d'être* was protection of the rights of political prisoners, its scope of activity soon broadened to include examination and critique of society at large and the regime which purported to govern it. In this latter effort KOR was joined by other dissident groups, by members of the Catholic critical intelligentsia, and even by a group of Party elders, including former Party First Secretary Edward Ochab, who in 1977 sent an open letter to Gierek criticizing his style of rule and calling for a thorough-going reform of public life. Further symptomatic of the ferment within the country was the coalescence of several of these forces in the form of a loosely knit discussion club calling itself "Experience and the Future" (DiP). Composed of dissident, Catholic, and Party intellectuals, the group was formally disbanded after a single meeting but nevertheless issued two exhaustive critiques of Polish society, prepared on the basis of questionnaires sent to its dispersed members.[132]

Perhaps the most important new element in the Polish societal equation was the election in October 1978 of Cracow's former cardinal Karol Wojtyla as Pope John Paul II and his triumphal return to Poland in June 1979.[133] Most obviously, the election of a Polish pope lent new political force and moral authority to the already powerful Polish Catholic Church in the battle for men's minds, souls, and allegiance. More than that, the election of Pope Wojtyla and the massive outpouring of public affection accorded him on his trip to his native land served to galvanize a disillusioned Poland around an alternative, but as yet not fully defined, vision of its national future.

All these concerns seemed, but of course were not, far removed from the deliberations of the 8th PUWP Congress. The tone was set early, when Party leader Edward Gierek proclaimed: "Close to 10 years ago . . . our Party adopted a socioeconomic strategy oriented toward man and his needs. . . . This strategy has brought great achievements to our country. It has proved correct in practice and has received the support of our nation. We shall continue."[134] This air of unreality persisted throughout the congress, as economic difficulties were acknowledged, but the essential correctness of the existing economic strategy was affirmed again and again, and statistics were presented to demonstrate the efficacy of the regime's strategy over the past ten years (the last five having been conveniently merged with the boom years of the early 1970s).

Such criticism as did emerge was confined to the general debate, a session instituted at the 6th Congress in December 1971 ostensibly to encourage broad participation in Party decisionmaking. Most of the criticism from the rank and file was directed at administrative mismanagement, official corruption, faulty execution, and other "subjective" errors, many of them attributed to the government of Prime Minister Piotr Jaroszewicz (but not to Gierek's Party). These attacks presaged the one real surprise at the Congress: the unexpected resignation from the Politburo and premiership of Jaroszewicz, clearly a scapegoat for the failures of the entire ruling team.[135]

In his place came Edward Babiuch, a member of Gierek's "Silesian Mafia" and reputed to be an effective administrator. Babiuch sought immediately to project a new image of competence and decisiveness in Poland's ruling circles, speaking candidly of the economic challenges facing the country and warning of the inevitable austerity measures to come. Mindful of the events of June 1976, Babiuch was determined to prepare the Polish population for impending food price increases, as in his April 3 address to the *Sejm* (Parliament). But Babiuch, like most of the rest of the world, had underestimated the gravity of the crisis gripping the country: when price increases were officially announced on July 2, 1980, protest strikes (or "work stoppages," as they were then called) broke out in several industrial plants, touching off the most remarkable and profound chain of events in the postwar history of Eastern Europe.[136]

Again, these concerns seemed far removed from the 8th PUWP Congress. In light of subsequent developments, it is no small irony that the most interesting aspects of the Congress were on international topics. This was the first inter-Party gathering since the December 1979 Soviet invasion of Afghanistan, and many foreign delegates hailed the "international support" given by the Soviet Union to the Afghan people in their struggle against the "reactionary conspiracy of the imperialists." Predictably, no one rose to condemn the invasion, and Cazacu, representing the Romanian Party, confined himself to a vague statement "renouncing the threat and use of force, and any form of [interference] in the domestic affairs of others."[137] The bulk of the discussion, however, was on the deterioration of East-West relations and the urgent need to strengthen the process of East-West détente. Gierek reaffirmed his commitment to peaceful coexistence and offered his own initiative toward reviving détente by disclosing that Warsaw would be prepared to act as host for a new conference on military détente and disarmament in Europe, an idea broached by the Soviet Union a month earlier and soon to become the centerpiece of Warsaw Pact proposals for East-West relations in the early 1980s.

A Summing Up

Imminent developments in Poland notwithstanding, the 8th PUWP Congress embodied a number of themes and trends characteristic of all the Party congresses in the 1970s. Above all, there was an almost compulsive emphasis on continuity and stability: top Party leaderships in all the countries remained generally intact throughout the period, and, with the partial exception of the Hungarian Party, there were few efforts to define new policies or seek innovative strategies to deal with the challenges of the decade. In external, intrabloc, and to a lesser degree domestic policies, the tone for the entire decade had been set at the 24th CPSU Congress in 1971, and only the Romanians showed any preparedness to deviate markedly from the prescribed Soviet line.

In international affairs, the CPSU "peace policy" defined the framework for Soviet and East European foreign policy throughout the period. In the early 1970s, Warsaw Pact Westpolitik was focused on preparations for the 1975 Conference on Security and Cooperation in Europe; in the latter half of the decade, it was geared toward keeping the Helsinki process alive through an unremitting peace offensive designed to preserve the fruits of détente while at the same time exploiting new fissures in the Atlantic alliance. Only the Romanians, and they only with limited success, endeavored to detach themselves from this overarching approach toward the West. Also common to all the Party congresses save the Romanian was the prominence given the supposed growing unity and cohesion of the socialist community. There is a strong element of ritualism in this, of course, but it should not obscure the very real steps taken throughout the decade to promote "socialist integration" in every sphere of Soviet–East European relations.

On the domestic aspects of the Party congresses, two themes stand out. The first is the considerable emphasis on ideological vigilance and strengthened propaganda efforts through the mass media. Linked initially to anticipated ideological dangers inherent in East-West détente, it later became tied to the reality of those dangers, as organized dissident groups sprang up throughout Eastern Europe. A second and ultimately more significant theme related to the mounting economic difficulties besetting all the countries of the region. None of the Party congresses could afford entirely to ignore these problems, but none save the Hungarian Party leadership showed any readiness to discard old nostrums and seek innovative solutions.

Closely related to this latter theme was the one key issue which divided the Soviet from the East European parties in the 1970s: the role of the consumer and the priority to be given his needs in formulating economic and social policy. Heralded by the 24th CPSU Congress but abandoned by the 25th, promises of further increases in the material standard of living had taken firm root in Eastern Europe. This stress on consumerism, or "goulash Communism," derives not so much from the materialism of the East European populaces (though this is a factor in Eastern Europe as elsewhere) as from the performance criteria on which their regimes came increasingly to be judged. Encouraged by the favorable economic forecasts of the early 1970s, the East European regimes (with the partial exception of the Romanian) had explicitly or implicitly linked the legitimacy of their rule to their ability to provide steady improvements in material living standards. By the end of the decade, of course, the East European economic situation had deteriorated sharply, and the gap between promise and performance, to say nothing of the gap between East and West, had become acute. Nowhere was this more apparent than Poland, where the Gierek regime found itself manifestly unable to deliver on the economic promises it had so loudly proclaimed a few years earlier.

Nor was the outlook any brighter as the East European parties entered the 1980s. Facing the prospect of continued economic deterioration but fearful of provoking a national backlash of the sort that engulfed Poland in the summer of 1980, the parties found themselves immobilized, entrapped by the promises of the early 1970s and the fundamental insecurity of their rule.[138]

5

Political and Military Relations: The Entangling Alliance

In celebrating its twenty-fifth anniversary on May 15, 1980, the Warsaw Pact had already established itself, historically speaking, as one of the more enduring alliance systems. Its history spans an international climate ranging from Cold War to détente—and partially back again—and a regional situation characterized by alternating periods of stability and disarray. Underlying the fits and starts of political and military relations in the region, however, has been a more consistent pattern of development: the expansion of the Warsaw Pact's once limited role to encompass a vast array of functions related to foreign policy coordination, military cooperation, and intrabloc alliance management.[1]

Although considerable attention has been given the Warsaw Pact's military evolution in the context of East-West relations, comparatively little has been said of its more significant internal transformation in recent years. As one analyst has observed, the Warsaw Pact is an "entangling alliance," whose primary aims are internal: "to contain, to police, and to maintain stability." Thus, he concludes, "its main uses are political, rather than purely military, and it serves as an iron corset to hold together the communist bloc. In a larger sense, the Warsaw Pact serves as an alliance system through which the Soviet leaders seek to entangle their unwilling allies in the web of Soviet national interests."[2]

Soviet spokesmen, too, repeatedly contend that the Warsaw Treaty Organization is not simply a mutual defense arrangement, but an "unbreakable military and political alliance of the fraternal countries, and a reliable guarantee of their socialist gains."[3] According to Foreign Minister Gromyko, the Soviet leaders regard the Warsaw Pact as the "chief coordinating center of foreign political activity of [the] fraternal countries," and an "effective mechanism for political, economic, and defense interaction of its member states."[4] Not only are Warsaw Pact relations linked in Soviet commentary to the broader pattern of interaction (*vzaimodeistvie*) in Eastern Europe, but they are held to be leading to the eventual creation of a "multi-faceted military-political union" of its member states.[5] By applying the Brezhnev Doctrine and the "class" understanding of sovereignty to Warsaw Pact relations, moreover, the Soviet leaders have sought to expand mutual defense obligations to include the overarching "internationalist duty" to "defend the socialist gains" against both internal and external enemies.

All this is not to suggest that the Warsaw Pact does not serve other objectives, or that those other aims are merely incidental. Soviet aims in Eastern Europe, as has been seen, are several: they include the preservation of a buffer zone between the Soviet Motherland and the center of "aggressive imperialism," the protection and consolidation of existing socialist regimes in Eastern Europe (and, derivatively, of the Soviet regime as well), the creation and extension of a base for the assertion of Soviet influence over all of Europe,[6] and a host of other ideological, political, economic, military, and strategic objectives related in one way or another to "fraternal relations" among the Warsaw Pact countries.

Nor should one overlook the role of the junior allies in Warsaw Pact affairs. Although the Romanians have been alone in frontally challenging Soviet primacy in major foreign policy initiatives or strategic doctrines, East European grievances have been more vocal and widespread on such issues as national control over the armed forces, defense modernization and expenditure, extension of defense obligations beyond Europe, and access to Warsaw Pact decision-making. All these points of contention emerged during the 1970s, and continued Soviet military preponderance was matched by growing East European assertiveness in Warsaw Pact deliberations.

How, then, does the Warsaw Treaty Organization fit into the broader patterns of Soviet–East European relations, what objectives does it serve, and how has its role changed during the period under investigation? Through its various deliberative bodies—the Political Consultative Committee, Committee of Defense Ministers, Military Council, and others—the Warsaw Treaty Organization provides forums for discussion of issues concerning pact foreign policy, strategic planning, and military operations. In military and strategic terms, it provides for the conduct of joint military training, elaboration of common defense doctrine and practice, and standardization of weapons development and employment. Finally and most generally, by drawing together the military establishments of the several states, including a wide range of defense-related enterprises and political organs, the pact serves as an instrument of Soviet bloc alliance management and cements, or helps cement, the complex relationship on which the stability—indeed the very existence—of the East European regimes depends.

Briefly, then, the Warsaw Pact's functions are three: political-consultative, military-strategic, and internal-policing.[7] In each of these areas, as will be shown, the role of the Warsaw Pact expanded in the 1970s: mutual consultation increased, through the new deliberative bodies and in others as well; East European defense forces were continually reequipped and coordinated through periodic joint military exercises; and the Soviet leaders turned increasingly to the Warsaw Pact as an instrument of alliance cohesion. Underlying these developments, however, was a more general and significant trend: the Warsaw Pact's evolution from an externally oriented military organization of limited aims to a complex and inner-directed political and military alliance entangling the East European states in the exigencies of Soviet global and regional ambitions.

Consultation in the Warsaw Pact

The main organ of the Warsaw Pact is the Political Consultative Committee (PCC), composed of Party first (or general) secretaries of the member states and convened ad hoc to discuss salient, usually foreign policy, issues of the day. Since about the mid-1960s, the PCC has been employed as a forum for issuing major foreign policy resolutions or adding the Warsaw Pact's collective weight to initiatives broached before, usually but not exclusively by the Soviet Union. Despite its statutory requirement to meet at least twice a year, the PCC has in fact met far less frequently, convening twice in 1970 but just once every two years for the remainder of the decade.[8]

Soviet influence over these deliberations is paramount, of course, but genuine, occasionally heated conflicts are known to take place. At the time of the 1969 Budapest meeting, for example, there was considerable intra-alliance wrangling over the emerging nature of Warsaw Pact Westpolitik; and thinly veiled Soviet–East German disputes over the "German question" surrounded the East Berlin summit in December 1970.[9] After the April 1974 PCC session in Warsaw, it was widely reported that Romania's Ceauşescu had seized the opportunity to reiterate his call for rotation of the post of WTO commander-in-chief among all member states and to reject (unspecified) proposals to tighten the Warsaw Pact command structure.[10] Ceauşescu's defiant posture at the Warsaw meeting, as has been seen, apparently led to the abrupt cancellation of the Crimea summit scheduled for August 1974.[11] In November 1978, this defiance erupted in far more dramatic form, as Ceauşescu rejected Soviet demands for increased defense expenditure and strengthened military integration, as well as for a collective admonition to the Chinese, and proceeded to air his grievances publicly upon his return to Bucharest.[12]

These relatively rare open clashes are only the most dramatic manifestations of a more general dilemma affecting PCC deliberations. As PCC declarations and resolutions are issued over the signatures of all participants and presumably require unanimous approval, they often appear to be the result of hard-fought compromise, or simply to have descended to the lowest common denominator. It is of course impossible to document the extent of East European influence in the drafting of PCC resolutions, but some of the Warsaw Pact's early initiatives toward détente, as well as post-Helsinki efforts to resuscitate it, bore the unmistakable imprint of East European coauthorship. More commonly, the junior allies clearly have been able to eliminate or moderate unacceptable formulations, as in the omission of any reference to China in the 1978 PCC resolution and the extremely mild reference to Afghanistan in 1980.[13]

These difficulties help account for the infrequency and irregularity of PCC sessions and also explain the Brezhnev leadership's repeated calls for "further perfecting" the Warsaw Pact in the area of foreign policy coordination. As is illustrated in Table 5.1, the PCC met just six times in the 1970s (compared with eight in the 1960s) and convened but twice between 1971 and 1975, the period in which East-West negotiations toward a European security conference were most intense. It may have been anticipated initially that some of the PCC's functions would be taken over by annual Crimea summit conferences, but these degenerated after 1974 to ritualistic bilateral encounters far less significant than the ambitious multilateral summitry of 1971–1973.

Beginning in 1969, however, Warsaw Pact foreign policy consultation increasingly devolved to periodic meetings of the Soviet and East European foreign ministers and occasional conferences among deputy foreign ministers as well. Prior to 1969, just three meetings of the foreign ministers had been held: in April 1959 (a meeting also attended by the Chinese foreign minister), June 1966, and February 1967. In the early 1970s, however, foreign ministers' conferences became a regular part of the Soviet–East European consultative process, convening six times during the period 1969–1975. Similarly, the deputy foreign ministers of the Warsaw Pact countries, who had met but once (in February 1968) before 1969, began to meet with some regularity in the early 1970s. These sessions, of course, went a long way toward fulfilling the long-standing Soviet desire for a permanent, high-level organ for foreign policy coordination,[14] and they had the distinct advantage of providing consultative forums outside the highly charged atmosphere of the Political Consultative Committee and other summit conferences.

The significance attached to the foreign ministers' conferences, and to foreign policy consultation more generally, was further demonstrated in 1976, when the PCC, meeting in Bucharest in November, announced the creation of "a Committee of Foreign Ministers and a Joint Secretariat as organs of the Political Consultative Committee."[15] With its formal incorporation into the Warsaw Pact consultative structure, the Committee of Foreign Ministers began to meet more regularly and frequently, normally convening once a year either in the late spring or early fall. (See Table 5.1.) More important, it began to emerge as a major forum in its own right, issuing such key foreign policy initiatives as the

December 1979 proposal for an East-West conference on military détente and disarmament.

Less is known of the second organizational change undertaken in 1976, particularly in that a Joint Secretariat had been created as early as 1956 but had apparently lapsed thereafter into desuetude.[16] As far as can be gathered, the new Joint Secretariat is a reincarnation of the former body, charged with coordinating

Table 5.1

Warsaw Pact Foreign Policy Consultation, 1969–1980

Year	Date	Location	Political Consultative Committee	Committee of Foreign Ministers	Deputy Foreign Ministers
1969	Mar. 17	Budapest	X		
	Oct. 30	Prague		X	
1970	Jan. 26–27	Sofia			X
	June 21–22	Budapest		X	
	Aug. 20	Moscow	X		
	Dec. 2	E. Berlin	X		
1971	Feb. 18–19	Bucharest		X	
	Nov. 30–Dec. 1	Warsaw		X	
1972	Jan. 25–26	Prague	X		
1973	Jan. 15–16	Moscow		X	
	Apr. 24	Moscow			X
1974	Apr. 17–18	Warsaw	X		
1975	Mar. 21	Warsaw			X
	Dec. 15–16	Moscow		X	
1976	July	Sofia			X
	Nov. 25–26	Bucharest	X		
1977	Feb. 20–22	E. Berlin			X
	Apr. 5–7	Moscow			X
	May 25–26	Moscow		X	
1978	Apr. 24–25	Sofia		X	
	Nov. 22–23	Moscow	X		
1979	May 14–15	Budapest		X	
	Dec. 5–6	E. Berlin		X	
1980	Jan.	E. Berlin			X
	May 15	Warsaw	X		
	July 8–9	Prague			X
	Oct. 19–20	Warsaw		X	

SOURCES: I. I. Iakubovskii, *Boevoe sodruzhestvo bratskikh narodov i armii* (Moscow: Voenizdat, 1975), pp. 285–93; V. G. Kulikov, ed., *Varshavskii dogovor: Soyuz vo imya mira i sotsializma* (Moscow: Voenizdat, 1980), pp. 272–93. Additional data compiled by the author.

NOTE: The list of deputy foreign ministers' meetings was compiled by the author and could not be verified by official sources for accuracy or completeness.

Warsaw Pact foreign policies between sessions of the PCC. It has been both praised for its work in overseeing the implementation of PCC decisions and criticized for alleged interference in the work of other Warsaw Pact organs, particularly the Joint Command and Joint Staff.[17] Since it is a permanent body charged with implementing the decisions of two ad hoc committees (the PCC and the Committee of Foreign Ministers), and since it is headquartered in Moscow under the jurisdiction of a Soviet deputy foreign minister,[18] the Joint Secretariat may well represent a new means for expanding direct Soviet influence and control over Warsaw Pact affairs, though no direct documentation to that effect can be adduced.

Figure 5.1 depicts the Warsaw Pact's new command/consultative structure after the 1976 reorganization and reveals the dramatic expansion of the pact's consultative mechanisms in recent years. Virtually the entire upper half of the now top-heavy organizational chart consists of influential new bodies incorporated since 1969: the Committee of Foreign Ministers and the Joint Secretariat, both added in 1976, and the Committee of Defense Ministers, the Military Council, and the Committee for the Coordination of Military Technology, all created in 1969.

The three last-named bodies, as has been seen, were created at the 1969 Budapest meeting of the PCC to facilitate military consultation and coordination in the Warsaw Pact.[19] The Committee for Coordination of Military Technology, charged with coordinating military research and development and facilitating modernization and standardization of weapons systems, has been shrouded in secrecy since its inception, and little is known of its operations. Acting in apparent conjunction with the Council for Mutual Economic Assistance (CMEA) Committee on Scientific and Technical Cooperation, it is known to have played some role in modernizing the non-Soviet Warsaw Pact armies and presumably facilitates Soviet supervision of East European defense-related industries.[20]

It is almost as difficult to define the precise functions of the other new military organs, the Committee of Defense Ministers (CDM) and the Military Council (MC), for the communiqués issued after their sessions have been generally unrevealing, hinting only obliquely at discussions of "problems pertaining to the current activity of Warsaw Pact military organs"[21] and the like. It is clear that the CDM is the senior of the two, but its relationship to the MC—or, for that matter, to the PCC or the Joint Command—remains obscure. Marshal Yakubovsky, former commander-in-chief of the Joint Armed Forces, explained that the CDM "elaborates coordinated recommendations and proposals"; but Lieutenant General K. K. Pashuk, WTO first deputy chief of staff, added that the committee "decides on issues" concerning combat readiness and defense capabilities. As to the Military Council, both Yakubovsky and Pashuk observed that it performs "consultative recommendatory functions" on such matters as administration, organization, weaponry and equipment, and combat readiness; but neither specified to whom these recommendations are issued.[22] Otherwise, what little we know of its operations comes from Marshal Yakubovsky, who noted that "the Military Council renders effective aid to the [Joint] Command," and from Marshal Kulikov, Yakubovsky's successor as Warsaw Pact commander-in-chief, who explained that the council analyzes "results of combat and

Figure 5.1
Structure of the Warsaw Treaty Organization, 1980

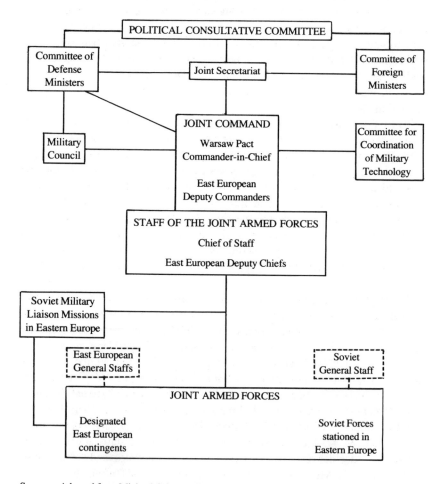

SOURCE: Adapted from Michael Csizmas, *Der Warschauer Pakt* (Bern: Verlag SOI, 1972).

operational activities of the preceding year and determines the tasks of the armies and fleets for the coming year.''[23]

Some light can be shed on these issues by examining patterns of military consultation in the Warsaw Pact from 1969 to 1980. As is illustrated in Table 5.2, the new consultative bodies have convened quite frequently and regularly, the Committee of Defense Ministers usually once a year and the Military Council almost always twice annually. Inasmuch as meetings of the MC in 1969 and 1970 immediately preceded sessions of the CDM,[24] it appeared initially that the council might be submitting recommendations directly to the defense ministers for approval. After 1971, however, the pattern became much less regular, and it seems clear that no such direct relationship exists. It further appears that the CDM does not serve the Political Consultative Committee in any regular and direct advisory capacity, for CDM sessions never have been scheduled immediately to precede those of the PCC. What is readily apparent from the table, however, is the extent to which the two new bodies have been institutionalized as part of the Warsaw Pact's consultative mechanism. From 1971 on, the Military Council met regularly twice a year, once in April or May and again in October or November, and by 1975 the Committee of Defense Ministers had settled on a regular year-end meeting. Both rotate their venue among each of the capital cities in turn, with the Military Council having met in Kiev and Minsk as well as in Moscow.

Thus, although considerable uncertainty still surrounds military consultation in the WTO, it is possible to draw a general picture of the Warsaw Pact command and consultative bodies and relations among them.[25] The Military Council is permanently chaired by the Warsaw Pact commander-in-chief and includes the East European deputy commanders-in-chief (all members of the Joint Command) as well as the Warsaw Pact chief of staff and other senior military officers. With areas of competence generally restricted to military operations and planning, the Military Council is the consultative arm of the Joint Command, which in turn reports to the Political Consultative Committee, either directly or via the Committee of Defense Ministers.[26] The CDM, then, is the highest military organ of the Warsaw Pact, consisting of the Soviet and East European ministers of defense (who apparently chair the meetings in rotation) and including the Warsaw Pact commander-in-chief and chief of staff, with chiefs of the general staffs of the national armies also in attendance. Concerned with the broader question of military doctrine and deployment, the Committee of Defense Ministers reports to the Political Consultative Committee and apparently serves as liaison between the PCC and the Military Council and Joint Command.

In any case, doubts concerning the functions and interrelationships of the Warsaw Pact consultative mechanisms should not obscure the more important fact that political and military consultation in the WTO increased dramatically in the 1970s. Entirely new bodies were created for formal consultation on foreign

Table 5.2
Military Consultation in the Warsaw Pact, 1969–1980

Year	Date	Location	Committee of Defense Ministers	Military Council
1969	Dec. 9–10	Moscow		X
	Dec. 22–23	Moscow	X	
1970	Apr. 27–28	Budapest		X
	May 21–22	Sofia	X	
	Oct. 27–30	Varna		X
1971	Mar. 2–3	Budapest	X	
	May 12–15	E. Berlin		X
	Oct. 26–29	Warsaw		X
1972	Feb. 9–10	E. Berlin	X	
	Apr. 11–12	Bucharest		X
	Oct. 17–20	Minsk		X
1973	Feb. 6–8	Warsaw	X	
	May 16–17	Sofia		X
	Oct. 30–Nov. 1	Prague		X
1974	Feb. 6–7	Bucharest	X	
	Mar. 26–28	Budapest		X
	Nov. 19–21	E. Berlin		X
1975	Jan. 7–8	Moscow	X	
	May 19–20	Warsaw		X
	Oct. 27–30	Bucharest		X
	Nov. 18–19	Prague	X	
1976	May 25–27	Kiev		X
	Dec. 10–11	Sofia	X	
1977	May 16–20	Prague		X
	Oct. 17–20	Sofia		X
	Nov. 29–Dec. 2	Budapest	X	
1978	May 16–19	Budapest		X
	Oct. 16–19	E. Berlin		X
	Dec. 4–7	E. Berlin	X	
1979	Apr. 23–26	Warsaw		X
	Oct. 29–31	Bucharest		X
	Dec. 4–6	Warsaw	X	
1980	Oct. 15	Prague		X
	Dec. 1–3	Bucharest	X	

SOURCES: I. I. Iakubovskii, *Boevoe sodruzhestvo bratskikh narodov i armii* (Moscow: Voenizdat, 1975), pp. 285–93; V. G. Kulikov, ed., *Varshavskii dogovor: Soyuz vo imya mira i sotsializma* (Moscow: Voenizdat, 1980), pp. 272–93.

policy and military planning, and activity expanded at all levels of the organization. All this adds up to a vast and growing infrastructure in the Warsaw Pact, whose internal evolution in the 1970s far outpaced its development in purely military areas.

Military-Strategic Relations

It is of course impossible to discuss the Warsaw Pact's military evolution outside the context of Soviet strategic objectives and the impressive expansion of Soviet strategic and conventional military capacity in recent years. Analytically, however, it is important to detach the strictly Soviet contribution from that of the Warsaw Pact *per se* to the combined strength of the Warsaw Pact countries. Seen in these terms, the military evolution of the Warsaw Pact has been far less impressive than is suggested by facile quantitative comparisons of NATO and the Warsaw Pact, including all Soviet and all East European forces. Indeed, to understand the military significance of the Warsaw Pact, one should view it not as an organization with intrinsic military power or potential but primarily as an extension and projection of Soviet military power in Europe.

Despite the extended Soviet occupation of Afghanistan, the commitment of some 500,000 Soviet troops to the Far East, and the consequent reorganization of Soviet forces into European and Asian theaters, Soviet military strategy continues to be oriented chiefly toward a European theater of operations—more specifically, toward the North Central European region, route of the historic German *Drang nach Osten*.[27] Soviet strategic concerns in Eastern Europe have centered around the "Northern Tier" countries—East Germany, Poland, and Czechoslovakia—as the core of the so-called "first strategic echelon," and the bulk of Soviet resources have been applied to that area.[28]

How does the Warsaw Pact serve these broader Soviet strategic objectives in Europe? Above all, the alliance provides the USSR with sites for the forward positioning of its own troops in key areas throughout North Central Europe.[29] Since the 1968 invasion of Czechoslovakia, an entire new army has been added to the total of Soviet forces stationed in Eastern Europe. With the addition of the Central Group of Soviet Forces (CGSF) in Czechoslovakia, Soviet forces in Eastern Europe now total thirty divisions: nineteen in East Germany (nine tank and ten motor rifle), four in Hungary (two tank and two motor rifle), two (tank) in Poland, and five in Czechoslovakia (two tank and three motor rifle). Thus, according to estimates by the International Institute for Strategic Studies, Soviet combat and direct support forces in Eastern Europe and along the western borders of the USSR now total some 785,000 ground troops and four tactical air armies.

As to the non-Soviet forces of the Warsaw Pact, their manpower levels actually declined in the 1970s, and the numbers of tanks and aircraft at their disposal increased only marginally. (See Table 5.3.) It should also be remembered that the East European forces, with the single exception of the East German, remain under strict national control; only those contingents specifically (and temporarily) designated by the national commands fall under the control of the Warsaw Pact Joint Command, and even those troops remain ultimately responsible to their own governments. Thus, the grand total of fifty-four non-Soviet divisions can in no way be counted in overall Warsaw Pact operational strength, if for no other reason than the fact that mobilizing these forces (assuming this could be done at all) would be such a cumbersome undertaking that the "surprise factor" so essential to Soviet military doctrine and practice would be utterly lost. As far as can be ascertained, Soviet war planning is predicated not on mass Warsaw Pact mobilization but on the transfer to a unified command of a relatively small number of specially designated East European formations, those included in the "first strategic echelon" and maintained at high levels of combat readiness.[30]

Some additional insight into the role of the East European forces can be gained by examining force modernization in the Warsaw Pact, of which much was said but less done in the 1970s. As is illustrated in Table 5.4, new Soviet tanks, missiles, and aircraft normally reached the East European inventories at least a decade after their introduction in the Soviet forces. An exception to this general

Table 5.3

Comparison of Warsaw Pact Force Levels, 1968, 1975, and 1980

Country	Manpower (in thousands)						Equipment					
	Ground forces			Air forces			Tanks			Combat aircraft		
	1968	1975	1980	1968	1975	1980	1968	1975	1980	1968	1975	1980
Bulgaria	125	131	105	22	25	34	2,000+	2,200+	1,900	250	253	210
Czechoslovakia	175	135	140	55	45	38	2,700	3,300	3,600	600	458	471
East Germany	90	105	108	31	36	38	1,800	3,115[a]	2,660[a]	270	441	347
Hungary	90	80	72	7	20	21	750	1,475	1,410	140	140	170
Poland	185	204	210	70	61	85	2,800	3,775	3,600	750	804	700
Romania	170	145	140	15	25	34	1,200	2,070	1,700	240	320	328
Soviet Union[b]	700	775	785	—	—	—	9,300	13,750	15,000	2,645	2,900	2,825

SOURCES: *The Military Balance* (London: International Institute for Strategic Studies, annual editions 1968–69 through 1980–81).

[a] Figures include 600 obsolete T-34 tanks in storage.

[b] Soviet totals include Soviet forces stationed in Eastern Europe or along the western borders of the USSR. Full manpower figures for Soviet air forces stationed in Eastern Europe are not available, but it is known that one tactical air army is attached to each of the four Groups of Soviet Forces stationed in Eastern Europe.

pattern—one not covered in the table—is in the delivery of the anti-tank guided weapons (ATGW's) Snapper, Sagger, and Swatter. These weapons, which proved so effective in the 1973 Middle East War, were introduced in the USSR in the mid-1960s and distributed to all the East European countries in 1971.[31] The tactical surface-to-air missiles SA-6 and SA-7 were also delivered to the East European forces somewhat ahead of schedule, but not until they had already been distributed to Syria and Iraq, and well after they were being manned by

Table 5.4

Modernization of Warsaw Pact Forces, 1969–1980

Weapons system	First in service in USSR[a]	Year of acquisition[b]					
		Bul.	CSSR	GDR	Hung.	Pol.	Rom.
Tanks							
PT-76	1952	1971	1970	1970	1970	1970	1974
T-62	1961	1971	1969	1971	1971	1971	1971
T-64/-72	1970	1980	1980	1980	1980	1980	1980
Missiles[c]							
SSM							
Frog	1957	1970	1970	1970	1970	1970	1971
Scud	1958	1971	1970	1970	1973	1970	1973
Scaleboard	1969						
SSNM							
Styx	1959	1972		1971		1971	1971
Goa						1977	
SAM							
SA-6	1967	1975	1977	1979	1977	1975	1978
SA-7	1967	1974	1975	1975	1978	1974	1978
SA-9	1975			1980	1977	1976	
Aircraft							
MiG-21	1958	1969	1969	1969	1969	1969	1969
Su-7	1958		1969		1974	1969	1974
Su-15	1969						
Su-17/-20	1971					1976	
MiG-23	1971	1978	1978	1980	1980		
MiG-25	1970						
MiG-27	1975						

Sources: *The Military Balance* (London: International Institute for Strategic Studies, annual editions 1969–70 through 1980–81).

[a] Best estimates available from various sources.

[b] *1969* indicates system acquired before or during 1969.

[c] Abbreviations stand for surface-to-surface (SSM), ship-to-surface (SSNM), and surface-to-air (SAM) missiles.

Soviet personnel in Egypt.[32] Similarly, SA-9's were distributed to Poland, Hungary and the GDR in the late 1970s, at about the same time they were sent to Soviet friends in the Middle East.

Although each of the East European states has been supplied with tactical, short-range, surface-to-surface missiles capable of delivering nuclear payloads (''Frog'' and ''Scud'' in their infelicitous NATO designations), there is no evidence that nuclear warheads have ever been supplied to the East European forces.[33] Of course, no East European country has ever been supplied with a strategic weapon of any kind, nor are any strategic weapons in the hands of the Soviet forces stationed in Eastern Europe.[34]

Despite their impressive numbers, tanks in the East European inventories are in a state of near obsolescence. World War II–vintage T-34's continue to be held in the inventories of some East European armies, and the mainstays of the East European tank forces are the serviceable but dated T-54/55's.[35] Even the T-62, which represents a marginal improvement over the T-55 but which still does not match its NATO counterparts, has had only limited distribution among the East European armies; and the more advanced T-64/72's were not distributed to Eastern Europe until 1980, and then only in very small numbers.[36]

A similar situation obtains in the East European air forces. In keeping with the short-range tactical role assigned the East European forces, their air arms include only a few long-range bomber squadrons consisting mainly of obsolete IL-28's. The venerable MiG-21, the most widely used combat aircraft in the world in the 1970s and still the most common aircraft in the Soviet inventory, provides the bulk of the East European air defense force. However, MiG-19's and even MiG-17s, both of which were first constructed in Stalin's day, are very much in evidence in Eastern Europe; and the newer generation of Soviet interceptors and fighter-bombers were only beginning to reach Eastern Europe in the late 1970s with the delivery of MiG-23's to Bulgaria, Czechoslovakia, Hungary, and East Germany (the Poles having opted earlier for the semivariable geometry SU-20).

The slow pace of Warsaw Pact force modernization cannot be attributed solely to Soviet niggardliness, of course, for the East Europeans have been manifestly reluctant to shoulder the additional financial burden thorough modernization would entail. As Table 5.5 illustrates, defense expenditure (as a percentage of gross national product) was low and steadily declining in every East European country save the GDR during the 1970s. As has been seen, this issue flared dramatically during the November 1978 PCC summit, when the Soviet leadership sought to counter NATO's Long-Term Defense Program by demanding of its allies an across-the-board increase in Warsaw Pact defense spending.[37] In a now famous public exposé, Romania's Ceauşescu returned to Bucharest to reject the Soviet proposal, arguing that the socialist states ''should offer an example to all peoples: not to choose the road of augmenting military expenditures but, instead, of inducing a strong current of opinion for their reduction."[38] In Moscow, meanwhile, Soviet Party leader Brezhnev was warning, "We shall not agree to the weakening of our defenses in the face of the growing military might of the imperialists, no matter what demagogic arguments are used to camouflage such calls."[39] We do not know the positions taken in the dispute by the other East European leaders, but it is known that the Poles were allowed to freeze their defense spending in 1978 out of consideration for their domestic economic difficulties.[40] Given the economic problems besetting all the East European countries and their continued reductions in defense outlays in the late 1970s, however, it is more than likely that the Soviet leaders were confronted with a clear East European consensus opposed to further increases in defense spending.

For these and other reasons, the bulk of Warsaw Pact modernization efforts has been applied to Soviet forces stationed in Eastern Europe: the Group of Soviet Forces, Germany (GSFG) and the Northern, Central, and Southern Groups of Soviet Forces (in Poland, Czechoslovakia, and Hungary, respectively). These forces have been reequipped, along with the home forces in the USSR, with advanced T-72 tanks, MiG-23 and MiG-27 aircraft, and other modern Soviet weaponry. It goes without saying that these forces are viewed by Soviet strategic planners as the first line of defense in the European theater.

Otherwise, Warsaw Pact modernization has centered on the Northern Tier countries—Poland, East Germany, and Czechoslovakia. As is shown in Table 5.6, the Northern Tier has always been the first to receive new Soviet equipment, though Hungary's (and more recently Czechoslovakia's) relatively low status is partially offset by indigenous production capacity. The elevation of the GDR in the Warsaw Pact order of priorities is particularly notable. Initially restricted

Table 5.5
Warsaw Pact Defense Expenditures

Country	Total expenditures ($million)			% of GNP (est.)		
	1970	1975	1980	1970	1975	1979
Bulgaria	279	457	1,140	3.1	2.7	2.1
Czechoslovakia	1,765	1,706	3,520	5.8	3.8	2.8
East Germany	1,990	2,550	4,790	5.9	5.5	6.3
Hungary	511	506	1,080	3.4	2.4	2.1
Poland	2,220	2,011	4,670	5.0	3.1	2.4
Romania	750	707	1,470	2.9	1.7	1.4
Soviet Union	53,900	124,000	—	11–13	11–13	11–13

SOURCES: *The Military Balance* (London: International Institute for Strategic Studies, annual editions 1971–72 and 1980–81).

because of the GDR's anomalous status and the overwhelming presence of the GSFG, Soviet deliveries of modern equipment and weaponry to the GDR increased markedly in the 1970s, reflecting the GDR's full incorporation into the Northern Tier and its growing role in the Warsaw Pact's "first strategic echelon."[41]

A related development has been the employment of specially designated Polish, East German, and Czechoslovak forces, equipped with the most modern weaponry in their inventories and maintained at the highest state of combat readiness, alongside first-line Soviet divisions in Warsaw Pact military maneuvers. This practice, manifested in the March 1975 ground assault maneuvers in the GDR and other joint maneuvers involving Northern Tier forces, may indicate the evolution of something approaching the concept of a Warsaw Pact "standing army"—albeit on a limited scale—so vigorously opposed by Romania in the past.[42] At the very least, it further indicates Soviet reliance on specially earmarked East European units, rather than mass mobilization, in Warsaw Pact doctrine and practice.

Thus, the non-Soviet forces are a part, though not an integral one, of the overall Warsaw Pact defense posture, and their military role certainly should not be considered negligible. East European units are expected to join Soviet forces in a conventional role in the European theater; and joint exercises and maneuvers, some of high levels of sophistication, are held periodically. As is illustrated in Table 5.7, exercises continue to be held most often among the Northern Tier countries, with the occasional participation of Hungarian forces as well.[43] In the period 1969–1979, twenty-five exercises were conducted exclusively within the Northern Tier, eight were held solely or partly in Hungary, and only nine were held exclusively among the Southern Tier countries. Additionally,

Table 5.6

Modernization of Warsaw Pact Forces: Order of Receipt of New Soviet Equipment, 1963, 1967, 1971, and 1975

	1963	1967	1971	1975
1	Poland	Czech.	Poland	Poland
2	Czech.	Poland	Czech.	GDR
3	Bulgaria	Hungary	Hungary	Czech.
4	Hungary	Bulgaria	GDR	Bulgaria
5	Romania	GDR	Bulgaria	Hungary
6	GDR	Romania	Romania	Romania

SOURCES: *The Military Balance* (London: The International Institute for Strategic Studies, 1963–64 through 1975–76); *The Soviet War Machine: An Encyclopedia of Russian Military Equipment and Strategy* (London: Hamlyn Publishing Group, 1976), p. 176.

Table 5.7
Warsaw Pact Military Exercises, 1969–1979

Year	Month	Type of exercise/ Code name	Participants (site italicized)
1969	Mar	combined forces	*GDR*, USSR (GSFG)[a]
	Mar–Apr	naval and air staffs	*Bulgaria*, Romania, USSR
	Mar–Apr	army (staff)/"Vesna 69"	*GDR, Poland, Czech.*, USSR
	Apr	air defense	*Hungary, Poland, Czech., USSR*
	May	army staff	*USSR*, Bulgaria, Romania
	June	army staff	*Hungary*, USSR (SGSF)[a]
	July	army staff	*Poland*, GDR, USSR
	July–Aug	army and air forces	*Poland, Czech., USSR*
	Aug	command staff	*Czech.*, USSR (CGSF)[a]
	Sept	combined/"Oder-Niesse"	*Poland*, GDR, Czech., USSR
	Oct	staff	*GDR, Poland, Czech., USSR*
1970	Mar	army (staff)/"Dvina"	*Bulgaria*, USSR
	July	combined staff	*Hungary*, USSR (SGSF)[a]
	July	air defense	*all Warsaw Pact countries*
	Aug	combined/"Taran"	*Czech.*, USSR (CGSF)[a]
	Oct	combined/"Brotherhood-in-Arms"	all Warsaw Pact (*GDR*); Romania observer
1971	May	air defense	all Warsaw Pact (*Czech.*)
	June–July	combined staff	*GDR, Czech.*, USSR
	July	air defense	*Poland, Czech.*, USSR
	July	staff/"Vistula-Elbe"	*Poland, GDR*, USSR
	Aug	staff/"Opal 71"	*Hungary, Czech.*, USSR
	Sept	army staff	*GDR, Poland*, USSR
1972	Feb–Mar	combined staff	*Poland, GDR*, USSR
	Mar	command staff	*Bulgaria*, Romania, USSR
	Apr	ground forces	*Poland*, USSR
	Apr	naval staff	Bulgaria, Romania, USSR (*Black Sea*)
	Sept	army (staff)/"Shield 72"	all Warsaw Pact (*Czech.*); Romania and Bulgaria observers
1973	Feb	staff mapping exercises	*Romania*, Bulgaria, USSR
	June–July	command staff	*GDR, Poland*, USSR
	Sept	army (staff)/"Vertes 73"	*Hungary*, USSR (SGSF)[a]
1974	Feb	staff mapping exercises	*Romania*, USSR
	May	command staff	*Hungary, Czech.*, USSR
	June	command staff	*Romania, Bulgaria*, USSR
	June	staff/"Leto 74"	*Poland*, USSR (NGSF)[a]
	Sept	naval staff	GDR, Poland, USSR (*Baltic Sea*)
1975	Mar	ground forces	*GDR, Poland*, USSR
	July	army staff	*Poland, Czech.*, USSR
1976	Sept	"Shield 76"	all Warsaw Pact? (*GDR*)[b]
1977	Mar	command staff/"Soyuz 77"	*Czech., Hungary*, USSR
	July	operational staff	GDR, Poland, USSR (*Baltic Sea*)

Table 5.7 (continued)

Year	Month	Type of exercise/ Code name	Participants (site italicized)
1978	Mar	staff mapping exercise	*Romania,* Bulgaria, USSR
1979	Feb	"Druzhba 79"	*Czech.,* USSR
	May	"Shield 79"	*Hungary,* Bulgaria, Czech., USSR; Romania observer

SOURCES: I. I. Iakubovskii, *Boevoe sodruzhestvo bratskikh narodov i armii* (Moscow: Voenizdat, 1975), pp. 286–93; V. G. Kulikov, ed., *Varshavskii dogovor: Soyuz vo imya mira i sotsializma* (Moscow: Voenizdat, 1980), pp. 272–93.

[a] Abbreviations stand for Soviet forces stationed in Eastern Europe:

> CGSF = Central Group of Soviet Forces
> GSFG = Group of Soviet Forces, Germany
> NGSF = Northern Group of Soviet Forces
> SGSF = Southern Group of Soviet Forces

[b] Listed as also "in attendance" were military delegations from Cuba, Mongolia, Vietnam, and Yugoslavia; listed as observers were military delegations from Austria, Denmark, Finland, and Sweden.

virtually all the major, large-scale exercises involving actual combat maneuvers have been held exclusively among the Northern Tier countries, with Romania playing a purely nominal role and Bulgaria sending little more than token contingents.

Most dramatic of all is the sharp drop in the frequency of Warsaw Pact exercises after 1974. (See also Fig. 5.2.) Except for the peak period 1968–1972, the Warsaw Pact has averaged about three exercises per year, with even fewer in the period 1975–1979. Similarly, the number of joint exercises involving combat troops was low throughout the 1970s and dropped to an average of fewer than one per year after 1973, apparently to present a low Warsaw Pact profile in the interest of Soviet détente initiatives.

It will not have escaped notice that all of these exercises have included Soviet participation; as far as can be gathered, the Warsaw Pact has never conducted a joint military exercise involving only the junior allies. Even in large multi-national exercises there is little contact among national forces except at the staff level, and East European units customarily maneuver side-by-side or in proximity with their allied counterparts rather than as part of an integrated operational force.[44] In this sense, Warsaw Pact exercises are simultaneous rather than "joint," quite dissimilar from the truly integrated (if occasionally chaotic) multinational NATO war games.

One other significant aspect of Warsaw Pact exercises is the extent to which they have been used to serve political rather than military or strategic objectives.

The March–April 1969 exercises in Bulgaria, for example, clearly were designed to elicit Romanian participation in Warsaw Pact activities in the wake of the March 17 Budapest meeting of the PCC.[45] Even more revealing were the "Vesna [Spring] 69" exercises, conducted partly on Czechoslovak territory in late March and early April, the time of the "ice hockey crisis" in the ČSSR.[46] It was surely no accident that the exercises coincided with the arrival in Prague of the USSR's Marshal Grechko and Deputy Foreign Minister Semenov; and it was more than coincidental that the ouster of Alexander Dubček from the Czechoslovak leadership came just six days after the conclusion of the "Vesna 69" exercises.[47] Even the 1970 "Brotherhood-in-Arms" (*Bratstvo po oruzhiiu*) maneuvers, the largest pact exercises ever held, were accompanied by a massive propaganda campaign stressing "unity and cohesion" among the "fraternal countries." As Marshal Yakubovsky, then commander-in-chief of the Joint Armed Forces, said in characterizing its military-political significance, "During the 'Brotherhood-in-Arms' exercise, there were exchanges of experience, meetings between servicemen, and meetings with the public. . . . The exercise was a clear manifestation of the unity and solidarity of nations in the socialist commonwealth and of their armed forces."[48] All these considerations lead to the somewhat paradoxical conclusion that Warsaw Pact joint exercises are primarily instruments of internal cohesion and only secondarily of military preparedness.

In any case, it should be remembered that the Warsaw Pact is fundamentally a peacetime organization; in the event of actual hostilities, designated Warsaw Pact contingents would probably be transferred directly to the Soviet High

Figure 5.2
Frequency of Warsaw Pact Military Exercises, 1969–1979

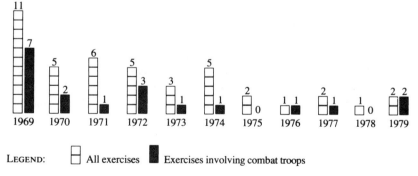

LEGEND: ☐ All exercises   ■ Exercises involving combat troops

SOURCES: V. G. Kulikov, ed., *Varshavskii dogovor: Soyuz vo imya mira i sotsializma* (Moscow: Voenizdat, 1980), pp. 272–93; Dale R. Herspring, "The Warsaw Pact at Twenty-five," *Problems of Communism,* September–October 1980, p. 6.

Command, as was the case in the Czechoslovak invasion.[49] This also was the command arrangement employed for joint Soviet–East European forces at the end of World War II, an arrangement cited in an authoritative military text by the late Marshal Sokolovskii as the basis for current Soviet military-strategic planning in the European theater.[50] There have been numerous reports that a Warsaw Pact Supreme Command has been established at Lvov, Ukrainian SSR, but it is not clear whether this command would be for operational command and control or for purely administrative jurisdiction over Warsaw Pact peacetime exercises.[51]

Whether Warsaw Pact wartime operations would be conducted through a WTO Supreme Command or directly through the Soviet High Command, it is almost certain that command and control would remain exclusively in Soviet hands. Strictly speaking, there exists no "Warsaw Pact Military Doctrine"; all military-strategic doctrine applied to the Warsaw Pact comes directly from Soviet strategic planning for the European theater.[52] Even in peacetime, many of the operational functions of the WTO are subordinated directly to the Soviet command: East European air defense units, for example, are subordinated to the Soviet commander of *PVO Strany*, whose WTO title as commander of air defense forces appears to be purely nominal.[53] Similarly, Polish and East German naval units attached to the so-called "Combined Baltic Sea Fleet" are in fact subordinate to the Baltic "Red Banner" Fleet of the Soviet Navy; and the infrequent Soviet-Bulgarian-Romanian joint naval exercises have been conducted under the direct operational control of the commander of the Soviet Black Sea Fleet.[54] Additionally, most of the Warsaw Pact's long-range bomber squadrons, the entire "blue water" navy, and all strategic forces are under the exclusive peacetime control of the USSR and of course would remain so under conditions of war.

Thus, despite the existence of a Warsaw Pact Supreme Command, Joint Command, Joint Staff, and other trappings of a genuine wartime military command, the Warsaw Treaty Organization remains in essence an administrative command, analogous to a traditional European War Office and controlled as if it were just another military district of the Soviet Union.[55] Its chief military functions are to ensure the combat readiness of units under its control and prepare them for timely mobilization, to promote integration of forces and standardization of equipment, and to supervise joint exercises and military maneuvers among staffs and combat units. It is not, however, an operational military command in the usual sense of the term.[56]

The "Entangling" Functions of the Warsaw Pact

It is difficult to detach the Warsaw Pact's role in purely military or consultative matters from its "entangling" functions, that is, from functions which serve to strengthen bloc solidarity and, derivatively, facilitate Soviet control and influence in the region. The creation of new bodies for consultation and policy coordination, for example, inevitably tends to tighten the bonds within the Warsaw Pact and restrict the latitude for independent action on the part of its East European members.

Even in areas which are seemingly of purely military concern, such as joint military exercises, the Warsaw Pact has been used as an instrument of Soviet influence over the junior allies. Indeed, some of the major joint maneuvers have had such a manifestly political content that their ostensible military purpose was rendered almost insignificant. The 1970 "Brotherhood-in-Arms" exercises, for example, served a whole series of political objectives: they provided a show of bloc-wide support for the Ulbricht regime in the aftermath of the Moscow-Bonn Pact, demonstrated the presumed "unity and solidarity" of all Warsaw Pact members (including Czechoslovakia and Romania), and implicitly reaffirmed the validity of the Brezhnev Doctrine. The nominal participation of the Bulgarians and Romanians in these, the first pact-wide exercises ever held, further revealed the political significance attached to the joint maneuvers. During and after the exercises, moreover, extensive press coverage throughout Eastern Europe stressed that the "Brotherhood-in-Arms" maneuvers, conducted in the spirit of "proletarian internationalism," had demonstrated the Warsaw Pact's commitment to "the inviolability of the GDR," to the deepening of "unity, cohesion, and combat cooperation" among the member states, and to "the defense of the socialist gains of their peoples and of the entire socialist community."[57]

A related practice has been the use of joint maneuvers to bring pressure to bear on wayward allies. Such "exercise pressure" was exerted several times against Czechoslovakia in 1968–1969: first to influence the course of domestic policy under Dubček, next to plan the invasion itself, then to help secure the ouster of Dubček from the Party leadership, and finally to accelerate the process of "normalization." In late 1968, as has been seen, the Soviet leaders used the threat of a major military build-up in Bulgaria to still Romania's criticism of the Czechoslovak invasion and to induce Ceauşescu to adopt a more conciliatory attitude toward Warsaw Pact and CMEA activities. Again in mid-1971, when fears of an emerging "Tirana-Belgrade-Bucharest axis" were running high, the Soviet leaders employed the threat of large-scale Soviet-Bulgarian maneuvers to bring pressure to bear on the Ceauşescu leadership.[58]

Similarly, a recurrent theme in Warsaw Pact relations for nearly two decades has been the Soviet effort to secure Romanian participation in joint military maneuvers and, derivatively, to elicit Romania's tacit acceptance of its "fraternal obligation" to promote pact solidarity. In 1967, as has been seen, Romania ended its three-year boycott of Warsaw Pact exercises by sending a contingent to the joint naval maneuvers held on the Black Sea; but in 1968, the Romanians again refused to participate in WTO maneuvers, and the Ceauşescu leadership sharply criticized "exercise pressure" directed against the Dubček regime.

In the aftermath of the 1969 Budapest Conference, the Romanians succumbed to strong Soviet pressure in agreeing to send limited staff contingents to the March–April exercises in Bulgaria and those held in the Soviet Union in May.[59] The scope and frequency of Warsaw Pact maneuvers in 1969 must have generated considerable concern in Bucharest, however, for in early 1970 President Ceauşescu publicly expressed his opposition to the idea of a supranational army and stressed that the Romanian military forces must remain under the exclusive control of the Romanian government.[60] These remarks were particularly interesting, for although General Shtemenko had admitted that Warsaw Pact military activity in 1969 was "a political exercise" designed to promote fraternal solidarity among the various armed forces,[61] the Soviet leaders had never publicly broached the possibility of a supranational WTO army. Whatever the motives of the Soviet leaders—and it seems clear that their objectives stopped far short of supranationalism—the Romanians came under intense Soviet pressure to participate in joint WTO exercises scheduled for early spring.[62]

Although the Romanians avoided joining the March 1970 "Dvina" maneuvers in Bulgaria, they did send a team of some 300 "observers" to the "Brotherhood-in-Arms" exercises held in East Germany in October. It is instructive that although Romania's participation was purely nominal, military leaders from the other Warsaw Pact states went out of their way to stress that "units from *all* of the Warsaw Treaty Organization are now participating" and that such joint action provides "renewed and convincing proof of the unity, cohesion, and military strength of the socialist allies."[63] Thus, according to East German Defense Minister Heinz Hoffmann, who commanded the exercises, "all the speculations by Western writers about ominous rifts in the Warsaw Pact have been proved by our Brotherhood-in-Arms exercises to be absurd."[64]

Hoffmann's reassurances notwithstanding, rifts in the Warsaw Pact loomed larger in 1971. Growing concern in Eastern Europe over the putative "Tirana-Belgrade-Bucharest axis" has already been discussed at some length, as have the difficulties surrounding the August 1971 Crimea conference and the subsequent anti-Romanian press campaign in Eastern Europe.[65] At the time of the Crimea session, joint "Opal 71" maneuvers were being conducted in Hungary, near the Romanian border, and plans were revealed for new joint exercises in Bulgaria. Although the precise nature of the plans was never made public, it was reported in the Western press that the Romanians not only declined to take part in the Bulgarian exercises but refused to grant Soviet troops rights of passage through Romanian territory.[66] In any case, the exercises, originally scheduled to begin August 1 and then postponed until later in the month, were finally cancelled altogether.

With preliminary negotiations toward a pan-European security conference scheduled to begin in Helsinki in late 1972, the matter of restoring a measure of unity in the Warsaw Pact acquired increased urgency. Soviet attempts to isolate the Romanians by dealing bilaterally with the Yugoslavs and Chinese had achieved some success by the middle of that year,[67] and the Romanians agreed to participate in limited WTO staff exercises held in Bulgaria in March and dispatched the Romanian defense minister to "observe" the "Shield 72" maneuvers in Czechoslovakia in September. Romania's rather more conciliatory posture, already revealed in its renewal of the last of its bilateral treaties with its WTO allies and Ceauşescu's participation in the August 1972 Crimea session, was underscored again in February 1973, when for the first time in more than a decade joint Warsaw Pact exercises were held on Romanian territory. While it is true that the 1973 exercises, like those of the following year, were limited mapping exercises which did not involve actual combat troops, the fact that the Ceauşescu government had permitted foreign military contingents on Romanian soil represented a significant success for Soviet efforts to erect a façade of fraternal solidarity.

On more fundamental issues, however, the Romanians remained adamant. At the PCC session in April 1974, as has been seen, Ceauşescu reportedly rejected Soviet proposals for a tightening of the Warsaw Pact command structure, and in June of that year it was reported that the Romanian government had complained that the Soviet Union was demanding extraterritorial transit rights through Romanian territory.[68] "In view of the contemporary international situation," Ceauşescu argued, not for the first time, at the 11th RCP Congress in November 1974, "the struggle to dissolve military blocs must be intensified."[69] Part and parcel of this aim have been efforts to strengthen national control over the Romanian armed forces. In the aftermath of the invasion of Czechoslovakia, for example, Romania's Grand National Assembly passed a law stipulating that only elected Party and state bodies, and not unspecified groups therein, are entitled to ask for political, economic, or military "assistance" from other socialist countries.[70] The 1972 Law on National Defense went a step further, requiring that the Grand National Assembly approve any employment of Romanian troops, regardless of whether such employment ostensibly is required by treaty obligations.[71]

These issues resurfaced in more dramatic fashion at the 1978 session of the Political Consultative Committee, when Ceauşescu rejected another Soviet call for tightening the Warsaw Pact Joint Command. Although details of the proposal were never made public, the Romanian leader left no doubt as to its general import. In a speech in Bucharest two days after the close of the PCC session, Ceauşescu warned that he would never accept a decision which would "prejudice the principle of the independence and sovereignty" of the country and its armed forces nor sign a document "that might affect the independence of our homeland and army." Commanding the national army, the Romanian Party Central Committee added, "is one of the main facets of exercising national sovereignty."[72]

These developments, in turn, bore adversely on the more fundamental "entangling" function of the Warsaw Pact: its facilitation of the Soviet-directed integration of the armed forces of its member states. As Soviet military leaders tirelessly repeat, "All fraternal armies are organized along common principles as regular, highly organized armies with a centralized leadership. . . . In general, the allied socialist armies have the same type of organizational structure, combat material, and armaments."[73] "Multi-faceted cooperation" among the Warsaw Pact armies, it is further argued, is a "manifestation of the objective tendency toward political, economic and military *rapprochement* [*sblizhenie*] of the socialist countries."[74]

Indeed, on several levels, military integration could hardly be more complete. Strategic doctrine for the Warsaw Pact, as has been seen, is totally subordinated to Soviet strategic planning for the European theater. Organizational structures of the East European defense forces are closely, if not fully, patterned after the Soviet model, and Warsaw Pact command and control principles are taken straight from Soviet military doctrine.[75] As Romanian and Czechoslovak critics have noted in the past, moreover, subordination to Soviet strategic planning serves to dictate East European defense priorities. By entangling the East European forces in the broader web of Soviet strategic considerations and assigning to those forces a primarily tactical role, Warsaw Pact doctrine requires that the East European states maintain unnecessarily large ground forces and deprives them of funds which otherwise might have been allocated to comprehensive defense modernization.[76] Thus, although the Romanians and to a lesser extent the Poles have implemented limited concepts of "territorial defense,"[77] Warsaw Pact military integration effectively precludes the development of fully rounded national defense postures among the East European members.

The development of national defense policies and structures is further restricted by the Soviet Union's near monopoly on manufacture of weapons systems and military equipment. Although several categories of military hardware are produced domestically in Eastern Europe and some Soviet equipment is constructed under license to the East European states, no East European country possesses a national manufacturing capacity sufficient to produce a full range of essential military equipment. Only the Romanians have looked beyond the pact to reduce their dependence on Soviet arms by purchasing French Alouette III helicopters and Chinese naval vessels, coproducing with Yugoslavia a jet fighter-trainer, and contracting with British firms for domestic production of British-designed aircraft; but even the Romanians remain heavily dependent on the Soviet Union for most categories of weaponry.[78]

Military dependence on the Soviet Union is further assured by the standardization—that is, Sovietization—of Warsaw Pact weaponry: ammunition of all calibers is almost entirely standardized, and most types of military equipment manufactured in Eastern Europe is constructed in conformity with Soviet specifications. In analyzing Warsaw Pact military preparedness, the extent of standardization can be exaggerated, inasmuch as the existence of wide variations in weapons systems and the weapons mixes of individual countries does considerable violence to easy assumptions of full interchangeability of components and ammunition.[79] In terms of Soviet control and influence, however, Sovietization is all but complete, for the USSR exercises close supervision over military research and development, planning, distribution, and deployment. Such supervision undoubtedly has been strengthened through the Committee for Coordination of Military Technology, which provides another vehicle for Soviet oversight of East European defense industries. Thus, while the Soviet Union no longer makes a practice of omitting from every East European military blueprint one vital part available only in the Soviet inventory,[80] standardization of Warsaw Pact weaponry is sufficient to ensure effective Soviet control over weapons procurement in Eastern Europe.

Military integration, of course, is supposed to extend to other areas as well. In addition to their other functions, joint training exercises ostensibly are designed to engender feelings of "fraternal solidarity" among soldiers of the Warsaw Pact. At the troop level, such solidarity appears to be largely bogus: even during war games there is strict segregation of forces, and Soviet soldiers are absolutely forbidden to fraternize with their East European counterparts.[81] Among senior Soviet and East European officers, however, regular contacts of this kind, as well as exchanges of military delegations of all types and the training of East European officers at Soviet military schools, almost certainly promotes a certain Warsaw Pact *esprit de corps*. This commonality of experience and interest among senior Warsaw Pact officers, in turn, constitutes a vital element of stability and pro-Soviet solidarity in Eastern Europe.

Similarly, contacts among Warsaw Pact ideological and political workers undoubtedly facilitates Soviet surveillance in the East European military establishments and the cultivation of loyalist groups therein.[82] The 1970s saw a considerable expansion of such contacts, ranging from meetings of Party political workers in the several armed forces to pact-wide conferences of army youth organizations and gatherings of editors-in-chief of central military journals. According to Marshal Yakubovsky, "Our commanders, political organs, party and Komsomol organizations have amassed an especially great wealth of experience on the international indoctrination of troops and on strengthening the class and military solidarity with personnel of the armies of socialist countries."[83]

More direct and regular Soviet supervision is achieved through the normal organizational channels of the Warsaw Pact. Attached to each East European Ministry of Defense is a Soviet Military Liaison Mission, headed by a two- or three-star general and composed of numerous senior Soviet army, navy, and air force officers. Although these missions apparently do not perform command functions, they clearly wield great influence in supervising and coordinating military activities throughout the bloc and transmitting Soviet military directives.[84] In addition to these officials are a variety of Soviet officers, advisors, and assorted functionaries (military attachés, KGB and other intelligence officers, and liaison personnel in the armed forces and defense-related industries) who serve as levers of Soviet control and influence in Eastern Europe. All these are linked, in turn, to Warsaw Pact headquarters, located in Moscow and attached to the Soviet Ministry of Defense.

Within the command and consultative bodies of the Warsaw Pact, Soviet dominance is assured not only by the political and military preponderance of the USSR, but by the overwhelming presence of Soviet officers in all key positions. The Warsaw Pact commander-in-chief and chief of staff (and first deputy commander-in-chief) are Soviet generals, the former also serving as head of the Military Council. The Committee for the Coordination of Military Technology is headed by a Soviet general, the Joint Secretariat by a Soviet deputy foreign minister. There is a Soviet deputy chief of staff, a Soviet inspector-general and a Soviet assistant commander-in-chief for logistics; and Soviet officers command Warsaw Pact ground, air, naval, and air defense forces.[85]

Finally and most generally, the omnipresence of the Soviet Union casts, in Kennan's words, a "psychological shadow" over Eastern Europe. It escapes no one's notice in the East that the only occasions since 1945 in which shots have been fired in anger by Soviet soldiers in Europe have been in actions taken against political developments in Eastern Europe itself. The continued presence of some thirty Soviet divisions in Eastern Europe, moreover, provides a constant reminder—one not altogether unwelcome among the leaders of the East European regimes—that the military might of the Soviet Union is the ultimate guardian of the political status quo in the region.

Doubly Entangled: The Bilateral Pact System

An adjunct to, and extension of, Warsaw Pact defense obligations is to be found in the web of twenty-one bilateral treaties of friendship, cooperation, and mutual assistance binding the Soviet Union and the states of Eastern Europe. Because the bilateral pact system provides a further layer of Soviet–East European mutual defense obligations, and because it provides the legal basis for many dimensions of Soviet–East European relations in the broader sense, these treaties are worth examining in some detail.

The earliest round of twenty-year treaties among the East European states already has been discussed, as have some of the treaty renewals of the late

1960s.[86] By 1969, several of the initial treaties, including most of those to which Romania was cosignatory, had expired and entered their automatic five-year extension periods. (See Table 5.8.) The matter of bringing all the treaties up to date acquired increased urgency, of course, after the issuing of the "Budapest Appeal" in March 1969 and the opening of East-West negotiations toward a European security conference.

With the conclusion of a new treaty between Bulgaria and Hungary in July 1969, all of the bilateral treaties had been renewed, save Romania's treaties with the USSR, Poland, Bulgaria, Hungary, and East Germany.[87] Initially postponed because of strains caused by Romania's independent exchange of diplomatic relations with West Germany, negotiations for a new round of treaties were again delayed in the wake of the Czechoslovak invasion. In mid-1969, with leaders of the other "fraternal countries" waiting to follow the Soviet initiative, the Soviet leaders finally opened treaty discussions with Romania, only to break

Table 5.8
The Bilateral Pact System in Eastern Europe, 1943–1980:
Treaties of Friendship, Cooperation, and Mutual Assistance
(Month and Year Signed)

	USSR	Bul.	Rom.	Hung.	Czech.	Pol.	GDR
Soviet Union		3/48	2/48	2/48	12/43	4/45	6/64
		5/67	7/70[a]	9/67	12/63	4/65	10/75[a]
					5/70[a]		
Bulgaria	3/48		1/48	7/48	4/48	5/48	8/50[b]
	5/67		11/70[a]	7/69[a]	4/68	4/67	9/67
							9/77[a]
Romania	2/48	1/48		1/48	7/48	1/49	8/50[b]
	7/70[a]	11/70[a]		2/72[a]	8/68	11/70[a]	5/72[a]
Hungary	2/48	7/48	1/48		4/49	6/48	6/50[b]
	9/67	7/69[a]	2/72[a]		6/68	5/68	5/67
							3/77[a]
Czechoslovakia	12/43	4/48	7/48	4/49		3/47	6/50[b]
	12/63	4/68	8/68	6/68		3/67	3/67
	5/70[a]						10/77[a]
Poland	3/47	5/48	1/49	6/48	3/47		7/50[b]
	4/65	4/67	11/70[a]	5/68	3/67		3/67
							5/77[a]
East Germany	6/64	8/50[b]	8/50[b]	6/50[b]	6/50[b]	7/50[b]	
	10/75[a]	9/67	5/72[a]	5/67	3/67	3/67	
		9/77[a]		3/77[a]	10/77[a]	5/77[a]	

[a] Treaties renewed, 1969–80.
[b] Treaties of "Friendship" (see Table 1.1).

them off after the announcement of President Nixon's forthcoming visit to Bucharest. It was only after a lengthy period of Soviet-Romanian "normalization" that leaders of the two countries agreed to sign the long-delayed Treaty of Friendship, Cooperation, and Mutual Assistance in July of 1970.

In the meantime, as part of another "normalization" process, Soviet and Czechoslovak leaders had concluded an early renewal of their 1963 bilateral treaty. The Soviet-Czechoslovak treaty of May 1970 is particularly significant in that it presents the most elaborate and ambitious formal statement of the Soviet interpretation of socialist internationalism.[88] Like the other bilateral treaties, the Soviet-Czechoslovak treaty provides for joint defense in the event of armed attack on either party, not only by a European aggressor, but "by any state or group of states." Thus, although the Warsaw Treaty could not legally be invoked in the case of an attack by China on the Soviet Union, Czechoslovakia would nonetheless be treaty-bound to render "all possible assistance, including military aid."[89]

A number of familiar shibboleths associated with the Brezhnev Doctrine and the Soviet understanding of socialist internationalism likewise find expression in the treaty, which specifies that it is an "internationalist duty of the socialist countries" to defend "the socialist gains" and strengthen the "unity and solidarity of all countries of the socialist commonwealth."[90] The signatories further pledged to promote the "international socialist division of labor" and "socialist economic integration" and expand "all-round cooperation" among state and public organizations and across a wide range of functional areas. One objective of such cooperation, according to the treaty, is a closer "drawing together [*sblizhenie*] between the peoples of the two states," a process explicitly linked in Soviet theoretical literature to the eventual "union," or "merger" [*sliianie*] of all the countries of the "socialist commonwealth."[91]

This language contrasts sharply with the text of the Soviet-Romanian treaty signed just two months later. Joint defense in the event of "armed attack by any state or group of states" is specified in both treaties; but in the Romanian treaty it is added that "the commitments envisaged in the Warsaw Treaty"—and, implicitly, obligations under the present treaty as well—are strictly limited to the European continent. In clear refutation of the Brezhnev Doctrine, moreover, it is emphasized that mutual defense obligations are limited to cases of external aggression and thus are not linked to any "internationalist duty" to "defend the socialist gains" from internal counterrevolution, real or imagined. The signatories further agreed to promote economic cooperation on the basis of the "international socialist division of labor," but no reference is made to "socialist economic integration," nor is there any hint of a gradual "drawing together" of peoples of the two countries. Finally, like relations between the Soviet Union and Czechoslovakia, Soviet-Romanian relations are said to be governed by "socialist internationalism," but the emphasis in the Romanian treaty is not on internationalist duties but on the national rights of the socialist countries: "sovereignty and national independence, equality, and non-interference in . . . internal affairs."[92]

Romania's treaties with Polish and Bulgaria, signed on November 12 and 19, 1970,[93] also followed the "Ceauşescu formula," differing only in three minor respects from the Soviet-Romanian treaty. Whereas the treaty with the USSR had included a specific call for the convocation of a pan-European security conference, Romania's treaties with Poland and Bulgaria hinted only vaguely at the desirability of "strengthening peace and security in Europe"; and while the Soviet treaty had restricted economic objectives to the framework of CMEA, the Polish and Bulgarian treaties added that economic cooperation should be encouraged "with the other socialist states" as well. If these differences reflect the stronger Soviet bargaining position in treaty negotiations, the final difference reveals Romania's continued determination to avoid ideological entanglement with the CPSU: whereas Romania's treaties with Poland and Bulgaria were signed by both the heads of state and the Party leaders, only the heads of state signed the Soviet-Romanian treaty.

Initially scheduled for signing in mid-1971, Romania's treaties with Hungary and East Germany were delayed for nearly a year in the wake of Ceauşescu's visit to China and the subsequent strains in Romania's relations with its allies. The Romanian-Hungarian treaty, finally signed in February 1972, was a virtual carbon copy of the 1970 treaties with Poland and Bulgaria.[94] Apparently because of continuing strains between Romania and Hungary, however, the treaty was signed only by the two heads of state, with the Party leaders merely attending the signing ceremony.

The Romanian–East German treaty of May 1972 differed from Romania's other treaties in that it included a few concessions to East German concern over the direction of interbloc negotiations in Europe. That these concessions were the products of hard-fought compromise is revealed in the cautiously worded defense of "the sovereign socialist GDR" and in this noncommittal observation in Article 10: "The high contracting parties believe that the establishment of normal relations of equality of rights between the two German states on the basis of international law would contribute substantially to safeguarding European peace and security."[95] As to relations among the socialist countries, however, the treaty amounted to a full endorsement of the Romanian interpretation of socialist internationalism.

The preferred East German formulation of socialist internationalism was presented in two subsequent documents: a joint Czechoslovak–East German declaration of October 1974 and the October 1975 Soviet–East German Treaty of Friendship, Cooperation, and Mutual Assistance. In the former, the East German and Czechoslovak Party and state leaders outlined their objectives for promoting "socialist economic integration" and "expanding fraternal cooperation.'' Paying "special attention to ideological cooperation," leaders of the two countries further expressed their "unswerving will . . . to promote the historic process of bringing them closer together" and pledged to strengthen the "unity and cohesion" of the entire "socialist community."[96] If anything, the Soviet–East German treaty went even further in affirming the Soviet view of relations among the socialist states. In addition to subscribing to the familiar litany of terms associated with the Soviet understanding of socialist internationalism—"internationalist duty," "defense of the socialist gains," "drawing closer together," and the like—the signatories revealed new plans for promoting "socialist economic integration" and agreed to "coordinate their national economic plans on a long-term basis."[97] All these objectives, it should be reiterated, stand in marked contrast to the much more limited objectives embodied in the Romanian treaties.

In addition to affirming the irrevocable eastward orientation of the GDR, the 1975 Soviet–East German Treaty also was designed to expunge any suggestions in the previous (1964) treaty that the "German question" might still be open. East German concerns over relations with the "other" Germany were also behind the treaties concluded in 1977 between the GDR and Hungary, Poland, Bulgaria, and Czechoslovakia to replace the only half-expired treaties of 1967. As the Bulgarian Party organ *Rabotnichesko Delo* explained at the time of the 1977 Bulgarian–GDR treaty, the premature signing of a new treaty was demanded by "qualitative changes in the international arena," presumably those issuing from West German Ostpolitik.[98] Common to all these treaties are affirmations of the sovereignty and independence of the GDR and the inviolability of existing European frontiers, including those between the two Germanies. On the question of Berlin, all the treaties endorse the East German interpretation of the 1971 Quadripartite Agreement: "Berlin . . . is not a constituent part of the Federal Republic of Germany and will not be governed by it in the future."[99]

East German sensitivity over the "German question" can hardly be exaggerated, and East German spokesmen have gone to some length to stress the significance of the new bilateral treaties as further affirmations of the sovereignty and independence of the GDR. Noting with satisfaction the GDR's increasingly important role within the socialist community, its membership in the United Nations, and its recognition by more than 120 states, East German scholars have explained that a new round of bilateral treaties was demanded by the "profound changes . . . in the GDR's international and domestic situation."[100] For these reasons, East German Foreign Minister Oskar Fischer claimed at the 7th plenum of the SED Central Committee in 1977, the new treaties have "cut the ground from under the feet of those still harboring illusions about the development of the socialist nation in the GDR."[101]

The 1977 round of treaties is further significant in that it marked the extension and elaboration of the Soviet interpretation of socialist internationalism. All the treaties contain references to the "drawing together" of socialist states, though the Polish and Hungarian treaties are couched in more perfunctory language, and all contain affirmations of the "internationalist duties" of socialist states to protect the "historic gains of socialism."[102] In this sense, "socialist internationalism" has, since the invasion of Czechoslovakia, become an implicit endorsement of the Brezhnev Doctrine, though the term was previously used without such a connotation.

The texts of these recent bilateral treaties are analyzed in Table 5.9. As can be seen in the table, there exists among the various countries a core of shared beliefs which in some sense can be said to constitute the "alliance ideology" of the Warsaw Pact countries. In external relations, all the countries subscribe to the general notion of "peaceful coexistence," and all are formally committed to the recognition of existing European boundaries. In intra-alliance relations, all are pledged to promote "unity and cohesion" on the basis of the "five principles" said to govern their mutual relations,[103] and all have subscribed to socialist internationalism, variously defined and interpreted. In the event of armed attack on any signatory state, all are bound by these and other treaties to render "all necessary assistance," including military aid.

Additionally, in all the treaties save the Romanian, the Soviet understanding of socialist internationalism is affirmed, along with the corollary Brezhnev Doctrine, which asserts that it is an internationalist duty of socialist states to defend the "historic gains" of socialism. All are pledged to promote "broad ties," toward the continual "drawing together" (*sblizhenie*) of all states of the "socialist commonwealth." In economic affairs, the previous commitment to the "international socialist division of labor" has been dropped in favor of measures agreed upon under the Comprehensive Program of 1971: socialist economic integration and coordination of national economic plans.

The Romanian treaties, as is readily apparent in the table, differ markedly from the others. In addition to eschewing commitment to the more entangling particulars of socialist internationalism, the Romanian treaties omit reference to socialist economic integration, plan coordination, or the desirability of constructing long-term ties among the socialist states. More important, particularly in light of past Soviet-Romanian disputes over the territorial limits of Warsaw Pact mutual defense commitments, is Romanian insistence that the military assistance clauses in its treaties be implicitly linked to cases of armed aggression in Europe, as specified in the Warsaw Treaty.

Clearly, much of the language contained in the bilateral treaties is rather *pro forma*, and there is a danger of reading too much into textual nuances and discrepancies. Nevertheless, as the treaties form the legal foundation for Soviet–East European relations in the broadest sense, their general content and even their precise wording are the subjects of intense negotiations between the signatories. The bilateral treaties constitute, moreover, the most authoritative

Table 5.9
Content Analysis of Bilateral Treaties, 1969–1980

Treaty (month and year signed)	External relations — Peaceful coexistence	External relations — European security system	External relations — Inviolability of European borders	External relations — Sovereignty of GDR	Bloc relations (general) — Socialist internationalism	Bloc relations (general) — "Five principles"	Bloc relations (general) — Strengthen unity and cohesion	Bloc relations (general) — Promote "broad ties"	Bloc relations (general) — "Socialist commonwealth"	Bloc relations (general) — "Drawing together"	Bloc relations (general) — Protect "historic gains"	Bloc relations (general) — "Internationalist duties"	Defense obligations — Defense against any attack	Defense obligations — Render all necessary assistance	Defense obligations — WTO obligations limited to Europe	Economic relations — Promote socialist economic integration	Economic relations — Coordinate nat'l. economic plans	Economic relations — Promote international socialist division of labor	Economic relations — Develop "long-term" ties	Economic relations — Encourage trade with other states	Signed by — Party leaders	Signed by — Heads of state
Bulgaria-Hungary (7/69)	X	X	X		X	X	X						X	X				X			X	X
Czechoslovakia-Soviet Union (5/70)	X	X	X		X	X	X	X	X	X	X	X	X	X		X		X			X	X
Romania-Soviet Union (7/70)	X	X	X		X	X	X						X	X	X			X				X
Romania-Poland (11/70)	X		X		X	X	X						X	X	X			X			X	X
Romania-Bulgaria (11/70)	X		X		X	X	X						X	X	X			X		X	X	X
Romania-Hungary (2/72)	X		X		X	X	X						X	X	X			X		X		X
Romania-East Germany (5/72)	X		X	X	X	X	X						X	X				X		X		X
Soviet Union-East Germany (10/75)	X	X	X	X	X	X	X	X	X	X	X	X	X	X		X	X			X	X	
East Germany-Hungary (3/77)	X		X	X	X	X	X	X	X	X	X	X	X	X		X	X		X		X	X
East Germany-Poland (5/77)	X		X	X	X	X	X	X	X	X	X	X	X	X		X	X		X		X	
East Germany-Bulgaria (9/77)	X		X	X	X	X	X	X	X	X	X	X	X	X			X		X		X	X
East Germany-Czechoslovakia (10/77)	X		X	X	X	X	X	X	X	X	X	X	X	X		X	X		X		X	X

formal expression of socialist internationalism, through which the East European states are entangled in the exigencies of Soviet regional and global objectives.

In light of recurrent Soviet and East European calls for the simultaneous dissolution of NATO and the Warsaw Pact, it is worth considering whether, or to what extent, the bilateral treaty system could supplant the Warsaw Pact in the broader context of Soviet–East European relations. It is true that the mutual defense commitments in the bilateral treaties duplicate and in fact exceed those embodied in the Warsaw Pact, and it is doubtless true that many of the functions of the latter could be taken over through bilateral arrangements between the Soviet Union and its East European allies. Yet, no other vehicle currently exists for the kinds of functions described at such length in the present chapter: foreign policy consultation and coordination; military cooperation through coordination, joint training, and assorted integration measures; and Soviet alliance management and supervision over the armed forces of the East European states. The expansion of the pact's internal role, as has been seen, was particularly striking during the 1970s, and some mechanisms would have to be found to replace those already in place under the aegis of the Warsaw Pact. In short, if the Warsaw Pact did not exist, some facsimile would have to be created.

From the perspectives of the Soviet and East European leaders, the Warsaw Pact remained at the end of the 1970s as important as it had ever been. Indeed, with the advent of rough strategic parity between the superpowers, the significance of the Warsaw Pact's conventional forces was probably greater than ever. In political terms as well, the Warsaw Pact continued to play a key role in reconciling Soviet interests with those of its allies and presenting a common front in negotiations with the West. Most dramatic of all, however, has been the Warsaw Pact's internal evolution from a defense arrangement of limited aims to a complex political-military alliance system entangling the East European states in Soviet aims in the region and beyond.

Only the Romanians, and they only occasionally, have challenged these objectives frontally. The other East European regimes have accepted the fundamental premises of Warsaw Pact relations as well as the military and political preponderance of the Soviet Union, and negotiations have proceeded on that basis. Those disputes which have surfaced have typically been of limited scope, centering on such matters as military burden-sharing and East European access to the levers of decisionmaking.

The Soviet invasion of Afghanistan, however, suggests another recurrent issue in Warsaw Pact deliberations: the possibility that the East Europeans might be called on to render some sort of military assistance in support of Soviet objectives beyond Europe. Although the East European states have signed formal ''friendship'' treaties with several Soviet allies in the Third World and have even sent limited military contingents, most notably the East German "Afrika Korps," outside the European continent, these are strictly bilateral arrangements unrelated to the Warsaw Pact *per se*.[104] In 1969, at the time of the Sino-Soviet border clashes, and again in 1978, during the Chinese incursion into Vietnam, however, it was widely reported that the Soviet leadership sought some sort of formal Warsaw Pact commitment to the Soviet cause. In the latter instance, the Romanian leadership swiftly reminded its allies that mutual defense obligations under the Warsaw Treaty are limited to cases of "armed attack in Europe," and warned that "nobody would be able to engage the country and the army in any action without the full approval of our entire people."[105] The prolonged Soviet occupation of Afghanistan, of course, points once again to the potential clash between Soviet global ambitions and the more limited concerns of the junior Warsaw Pact allies.

Yet, these strains and difficulties should not obscure the enduring importance of the Warsaw Pact for the Soviet and East European regimes. For the Soviet leaders, the Warsaw Pact has shown itself to be a nearly indispensable instrument for projecting Soviet power in Europe and promoting stability and unity among its allies; and for the East European leaders, even Ceauşescu, it forms part of the complex alliance system on which they depend for the stability—indeed the very existence—of their regimes.

6

Economic Relations: Dilemmas of Dependency

For more than three decades, Soviet–East European trade relations have been frustrated by a host of seemingly insuperable political and economic impediments to expanded economic cooperation: the disparity in size, influence, and resource endowment of the states concerned; differences in levels of economic development; the political-ideological commitment of the several regimes to comprehensive industrial development at the expense of export specialization; low mobility of labor and capital across state boundaries; failure to develop a rational system of price formation; and problems of trading procedure, compounded by the absence of a convertible currency. To these should be added growing conceptual divergences in the Council for Mutual Economic Assistance (CMEA) surrounding the notion of socialist economic integration. Despite the wide range of generally shared economic and political goals among the Soviet and East European regimes, improved economic cooperation has foundered on East European fears (voiced most forcefully by the Romanians and Hungarians) that Soviet-style integration is tantamount to economic dependency on the Soviet Union. For their part, the Soviet leaders have been equally loath to countenance genuine integration—that is, integration among free and equal partners—for fear of losing their grip on important levers of control in Eastern Europe.[1]

Caught between the opposing conceptions of supranationalism (which the Soviet leaders sought unsuccessfully to impose in the early 1960s) and market-style integration (for which the Hungarians and others had been lobbying), CMEA settled in 1971 for the hybrid "Comprehensive Program," which sought to promote integration through joint economic planning—both long- and short-term, bilateral and multilateral—and joint production ventures, embodied in CMEA's new "target programs" in key areas of economic activity.[2] Yet, for all the measures taken to promote multilateral cooperation in CMEA, Soviet–East European trade relations can best be characterized as "multiple bilateralism,"[3] a pattern in which an elaborate multilateral superstructure has been erected over an essentially unaltered system of bilateral trade relations in the region.

There is a danger, of course, of emphasizing political to the exclusion of economic factors affecting Soviet–East European trade. Indeed, a fundamental feature of CMEA economic relations in the early 1970s was the favorable impact of the global economic boom of the late 1960s. For the East European leaders, the prospect of greater economic prosperity offered the hope of strengthening political security by redirecting economic policy toward the production of consumer goods. Throughout the region in the early 1970s, as has been seen, this stress on consumerism, or "goulash Communism," was manifested in a new-found "concern for the man" and the "material well-being of the people" expressed at the Soviet and East European Party congresses.[4] The lessons of the labor unrest in Poland in December 1970 were clear enough: no degree of "socialist solidarity" could sustain the rule of a leader—viz., Gomulka—whose populace was prepared to resist continued suppression of living standards.[5]

There was another lesson fresh in the minds of Soviet and East European leaders, however: that of the Prague Spring, in which economic reformists had joined hands with political reformists to topple established methods of Party rule. Thus, for the Soviet and East European regimes a reorientation of economic policy was not to be accompanied by serious economic reform; indeed, a successful consumerist policy offered the attractive possibility of defusing demands for fundamental economic reform, or at least of easing the social discontent which might lend strength to reformist ideas. Central to this strategy was the rapid expansion of East-West trade, which was seen as the motor of sustained economic progress in Eastern Europe. By gaining access to Western finished products, employing Western credits for domestic investment, and taking advantage of the latest in Western technology, the East European states sought to increase productivity and efficiency (and thereby satisfy consumer demands) without embarking on the perilous course of economic reform.

Within CMEA, a dual approach began to take shape: new cooperative efforts to facilitate the exploitation of Western technology and offset the potentially disruptive impact of greatly expanded trade with the capitalist West, and a vigorous, Soviet-led drive toward economic integration on the basis of the newly adopted Comprehensive Program. New agreements on joint planning and production were drawn up, and long-term "target programs" were formulated to promote intensive, multilateral cooperation in key economic sectors, notably fuels, energy sources, and other raw materials. Unlike the abortive Soviet effort toward supranationalism in the early 1960s, which sought to impose integration from above through a powerful central planning organ, these measures were designed to promote integration "from the bottom up" by bringing more and more of CMEA planning and trade activity under a coordinated multilateral plan embracing all the East European economies.

These, then, were the key elements of Soviet and East European economic strategies in the early 1970s: rejection of economic reformism; adoption of import-led growth programs, particularly through imports of Western technology; and intensified efforts toward CMEA integration through plan coordination, joint investment projects, and long-term target programs.[6] For several years, the strategy appeared to have been vindicated: growth rates increased almost everywhere, particularly in the industrial sector, and material living standards visibly improved throughout the region.

By 1975, however, this grand strategy had begun to unravel. The dramatic increase in OPEC oil prices in 1973–74 had a profound, if somewhat belated, impact on the East European economies, newly sensitized to international economic fluctuations. Under the combined influence of global recession and inflation, trade with the West began to founder, as the East European states found it increasingly difficult to purchase Western products at their newly inflated prices or find markets in the West for East European exports. Western credits, on the other hand, were easier to come by than ever: with the glut of OPEC-generated funds on world financial markets coming at the very time that recession had sharply reduced credit demand among Western corporations, Western lenders were eagerly seeking investment opportunities abroad. Not surprisingly, the East European states most heavily committed to trade with the West—notably Poland—succumbed to the temptation to defer economic austerity by running up enormous Western debts.

If chronic East European balance of payments problems with the West were exacerbated in the late 1970s, terms of trade with the USSR suffered an equally debilitating reversal as a result of the precipitous increase in prices of Soviet oil deliveries. Implemented in January 1975 in response to price rises by the OPEC oil cartel, Soviet oil price increases had an immediate impact on the East European economies, most of which are heavily dependent on foreign (primarily Soviet) energy sources. Accordingly, the East European states found themselves in a double bind, forced to divert trade eastward to compensate for increased Soviet oil prices and westward to repay growing hard currency debts to Western creditors.

Mounting economic difficulties, then, exacerbated perennial differences in CMEA over the scope and direction of "socialist economic integration." The Comprehensive Program acknowledged but did not resolve these differences, seeking instead to promote economic cooperation through the voluntary coordination of national economic plans. Thus, throughout the 1970s, sessions of the CMEA Council, Executive Committee, and specialized commissions were devoted to the task of resolving the political and economic cross-purposes which had bedevilled CMEA planners from the beginning.

From the 26th to the 34th Council Sessions: Toward a "CMEA Plan"?

The hectic pace of CMEA negotiations preceding adoption of the Comprehensive Program gave way to a period of quiescence, as CMEA representatives sought to translate the contradictory aims embodied in the program into a set of workable measures for CMEA economic cooperation. The 26th, 27th, and 28th CMEA Council sessions were largely uneventful, although a revised CMEA charter was enacted at the 28th session in 1974. A number of new cooperative ventures were undertaken during this period, however, and efforts continued toward the elaboration of a joint, coordinated CMEA plan, finally announced at the 29th Council session. (See Table 6.1.) The relative quiescence in CMEA activities during the period should not, therefore, obscure the very serious conflicts surrounding implementation of the Comprehensive Program. After

Table 6.1

Sessions of the CMEA Council, 1969–1980

No.	Date	Location	Agenda
22nd	Jan. 1969	E. Berlin	integration, coordination of national economic plans
23rd[a]	Apr. 1969	Moscow	decision to draft comprehensive integration program
24th	May 1970	Warsaw	integration, decision to create International Investment Bank
25th	July 1971	Bucharest	adoption of "Comprehensive Program" for socialist economic integration, creation of new CMEA Council committees
26th	July 1972	Moscow	integration, coordination of national economic plans
27th	June 1973	Prague	integration, multilateral plan coordination measures
28th	June 1974	Sofia	integration, multilateral plan coordination, adoption of new CMEA Charter
29th	June 1975	Budapest	adoption of "Coordinated Plan for Multilateral Integration Measures for 1976–80," agreement on "joint projects"
30th	July 1976	E. Berlin	long-term "target" programs, convertibility, relations with the EEC
31st	June 1977	Warsaw	long-term target programs, plan coordination, EEC relations
32nd	June 1978	Bucharest	target programs for fuel, energy, and raw materials, organizational issues
33rd	June 1979	Moscow	target programs on consumer goods and transport, Charter changes
34th	June 1980	Prague	plan coordination problems, energy and raw materials

[a] "Extraordinary" session attended by Soviet and East European Party leaders.

1971, every session of the CMEA Council was attended by most or all of the prime ministers themselves, and the Soviet leaders began almost immediately to use the new Council committees and other CMEA organs to promote bilateral and multilateral plan coordination.

At the 26th CMEA Council session, held in Moscow in July 1972, it was argued that negotiations since the 25th session had "confirmed the rightness of the orientation toward . . . the development of socialist economic integration."[7] In surveying the progress made in fulfilling the directives of the Comprehensive Program, the communiqué noted a number of specific measures undertaken during the year, including the creation of twenty coordination centers, seven scientific coordination committees, two international collectives of scientists, and one scientific-production association. More importantly, CMEA members agreed to develop national economic plans incorporating bilateral and multilateral arrangements with other CMEA states, so that the next five-year plans (1976–1980) could be harmonized with a joint CMEA plan effective for the same period.[8]

By the time of the 27th Council session, however, CMEA spokesmen had acknowledged the existence of "difficulties and problems" in CMEA plan coordination. Chief among these was the problem of establishing joint production plans without simultaneously coordinating the domestic investment plans of CMEA countries. As Czechoslovak Prime Minister Lubomir Strougal put it, "Integration [requires] a far deeper economic linkage among the individual fraternal states. It has so far been ensured mostly through agreements on mutual supplies. Now it is necessary to attain a closer linkage among states in the fields of production, science, technology, and investment."[9] In other words, without a region-wide plan for economic investment and development, CMEA cooperation necessarily would be limited to a relatively small percentage of the total economic activity of the CMEA countries. Thus, as a Hungarian economist argued, "The basic and decisive task of plan coordination would consist [of] coordinating such investments as will determine structural change." He was quick to point out, however, that coordination of domestic investment plans had been strongly resisted by the Romanians (and perhaps others), who have "shown little inclination to subject the structural development of [their] industries to regional coordination."[10]

These difficulties notwithstanding, representatives at the 27th Council session, held in Prague from June 5 to June 8, 1973, moved ahead with efforts to coordinate national economic plans. Although the communiqué issued after the session hinted only vaguely at new measures toward plan coordination, it soon became apparent that an agreement had been reached for the preparation of a multilateral five-year integration plan for CMEA. Speaking in Minsk later in the year, Soviet Premier Aleksei Kosygin revealed: "The Soviet Union proposed to the 27th Comecon session . . . that measures for socialist economic integration should form part of the state plans of each country, on whose basis a multilateral five-year plan would be drawn up. . . . [All] the countries participating in the session adopted the proposal and are now working jointly on implementing the session's decisions."[11] Despite Romanian Premier Maurer's suggestion that these "interesting proposals . . . need to be examined in great detail," CMEA's newly created Committee for Cooperation in Planning had already begun work on a plan for multilateral integration by the time of its fifth session, held in Moscow on October 30 and 31, 1973.[12]

Clearly, the kind of plan coordination envisioned in the directives of the 27th CMEA session would be quite restricted in scope. Soviet spokesmen noted that joint planning would focus on a relatively few areas of production: gas and oil, power stations and transmission lines, ore and non-ore minerals, and metallurgical and chemical industries. "As experience is accumulated," it was argued elsewhere, joint planning will be extended to other areas as well, but it will not be until the "second stage of socialist economic integration"—to commence some time in the mid-1980s, ostensibly—that plan coordination "will be characterized by profound penetration of the national economies."[13]

In the meantime, difficulties continued to surface in the campaign to implement the first stage of economic integration, whose principal vehicle was to be the voluntary coordination of national economic plans. Articles in the East European press preceding the 28th Council session indicated that the chief source of these difficulties was the Romanian leadership, which had accepted in principle the aims embodied in the Comprehensive Program but continued to oppose specific measures considered incompatible with its defense of state sovereignty. "The new forms of co-operation in planning," wrote one Romanian analyst, must be "based on the idea that they do not affect the problems of internal planning."[14] Similarly, a leading Romanian economist rejected talk "about 'the socialist world economy' and about 'the world co-operative,' with a joint plan and suprastate bodies," noting that "socialist economic integration does not mean contradicting national sovereignty."[15]

Continuing disputes over the issue of joint planning may explain why Party leaders did not attend the 28th Council session, commemorating CMEA's twenty-fifth anniversary. In his opening remarks, CMEA Secretary General Fadeyev acknowledged "difficulties in the organization and development of co-operation," and Soviet Premier Kosygin added that "much work" remained to be done if coordination was to be achieved in time for the next planning period (1976–1980).[16] A major topic of concern at the meeting, of course, was the recent increase in Middle Eastern oil prices. The Soviet leaders, having forewarned their East European counterparts that they, too, would have to shoulder some of the burden of these increases and that future Soviet oil deliveries would fall short of initial forecasts, stressed the necessity of joint action in developing CMEA energy resources. Toward that end, representatives to the 28th CMEA session agreed to establish a new Council Committee on Material and Technical

Supply and approved plans for joint construction of the massive Orenburg gas pipeline and expansion of the *Mir* ("Peace") powergrid. With the incorporation of these measures into national economic forecasts, moreover, the communiqué on the 28th session could claim that "a number of countries" have "for the first time" included in their new national economic plans "specific sections for . . . socialist economic integration."[17]

Beyond these measures, the 28th session was notable chiefly for its lack of progress on fundamental economic issues, including standardization, labor mobility, price formation, and currency convertibility. The session did, however, approve a new CMEA charter, which replaces the original charter signed in 1959 and amended in 1962. This is not the place for a detailed assessment of these latest revisions, many of which simply codified measures already adopted under the Comprehensive Program, but it should be noted that the revised Article 1 listed "the development of socialist economic integration" among the aims of the organization. More to the point, although member countries were not specifically required to develop joint economic plans, CMEA was empowered, under the terms of the new Article 3, to promote joint economic cooperation by "co-ordinating national economic development plans."[18]

By the time of the 29th CMEA Council session, the economic context of CMEA negotiations had changed dramatically. With the general deterioration of the economic situation in Eastern Europe and the announcement that effective January 1, 1975, the price for Soviet oil deliveries would be drastically increased, joint planning in the area of energy resources had become a matter of necessity for most of the East Europeans. Thus, although no details were revealed, the April 1975 meeting of CMEA's Executive Committee announced that basic agreement had been reached on the "draft of a coordinated plan incorporating multilateral measures for the integration of the Comecon countries for the years 1976–80."[19]

Odd men out in this drive toward joint planning were the recalcitrant Romanians, who viewed centralizing tendencies in CMEA with growing concern. In a series of articles published just before the convening of the 29th Council session in June 1975, the Romanian leaders strongly condemned "various erroneous opinions," including "those about the so-called 'necessity' to set up 'a unified economic complex.' " In the Romanian view, economic integration must not be "prejudicial to national independence": "Thus, it is clear that it cannot involve planning methods and forms of suprastate organization; it cannot affect questions of internal planning, financing, and economic self-administration of production units in each country—an essential and inalienable prerogative of the national sovereignty of each Comecon member country."[20] These strictures had a familiar ring, of course, and were in fact almost identical to those raised by the Romanians in rejecting the 1962 "Basic Principles" plan for economic integration.[21] The Romanian attack in 1975, however, was levelled more specifically at proposals for joint planning, particularly those involving large multilateral ventures, recently expressed by "some economists" in "works published abroad."[22] Although the targets of this criticism were never identified, it is clear that the Romanians had in mind the Soviet leaders, who had been arguing for "the step-by-step shaping of large international complexes," and the Bulgarians, who had chimed in with their own proposals for "joint planning within the framework of [unified production-technical] complexes."[23] The Hungarians, Poles, Czechoslovaks, and East Germans, it should be noted, offered no statements of support for the Soviet-Bulgarian position, but neither did they echo Romania's strong condemnation.[24]

It was against this background that the 29th Council session convened in Budapest in June 1975. Although the communiqué issued after the meeting was typically unrevealing, it was clear from the outset that joint planning in CMEA would proceed on two related but distinct levels. On the multilateral, "macro-planning" level—clearly the more important of the two—"interested" countries were to enter into large-scale multilateral production ventures, chiefly in the area of energy resource development. On the bilateral, "micro-planning" level, CMEA members were urged to negotiate agreements for coordinating their national economic plans in specific spheres of foreign trade activity. Even taken together, of course, these measures fell far short of Khrushchev's early aim of molding "the socialist world economy into a single entity."[25]

Progress was particularly slow in the area of bilateral plan coordination. The official communiqué on the 29th Council session hinted vaguely at the desirability of the "further deepening and perfecting of co-operation" in this area, but there was no indication that such coordination would encompass domestic investment planning.[26] Rather, CMEA members began negotiations to coordinate foreign trade plans—which represent, of course, only a small percentage of their total economic activity—for the limited purposes of forecasting import/export quotas and stimulating bilateral trade in specific production areas. Toward those ends, foreign trade delegations exchanged visits throughout 1975, and by the end of that year several plan coordination protocols had been signed. From assessments of the protocol agreements signed to date, however, it appears that bilateral plan coordination in its current conception will neither generate greater trade activity nor significantly affect domestic economic planning.[27]

Of far greater potential importance was the so-called "Coordinated Plan for Multilateral Integration Measures for 1976–80," adopted at the 29th CMEA Session. Although the text of the plan was never published, assessments by various CMEA spokesmen, including N. K. Baibakov, chairman of the USSR State Planning Committee, provided some indication of its scope and intent.[28] It should be noted first that the Coordinated Plan was linked indirectly to the bilateral protocols discussed above and to CMEA's new "Complex Target-

Programs," which are long-term (ten- to fifteen-year) plans for developing multilateral collaboration in five general areas of production.[29]

The chief feature of the Coordinated Plan, however, was the section on joint projects. These included ten new ventures for the joint development of fuel and energy resources, including atomic energy, and other primary product sectors. Seven projects—five in the USSR, one in Cuba, and another in Mongolia—were already under negotiation by the time of the 29th session; and three others, all to be on Soviet territory, were outlined in the plan. As outlined, these ventures provided for joint production in electricity transmission, gas transport, iron and ferro-alloys, coking coal, nickel, asbestos, cellulose, isoprene rubber, and fodder yeasts.[30] Financing for these projects, to be borne jointly by the participating countries, was incorporated into the national five-year plans, under special sections on CMEA integration measures.

In economic terms, the significance of these projects was not overwhelming. Their total cost, said to be about 9 billion transferable rubles (TR's), was estimated to be only 1 to 2 percent of total CMEA investment expenditures for the period 1976–1980.[31] Politically, however, these measures were highly significant, for they established for the first time something approaching a "CMEA Plan"—albeit of limited scope—whereby national economic plans, including investment plans, were subordinated to efforts toward multilateral integration in CMEA. It was on these grounds, and not on the purely economic merits or demerits of the projects, that the Romanians and others in Eastern Europe resisted "Soviet-style" integration.

By the time of the 30th CMEA Council session, held in East Berlin from July 7 to 9, 1976, difficulties were already beginning to surface over the Coordinated Plan and its associated target programs and joint production ventures. While criticism of the new joint ventures centered largely on economic considerations— the "value aspect," as Czechoslovak Prime Minister Lubomir Strougal put it[32]—familiar political differences continued to plague efforts toward joint planning. Even as Bulgarian Prime Minister Stanko Todorov was hailing the Coordinated Plan as a "qualitatively new step in promoting integration and expanding the sphere of joint planning,"[33] Romania's Manea Manescu was lecturing the Council on "the constantly increasing importance of state plans in the socioeconomic development of each country." Warming to his topic, and indirectly rejecting the premise of CMEA-wide planning, Manescu went on to laud the state plan as "an expression of national will, . . . a uniform and indivisible entity."[34] The communiqué issued at the end of the session implicitly acknowledged these differences, referring only vaguely to the desirability of expanded joint planning.[35]

Similar lack of progress was evident in the session's discussion of CMEA's long-term target programs, heralded by Soviet and Bulgarian spokesmen as a step in the direction of CMEA-wide supranational planning but curbed in practice by the "interested party" principle, which preserved the right of individual CMEA members to opt out of specific joint undertakings. The voluntary nature of the joint projects was stressed by several speakers, and Romanian Prime Minister Manescu underscored his country's determination to exercise its right of abstention by absenting himself from the session's ceremony inaugurating the CMEA International Management Institute. These difficulties notwithstanding, the communiqué noted that the Council had instructed the Committee on Cooperation in Planning to draw up a draft of "long-term, specific cooperation programs" for presentation to the next (31st) CMEA Council session. The Planning Committee was further enjoined to look into "the style and methods of operation of Comecon organs," a vague mandate which prompted the Romanian prime minister to warn that "any measures taken in this area will have to be based on full respect for the fundamental principles of relations among our states," by which he presumably meant the guarantees of "interestedness" and voluntary participation.[36]

Progress was so scant over the following year that the 31st Council session, meeting in Warsaw from June 21 to 23, 1977, decided to defer action on both these issues for another year.[37] In reviewing the problems of drafting the target programs, Czechoslovakia's Strougal admitted, "Work on long-term programs has been lagging, partly because people tend to push aside the difficult and demanding questions and deal with new matters where the necessary experience is only now being acquired."[38] Mindful of these delays, and giving clear priority to the growingly critical energy and consumer sectors, the Council decided to abandon temporarily the last two target programs and concentrate on the first three: fuel, energy, and raw materials; foods and consumer durables; and machinery and equipment, particularly those products related to the first two target programs. Problems were also evident in the related area of bilateral (five-year) plan coordination, as Manescu suggested that Romania's domestic planning was being hampered by persistent delays in finalizing joint cooperative ventures.[39] On the question of organizational and procedural changes raised at the 30th session in 1976, lingering but still unspecified differences were suggested by the fact that the 31st session returned the matter to the Executive Committee for further consideration.[40]

The nature of this procedural dispute was revealed on the eve of the 32nd Council session by the Romanian leadership via the Yugoslav news agency Tanjug. Citing "well informed sources" in Bucharest, Tanjug reported the proposed statute changes specified that "any decisions adopted by majority vote would be binding upon all, including those countries that voted against the decisions."[41] Although the proposal presumably would not have affected the voting procedures of major CMEA bodies (Council, Executive Committee, Council committees, and others) whose statutes fall under the CMEA Charter (and hence could be changed only by unanimous consent), it clearly engendered Romanian fears of tyranny of a Soviet-led majority in some of CMEA's joint ventures and affiliated international organizations.[42] The Romanians further feared, according to the Tanjug report, that expansion of CMEA's collective power over individual members might be used to consign Romania to the status of "producer of semi-finished goods and raw materials" (as Khrushchev had sought to do in the early 1960s) and delimit Romania's economic and political independence. To erase any doubts on this latter score, the Romanian Party organ *Scinteia* put the case plainly on the eve of the 32nd Council session: "The full realization of national sovereignty is incompatible with any form of supranational management, with any type of supranational organism."[43]

In the event, the proposed changes came to nothing, and Comecon Secretary General Nikolai Fadeyev sought to rise above the unseemly bickering by remonstrating, "I do not know who thought that up and started all the fuss, and I ask myself whose purposes such an invention serves."[44] This issue behind them, delegates to the 32nd Council session (held in Bucharest on June 27–29, 1978) concentrated on reviewing and approving draft plans for the first three target programs. Intended to chart the course for joint planning and joint action over the period 1981–1990, the draft programs clearly amounted to little beyond general statements of common purpose, and Soviet Premier Aleksei Kosygin warned that it would be necessary to move quickly toward specific agreements if the target programs were to be completed by 1980.[45] Little was revealed of the programs themselves, but the attention given to the first—fuel, energy, and raw materials—made it clear that soaring energy costs and diminishing supplies were the predominant concerns of the CMEA states.

Indeed, the immediacy of the energy dilemma facing Eastern Europe had rendered increasingly irrelevant the grandiose efforts toward long-term, multilateral planning in CMEA. As Poland's Premier Jaroszewicz noted during the meeting, the elaboration of the CMEA target programs, however useful they might prove in the long run, would not help Poland meet its short-term energy needs or solve its immediate economic problems.[46] Unstated but clearly implied in Jaroszewicz's remarks was the conviction that CMEA's target programs, Coordinated Plan, and other integration measures were no solution to the acute difficulties confronting the East European economies in the late 1970s: declining growth rates, soaring energy costs, mounting indebtedness, and steadily deteriorating terms of trade.

For all these reasons, as well as the announcement of yet another OPEC oil price increase, Comecon's thirtieth anniversary, commemorated briefly at the 33rd Council session in Moscow from June 26 to June 28, 1979, was not a particularly festive occasion. Neither Soviet Premier Kosygin nor planning chief Baibakov (also chairman of the CMEA Council Committee on Cooperation in Planning) held out any prospect of increased Soviet oil deliveries, and the presentation of the 1981–1985 economic plans revealed sharply scaled-down growth targets throughout the region, particularly in Poland, Hungary, Czechoslovakia, and East Germany. Otherwise, the session approved unanimously— i.e., with Romanian consent—"certain changes" to the Comecon Charter[47] and unveiled the final two target programs (on consumer goods production and transportation). Dissatisfaction was registered once again, however, over delays in implementing the long-term projects associated with the target programs and in coordinating the five-year national economic plans.[48]

The full extent of these delays became evident at the next CMEA Council session (the 34th, held in Prague on June 17–18, 1980), when it was admitted that the 1981–1985 Coordinated Plan was still not complete and would have to be deferred until the next Council session, scheduled for the summer of 1981, six months into the planning period which the agreement was supposed to cover.[49] Thus, the call at the 34th session for "speedy completion of work on the coordination of plans" betrayed a note of exasperation, as did the sharply critical remarks of Czechoslovakia's Strougal and Romanian Premier Ilie Verdet on the nature and pace of CMEA joint planning.[50] Verdet was particularly blunt, reiterating the Romanian complaint that delays in concluding the Coordinated Plan caused domestic planning bottlenecks and decrying CMEA's failure to meet the energy needs of its member countries. He ended his speech with a dramatic call for the speedy convocation of a CMEA summit meeting at "the highest possible level of party and state dignitaries led by first secretaries" to discuss problems of plan coordination and "the deepening of cooperation" among CMEA countries, particularly in the area of fuels, energy sources, and raw materials.[51]

This surprising Romanian *volte face* on the desirability of CMEA cooperation, though hardly an acquiescence to Soviet-style integration, reflected the urgency of the economic dilemmas facing East European leaders and their growing disenchantment with CMEA economic strategies. Comecon, it seemed, had arrived at an impasse. Joint planning, the hallmark of the 1971 Comprehensive Program, had shown itself largely irrelevant to the economic challenges of the day, and the East Europeans were becoming increasingly restive over its failures and those of the highly touted multilateral ventures inaugurated in the 1970s.

Multilateralism in CMEA: Incipient Supranationalism?

"Multilateralism" in CMEA, it should be reiterated, is better understood as "multiple bilateralism," in which an increasingly complex multilateral infrastructure has been developed to facilitate what remain primarily bilateral trade relations in the region. Multilateralism in CMEA, thus understood, covers a broad array of joint endeavors, ranging from the standing commissions and Council committees, endowed only with recommendatory and advisory functions, to the more substantive bodies, such as the international banks, joint construction projects, and the many interstate and international economic organizations. Most of these generated little opposition in Eastern Europe, for the economic imperatives of closer CMEA cooperation had become increasingly clear. If there were economic advantages to be had, even the Romanians did not object to multilateralism *per se*; and the other East European leaders generally were willing parties to new cooperative ventures, so long as those ventures did not impinge on matters of internal planning and CMEA's procedural rules ensured decisionmaking by consent.

Institutional Issues

Conflicts surrounding the new forms of multilateral cooperation in CMEA focused on East European fears of increased Soviet domination through a tighter, even a supranational, CMEA infrastructure. Specifically, tendencies toward supranationalism *cum* Soviet domination were manifested in three areas: elaboration of new, less restrictive procedural rules, particularly those governing the powerful Council committees; expansion of the power of the new international economic organizations; and creation of what the Romanians have called "megastructures," in the form of new international production complexes.

Disputes in CMEA over the implementation of the new principles of "voluntarism" and "interestedness" already have been discussed in some detail.[52] Initially applied only to newly established CMEA bodies, such as the International Investment Bank and the many interstate economic organizations, the "interested party" principle was extended in 1974 to the CMEA standing commissions as well.[53] Further motivated by CMEA's efforts to establish relations with the Common Market and the attendant need to coordinate economic policies in CMEA,[54] representatives to the 28th CMEA Council session agreed to extend the "interestedness" principle to the creation of new standing commissions and to recommendations issued by those already in existence. For the East Europeans, of course, this meant that while they could not be compelled to participate in new standing commissions or joint projects, neither could they prevent the establishment of new multilateral ventures in spheres where they might have preferred to maintain bilateralism in CMEA trade.

Of far greater significance were the new CMEA Council committees, which were accorded much broader authority than the standing commissions. Although their primary functions are recommendatory and advisory, they also are empowered to submit proposals for consideration by sessions of the CMEA

Council, establish various "working groups," and solicit material and information from subsidiary organizations.[55] (See Fig. 6.1.) The most important of these is the Committee for Cooperation in Planning, which Soviet spokesmen acclaimed as the "real headquarters of planned socialist integration."[56] Composed of the chairmen of the powerful central planning committees of CMEA countries and empowered to "influence" the work of other CMEA organs, the committee is charged with "forecasting, joint planning, the co-ordination of five-year plans and plans for the long-term perspective" and specialized planning in "individual industries and types of production."[57] Similarly broad powers were accorded the Committee on Scientific and Technical Cooperation, under whose aegis has been established a vast network of research institutes, laboratories, and coordinating centers. At the 28th CMEA Council session, as has been seen, Soviet and East European leaders further agreed to create a Committee on Cooperation in Material and Technical Supply, whose chief purpose has been to facilitate high-level cooperation in the development and utilization of CMEA energy resources.[58]

For the Romanians and others, such centralizing tendencies presented clear difficulties. While Romanian spokesmen emphasized that their country is "eager to attract the resources of [other CMEA] states" and that "Romanian planning bodies and economic organizations are actively participating" in joint planning endeavors, they were quick to warn that such cooperation must not take the form of "one single set of guidelines, one over-all policy for all Comecon members."[59] Thus, the lowest common denominator in CMEA activities, including the Council committees, has been strict observance of the "interested party" principle, which preserves for each member the right to opt out of any new venture.

Another Romanian concern was the proliferation of new interstate and international economic organizations. Interstate economic organizations have been in existence since 1956, but—as is illustrated in Table 6.2.—their number more than doubled in the 1970s. According to the Comprehensive Program, the main function of these organizations is "to co-ordinate the actions of participating countries [in] definite fields of the economy" through joint research and planning, standardization, specialization, coordination of national production plans, and the like. Although various lower-level economic bodies are allowed to participate, the organizations themselves operate primarily at the intergovernmental level. Their activities are governed by the "interested party" principle; but the "unanimity" provision is required only for "key questions," as defined at the time of the organization's creation, while decisionmaking procedures on other issues are to be determined by the participating countries.[60]

These organizations are understandably confused with the international economic organizations, which, as one Soviet spokesman tried to explain, "perform roughly the same functions as interstate organizations."[61] The chief

Figure 6.1
Organization of the CMEA Council Committees

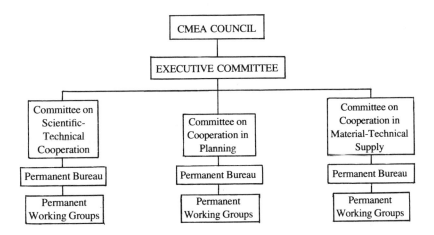

Attached to each Council Committee is a group of subordinate or affiliate organizations. E.g.:

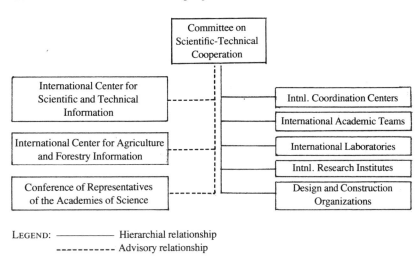

LEGEND: —————— Hierarchial relationship
- - - - - - - - - - Advisory relationship

SOURCES: *The Multilateral Economic Cooperation of Socialist States* (Moscow: Progress Publishers, 1977); *Grunddokumente des RGW* (Berlin: Staatsverlag der DDR, 1978); Harry Trend, "Comecon's Organizational Structure," RAD Background Report/114 (Eastern Europe), *Radio Free Europe Research*, July 3, 1975.

Table 6.2
CMEA's Multilateral Economic Organizations

Organization	Functional area	Year created
Interstate economic organizations		
Org. for Railroad Coop.	rail equip. and operations	1956
Central Dispatching Admin.	control of Mir power grid	1962
Joint Freight Car Pool	dispatching of freight cars	1963
Agromash	agricultural machinery	1964
Intermetal	rolled steel products	1964
Interpodszypnik	roller bearing industries	1964
Medunion	medical equip. and facilities	1967
Interkosmos	research on use of space	1967
Interkhim	chemical industries	1969
Intergormash	mining equipment	1971
Intersputnik	space communication systems	1971
Interkabel	international communications	1972
Interelektro	electrical equipment	1973
Joint Container Pool	air, sea, and rail transport	1974
Intertransplant	experimental medicine	1980
Intermorgeo	sea geology	?
International economic organizations		
Interetalonpribor	precision measuring devices	1972
Interatominstrument	equipment for nuclear reactors	1972
Interatomenergo	nuclear power plants	1973
Interelektrotest	high voltage laboratories	1973
Interkhimvolokno	artificial fibers	1974
Intertekstilmash	textile machinery	1974
Interenergoremont	electrical assembly, repair	1974
Interkhimmash	machinery for chemical ind.	1974
Intervodoochistka	water decontamination	1977
Internefteprodukt	petroleum products	1978

Sources: Harry Trend, "Comecon's Organizational Structure," RAD Background Report/114 (Eastern Europe), *Radio Free Europe Research,* July 3, 1975; *The Multilateral Economic Cooperation of Socialist States* (Moscow: Progress Publishers, 1977); *Grunddokumente des RGW* (Berlin: Staatsverlag der DDR, 1978), pp. 321–41.

Notes: Participants include all European members of CMEA except in the following: Intermetal, Interatominstrument, Internefteprodukt (Romania not a member); Medunion (Bulgaria and Romania not members); and Agromash (founded by Bulgaria and Hungary, later joined by the USSR, the GDR, and Poland).

Some sources list Interetalonpribor as an interstate economic organization.

distinctions between the two concern what powers they are accorded and at what level they exercise those powers. In contrast to the interstate organizations, the international economic organizations have been created to facilitate "direct links" among lower-level economic units—"enterprises, trusts, associations, . . . research institutes, design offices, etc."—across national boundaries. They, too, are governed by the unanimity requirement for key questions, but in their procedural rules the principle of "voluntarism" has been dropped in favor of the less stringent provision that they "shall in no way infringe upon the interests of individual CMEA member-countries."[62] They are, moreover, intended to be production-oriented "amalgamations," rather than simply coordinating centers, designed to promote the "internationalization of production" in CMEA.[63]

Information on the international economic organizations is sparse and conflicting, even as to the number currently in operation,[64] but Table 6.2 presents a list of those established in the 1970s. Headquartered in various member-countries and directed by a national of the host country, the organizations apparently operate on a semi-autonomous basis to promote joint research, design, production, and distribution of their specialized product lines.[65]

Although we know little of the operations of the international economic organizations, it is clear that they have come under fire from several of the East European participants. The Romanians, as usual, were quick to criticize anything that smacked of supranationalism in CMEA. Writing in 1974, for example, a Romanian economist contrasted "three political conceptions of economic integration": "*(a) interstate economic integration,*" which implies economic integration through "organizations whose statutes are limited to the functions and powers unanimously conferred" and whose decisions are "entirely subordinate" to the governments concerned; "*(b) superstate economic integration,*" which involves the creation of "representative bodies" governed by "the majority will" and operating independently of the national governments; and "*(c) transstate economic integration,*" in which "international economic organizations of the type of multinational corporations are set up, whose decisions are not subordinate to the governments." Not surprisingly, the writer rejected the last two conceptions: "By its very nature, socialist economic integration can only be of the *interstate* type. . . . Socialist economic integration, as a form of economic cooperation, involves mutual economic links among the states; it is based on the development of national economies as independent entities."[66]

Hungarian criticism of the new forms of cooperation in CMEA has been quite different. Far from rejecting the notion of "transstate" corporations, the Hungarians sought to improve the mechanisms for "direct links" among enterprises by urging a move toward full convertibility and greater use of "market mechanisms." "As is the case with Comecon's other international associations," one Hungarian journal noted, "Interatomenergo has failed to solve certain problems of financial accounting,'' by which was meant the inadequacy of pricing policies and the lack of a convertible currency. Consequently, the article concluded, the organization has not been able to fulfill its intended functions and will require another five years to develop an adequate "framework for co-operation."[67]

Elsewhere in Eastern Europe, the Poles had become, along with the Hungarians, the chief advocates of collective currency and "commodity-market" relations, and the Czechoslovaks and East Germans had offered similar proposals for overcoming the "comparative isolation of the national markets."[68] These differences reflected the continuing division in CMEA between the more advanced East European countries, who were pushing for decentralization and the "freeing of domestic markets," and the Soviet Union and Bulgaria, who continued to emphasize plan coordination and increased centralization. For their part, the Romanians sided more with the first group than the second but continued to resist any form of "penetration" of the national economy.

Indeed, the section of the Comprehensive Program on "direct links" had been included only on the urging of the more advanced East European states, who then proceeded to take advantage of improved opportunities for direct cooperation at the enterprise level. Between 1971 and 1973, the East Europeans were particularly active in establishing joint production ventures, such as the Polish–East German cotton mill at Zawiercie, established in 1972 under joint management. This was just one of a growing number of bilateral and trilateral production ventures undertaken in such diverse fields as electric motors, footwear, textiles, construction materials, and factory machinery.[69] (See Table 6.3.) Although the exact number of such agreements is not known, in 1975 the East German journal *Einheit* listed thirteen bilateral production organizations, nine of which included the GDR.[70]

Interestingly, to take advantage of this new form of bilateral cooperation, the Soviet leaders moved in 1973 to create new middle-level production associations, which conformed roughly to the "trusts" already in existence in East Germany and Poland.[71] Commenting on this innovation just before the establishment of the Soviet–East German amalgamation Assofoto, SED Party leader Erich Honecker noted, "Thanks to the resolution of the Central Committee of the C.P.S.U. we have, in the production associations and industrial associations of the Soviet Union, new partners for our V.V.B.'s and our Kombinats for the development of cooperation in science and production."[72]

Now this was surely a case of the tail wagging the dog, and the Soviet leaders cannot have been wholly satisfied with the drift toward bilateral "direct links" in CMEA economic relations, for it implied an eventual loosening of CMEA-wide planning and ran counter to Soviet efforts to promote integration through a tighter CMEA infrastructure susceptible to Soviet control. It was at this juncture, therefore, that the Soviet leaders began to accelerate the drive toward coordination of national economic plans through the CMEA Committee for

Cooperation in Planning and discuss the possibilities of multilateral plan coordination. Thus, by 1974, the pendulum had swung once again from the "market" to the "plan" conception of CMEA integration and, in the words of one Western analyst, toward the pattern of integration "most conducive to increasing Soviet economic and political hegemony in Comecon."[73] This reorientation was facilitated, of course, by the confluence of a number of external economic pressures facing Eastern Europe, most notably those arising from the dramatic increase in world oil prices.

Economic Issues

It is no small irony that Soviet efforts to restore "plan" discipline in CMEA were undertaken in conjunction with a "market" measure of the first order—the 1975 decision to tie prices for Soviet oil deliveries to Eastern Europe to prevailing world market prices according to a five-year moving average, recalculated annually. To further offset the "opportunity cost" of Soviet oil deliver-

Table 6.3
Joint Enterprises in CMEA

Enterprise[a]	Functional area	Participants (site italicized)	Year created
Wismut[b]	uranium production	*GDR*, USSR	1954
Haldex	coal products	*Poland*, Hungary	1959
Intransmash	mechanical handling equipment	*Bulgaria*, Hungary	1964
Friendship Mill	cotton yarns	*Poland*, GDR	1972
Mongolsovzwetmet	nonferrous metal ores	*Mongolia*, USSR	1973
Erdenet	copper and molybdenum ores	*Mongolia*, USSR	1973
Petrobaltic	oil/gas exploration and drilling	*Poland*, USSR, GDR	1975
Interprogramma	computer programming	*Bulgaria*, USSR	1976
Interlighter	river/sea transport	*Hungary*, Czech., Bulgaria, USSR	1978

SOURCES: Various; compiled by the author. For a partial list, see *Grunddokumente des RGW* (Berlin: Staatsverlag der DDR, 1978).

[a] This list is generally confined to joint *production* enterprises, excluding such purely service enterprises as Baltamerika (chartering), Dunarea (marketing), and Intermorput (dredging and rescue). Interlighter, though primarily a service enterprise, apparently has production branches as well; Petrobaltic and Interprogramma occupy the vague middle ground between production and service.

[b] Wismut, founded in 1946 as one of the notorious "joint stock companies" for war reparations, was converted in 1954 to a joint enterprise and is apparently the last of the original joint stock companies still operating in Eastern Europe.

ies to Eastern Europe, as has been seen, the Soviet leaders served notice that the East Europeans would be expected to contribute capital and labor through joint investment projects for the development and transport of Soviet energy resources.

Unlike the spontaneous, ad hoc, and largely bilateral "joint enterprises" described above, the joint investment projects unveiled at the 29th CMEA Council session in 1975 were linked to the long-term target programs, as well as to the broader "Coordinated Plan for Multilateral Integration Measures, 1976–80," and bore the heavy imprint of Soviet authorship.[74] Of the projects an-

Table 6.4
Joint Investment Projects in CMEA

Location		Project[a]	Agreement signed	Project operational	Participants[b]
USSR	(Ust Ilimsk)	cellulose mill	1972	1980	All but Czechoslovakia
USSR	(Kiembaev)	asbestos combine	1973	1980	All
USSR	(Orenburg)	natural gas pipeline	1974	1980	All; limited role for Romania
USSR	(Kursk Magnetic Anomaly)	iron ore mining and dressing	1974	1977–80	All but Romania
USSR	(Vinnitsa-Albertirsa)	electric power transmission line	1974	1978	All but Romania
USSR	(various)	ferroalloys production	1974	1979–80	All
Cuba	(Las Camariocas)	nickel and cobalt production	1975	?	All
USSR	(Khmelnitsky)	nuclear power station and power line	1979	(1984)	All
USSR	(Konstantinovka)	nuclear power station and power line	1980	(by 1990)	Romania, Bulgaria, USSR; other participation not yet clear

SOURCES: John Hannigan and Carl McMillan, "Joint Investment Projects in Resource Development: Sectoral Approaches to Socialist Integration," in U.S. Congress, Joint Economic Committee, *East European Economic Assessment,* Part II, pp. 259–95 (Washington, D.C.: Government Printing Office, 1981); Arthur J. Smith, "The Council for Mutual Economic Assistance in 1977," in U.S. Congress, Joint Economic Committee, *East European Economies Post-Helsinki* (Washington, D.C.: Government Printing Office, 1977), pp. 152–73; Cam Hudson, "CMEA Joint Investments in Soviet Nuclear Power Stations," RAD Background Report/11 (Eastern Europe), *Radio Free Europe Research,* January 20, 1981.

[a] Excludes strictly bilateral investment projects such as the Adria pipeline and a number of bilateral hydroelectric projects. Three additional multilateral projects, on which few details are available, have been reported for the production of coking ore (in Mongolia), fodder yeasts (USSR), and isoprene rubber (USSR).

[b] Except where noted to the contrary, participants include all European members of CMEA.

nounced to date, not one is situated in Eastern Europe, and all are subject to Soviet control over conception, planning, production, and distribution.[75]

Table 6.4 lists the known joint investment projects among the CMEA countries. Typically, these projects involve participation by most or all of the East European countries in the development of energy-related production or transport facilities in the Soviet Union. The East Europeans contribute investment funds, equipment, materials and/or labor and in return receive guaranteed supplies of the products of the enterprise. They do not, however, become co-owners of the enterprise itself.

The most highly publicized of these ventures is the Orenburg natural gas project, which involved the joint development of a huge natural gas field near Orenburg, in the southern Urals, and construction of a 1,733-mile pipeline from Orenburg to the Soviet-Czechoslovak border near Uzhgorod, where it connects with the Friendship Pipeline, constructed in 1967, and other links in the system. Although all European members of CMEA contributed labor and capital to the project, Romania's participation was limited to the building of a gas-processing plant. To oversee the project, each country created its own coordinating center, subordinate to an "intergovernmental commission" chaired by Soviet Deputy Premier Mikhail Lesechko.[76]

Like the other multilateral ventures, the Orenburg project is a quasi-supranational enterprise, whose tasks include the management of new economic and legal forms of property, now referred to by Soviet spokesmen as "international socialist property."[77] The term is misleading in the extreme, however, for only the products of the enterprise are in any sense "international"; all plants and facilities built through these joint efforts become the exclusive state property of the host country—viz., the Soviet Union. Thus, the projects are jointly built and financed, but control over their operations has been delegated to CMEA's new "multinational corporations" (in the form of the intergovernmental commissions), whose most influential "share-holder" is the Soviet Union, and the productive capital they generate devolves to the exclusive benefit of the USSR.

Not surprisingly, the Romanians reserved their most shrill condemnation for these new "megastructures" and the related "theses about 'the internationalization of the process of socialist production and the establishment of a single international production process.' "[78] Romanian spokesmen further argued that by erroneously identifying increased economic interdependence with the need for "regional economic integration," the (unspecified) authors of such "theses" were guilty of "subjectivism" and "infringing upon the basic principles governing socialist intrastate relations."[79] Yet, Romanian policy toward these new multilateral projects followed a familiar pattern: an initial refusal to participate, accompanied by an unremitting press campaign decrying attempts to interfere in Romania's internal affairs, but—once the economic costs of nonparticipation had been weighed—a belated decision to join, usually on a limited basis.[80]

Once again, criticism from the other East European states was somewhat different. A Hungarian economist, for example, alluding to "numerous un-solved problems" in the joint enterprises, repeated the familiar Hungarian demand for "more active commodity and money relations." The main thrust of this critique, however, was that participants in the joint ventures were required to supply labor and capital for the expansion of productive capacity in the host country but were denied any share of the "profits" from the facilities they helped construct, since those facilities became the exclusive property of the host country. Thus, unlike domestic investments, which yield both goods and cap-ital, investments in the joint enterprises yield only goods, in the form of raw materials delivered in repayment to the investing countries. "In principle" (but presumably not in practice), the writer concluded, "a joint enterprise ensures both the supply of the necessary products and the provision of income."[81]

Expressing similar reservations about the "value aspect . . . of the joint projects" and "the relation of the expected expenditure to the anticipated effect of the joint undertaking," Czechoslovak Prime Minister Lubomir Strougal argued, "We think the contribution of interested states to individual integration projects need not always take the form of immediate participation through loans or sharing in a given project. In our view the advantages stemming from integration projects can also be enjoyed in other ways." These other ways, he continued, would involve domestic investments by the East Europeans for the production of goods and materials to be used in the joint enterprises. As an alternative to the existing system of joint investments, which clearly favored the raw material supplier, Strougal proposed the "principle of equivalence," whereby goods supplied by the East European participants would be considered "equivalent to supplies of fuel, energy, and raw and other materials."[82]

These reservations by the East Europeans, as well as various problems of labor mobility and organization, have had very practical consequences, partic-ularly in the case of the Orenburg project. Originally, responsibility for con-struction of the five sections of the Orenburg-Uzhgorod pipeline was assigned to the five East European participants: Poland, Czechoslovakia, Hungary, the GDR, and Bulgaria. In May of 1975, however, the Hungarians transferred responsibility for their assigned pipeline section to the Soviet Union and offered compensation in the form of increased commodity shipments and a pledge to build four compressor stations. By the end of that year, the Bulgarian and Czechoslovak governments also had reneged on their pipeline assignments, and the East Germans had turned over half of their stretch to Soviet builders. Only the Poles—and they only after considerable delay owing to an early switch of their assigned pipeline segment—ultimately fulfilled their construction agree-ment, leaving the Soviet Union, initially assigned no construction tasks at all, to assume responsibility for building more than two-thirds of the pipeline.[83]

Given the considerable difficulties in bringing the Orenburg project to a belated conclusion and the growing chorus of East European voices questioning the economic merits of such joint undertakings, it is not surprising that the Soviet Union began in the late 1970s to reconsider the viability of joint investment projects. After the flurry of agreements at mid-decade (see Table 6.4), only two new projects were undertaken in the last half of the 1970s, both involving joint investment in Soviet nuclear energy development.[84] The first, a nuclear power station in Khmelnitsky, involves East European contributions of investment capital, equipment, and materials (but almost no labor) in return for guaranteed deliveries of electricity at fixed prices for a period of twenty years. Mindful of the Orenburg experience, the participants agreed that the transmission lines carrying electricity from the USSR to Eastern Europe will be constructed according to the format of the Druzhba (Friendship) oil pipeline: the Soviet Union will have construction responsibility for the segment of the power line in the USSR, while Poland, Czechoslovakia, and Hungary will build only the East European segments of the line.[85] Although little is known about the second nuclear power project, to be located in Konstantinovka, Ukrainian SSR, it appears that similar arrangements will be made for construction of the station and installation of the Soviet-Romanian-Bulgarian transmission line.

In addition to scaling down the number and scope of joint investment projects, CMEA has been seeking other ways of developing Soviet–East European collaboration in the energy sector. One such approach is embodied in the "General Agreements on Multilateral Investment Cooperation" adopted at the January 1979 meeting of the CMEA Executive Committee.[86] By providing for coordination of investments in key sectors of the individual economies, these agreements are designed to upgrade export commodities with which the East European countries can compensate the Soviet Union for future deliveries of energy and raw materials. The agreements are multilateral only in a very limited sense, of course, and represent a significant retreat from the grandiose joint investment projects heralded in the mid-1970s.

Thus, by decade's end the elaborate multilateral framework established in CMEA had largely failed to yield practical results. On the surface, substantial progress had been made in fleshing out the bare bones of the 1971 Comprehensive Program: new procedural rules had been implemented which minimized the potential for Romanian divisiveness, powerful Council committees had been created, and new international economic organizations had been established and invested with powers which began to encroach on matters of domestic economic planning. Finally, at Soviet urging, new joint production complexes, supervised by intergovernmental commissions with quasi-supranational authority, had begun operations. All these measures, moveover, were incorporated into the so-called Coordinated Plan, whose objectives included the gradual transfer of planning prerogatives from national authorities to central planning organs in CMEA.

For its part, the Soviet Union had begun to make greater use of its considerable economic power, particularly its near-monopoly on CMEA energy resources, to compel a reorientation of Soviet–East European economic relations. The essential features of the Soviet "integration program," opposed in one way or another by all the East European countries save Bulgaria, seem to have been these: to utilize East European products, labor, and capital to develop the productive capacity of Soviet energy-related enterprises, and in so doing to ensure the eastward diversion of CMEA trade; to expand Soviet influence through a tighter CMEA infrastructure; to link more and more elements of East European economic planning to CMEA's bilateral and multilateral planning arrangements; and to incorporate joint production ventures into a constantly expanding Coordinated Plan.

For all this, the actual conduct of Soviet–East European economic relations remained essentially unaltered: only about 5 percent of total intra-CMEA trade actually was settled on a multilateral basis, and even the halting efforts toward genuine multilateralism, most notably through joint investment projects, were scaled down considerably in the face of growing doubts in Eastern Europe as to their economic viability. Familiar political and conceptual disputes doubtless accounted for much of the failure of Soviet-led integrationist efforts in the 1970s; more important still were the increasingly acute economic difficulties facing all the East European countries in the late 1970s and the manifest inability of CMEA integration schemes to address the real economic dilemmas of the day.

The East European Economies between East and West

Underlying the development of CMEA economic relations in the 1970s were two fundamental and interrelated sets of factors: the rapid expansion of East-West trade and the radical alteration of CMEA terms of trade occasioned by soaring world energy prices. At the beginning of the 1970s the attraction of Western goods, technology, and credits exerted a powerful westward pull on East European regimes anxious to usher in a new era of prosperity and stability in Eastern Europe. In the wake of the 1973–74 oil price increases by the OPEC cartel, however, the East European economies began to experience a countervailing eastward pull, as trade was diverted toward the East to compensate for Soviet oil deliveries at their newly inflated prices.

The energy crisis of 1973–74, in turn, generated a series of unforeseen developments—double-digit inflation in most of the advanced industrial democracies, growing balance of payments problems in the West, and constriction of Western markets for East European exports—all of which severely exacerbated the chronically poor East European terms of trade with the West. Thus, by the late 1970s the East European states found themselves in a double economic bind, trying to salvage rapidly deteriorating trade relations with the West while coping with an equally severe economic reversal in the East.

It would be an error to see the January 1975 Soviet oil price rises as a political decision designed to increase East European economic dependence on the USSR, though such was their initial effect. Soviet oil deliveries to Eastern Europe, for years priced well below prevailing world market prices, by 1974 had begun to levy an unacceptable economic burden on the USSR.[87] Not only had price increases by the OPEC oil cartel radically raised the "opportunity cost" of cut-rate Soviet oil deliveries to CMEA countries,[88] but the requirement of supplying a huge volume of oil to Eastern Europe conflicted with Soviet foreign trade objectives, which involved the exchange of Soviet oil and other energy sources for Western goods and technology. The East Europeans, beset with foreign trade and domestic problems of their own, could do little more than appeal to Soviet interests in preserving economic and political stability in the region. With these considerations in mind, the Soviet leaders moved in late 1974 toward a compromise solution to renegotiate the price of oil supplied to Eastern Europe.[89]

Under the old system (the "Bucharest formula"), Soviet oil sent to the CMEA countries for the period 1971–1975 was set at a fixed rate, based on average world market prices for the preceding five-year period (1966–1970). According to the "rolling average" price system adopted by CMEA's Executive Committee in 1974 to be introduced in January 1975, however, the price for oil and other commodities is revised annually to conform to the world average for the five years immediately preceding. Although the new formula (the "revised Bucharest formula") left CMEA prices substantially below world market levels, the impact on the East European countries was profound: while the prices for (primarily East European) manufactured goods were raised by about a third, prices for (mainly Soviet) raw materials were increased by about 130 percent.[90] To make matters even worse, 1975 prices were to be recalculated according to 1972–1974 world averages, presumably to capture the peak rates in world oil prices, and the East Europeans were put on notice that goods supplied in repayment "must be of the first quality and . . . a proportion of them must consist of products made from import materials or under foreign license."[91]

The impact of these changes on Eastern Europe, dependent on Soviet sources for 80 percent of its oil supply, was tremendous. Hardest hit were Hungary, Czechoslovakia, the GDR, and Bulgaria, which depended on the Soviet Union for roughly 90 percent of their oil.[92] For Romania and Poland, themselves net exporters of raw materials, the burden was less severe, but they too experienced some adverse effects in their balance of payments. (See Table 6.5.)

The impact of the price rises was admitted most swiftly in Hungary, where spokesmen for the Kádár regime spoke candidly of economic reversals on the horizon. Reacting to the revised pricing system, Hungarian Foreign Minister

József Bíró put on a brave front, terming it "a very rational and equitable solution for the price problem which prevents both the acquisition of unjustified gains and the exploitation of those pressed by straitened circumstances," but he acknowledged that these new circumstances would require the charting of a difficult course for the future:

> We must clearly recognize that the situation in the capitalist market, the price changes and their interrelations will continue to affect the ruble-designated market. We must therefore reckon on a further worsening of the terms of trade in exchanges for goods among the socialist countries. Hungary will have to offset the resulting burdens, mainly by increasing exports.[93]

The cumulative effect of these difficulties, as has been seen, led to a partial retrenchment in the Hungarian New Economic Mechanism in 1974 and 1975 and to the resignation of one of its chief exponents, Prime Minister Jenő Fock.[94] Overcoming these economic problems, Party leader János Kádár has acknowledged, will require "much better utilization than previously of the great opportunities inherent in the economic cooperation of the socialist countries."[95]

Hungary, of course, was far from alone in feeling the pressure of soaring energy costs: the altered pricing system forced all the East European states except Poland and Romania to increase their exports to the USSR by about 10

Table 6.5

Effects of the 1975 Price Changes on CMEA Terms of Trade, 1975
(1974 = 100)

	Soviet export prices		Soviet import prices		Terms of Trade Index	
	1974 weights	1975 weights	1974 weights	1975 weights	1974 weights	1975 weights
Bulgaria	139	156	130	137	107	112
Czechoslovakia	142	144	123	121	115	119
East Germany	147	154	121	125	121	125
Hungary	140	150	127	129	110	116
Poland	141	151	139	144	102	104
Romania	134	143	132	138	102	105
East Europe combined	142	151	128	132	111	114

SOURCE: *Vneshnaya Torgovlya SSR 1975* (Moscow: Soviet Foreign Trade, 1975), as cited in Martin J. Kohn and Nicholas R. Lang, "The Intra-CEMA Foreign Trade System: Major Price Changes, Little Reform," in U.S. Congress, Joint Economic Committee, *East European Economies Post-Helsinki* (Washington, D.C.: Government Printing Office, 1977), p. 141.

percent—or roughly 1 percent of GNP for Bulgaria, Hungary, and the GDR, and more than 0.5 percent for Czechoslovakia.[96] Moreover, at the same time that East European terms of trade within CMEA were deteriorating sharply, an even more serious reversal was manifesting itself in East-West economic relations. Under the impact of Western recession, trade with the West was proving a double-edged sword, and the high hopes of the early 1970s had led many of the East European states to undertake commitments which became increasingly onerous burdens by the end of the decade.

The expansion of East-West trade, which proceeded incrementally in the 1960s, began to reach take-off proportions in the early 1970s. The total volume of East European trade with the West tripled in the first half of the decade, accounting for shares of total trade ranging from about 20 percent for Bulgaria and Czechoslovakia to 40 percent and higher for Poland and Romania. (See Table 6.6). Most dramatic of all was the case of Poland, where the Gomulka regime supervised an actual (percentage) reduction of trade with the West in the 1960s, while the successor regime of Edward Gierek, committed to rapid industrial growth and visible improvements in material living standards, drastically reversed Poland's foreign trade in the direction of the industrial West. As Andrzej Korbonski nicely put it, "Considered as practically the root of all evil only a short time earlier, foreign trade was now proclaimed as the engine of

Table 6.6
East European Trade with the West, 1971, 1975, and 1979 (percentages)

Country	1971		1975		1979	
	Total turnover	Exports/ imports	Total turnover	Exports/ imports	Total turnover	Exports/ imports
Bulgaria	15.3	13.8/16.8	17.0	9.3/23.6	15.0	14.4/15.5
Czechoslovakia	22.5	20.3/24.8	22.4	19.8/24.6	22.1	19.9/24.1
East Germany	24.2	21.1/27.5	25.9	22.4/29.0	26.0	20.8/30.8
Hungary	27.4	25.2/29.3	24.4	21.4/27.0	35.2	32.3/37.9
Poland	28.5	29.8/27.3	41.3	31.5/49.3	34.6	31.1/37.9
Romania	36.8	34.1/39.6	36.7	31.5/41.9	—	—
Soviet Union	21.5	20.0/23.2	31.3	25.6/36.4	32.1	29.5/35.0

SOURCES: *Statisticheskii ezhegodnik stran-chlenov SEV* [Statistical yearbook of member states of CMEA] (Moscow: Statistika, annual editions 1971–80).

NOTE: Figures reflect all trade with "developed capitalist states," expressed in percentage of total trade turnover, percentage of exports, and percentage of imports.

progress which would not only put the economy back on the track but would also propel it on the path of rapid growth.''[97]

Of course, not all the East European countries embraced trade with the West in the early 1970s so unreservedly as did Poland under Gierek, and there were significant variations in approach. Poland and Romania, as has been seen, were the most eager trade partners with the West; Romania and Hungary were the most active in encouraging joint equity ventures with Western corporations; and Bulgaria swiftly ran up the highest debt burden until being overtaken at mid-decade by Poland, Hungary, and the GDR.[98] To one degree or another, however, all the East European countries hinged their economic strategies for the 1970s to expanded trade with the West and embarked on economic policies geared toward rapid growth through imports of Western technology, finished products, and credits.

These strategies worked well enough for a time. In Gierek's Poland, average annual growth rates (of per capita net material product) soared to 9.0 percent in 1971–1975, up from 5.2 percent in the preceding five-year period; Romania's growth rates were equally encouraging, rising from an average of 6.2 percent in 1966–1970 to 10.1 percent in 1971–1975.[99] Elsewhere, growth rates were less impressive but sufficiently strong to offer some vindication of import-led growth strategies.

All this changed abruptly at mid-decade, when the announcement of drastic OPEC oil price increases introduced a prolonged period of Western ''stagflation,'' under the combined impact of recession, inflation, and general economic slowdown. These economic reversals quickly made themselves felt in Eastern Europe, as inflation served to increase the prices of imports from the West, recession reduced demand for East European exports (except fuel), and balance of payments problems induced the Common Market countries to apply new protectionist measures, most notably those embodied in the Common Commercial Policy and Common Agricultural Policy.[100]

As is illustrated in Table 6.6, all the East European countries save Czechoslovakia began to encounter serious export/import imbalances in their trade with the West. In the case of Poland, for example, imports from the West accounted for 49.3 percent of Poland's total imports in 1975, while exports to the West during the same year amounted to only 31.5 percent of total exports. Imbalances were equally acute for Bulgaria, nearly so for Romania, the USSR, the GDR, and Hungary; and Eastern Europe's traditionally favorable balance of payments vis-à-vis the developing world had reversed dramatically with the rising prices of raw materials on the world market.

By the end of the decade, all the East European countries except the GDR had reduced their balance of payments deficits with the West, but only Hungary had managed to do so by pushing up its share of exports to the West. For the others, the expected expansion of exports to the West that would have paid for continued technology imports had failed to materialize, and they had begun with varying degrees of determination to cut back imports from the West. To redress the resulting imbalances in the domestic economies, three basic options presented themselves to the East European regimes: reduce investments, thereby abandoning the growth strategies on which they had recently embarked; raise prices, thereby reneging on the oft-repeated promises of real improvements in material living standards; or borrow, thereby mortgaging their future but buying time on the investment and consumer fronts. As Table 6.7 suggests, many chose to borrow.

One of the paradoxical consequences (at least so it seems to the layman) of the Western recession in the late 1970s was to open up new credit opportunities on Western financial markets, newly inundated with OPEC-generated funds but short of borrowers within constricted Western business circles. In this favorable borrowing climate, moreover, the East European countries were able to obtain credits on terms only slightly less favorable than those accorded members of the Organization for Economic Cooperation and Development (OECD).[101] Table 6.7 indicates the extent of East European borrowing from Western governments and private financial institutions in the 1970s. East European indebtedness, held within manageable proportions until the mid-1970s, began thereafter to increase dramatically, particularly in Poland, where the debt soared from $4.6 billion in 1974 to more than $20 billion in 1979.

Table 6.7
East European Indebtedness in the 1970s: Gross Debt in
Billions of Current U.S. Dollars

Country	1971	1972	1973	1974	1975	1976	1977	1978	1979
Bulgaria	0.7	1.0	1.0	1.7	2.6	3.2	3.7	4.3	4.5
Czechoslovakia	0.5	0.6	0.8	1.0	1.1	1.9	2.6	3.2	4.0
East Germany	1.4	1.6	2.1	3.1	5.2	5.9	7.1	8.9	10.1
Hungary	1.1	1.4	1.4	2.1	3.1	4.0	5.7	7.5	7.8
Poland	1.1	1.6	2.8	4.6	8.0	11.5	14.0	17.8	20.5
Romania	1.2	1.2	1.6	2.7	2.9	2.9	3.6	5.2	6.9
Eastern Europe[a]	6.1	7.4	9.7	15.4	23.0	29.5	36.7	46.9	53.7
Yugoslavia	3.2	3.9	4.7	5.4	6.6	7.9	9.5	11.8	15.0
Eastern Europe with Yugoslavia	9.3	11.3	14.4	20.8	29.6	37.4	46.2	58.7	68.7

Source: Paul Marer, "Economic Performance and Prospects in Eastern Europe: Analytical Summary and Interpretation of Findings," in U.S. Congress, Joint Economic Committee, *East European Economic Assessment* (Washington, D.C.: Government Printing Office, 1981), pt. 2, p. 57.

[a] Sums are not exact because of rounding.

More revealing than the absolute values of East European debts are their debt burdens, expressed in Table 6.8 through three different measures. The first measure reveals, for example, that in the early 1970s Bulgaria, not Poland, Hungary, or the GDR, was accumulating the highest debt per capita among the East European countries. The per capita increase in indebtedness during the 1970s was dramatic in almost every case, however; and, as the second measure indicates, Poland, Bulgaria, Hungary, and the GDR were incurring debts at a rate fast outstripping their capacity to pay (through exports generating hard currency).[102] Most dramatic of all was the immediate impact of East European debt burdens, indicated in the third measure by a ratio of debts falling due to hard currency exports. By 1979 these figures ranged from Czechoslovakia's 22 percent (itself relatively high by international standards) to a staggering 95 percent for Poland, whose debt maturity structure had brought it to the point where bankruptcy could be averted only by a massive rescheduling of its debt or by further borrowing.[103]

Thus, while heavy reliance on Western credits had bought a few years' time, it had failed to solve the increasingly acute East European economic crisis brought on by steadily deteriorating terms of trade with both West and East. Debt repayments were falling due, and more and more exports were required to repay credits already spent rather than finance new domestic investment projects through which export capacities might have been raised. To complete the vicious cycle, most of the East European countries were required to seek

Table 6.8

Eastern Europe's Debt Burden in the 1970s

Country	Debt per capita (U.S. dollars)			Debt/export ratio[a]			Debt service/export ratio (%)[b]		
	1971	1975	1979	1971	1975	1979	1970	1975	1979
Bulgaria	85	259	431	1.60	2.41	1.65	35	33	36
Czechoslovakia	11	56	207	0.13	0.35	0.88	8	14	22
East Germany	71	211	537	0.89	1.16	2.00	20	25	55
Hungary	82	208	702	1.13	1.30	2.23	20	19	36
Poland	23	217	568	0.52	1.79	3.16	20	30	95
Romania	60	115	306	1.30	0.85	1.26	36	23	25

SOURCE: Paul Marer, "Economic Performance and Prospects in Eastern Europe," in U.S. Congress, Joint Economic Committee, *East European Economic Assessment* (Washington, D.C.: Government Printing Office, 1981), pt. 2, pp. 67–68.

[a] Size of outstanding debt relative to annual hard currency exports (i.e., exports generating hard currency).

[b] Interest on outstanding debt and principal payments on medium- and long-term debts relative to hard currency exports. (Excludes service revenues and short-term debts.)

substantial new Western credits to refinance old debts, thereby adding to the debt burden for the 1980s without retaining sufficient surplus capital even to keep old investment projects afloat.

One further and related set of factors in the East European economic decline issued from the domestic economic strategies of the early 1970s, which favored massive industrial investment at the expense of the agricultural sector and a consumerist approach that demanded steady improvements in material living standards regardless of the objective capacity to pay. The consequences of these policies were demonstrated almost everywhere in Eastern Europe during the 1970s, as agricultural production slowed or even declined and agricultural imports increased, often drastically, in every country except Hungary and Romania.[104] Once the generator of surplus capital for industrial development, agriculture had become a growingly inefficient drain on other economic sectors, and official commitment to stable food prices demanded ever-increasing agricultural subsidies. Given the deteriorating balance of payments affecting all of Eastern Europe, the cost of such imports and subsidies, as well as supplies of affordable consumer products, could be borne only by still further reliance on Western credits.

Poland, of course, is the most dramatic case study in East European economic mismanagement in the 1970s. Poland's terms of trade and indebtedness dilemmas have already been discussed. Domestically, the Gierek regime's pursuit of rapid industrial growth, particularly through such massive projects as the Huta Katowice steel mill, was accompanied by utter neglect of agriculture, still largely in the hands of private farmers. Agricultural production declined for want of adequate inputs, incentives, or overall policy, and agricultural imports from the United States rose dramatically, from a cost of about $80 million in 1972 to $650 million in 1979.[105] Even in industry, many of the investment projects designed to reduce import dependence on consumer products backfired, as Poland found itself short of exportable commodities capable of offsetting growing terms of trade deficits.

Until the mid-1970s, however, Poland's economic strategy, while more ambitious, was not drastically different from that pursued by, say, Hungary or the GDR. What distinguished (if that is the appropriate term) Poland's economic experience in the 1970s, rather, was the manifest unwillingness or inability of the Gierek leadership to fashion policies to deal with much altered circumstances —to cut back investments, reduce trade with the West, stimulate agricultural production, place a moratorium on new credits, raise retail prices, and introduce austerity measures. With the failure of the belated and ill-conceived effort to raise food prices in 1976, itself the product of generally perceived economic ineptitude, the Polish leadership largely relapsed to the conspicuously ineffective economic policies of the early 1970s, reducing imports where possible and curtailing some investments, but relying on Western credits to keep the economy

Table 6.9
Declining Growth Rates in Eastern Europe: Percentage Change in Net Material Product

Country	1971–75 actual	1976 Plan	1976 Actual	1977 Plan	1977 Actual	1978 Plan	1978 Actual	1979 Plan	1979 Actual	1980 Plan	1980 Actual	1976–80 Plan	1976–80 Actual	1981–85 plan
Bulgaria	7.3	9.0	6.5	8.2	6.3	6.8	5.6	7.0	6.5	5.7	5.7	7.7	6.1	4.6–5.4[a]
Czechoslovakia	5.0	5.0	4.1	5.2	4.2	4.9	4.1	4.3	2.6–2.8	3.7	3.0	4.9	3.6	2.7–3.0[a]
East Germany	5.7	5.3	3.7	5.5	5.2	5.2	3.6	4.3	4.0	4.8	4.8	5.1	4.3	5.1–5.4
Hungary	6.0	5.0–5.5	3.0	6.0–6.5	8.0	5.0	3.9	3.0–4.0	1.0–1.5	3.0–3.5	−1.0	5.4–5.7	3.0	2.7–3.2
Poland	9.0	8.3	6.8	5.7	5.0	5.4	3.0	2.8	−2.0	1.4–1.8	−4.0	7.0–7.3	1.8	—
Romania	10.2	10.5	10.5	11.3	9.0	11.0–11.5	7.4	8.8	6.2	8.8	2.5	10.0–11.0	7.1	6.7–7.4
Eastern Europe	7.2	7.0	5.7	6.6	5.8	6.1	4.3	4.6	2.3	4.2	1.1	6.6	3.8	4.4–4.9[b]

SOURCE: Cam Hudson, "Constraints on Economic Performance in Eastern Europe," RAD Background Report/107 (Eastern Europe), *Radio Free Europe Research*, May 8, 1980. Additional data compiled by the author.
[a] Draft plan.
[b] Excludes Poland.

afloat and continuing to the end to proclaim the efficacy of the regime's economic strategy.[106] When the next real test came, with the price increases adopted in July 1980, the response would be not merely isolated strikes and protests but the beginning of a wholesale revolt against the Party and government of People's Poland.

The virtual collapse of the Polish economy was but the most severe manifestation of a more general deterioration in Eastern Europe whose full impact—because of heavy reliance on Western credits—was felt only toward the end of the 1970s. As Table 6.9 illustrates, economic growth rates in Eastern Europe were impressive in the first half of the decade and, buoyed by Western credits, remained generally respectable until about 1978, though the gap between planned and achieved growth was widening perceptibly. By 1979, however, all the East European countries save Bulgaria had significantly reduced their planned growth rates, and none was able to meet even the scaled-down growth targets. Indeed, Poland became the first East European country since Czechoslovakia in 1962–1963 to endure negative economic growth, and Poland was joined by Hungary a year later. At decade's end, Poland, Hungary, and Czechoslovakia all were facing the prospect of zero growth for some years to come, with growth targets sharply down for the other countries as well.

These developments naturally altered the context of CMEA deliberations in the late 1970s and placed new strains on Soviet–East European economic relations. Chief among the issues of contention was the still rising cost of Soviet energy deliveries and its impact on economic viability, and ultimately on political stability, in Eastern Europe.

The adoption of the ''revised Bucharest formula'' at mid-decade had been grudgingly accepted in Eastern Europe on the assumption that prices for Soviet oil (and other raw materials) would rise to conform to world market rates, then stabilize at their new, higher level. The East Europeans, of course, did not entirely foresee that OPEC oil prices, and with them Soviet oil prices, would continue to rise, and they certainly did not anticipate the dramatic 75 percent world market price increases of 1978–1979. Although the new pricing system assured a certain lag in the full implementation of world market prices, it nonetheless guaranteed that within five years the price for Soviet oil deliveries would more than double.[107]

In the wake of the 1975 price rises, the East Europeans tried with indifferent success to curtail energy consumption and find alternate supplies of energy for above-plan needs. Because of the structure of domestic consumption and the prevalence of energy-inefficient industrial facilities, however, the East Europeans were unable to follow the United States and Western Europe in reducing per capita energy consumption. Only in Hungary was there a certain levelling off in per capita consumption; in Eastern Europe as a whole, per capita consumption rose more rapidly than in any other area of the world.[108] To fill the gap between rising consumption and fixed Soviet oil deliveries (i.e., by the 1976–1980 five-year plan), of course, the East Europeans were required to satisfy more and more of their total import needs through hard currency purchases on the world market.

Initially, as has been seen, the impact of the new pricing system on CMEA terms of trade clearly redounded to the benefit of the Soviet Union, whose leaders seized the opportunity to promote their vision of multilateral integration in CMEA. Far from revelling in their enhanced ability to exert economic leverage on their East European allies, however, the Soviet leaders found it necessary in the late 1970s to retreat from a rigorous application of the new pricing formula and offer relief to the countries most adversely affected by balance of payments reversals. Hungary's economic burden, for example, was eased by low-interest ten-year Soviet loans; and substantial Soviet credits were extended to East Germany and Poland, the latter receiving credits in the amount of one billion rubles in the aftermath of the June 1976 upheaval.[109] It is also apparent that the prices actually paid for Soviet oil have remained well below the levels envisioned under the new pricing system, for all the East European countries ran up deficits with the Soviet Union in 1976–1980. These deficits, in turn, produced substantial Soviet trade surpluses which amounted to de facto grants, in that "banked" transferable rubles in the CMEA financial system are purely bookkeeping units, not currency surrogates with real exchange value. In the period 1976–1980, these de facto Soviet grants reached a level of nearly 8 billion transferable rubles.[110]

In light of the acute economic crisis in Eastern Europe, therefore, Soviet energy "leverage" remains at best a potential rather than a usable asset, whose possible economic and political costs outweigh any foreseeable gains. As Soviet oil prices begin to conform more closely to those on the world market and the East Europeans begin to find alternate supplies of oil, moreover, even this potential leverage will probably diminish. Over the longer term, the likelihood that Soviet oil production will level off, perhaps as early as the 1980s, suggests that economic considerations, and not those of political advantage, will dictate future intra-CMEA oil prices. In the meantime, oil exports continued to figure prominently in the Soviet Union's own strategy in East-West trade, accounting in 1977 for 37 percent of total Soviet exports to nonsocialist countries. For all these reasons, the Soviet decision to raise CMEA oil prices was designed not to increase East European energy dependence on the USSR but to reduce it, so that the Soviet Union could meet growing domestic requirements and retain a sufficient surplus for exchange on the world market.[111]

These considerations, of course, ameliorated but did not fundamentally alter the tremendous negative impact of constantly rising energy costs on the East European economies. From the beginning, complaints were raised in Eastern Europe over the selective application of world market prices for intra-CMEA trade. Taking note of the fact that "not all goods have a world price to provide us with a base," one Polish economist argued: "Although the adoption by the CMEA Executive Committee of this system of 'creeping' prices for reciprocal settlements among member countries will undoubtedly help to improve the mechanisms of economic cooperation and of socialist integration, pricing remains a weak spot in the mechanism of cooperation, which will require continuous improvement if we want cooperation to be optimally systematic."[112] Similar complaints, voiced in one way or another by all six East European members of CMEA, centered on two growing imbalances in intra-CMEA pricing procedures: world market prices were rising far faster for oil and raw materials than for manufactured goods, thus imposing a mounting economic burden on the East European economies; and the application of world market prices was inherently inequitable, since it was easier to fix world market rates for Soviet oil and other raw materials than for buses, industrial equipment, and other East European export goods.

By the end of the decade, East European complaints had crystallized into a more general critique of intra-CMEA pricing procedures, and a consensus was beginning to emerge that some overall reevaluation of CMEA integration measures was in order.[113] Ceauşescu's 1979 call for a summit meeting of Party leaders and heads of state to discuss economic problems should be seen in this context, as should growing calls from Hungarian and to a lesser extent from Czechoslovak, Polish, and East German officials for economic cooperation along market economy lines through currency convertibility, direct links among enterprises, and the like.

Thus, by 1980 CMEA seemingly had reached another procedural and conceptual impasse.[114] The integration programs of the early 1970s, like the Soviet and East European economies themselves, were in a state of considerable disarray: joint investment projects had been sharply cut back, the long-term target programs had amounted in practice to little more than vague statements of intent, and plan coordination had foundered on growing delays in implementation, most notably in the still incomplete 1981–1985 Coordinated Plan. More important, CMEA economic integration as conceived a decade earlier had proved largely irrelevant to the increasingly acute economic difficulties besetting all the East European economies.

Some progress undeniably was achieved with the less ambitious elements of the Soviet integration program in the 1970s, particularly in the areas of coordination and specialization of production. In the transport sector, for example, Hungary produces most of the buses used by CMEA countries, while the USSR builds most of the large-capacity trucks and Bulgaria specializes in the construction of electric trolleys. A similar situation obtains in the shipping industry, in which the East Germans build most of the smaller ships (up to 6,000 tons), the Soviets are responsible for medium-sized ships (5,000–16,000 tons), and the

Poles construct most of the largest vessels (20,000–60,000 tons).[115] Coordination and specialization of this kind, which is to be found in most of the major areas of production,[116] lead almost inevitably to increased interdependence and certainly promote a kind of economic integration, at least to the extent that domestic production decisions are based on region-wide considerations and depend on vital products from the other CMEA member-countries.

Such efforts have been facilitated by the proliferation of new CMEA organs— standing commissions, Council committees, interstate and international economic organizations, and coordinating centers—which operate at various levels to promote cooperation in specific spheres of production. Multilateral planning and production, moreover, have developed with the creation of joint production complexes and the elaboration of bilateral and multilateral planning agreements, all of which are tied in to the Soviet-sponsored "Coordinated Plan for Multilateral Integration Measures." All this adds up to a vast and growing CMEA infrastructure, whose strengthened central authority provides for increased Soviet influence and generates growing fears in Eastern Europe over supranational tendencies in the organization.

For the present, however, trade relations in CMEA amount to considerably less than meets the eye, for beneath the impressive array of CMEA councils, committees, agencies, commissions, and institutes, the actual conduct of trade relations in the region remains essentially unchanged. Despite recent efforts toward multilateralism, as has been seen, only about 5 percent of total CMEA trade is actually settled on a multilateral basis. Similarly, "convertibility" and "transferability" have been debated in CMEA for years, but hard-currency transactions amount to but a small fraction of overall CMEA trade, and the much-discussed "transferable ruble" has been employed, not as a currency surrogate with exchange value, but as a unit of account applied after a transaction has been completed.[117] As to the supposed achievements in bilateral and multilateral coordination of national economic plans, it should be noted that aside from the few joint investment projects, CMEA plan coordination has been limited to joint forecasting of foreign trade deliveries, while matters of domestic investment remain under the exclusive control of national planning bodies. "Joint planning came to the fore," one Hungarian economist explained, "but it was never applied in practice" because of "its political implications." Thus, he argued, "the fact must be reckoned with that beside the universal interests of Comecon integration, the separate interests of the individual countries and enterprises continue to exist and vigorously assert themselves."[118]

Indeed, these "political implications" have proved the most persistent impediments to the development of CMEA integration. For fear of losing their grip on important levers of control in Eastern Europe, the Soviet leaders opposed the "spontaneous" integration which was developing among the more advanced East European states in the early 1970s. The East European leaders, conversely, have acknowledged the economic benefits to be derived from closer CMEA cooperation but have continued to resist Soviet-imposed plan integration on the grounds that it would involve the transfer of economic and political prerogatives to supranational CMEA organs susceptible to Soviet manipulation. Their preference, rather, has been for a kind of market integration, a more loosely knit, decentralized free trade area in which member countries would voluntarily coordinate their trade relations on the basis of economic advantage and facilitate direct contacts among individual enterprises. Thus, CMEA is caught between the plan and market conceptions of integration, and pressures for economic change, much greater in Eastern Europe than the Soviet Union, continue to push the more advanced East European states in the market direction and toward increased trade with the West.[119]

Similarly, CMEA is caught between East and West—that is, between an economic orientation which emphasizes the development of ever more intricate ties within CMEA and one which relies more heavily on the potential advantages inherent in expanded trade with the advanced industrial democracies. For the time being, opportunities for economic relief are severely circumscribed on both fronts, as the East European states find themselves in a double economic bind resulting from seriously deteriorating terms of trade with both East and West. Over the longer term, however, most of the East European regimes recognize that the ultimate solutions to their economic difficulties are to be found not in the East but in the West, for only there can they acquire the kind of technology and capital required for rapid economic growth. The key task for the 1980s, therefore, was to reconcile the imperatives of closer cooperation within CMEA, particularly in the energy sector, with the undiminished, but vastly more problematic, desire for expanded trade with the West.

7

On the Ideological Front

One of the most striking paradoxes of the era of détente is that it was accompanied in Eastern Europe by an intensive, coordinated campaign toward ideological unity and regeneration. Far from relaxing tensions on the ideological front, the Soviet leadership supervised a drive to strengthen ideological vigilance through the reimposition of domestic orthodoxy, coordinated through multilateral Soviet–East European efforts in the spheres of ideology and culture.

From the Soviet perspective, the process of détente may have reduced the danger of military confrontation and offered attractive economic benefits, but it also brought with it new perils in the form of ideological "infection." As one Soviet writer explained, there could be no ideological coexistence:

> Today, when the process of détente and normalization of relations is advancing and . . . contacts between socialist and capitalist countries are increasingly developing, the ideological struggle demands particular attention on the part of the Marxist-Leninist parties and socialist states, since the ideological adversaries delude themselves with the illusions that the people of socialist countries will become more "susceptible" to hostile ideology, above all, to bourgeois nationalism.[1]

For these reasons, the Soviet leaders moved in the early 1970s to restore ideological orthodoxy and construct new forums for ideological consultation in Eastern Europe.

Conducted under the banner of "socialist internationalism," this drive was manifested at all levels: in efforts to restore Soviet primacy in the international Communist movement, and in a regularization and intensification of ideological contacts of all sorts within the "socialist commonwealth." In cultural affairs, too, the 1970s saw a tremendous expansion of Soviet–East European contacts in such diverse fields as radio and television programming, the visual arts, music, literature, the natural and social sciences, and sports. All these efforts, it was argued, were designed to usher in a ''new culture,'' which would be ''socialist in content, national in form.''

Of equal importance to the Soviet–East European ideological offensive was the task of restoring the ideological leading role of the CPSU in the international Communist movement. Indeed, for the Soviet leaders the restoration of some sort of inter-Communist unity was seen as the logical concomitant to détente, and efforts began in the early 1970s to convene an international Communist conference which they hoped would reaffirm Soviet primacy in the Communist world at the same time that the Helsinki conference was affirming Soviet cosponsorship of East-West détente.

Inter-Communist Conflict

''At this time when there is no leading center of the international communist movement,'' declared the International Conference of Communist and Workers' Parties in 1969, ''voluntary coordination of the actions of parties acquires increased importance.''[2] The fallout from the 1968 invasion of Czechoslovakia, the disarray evident at the 1969 conference and its rejection of any ''leading center'' of the international Communist movement—these were but a few manifestations of mounting Soviet difficulties in the Communist world.[3] To these should be added the widening Sino-Soviet rift, whose full magnitude was revealed in the March 1969 border clashes along the Ussuri River, and the emerging specter of ''Eurocommunism,'' itself strengthened by widespread revulsion over the fate of the Czechoslovak reform movement.[4] As Spanish Communist party (PCE) leader Santiago Carrillo put it, ''Czechoslovakia was the straw which broke the camel's back. . . . That kind of 'internationalism' had come to an end as far as we were concerned.''[5] In its place the Spanish and Italian Communists proposed a ''new internationalism,'' predicated on collaboration with all ''progressive'' forces, rejection of any ''center'' of the Communist movement, and commitment to the equality and independence of all parties.[6]

In addition to the ''new internationalism,'' which touched a responsive chord among even the orthodox nonruling Communist parties, the Eurocommunist challenge to Soviet primacy was manifested in the growing electoral strength and political autonomy of the major West European parties. In 1972, the French Communist party (PCF) endorsed the ''Common Program'' of the French Left, agreeing among other things to work for the further development of the European Community; a year later the Italian Communist party (PCI) issued its *compromesso storico* (historic compromise), offering to join a broad coalition of

Italian parties and moderating its posture toward NATO and the European Community. While the PCI and especially the PCF maintained fidelity to the broad aims of the CPSU line, their growing autonomy with regard to Soviet aims in Europe was being viewed with increased alarm in the Kremlin, as were thorough-going Eurocommunist critiques of Soviet-style "real" socialism in Eastern Europe.

Of additional concern in Soviet eyes were cautious efforts toward *rapprochement* with the Chinese Communists by the Spanish and Italian parties and, closer to home, by the Yugoslavs and Romanians as well. By 1971, as has been seen, Yugoslav-Chinese relations had warmed dramatically, and Romania's long-standing close ties with China were further strengthened by Ceauşescu's personal visit to Peking in June 1971.[7] A few months later, and with the apparent assistance of the Romanians,[8] a PCE delegation headed by Carrillo also visited Peking, in an unsuccessful but promising effort to restore normal inter-Party relations. Although the Italian Communists were unable to mount a serious effort toward normalization until after the death of Mao Tse-tung (Zedong) in October 1976, they too seized every opportunity to cultivate inter-Party contacts, as several lower-level PCI delegations visited China in the early 1970s. Relations between the Eurocommunist parties and the Yugoslavs and Romanians likewise were becoming more cordial, and the danger was arising of an incipient Eurocommunist challenge to "actually existing socialism" (to borrow Honecker's favored expression) in Eastern Europe.

For all these reasons—to support their own détente initiatives by a flanking operation within the Communist movement, to counter the Eurocommunist challenge and reassert Soviet influence among the West European Communist parties, to condemn Maoism and rebuke parties linked in one way or another to the Chinese Communists, and to arrest ideological erosion in Eastern Europe— the Soviet leaders began in late 1973 and early 1974 to put out feelers toward the convocation of another international Communist conference. Indeed, the Soviet leaders already had been working behind the scenes to gather support for not one but two inter-Communist summits: a second European Communist conference, to be followed by a fourth world Communist conference.[9] The task of issuing formal calls for these conferences, however, was discreetly left to others. In November 1973, the leader of the miniscule West German Communist party (DKP) averred that "the time is maturing for a new world conference," noting further that a pan-European conference "could also serve to prepare a world meeting."[10] The call was picked up a month later by Hungary's Kádár and Bulgaria's Zhivkov, who also seized the opportunity to level strong attacks at the Chinese.

Given the anti-Chinese context of these calls, it is not surprising that the Romanian, Spanish, Italian, and other parties reacted warily, rejecting what PCE spokesman Manuel Azcárate termed efforts "to rally a series of parties around the CPSU and condemn the Chinese CP."[11] Similarly, Sergio Segre, head of the PCI Central Committee's foreign section, declared his party's "resolute opposition to any Communist conference which has as its main aim the condemnation of the Chinese comrades and the creation of a new Comintern."[12] Most other parties reacted not with polemics but with silence to the conference proposals, and by the end of 1974 only about one-third of the world's Communist parties had endorsed the idea of a new world conference. For their part, the Soviet leaders stayed largely in the background of this inter-Communist sparring, then quietly allowed the world conference idea to recede while they sought to drum up support for the more limited idea of a European Communist conference.

Reasonably sure of the endorsement of the smaller West European parties, the Soviet leaders sought to win over the "independents"—that is, parties which had declared themselves independent of Moscow's tutelage—in a series of secret inter-Party negotiations in early 1974. After further exploratory talks in the summer and early fall, representatives of twenty-eight parties (out of a possible thirty-one), meeting in Warsaw in October 1974, agreed to hold a conference of European Communist and workers' parties in East Berlin "no later than mid-1975," under the title "The Struggle for Peace, Security, Cooperation and Social Progress in Europe."[13] The timing and theme of the proposed conference left no doubt as to its intended purpose: this was to be the Communist counterpart to Helsinki, designed to affirm inter-Communist solidarity on the major East-West issues of the day. For the Soviet leaders, moreover, East Berlin was intended to demonstrate decisive Soviet influence over substantial segments of political life in Western Europe at the same time that Helsinki was affirming the Soviet Union's coequal status at the interstate level.

From the beginning, however, the Soviet leaders and their more orthodox comrades in Eastern Europe labored in vain to retain control over the preconference proceedings without alienating the independent parties—the Yugoslav, Romanian, Italian, Spanish, and others—in the process. This task had become progressively more difficult with each succeeding international conference; and by the mid-1970s, with the widening rift between Peking and Moscow and the growing trend toward collective regional identity among the major West European parties, the problem of forging a semblance of unity in the Communist world loomed even more formidable.

To win endorsement of the conference proposal and secure the participation of the Romanians and Yugoslavs, the Soviet leaders already had been forced to accept significant procedural changes. These concessions, adopted on the demands of the Romanians, Yugoslavs, Italians, and others at the Warsaw meeting and affirmed at the second preparatory meeting at Budapest in December, included the provisions that decisionmaking be consensual and that the eventual conference declaration be nonbinding. More than that, the independents succeeded in their demand that the final declaration be acceptable to all the participants, a provision certain to mean that the lowest common denominator would prevail.[14]

Indeed, one of the consequences of the preparatory negotiations was to forge a growing "independent alliance." This included the Yugoslavs and Romanians, bent on expanding their autonomy on ideological and foreign policy matters, and the major West European parties, united by electoral strategies predicated on cooperation with non-Communist parties and foreign policy positions divergent from those of the CPSU on such issues as membership in NATO and the European Community.[15] As the preconference debates wore on, the alliance of independents coalesced around a more broadly based opposition to Soviet efforts to impose a "general line" on the proceedings. In this the Yugoslav, Romanian, Italian, and Spanish parties were joined by the British and Swedish parties and later by the French, soon to collaborate with the PCI in what amounted to a "Eurocommunist Manifesto."[16]

As sessions of the Editorial Commission dragged on through 1975, it soon became apparent that the conference could not be arranged in time to coincide with the final session of the Conference on Security and Cooperation in Europe, which met in Helsinki in late July.[17] Rather, the Soviet leaders, through their East German comrades, who as hosts were charged with preparing the draft resolution, sought to introduce something approaching a general ideological line in a series of drafts presented in April, July, October, and November. The independents remained intransigent, however, refusing even to permit inclusion of "proletarian internationalism" in the text of the draft resolution.

Apparently persuaded there could be no conference without substantial concessions to the independents, the Soviet leaders began in early 1976 to reconsider some of the offending particulars of the draft resolution.[18] Progress was evident at sessions of the Editorial Commission in January and March, and the communiqué issued after the next session (held in early May) noted that the final meeting of the commission would convene in early June and that the full conference could be held "in the near future." In the event, the "final" session adjourned abruptly for another round of secret inter-Party negotiations, during which the Soviet side apparently dropped the demand that its version of "internationalism" be included in the resolution.[19] Thus, when the "final" meeting reconvened a few days later, it was only to announce that the conference at long last would be held in East Berlin on June 29 and 30.

As Yugoslav Communist party secretary Stane Dolanc noted on the eve of the session, "The preparations for this conference have shown that there has been a great and serious change . . . in the workers' and communist movement."[20] More than two years in the making and a full year behind schedule, the conference itself came as something of an anticlimax, for the essential concessions had been made in the lengthy negotiations which preceded it. Similarly, the chief lines of contention had been staked out long before the conference opened, and the main speeches delivered at East Berlin revealed the expected divergencies between the CPSU loyalists and the independents. Carrillo of the PCE was the most controversial of all the speakers. "Moscow," he said, "was for a long time a kind of Rome for us. We spoke of the Great October Socialist Revolution as if it were our Christmas. This was the period of our infancy. Today we have grown up [and have come] out of the catacombs." In similar if less heretical terms, the PCI's Berlinguer called on all parties to acknowledge the permanency of changes in their mutual relations, urging that "methods which are now outdated . . . be abandoned" and replaced by new ones assuring inter-Party equality and diversity of views. On the PCI's strategy, Berlinguer stressed his party's commitment to political pluralism, cooperation with non-Communist parties, and democratic principles, all of which were to operate "within the framework of international alliances [i.e., NATO and the EEC] to which our country belongs."[21]

Soviet Party leader Brezhnev delivered a surprisingly evenhanded speech, leaving the strident defense of orthodoxy to others. Acknowledging the right of individual parties "to shape their tactics and strategy according to the concrete situation in their respective countries" and eschewing any intention of establishing a "leading center" in the Communist world, Brezhnev clearly sought to assume the mantle of conciliation at the conference. At the same time, however, he reminded his listeners that "all of us are participants in a single struggle" and issued a spirited defense of proletarian internationalism, which he termed "a powerful and tested tool of the communist parties and the workers' movement more generally."[22]

These brave words found little echo in the much-amended conference resolution, which was more interesting for its omissions than its assertions. In place of the traditional affirmation of proletarian internationalism came a patently Eurocommunist formulation:

[Parties] will develop their internationalist, comradely and voluntary cooperation on the basis of the great ideas of Marx, Engels and Lenin, strictly adhering to the principles of equality and the sovereign independence of each party, noninterference in internal affairs, and respect for their free choice of different roads in the struggle for social change of a progressive nature and for socialism.[23]

Eurocommunist traces were further evident in the document's expressed commitment to dialogue and collaboration with "all other democratic forces" and the disclaimer that the parties "do not consider all those who are not in agreement with their policies . . . as being anticommunist." For the Yugoslavs and to a lesser extent the Romanians, there was for the first time ever in a collective document of this sort explicit recognition of the nonaligned movement as "one of the most important factors in world politics." As agreed early on in the preconference negotiations, moreover, even these bland particulars of the conference resolution were in no way binding on the participants, who had not been required even to sign the document.

From the Soviet perspective, the East Berlin conference had proved an almost unmitigated failure. The Soviet foreign policy line received a favorable endorsement, but the CPSU's status as *primus inter pares* in the Communist world was accorded only the slightest deference, and international proletarian solidarity was shown to be a myth of the Cominternist past. More than that, in establishing procedural rules assuring the consensual, nonbinding nature of the resolution, the East Berlin conference had set a precedent which amounted to the institutionalization of diversity among the Communist parties.[24]

Surveying this spectacle of inter-Party discord, PCF leader Marchais put the matter baldly at the close of the conference: "Since any elaboration of a strategy common to all our parties is henceforth absolutely ruled out," he said, "conferences like this one do not appear to us to correspond any longer to the needs of our time."[25] If the Soviet leaders still entertained any hopes of putting together a world Communist conference, the attitudes of the French and other West European parties surely offered little grounds for encouragement; indeed, the shambles of East Berlin must have given the Soviet and loyalist parties second thoughts as to the desirability of such a project.

The depth of Soviet and East European embarrassment over East Berlin was revealed eloquently in the selective coverage of the conference in the official media. As hosts the East Germans were obliged to report the proceedings fully in the Party daily *Neues Deutschland,* but the Soviet, Bulgarian, Czechoslovak, and other regime media subjected the debates to heavy censorship and sought to put the affair in the most favorable light possible.[26] Indeed, so blatant was the censorship and distortion that the Yugoslavs were moved to remonstrate that the Soviet and East European parties were guilty of "falsification of the consensus reached in Berlin."[27]

The Eurocommunists and independents, by contrast, emerged from East Berlin considerably strengthened, their ideological autonomy seemingly vindicated. For the Italian, Spanish, and French parties, East Berlin helped forge a new sense of solidarity and common purpose which led to the Eurocommunist summit at Madrid in March 1977. Expressing their shared commitment "to build socialism within democracy and freedom," the three Party leaders stopped short of direct criticism of Soviet-style "real" socialism but left no doubt as to their determination to retain their ideological autonomy.[28] The common expression of a Eurocommunist perspective was paralleled by new initiatives in the realm of political action, as the PCI joined the governmental majority in the Italian parliament in March 1978, the same month that the French Communists allied themselves with François Mitterrand's Socialist Party (PS) in the parliamentary elections which very nearly brought a PS-PCF victory. Even the PCE, despite its poor electoral showing after the Party's legalization in 1977, gained sufficient influence, particularly among the trade unions, to be brought into key negotiations with the government of Prime Minister Adolfo Suarez.[29] Still more heretical in Soviet eyes was the joint PCE-PCI "Euroleft" initiative of October 1979, which called for greater collaboration among all "progressive and democratic forces" (especially among Communist, socialist, and social-democratic parties).[30]

During this same period, the Eurocommunist parties were moving toward the normalization of relations with the Chinese Communists, a process of gradual *rapprochement* given new impetus by Mao's death in October 1976 and Chairman Hua Guofeng's historic visit to Romania and Yugoslavia in August 1978. This, clearly, was an expression of the "new internationalism" through which the PCE and PCI (and for a short while the PCF as well) sought to replace the old (i.e., proletarian) internationalism with a new pattern of relations based on inter-Party equality and autonomy. United by their common opposition to Soviet hegemony in the Communist world, the Chinese and the two West European parties moved rapidly toward inter-Party normalization, formally codified during Berlinguer's visit to China in April 1980 and Carrillo's the following October.[31]

Disturbing as these trends were from the Soviet perspective—the growing ideological autonomy of the major West European parties, their independent political strategies, and their new links to post-Mao China—there was another, more immediate challenge posed by Eurocommunism. This was the growing influence of Eurocommunism within Eastern Europe itself, where Charter 77 in Czechoslovakia, KOR (the Workers Defense Committee, later the Committee of Social Self-Defense, KSS "KOR") in Poland, and dissident intellectuals in East Germany and elsewhere drew moral, political, and in a few cases even financial support from the Eurocommunist parties.[32] The mere symbolic presence of Eurocommunism was not without its practical applications, as former Czechoslovak Foreign Minister (and Charter 77 signer) Jiří Hájek noted: "[The] Eurocommunists are my strongest card in my constant talks with our authorities. I say, do you really believe that our 'Charter 77' is antisocialist? But then what are these articles in the French, Spanish and Italian parties' presses which support us? Are they also antisocialist?"[33]

The Yugoslavs in the 1950s, the Chinese in the 1960s, and now the Eurocommunists in the 1970s (the differences need not detain us here) served as sources of ideological erosion in Eastern Europe, and this time the challenge also carried with it a distinct appeal within dissident intellectual circles. Among the East European regimes the sharpest attacks on Eurocommunism came from the Czechoslovaks, Bulgarians, and East Germans, who lost no opportunity to condemn any ideological deviation as anti-Soviet. The Poles and Hungarians were far less vocal in their criticism; and the Hungarians in particular sought to maintain correct inter-Party relations, hosting both Berlinguer and Marchais in Budapest in 1977 and couching their critiques of Eurocommunism in conciliatory terms, as they had done with regard to China in the early 1960s. The Romanians, of course, cultivated close and cordial relations with the Eurocommunists, frequently playing host to Party delegations and (like the Yugoslavs) allying themselves fully with Eurocommunist positions on inter-Party relations and the new internationalism.[34]

The Soviet response to this set of challenges was varied. Within Eastern Europe, as will be seen, the Soviet leadership supervised a coordinated, multilateral effort toward ideological unity and regeneration. The Soviets sought to win the Eurocommunist parties back with a combination of threats and blandishments, wielding their not inconsiderable influence among large segments of the West European parties. Most important of all, perhaps, they simply waited for the internal contradictions of the Eurocommunist position to manifest themselves. This came particularly swiftly in the case of the PCF, which found itself unable to maintain a "Eurocommunist" identity distinct from the Socialists and soon abandoned the "Euroleft" for a more congenial pro-Moscow orthodoxy.

With the French defection from the ranks of the Eurocommunists in 1977–1978, the challenge facing the Soviet leaders altered considerably: no longer were they confronting a nascent Eurocommunist bloc in Western Europe but rather a mixed independent alliance consisting of one powerful Eurocommunist party (the Italian) and one smaller but more outspoken party (the Spanish), with sporadic opposition from some of the smaller West European parties. But if Eurocommunism as a movement had receded, at least for the time being, its influence continued to make itself felt, particularly in its espousal of the equality and autonomy of parties under the "new internationalism."

One further element of Soviet inter-Party strategy was an ideological war on revisionism and Eurocommunism, waged chiefly through meetings of the East European parties and lower-level ideological gatherings among representatives of the nonruling parties. The campaign began with the Sofia meeting of Central Committee secretaries (for ideological and international affairs) in March 1977, designed to be the orthodox counterpart to the Eurocommunist summit then being held in Madrid.[35] This was followed by a long series of conferences commemorating the sixtieth anniversary of the October Revolution; among the most significant were the April 1977 Tashkent conference on the October Revolution and "the triumph of proletarian internationalism," the June 1977 Prague conference hosted by *Problems of Peace and Socialism* (*World Marxist Review*, in its English-language edition) and attended by representatives of seventy-five parties, and the gala in Moscow on the anniversary itself, attended by seventy parties. Throughout the next two years, a whole host of inter-Party theoretical conferences were devoted to such themes as "Democracy and

Human Rights under Socialism'' (in Budapest in late February and early March 1978), "Construction of Socialism and Communism and World Progress" (Sofia, December 1978), "Revolution, Democracy, and Socialism" (Tihany, Hungary, April 1979), "Democratic Freedoms and Human Rights under Socialism" (Warsaw, September 1979), and "Relations with the Social-Democratic Parties" (Tihany, December 1979). These and similar conferences, as well as various meetings of Central Committee secretaries and assorted anniversary celebrations, all aimed toward a set of underlying purposes: to extol the virtues of "real," or "actually existing," socialism and contrast them with the abstract (presumably "unreal") promises of Eurocommunism; to insinuate the Soviet and loyalist parties into the inter-Communist debate in Western Europe; and to isolate the Eurocommunist parties while at the same time leaving the door open for their possible return to the orthodox fold.[36]

These efforts toward inter-Party rapprochement were cut short in December 1979 by the Soviet invasion and subsequent occupation of Afghanistan. For many among the world's Communist parties this was further proof, if any were needed, of the real nature of Soviet-style "internationalism," and several West European parties lost no time in condemning the action as a violation of international law, to say nothing of acceptable inter-Party relations among Communists. The Italian and Spanish parties were particularly outspoken in denouncing the invasion, attributing it to "the logic of blocs" and even to Soviet "imperialism."[37] The French Communist party, by this time thoroughly disenchanted with Eurocommunism and its new internationalism, endorsed the Soviet action, but the chorus of attacks was soon joined by the Japanese, British, Swedish, Yugoslav, and Romanian parties.[38]

To arrest this process, and to win some Communist backing for their flagging peace campaign directed at Western Europe,[39] the Soviet leaders set about almost immediately to convene some sort of pan-European Communist conference. The precedent of East Berlin proved difficult to reverse, however, and the Italian, Spanish, Yugoslav, and Romanian parties let it be known from the outset that they would countenance no inter-Communist conclave which did not ensure free and open debate or whose resolutions were not based on the principles of consensus established at East Berlin in 1976. Mindful of the protracted and difficult preparations for the 1976 conference, the Soviet leaders opted in 1980 for a new approach to inter-Party consultation: rather than attempt to gather support for a full-fledged summit along the lines of the East Berlin conference, they proposed instead a thematic gathering of parties under the rubric "for peace and disarmament in Europe." But if the approach was novel, the methods employed to bring it about were old, harking back to Cominternist practices, for the Soviet leaders simply appointed the Polish and French parties to draw up an agenda and send out invitations for a conference to be held in Paris in late May.

The Eurocommunist response to these dictatorial methods was predictably sharp. As Antonio Rubbi, PCI Central Committee secretary for foreign affairs, put it: "Here we found ourselves faced with a proposal on which our own and other parties had passed a negative judgment from the first. . . . Then, unexpectedly, in mid-March, it was put forward again, the dates, procedures and contents having been fixed without the agreement of the parties invited—the latter being simply summoned to an initiative in which they had in no way participated.''[40] These sentiments were soon echoed by the Spaniards and Yugoslavs, later by the British, Swedish, and other parties, and finally by the Romanians, all of whom declared their intention to boycott the conference. The Romanians were of course in a particularly delicate position. Having maintained a discreet silence while the list of likely absentees mounted, the Romanian Party weighed in late and cautiously, expressing the RCP's opinion that "it would be better if the Paris meeting were postponed . . . or at least its character changed" to ensure adequate preparation and prior agreement. If these conditions were not met, the Romanians averred, they would not be prepared to attend.[41]

Thus, when the Paris conference convened on April 28–29, 1980, it was considerably less than the "pan-European" affair its organizers intended it to be. The absentee list included a third of those invited—nearly half of the West European parties plus two ruling parties, the Yugoslav and Romanian.[42] The conference resolution was what one would expect from a selective gathering subjected to such heavy-handed prior orchestration: Afghanistan was not even mentioned, the bulk of the text (issued brazenly in the name of "the communists of all of Europe") being devoted to an appeal to all "peace-loving forces" in Europe for new efforts toward détente and disarmament.[43] Rather than healing the rifts among the Communist parties, the Paris conference merely accentuated them; far from closing ranks, an unprecedented number of parties chose to break them.

Forgotten as soon as it ended, the Paris conference represented yet another failure of the Soviet Union to reassert decisive influence in the Communist world. Indeed, the 1970s had seen a steady erosion of that influence: the fissures evident at the 1969 Moscow conference were magnified and institutionalized at East Berlin in 1976; the divisions of Berlin were reconfirmed by the defections from Paris in 1980; and imminent convulsions in Poland cut short any new efforts toward inter-Communist solidarity.[44] In Eastern Europe meanwhile, the ideological war was being waged on another front, as the 1970s brought a tremendous expansion of Soviet–East European contacts in the ideological sphere.

Soviet–East European Ideological Relations

Speaking at the close of the July 1973 summit meeting of East European Party leaders in the Crimea, CPSU General Secretary Brezhnev noted, "Participants in the Crimea meeting were unanimous in the opinion that at the present stage it is essential to improve considerably the standard of ideological cooperation among the fraternal countries and parties.''[45] The immediate stimulus for this concern came from the opening of the Conference on Security and Cooperation in Europe, whose first stage was held in Helsinki from July 3 to July 7, just three weeks before the Crimea summit, and whose second stage was scheduled to commence in September. This linkage was made explicit in an article in the Czechoslovak Party daily *Rudé Právo*, which explained that the Crimea conferences had been held because the prospect of East-West détente had ''activated anti-communist propaganda.'' Thus, the article concluded, the ''ideological consolidation'' of the socialist countries was required to ''protect the building of socialism at home against the endeavors of aggressive imperialism.''[46]

Throughout the 1970s, as has been seen, a familiar theme in Soviet and East European commentary was that the process of East-West détente carried with it potentially destabilizing tendencies in the form of greatly expanded economic, human, and cultural contacts with the West. Predicated initially on diffuse fears of some sort of ideological ''softening up,'' Soviet and East European concern for ideological vigilance soon became tied to the reality of those dangers, as small but influential dissident human rights groups sprang up everywhere. Emboldened by the ''spirit of Helsinki'' and attracted by new political currents in the West, such groups as KOR in Poland, Charter 77 in Czechoslovakia, and ''Helsinki Watch'' organizations throughout the region, as well as disparate trends like the ''Democratic Movement'' in the USSR, emerged to challenge some of the fundamental premises of Communist rule.

There were, of course, powerful domestic concerns at work from the beginning of the decade. No sooner had postinvasion normalization yielded an uneasy stability in Czechoslovakia than a fresh challenge emerged in Poland, where the December 1970 workers' riots had brought down the regime of Wladyslaw Gomulka and opened a new chapter in popular resistance to Party rule in Eastern Europe. Motivated by the portentous lessons of Czechoslovakia in 1968 and Poland in 1970, all the East European regimes embarked to one degree or another on domestic strategies which combined an overtly consumerist approach—geared to greatly increased trade with the West and the economic prosperity it was supposed to engender—with new efforts toward ideological consolidation through the strengthening of the Party's leading role.[47] Manifestations of ideological retrenchment were evident throughout Eastern Europe in the early 1970s: in the GDR special attention was paid to *Abgrenzung*, the policy of ''demarcation'' and sharpening of the ideological struggle, particularly between the two Germanies;[48] in Romania, the Ceaușescu regime unveiled the so-called cultural revolution; and the Kádár regime in Hungary beat a hasty retreat on the NEM (New Economic Mechanism) and sought to strengthen Party control, particularly in economic policy.

None of this was entirely new, of course, and efforts in the ideological sphere acquired far less sweeping proportions in Poland and Hungary than, say, in Czechoslovakia or the Soviet Union. What was distinctive about the ideological drive of the 1970s, rather, was that it was a multilateral, bloc-wide affair, coordinated through various inter-Party meetings and agreements and manifested in a tremendous expansion of ideological contacts at every level. As one Soviet theorist put it, "A new stage in the sphere of [ideological] cooperation between the socialist countries . . . began early in the 1970s. Its distinguishing feature is the formation of a complex mechanism of ideological cooperation on a multilateral basis embracing all its major sectors."[49]

Waging the Ideological Struggle

In December 1973 Soviet and East European Central Committee secretaries for ideological and international affairs met in Moscow to "lay the groundwork" for the "broadening of multilateral ideological cooperation." At the top of the agenda were problems associated with détente and the "ideological struggle": "defense and dissemination of the ideas of socialism," "vigorous counteraction to anticommunism," and overcoming attempts on the part of "aggressive imperialist forces to torpedo the relaxation of world tension."[50] The first such meeting of its kind, the conference was called, according to one Czechoslovak ideologist, "on the basis of the conclusions of the [1973] Crimean meeting" to outline "the directions ideological cooperation should follow." Because of the "masked tactics of bourgeois ideology" under conditions of international détente, the writer continued, it was agreed that "the socialist countries . . . start a broad, well-planned ideological offensive."[51]

The key role in coordinating this offensive evidently was assigned to the Central Committee secretaries for ideological and international affairs, who convened regularly, usually once a year, after their initial meeting in 1973.[52] These, it should be emphasized, are high-level gatherings: in addition to the secretaries themselves, nearly all of them members or candidate members of their respective Party Politburos, delegations customarily include heads of the Party international departments and other high-ranking officials. Although their communiqués are typically unrevealing, alluding in unremarkable terms to salient international or inter-Party issues, these conferences clearly have played important roles in directing and coordinating ideological activity in Eastern Europe. After the 1978 meeting in Budapest, for example, it was revealed that the secretaries had "briefed one another on their parties' ideological work," "exchanged views about joint [ideological] activities," and worked out specific agreements for collaboration in the social sciences, education, culture, and the mass media, as well as for celebrating forthcoming anniversaries (Comecon's and the GDR's thirtieth, and the Cuban revolution's twentieth, all in 1979).[53]

These efforts were buttressed in the early 1970s by the first series of bilateral ideological agreements among the Soviet and East European Party central committees.[54] Although little is known of their substance, they appear to be short-term (usually two-year) agreements outlining specific cooperative measures in support of the desiderata expressed in the conferences of Central Committee secretaries. The 1973 Polish-Hungarian agreement, for example, provided for "large-scale exchange of experience" on ideological activities and "further development of cooperation between mass media, scientific and cultural institutions and higher party schools of the two Central Committees."[55] Reporting of these agreements in the official media is too spotty and cryptic to permit an accurate count of the number signed in the 1970s, but it is known that they are periodically renewed and that the Soviet Union and that all the East European countries are participating in these expressions of ideological solidarity.

The third chief vehicle of Soviet–East European ideological coordination comes through a regular system of links among the Soviet and East European academies of science, which are bound to a "common ideological program" established by a multilateral treaty signed in Moscow in 1971 and administered through a standing multilateral commission and a network of international research centers.[56] Vice-presidents or other representatives of the various academies hold periodic, apparently annual, multilateral meetings to review existing programs and plan future collaboration; and regular conferences and symposia are arranged among directors of the several philosophy institutes, historians, sociologists, and "scientific workers" associated with the academies of science. Additionally, a series of bilateral agreements among the academies has been concluded, and standing bilateral commissions of historians, philosophers, economists, and researchers "on the problems of the international communist and working class movement" have been created to encourage "joint creative activity by social scholars."[57]

Beneath the level of these top coordinating forums are a bewildering array of more specialized meetings in specific spheres of ideological activity, particularly those involving the mass media. Among the most important of these are the annual multilateral meetings of chairmen of the Soviet and East European journalists' unions, usually attended also by editors-in-chief of the Communist party dailies. Supplemented by a network of bilateral agreements among the journalists' unions, these meetings typically involve the usual "exchange of experiences" as well as coordination of approaches toward salient topics of the day.[58] A more direct role in this latter effort is played by annual conferences of directors of the Soviet and East European news and press agencies, whose November 1976 meeting, for example, was devoted to problems of covering the East Berlin conference of European Communist and workers' parties.[59]

In addition to these key meetings, regular multilateral conferences are held among editors of Party dailies, military journals, literary magazines, Party theoretical journals, and youth papers, as well as among foreign political commentators and representatives of specialized periodicals of the most diverse sort. The premises underlying heightened vigilance among the media have been stated explicitly. Commenting on a September 1974 conference of editors of the various Party history journals, for example, an article in the Hungarian press noted, "The information explosion which resulted in the development and spreading of mass communication media, the growing scientific, cultural, technical, and political co-operation between the socialist and capitalist countries, as well as the frequent personal contacts in connection with these programs, offer ample opportunity for . . . ideological confrontations." Thus, the article concluded, "the role of the ideological struggle grows more important in the peaceful competition between the two social systems."[60]

At the same time, however, many of these efforts have involved overt efforts toward the "Sovietization" of the East European mass media. The USSR has sponsored periodic conferences, for example, designed to educate East European journalists in the Russian language, Russian and Soviet literature, and work by Soviet social scientists on the "theory and practice of Communist journalism."[61] Soviet and East European journalism schools are involved in collaborative efforts, too, and a multilateral agreement signed in 1975 provided for the development of common journalism textbooks and curricula modeled after the "great efforts in this direction" made by Moscow State University's School of Journalism.[62]

The most ambitious efforts in the field of journalism have been the massive conferences of the editorial board of the Prague-based journal *Problems of Peace and Socialism* (*World Marxist Review*). Since the 1969 conference, the first in nearly a decade, such gatherings have been held roughly once a year, with representatives of most of the world's Communist parties in attendance. Disputes periodically surface at these affairs, and the Romanians have come under heavy criticism for regularly removing articles distributed by the central editorial board in Prague from the Romanian edition of the journal (*Probleme ale Păcii şi Socialismului*).[63]

Of greater significance than the board meetings of *Problems of Peace and Socialism*, however, are their associated theoretical conferences, typically organized under such ponderous themes as "building up of socialism and Communism and world progress" or "the joint struggle of the workers' movement and the national liberation movement against imperialism, for social progress." These conferences have gained added weight since the mid-1970s, moreover, by being periodically cosponsored by one of the East European Communist parties, and have acquired considerable international and inter-Party significance.[64] Indeed, they have been compared favorably by some East European spokesmen to the 1976 East Berlin conference of European Communist parties, and at least one West European delegate is known to have expressed concern that they might represent a new Soviet effort to establish a "world center" of the Communist movement.[65]

In any case, these were but a few of the many ideological conferences held in Eastern Europe in the 1970s. Radio Moscow noted that more than fifty "international theoretical conferences" were held between 1970 and 1975;[66] if anything, their frequency increased in the latter half of the decade. Their character was too diverse, their substance too dreary, to warrant enumeration here, but a brief review of those held in one four-month period should give some indication of their scope. In late September 1975 representatives of the Soviet and East European Communist parties met in Moscow to discuss the "dissemination of political and scientific knowledge"; a few days later Soviet and East European members (less Romania) of the institutes of international relations convened in Prague to review the results of the Helsinki conference. In late November, while Soviet and East European scientists and social workers were meeting in Sofia to discuss the "ideological struggle of youth under conditions of peaceful coexistence," representatives of forty-six Communist parties were gathered in Prague to debate "Lenin's teaching on imperialism and possibilities of the present stage of the crisis of capitalism." No sooner had that ended than Prague also hosted a colloquy on "the struggle against the ideology of 'democratic socialism'" cosponsored by the Czechoslovak and Soviet parties' institutes of Marxism-Leninism. Also in early December, Sofia played host to an international conference on "the struggle against ideological diversion in the field of sciences." As the foregoing suggests, scarcely a month went by in the 1970s without a Soviet–East European ideological conference of one sort or another.

One final dimension worth noting in the Soviet–East European ideological offensive has been in new efforts designed to strengthen Party control and facilitate inter-Party coordination. Ranging from the annual conferences of Central Committee secretaries for ideological and international affairs and regular meetings among secretaries for Party organizational matters down to lower-level contacts among Party political workers, such efforts were manifested in a tremendous expansion of inter-Party contacts at every level and across every aspect of public life. Leaders of Komsomol and other Communist youth organizations, for example, held annual multilateral conferences throughout the 1970s, and frequent youth symposia were arranged under such themes as "socialist personality development of young workers and students."[67] Among Party activists in the Warsaw Pact armed forces as well, regular conferences were held among heads of the (Party) main political administrations to promote ideological work, increase combat readiness, and gird against "imperialist diversion."[68] Finally, rectors of higher Party schools and directors of institutes of Marxism-Leninism maintained regular contacts,[69] and new inter-Party links were established between enterprise Party organizations, twin cities, trade unions, and local Party committees.[70]

All this adds up to a vast infrastructure for Soviet–East European ideological coordination in virtually every area of political life. The chief aims of these efforts seem to have been these: to strengthen the ideological foundations on which the various regimes legitimize their rule, facilitate Soviet supervision over ideological work throughout Eastern Europe, and bolster Party discipline and international (i.e., pro-Soviet) solidarity by developing cadres of loyal ideologists and agitprop (agitation and propaganda) workers throughout the region.

One particularly interesting commentary on the nature of the "ideological offensive" issued from a coordinating conference of vice-presidents of the academies of science of the socialist states in early 1975. In a paper presented to the conference and subsequently published in the CPSU theoretical journal *Kommunist*, P. D. Fedoseev, director of the USSR's Institute for Marxism-Leninism, outlined what amounted to a blueprint for the uniform development of socialist states. "The construction of socialism is a complex process," Fedoseev acknowledged, but its "basic principles have been laid down in the resolutions of the Twenty-fourth Congress" and other documents issued by the CPSU. These principles, he continued, which constitute the "*zakonomernost* [conformity with a law-governed pattern] of constructing and perfecting developed socialism" and are applicable to all states of the "socialist commonwealth," include perpetuation of the dictatorship of the proletariat until "the full and final victory of socialism" and, in keeping with "the principles of Lenin, . . . the maintenance of iron discipline." In economic affairs, "commodity-money relations" and *khozraschet* (enterprise accountability) will persist throughout the process of socialist construction, but "revisionist theories of 'a socialist market' are rejected since they lead to the undermining of the planned development of Socialist economies." The development of socialism on the national level, moreover, must go hand in hand with the economic and ideological integration of the "socialist commonwealth."[71]

None of these strictures was entirely new, of course, and Fedoseev's arguments might have gone unnoticed had it not been for their reappearance some months later in an article by a Hungarian analyst. In terms almost identical to the Fedoseev article, the Hungarian writer assessed the results of the 11th Hungarian Party Congress, of March 1975: "The policy of the Party must be built on . . . the general *zakonomernost* of socialist construction, the leading role of the working class and its Party, the dictatorship of the proletariat, the union of workers and peasants, and a planned economy." In an apparent allusion to the retrenchment evident in Hungary's New Economic Mechanism and the so-called social contract, the author further noted that "measures have been taken and will continue to be taken against undesirable phenomena in social development." "The process of construction of mature socialism," he concluded, will require greater "ideological unity of the masses under the guidance of the Party" and increased utilization of "the possibilities for integration with the economies of the socialist countries."[72]

Seen in these terms, it is apparent that the Soviet–East European ideological offensive of the 1970s, undertaken initially to counteract the perceived danger of ideological "infection" inherent in East-West détente, was part of a broader Soviet-led integrationist effort designed to promote the "unity and cohesion" of the socialist states in every sphere of their mutual relations. Even allowing for the self-congratulatory rhetoric associated with these efforts and their manifest failure to promote any sort of ideological regeneration among the peoples of Eastern Europe, they were unquestionably part of a very serious Soviet effort toward ideological consolidation in Eastern Europe. One further element in this drive was in the rapid expansion of Soviet–East European collaboration in cultural affairs.

Toward a "New, Socialist Culture"

Cultural cooperation among the socialist countries, according to Soviet theorists, is a process leading to the development of a "new culture, . . . socialist in content and national in form," in which the national cultures will retain their distinctive character but "will continue to draw ever closer together in their aims . . . and in their method and themes."[73] Such cooperation, it is argued, "is not directed from the top, as some supranational process, but is governed by the inner logic of development of every national socialist culture."[74] It is manifested, Soviet spokesmen claim, "in the fusion of the socialist cultures of fraternal nations" and in efforts to build "a world culture, a culture of militant goodness and love of mankind."[75]

These rhetorical excesses aside, it is undeniable that cultural cooperation among the "fraternal countries" expanded dramatically in the 1970s. According to Soviet sources, the overall volume of cultural links between the USSR and other socialist countries, chiefly East European, almost trebled in the 1970s, and there are now in effect more than 70 agreements concerning problems of interstate cultural cooperation and 200 protocols and conventions in specific spheres of cultural relations.[76] Ranging from "Days of Culture" and "Friendship Months" celebrating the cultural achievements of the socialist states to more substantive agreements on cultural exchanges or joint activities, these contacts constitute an intensive, bloc-wide effort toward intercultural penetration in Eastern Europe.

The foundation for cultural cooperation is derived from the bilateral treaties of friendship, cooperation, and mutual assistance binding the socialist states, all of which now include virtually identical sections providing for the development of cooperation in the fields of science, education, culture, the press, radio, television, films, tourism, health, and physical education. Although no single coordinating center has been established, most of the central direction for these efforts has come from four sources: regular, apparently annual, multilateral conferences of Soviet and East European ministers of culture; extensive contacts among the academies of science, linked through a multilateral treaty signed in 1971; a series of bilateral cultural cooperation agreements and associated protocols; and, since 1974, annual conferences of directors of the Soviet and East European institutes of culture. In specific spheres of cultural activity, regular conferences are also held among Soviet and East European tourist organizations, Soviet Friendship societies, and writers' unions, whose sixteenth annual meeting (held in Bucharest on October 17–18, 1979) was devoted to "the role of literature in the formation of socialist conscience."[77] In addition to these forums, a wide variety of conferences, symposia, and standing commissions of artists' and writers' unions, Friendship societies, theater representatives, research institutes, and the like have been created to facilitate coordination of cultural relations.[78]

In the field of education, Soviet writers note with pride that in the academic year 1970–71 some 187,000 university students and 1,200 graduate students from "fraternal socialist states" studied at Soviet institutions.[79] These figures apparently include summer school and other temporary students, however, for it is elsewhere estimated that about 14,000 students from the "fraternal states" have been enrolled in Soviet universities annually since 1970.[80] In any case, cooperation in the field of education has extended to the establishment of direct contacts among universities and research institutes, and various bilateral and multilateral research projects have been undertaken. Faculties of Moscow's Plekhanov Institute of the National Economy and the Karl Marx Economic University in Budapest, for example, participate in regular exchanges of scholars and joint research endeavors.[81] According to some Soviet spokesmen, moreover, the ultimate result of such cooperative efforts will be the full or partial integration of the educational systems of the socialist states. Discussing the prospects for educational cooperation over the next quarter century, for example, Academician R. Khokhlov, rector of Moscow State University, predicted, "It appears that there will come about an integration of the systems of higher education in the socialist countries that will provide their citizens with free access to all institutions of higher learning in the countries of the Socialist Commonwealth."[82]

In literature and the arts, too, new contacts have been cultivated under the guidance of the ministers of culture and the various artists' and writers' unions in the form of international film festivals, joint theatrical productions, literary translations, joint publications, exchanges of artists, and cultural exhibitions. From 1970 to 1975, some 200 "cooperative publications" were issued, and translations of literary works by authors in the "fraternal countries" reached a circulation of 300 million in the USSR.[83] During the same period, more than 100,000 Soviet "artistic workers" were involved in exchanges with the socialist countries, and some 1,000 "art societies" traveled to the fraternal countries to exhibit "masterpieces of socialist art" or to hold dramatic, musical, or ballet performances.[84] Similarly, Radio Moscow proudly noted that Soviet musicians performed 100 concerts in Romania in a single year (1975).[85] "The Soviet experience," one writer drily explained, "helps the fraternal socialist countries in the development of their national cultures."[86]

Similar activities have been undertaken in virtually every field of potential intercultural cooperation—the social sciences, history, the natural sciences, physical education, radio and television programming, journalism, tourism, and many others. To promote cooperation in sports in the 1970s, for example, a series of long-term bilateral agreements were signed between the Soviet Union and East Germany (1966), Bulgaria (1969), Poland and Hungary (1971), Czechoslovakia (1972), and Romania (1973); and hundreds of bilateral and multilateral sporting events are held each year to "strengthen fraternal cooperation and friendship and develop a sense of patriotism and internationalism among people of socialist states."[87] To commemorate the fiftieth anniversary of the USSR in 1972, eighty-seven climbers from the Soviet Union and the East European states assaulted "Peak Communism," the highest mountain in the USSR, to plant the flags of their respective countries. Lest the significance of this achievement be lost on the uninitiated, *Sport v SSSR* declared it to be a "symbol of unshakable friendship . . . inspired by the ideals of proletarian internationalism."[88]

It will not have escaped notice that most of these cooperative efforts have been distinctly one-sided affairs, usually involving the "sharing" of Soviet (and/or Russian) culture with the peoples of the "fraternal countries." Although cultural contacts among East European states also expanded during the 1970s, the great majority of efforts toward "cultural cooperation" include heavy Soviet participation and bear more than a coincidental resemblance to the processes of "Russianization" and "Russification" followed in the multinational Soviet state.[89] Indeed, one of the most striking features of cultural cooperation among the "fraternal countries" has been its linkage in Soviet theoretical literature to the "national in form, socialist in content" formula applied in policies toward the minority nationalities in the USSR. Alluding to the precedent of national unification in the Soviet Union, for example, one writer argued, "The principles of friendship of the people, the mutual enrichment of cultures, which are socialist in content and national in form, have now been successfully adopted in relations between the socialist countries."[90]

Other authoritative Soviet sources have offered even more sweeping applications of the Soviet experience to relations within the "socialist commonwealth." In one recent work by Soviet theorists, for example, the creation,

consolidation, and development of the "Soviet multinational state" were held
out as a "living embodiment" of the principles of proletarian internationalism
and the "basis of the interstate relations of the socialist countries."[91] And as
another Soviet analyst put it, "The Marxist-Leninist teaching on the nationality
question [and] Lenin's concepts of the ways and forms of national-state development under socialism . . . point up one of the fundamental tasks of the working
class and communist parties: to work to the utmost for the consolidation of the
unity of the peoples in the socialist community."[92] According to the CPSU
Party Program, moreover, "the establishment of the Union of Soviet Socialist
Republics" and the creation and development of "the world socialist system"
are parts of a single historical process leading ultimately to the "all-round
association" of peoples and nations on a global scale.[93]

Efforts toward cultural and ideological integration, in turn, are linked to the
sblizhenie–sliianie formulation, which postulates the ineluctable "drawing together" of the socialist countries, toward their eventual "merger."[94] These
efforts, as well as those in the areas of political, economic, and military relations
among the socialist states, are said to constitute "thousands of unbreakable
bonds [among] the peoples of the new world, facilitating their union."[95] "This
process of the socialist countries gradually drawing together," General Secretary Brezhnev further noted at the 25th CPSU Congress, "is now operating quite
definitely as an objective law."[96]

Ritual and Reality

Needless to say, abstract notions of the "merger" or "union" of the "peoples of
the new world" bear scant resemblance to the actual development of Soviet–
East European relations in the 1970s. Indeed, for all the attention paid in the
official media to cultural collaboration, nothing is more striking after thirty-five
years of Communist rule in Eastern Europe than the persistence of national
cultural traditions among the peoples of the region and the imperviousness of
their societies to alien influences. Similarly, despite the very serious efforts
toward ideological consolidation, it is clear that the 1970s saw a continuation of
ideological erosion in Eastern Europe, variously manifested in apolitical resignation, growing consumerism, or overt dissent. The extent of this erosion was
revealed in sharp relief with the publication in April 1981 of the Solidarity
"Theses," which made it clear that the great majority of Polish workers
considered any form of Communist ideology to be basically irrelevant.

The composition of Solidarity, many of whose top leaders were still in their
twenties, was symptomatic of a further and ultimately more profound development: the growing ideological disaffection of East European youth. Almost
imperceptibly, an entire new generation had arisen in Eastern Europe—a genera-

tion which did not know the horror of war or the terror of Stalinism, whose formative years were those of East-West détente and rising material and political expectations. As Solidarity's Young Turks demonstrated, the rising generation does not feel itself constrained by Eastern Europe's geopolitical fate or bound by the taboos of the past. Its orientation is Western, humanistic, anti-ideological; it is increasingly religious-minded, but it seeks from the Church (Roman Catholic, Protestant, Orthodox, or other) not solace and ritual but a positive set of moral values and an active engagement in Eastern Europe's social and political life. More than any other single factor, perhaps, Eastern Europe's new generation poses a growing, and growingly intractable, challenge to political stability in the region.

The decline of ideology as an energizing force was similarly evident in the political actions of the East European regimes, whose strategies for the 1970s were predicated on explicit consumerist policies, to be realized through greatly expanded trade relations with the "class enemies" in the West. Yet even while practice was belying ideology, inter-Party efforts on the ideological front were becoming more determined than ever. This seeming contradiction was addressed in a different but related context by Robert Tucker, who explained:

> Not only would a . . . Communist movement in the process of deradicalization go on proclaiming its adherence to the final goals of the movement; it would, by virtue of the dialectic of the process, reaffirm the goals in very strong terms, as it has done. For intensified *verbal* allegiance to ultimate ideological goals belongs to the pattern of deradicalization.[97]

While reaffirming their commitment to ideological orthodoxy and socialist solidarity, the East European regimes were in fact embracing what amounted to a new "social contract"—approaching a new ideology—which sought to secure political acquiescence through visible improvements in material living standards.[98] This new orientation, as has been seen, rendered the East European regimes particularly vulnerable to the economic reversals of the late 1970s, as they found themselves unable to satisfy the economic criteria on which fulfillment of their half of the social contract depended. Thus, by the beginning of the 1980s, the Soviet and East European regimes were facing a new crisis of legitimacy, unable to fulfill the economic promises of the early 1970s or harness public support through their increasingly ritualistic efforts toward ideological consolidation.

Conclusion: Pax Sovietica without Peace

To the extent that a single line of development characterizes Soviet–East European relations in the period 1968–1980, it is this: in the aftermath of the invasion of Czechoslovakia, the Soviet leaders moved to restore unity and cohesion in Eastern Europe through the reassertion of Soviet authority in the region, the reinstitution of domestic orthodoxy, and the elaboration of a comprehensive integrationist program in every sphere of Soviet–East European relations. Soviet in inspiration but collective in practice, these combined measures yielded a degree of stability in Eastern Europe during the early 1970s. In the latter half of the decade, however, efforts toward Soviet–East European consolidation were eroded by new political conflicts—between East and West, between the Soviet Union and its East European allies, and within the East European societies—and the grandiose integrationist designs of a few years earlier proved largely irrelevant to the pressing political and economic challenges confronting Eastern Europe.

Beyond this general line of development were a number of interrelated trends and factors affecting Soviet–East European relations in the era of détente. In the early 1970s, Soviet and East European diplomacy aimed at regulating the process of détente so as to maximize its political and economic benefits while minimizing the potentially destabilizing tendencies inherent in expanded contacts with the West; toward the end of the decade it was geared to keeping détente alive in the face of growing misgivings in the West. Even while engaging in an energetic post-Helsinki "peace offensive" designed to reinvigorate détente, however, the Soviet and East European regimes were grappling with the consequences of its ambiguous legacy. Despite their anxious countermeasures, the rapid expansion of contacts with the West had exposed the East European societies as never before to the cultural and economic lure of the West. The emergence of self-styled human rights and "Helsinki watch" groups were but the most visible manifestations of this influence; more important still were the diffuse consequences of Western cultural penetration and the belated "demonstration effect" of sustained economic prosperity in Western Europe.

Even the eagerly sought expansion of trade with the West had failed to live up to its early promise. Seen as the motor of economic regeneration and prosperity in Eastern Europe, trade with the West began to founder at mid-decade under the impact of soaring energy costs and their attendant disruptions on the global economy. By decade's end, economic growth rates were sharply down throughout Eastern Europe, balance of payments reversals were acute, and debts to Western lenders huge and still growing. Everywhere in Eastern Europe, the buoyant optimism surrounding the import-led growth strategies of a few years earlier had given way to profound concern over the mounting economic crisis confronting the entire region. For all this, Western trade, credits, and technology remained central to any hopes of economic recovery, and trade with the West had been introduced as a key, seemingly permanent feature of East European economic life.

One further consequence of the détente process was that it afforded scope for East European diplomatic activity on a scale unthinkable in the 1950s or early 1960s. It was the East Europeans who took the lead in promoting European détente—before their initiatives were subsumed within a Soviet-directed Warsaw Pact Westpolitik; and it was they who sought most urgently to revive it a decade later, when they saw their carefully cultivated contacts with the West threatened by superpower conflicts not of their making. In the interim, the Soviet leaders sought to channel and control this activity, and contain the continued independent-mindedness of the Romanians, through the Warsaw Pact's Political Consultative Committee and Committee of Foreign Ministers, annual summit meetings in the Crimea, and other forums for foreign policy coordination. Far from amounting to a genuine conciliar system, these combined measures were part of a Soviet effort to ensure "directed consensus" in Eastern Europe by according the junior allies new consultation privileges and giving a degree of political and institutional expression to their growing role in East-West affairs.

A similar pattern was revealed in intrabloc affairs during the period, as some of the dysfunctional control devices of the past were replaced by a more collectivist and participatory, though still Soviet-dominated, pattern of relations. In this regard, the Soviet leaders confronted the tasks of alliance management rather more creatively than in the past, supervising various integrationist schemes and erecting new multilateral forums for consultation and joint action. Soviet influence in alliance affairs remained paramount, of course, and there could be no demur in matters where vital Soviet interests were at stake; but considerable, sometimes decisive, East European influence was evident in a host of lesser issues, ranging from defense expenditures and joint economic ventures to the broader questions of Warsaw Pact decisionmaking and the shaping of an economic integration program.

If interstate relations in Eastern Europe during the era of détente were marked by a certain flexibility and innovation, at least initially, the same cannot be said of domestic policies in the region. At the beginning of the 1970s Soviet and East European domestic strategies were shaped, above all, by the legacy of the Prague Spring of 1968 and the outbreak of workers' riots along Poland's Baltic coast in protest against food price increases in late 1970. If the Prague Spring had persuaded the Soviet leaders and their more orthodox East European comrades that economic reform was fraught with unacceptable political risks, the convulsions in Poland just two years later revealed the dangers inherent in prolonged suppression of material living standards. Accordingly, Party programs for the 1970s stressed domestic orthodoxy and eschewed reformism in social and economic policy, but they also aimed at satisfying the material demands of the populations by shifting economic priorities toward the production of consumer goods.

This domestic orientation, in turn, fueled another, less conspicuous development affecting Soviet–East European relations in the era of détente: the decline of ideology as an energizing element in East European political life. The ideology of Soviet-style socialism, as the Italian Communists were to conclude in 1982, was a "spent force," and the strenuous but largely ritualistic paeans to ideology could not disguise its steady erosion, even (or especially) within the ruling apparats. The crushing of the Prague Spring had dealt the final blow to any residual revolutionary élan in Eastern Europe; after 1968, Party programs were based on an increasingly cynical combination of rigid orthodoxy and overt consumerist appeals. For the East German, Polish, Czechoslovak, and Hungarian regimes especially, "goulash Communism" supplanted the vision of socialist development as the linchpin of a new "social contract," which sought to win popular acquiescence in return for steady improvements in material living standards. In Hungary the process was broadened to embrace a cautious reformist course and conciliatory social policy; elsewhere a reorientation of economic policy was seen as a palliative—a substitute for, rather than concomitant of, social or economic reform.

To achieve the economic goals on which their rule came increasingly to be judged, the East European regimes (with the notable exception of the Czechoslovak) relied heavily on Western trade, credits, and technology, which were expected to propel the East European economies along the path of rapid growth and material abundance. Consequently, when East-West trade began to founder in the late 1970s, so too did East European economic strategies for the 1970s, and Eastern Europe was facing a political as well as an economic crisis. Unable to fulfill the early promises of a bright socialist future or even the far more limited aims embodied in the new social contract, the East European regimes were confronted with a new crisis of legitimacy, entrapped by their pledges of a few years earlier and the fundamental insecurity of their rule.

Within the East European societies, meanwhile, a parallel and largely subterranean transformation was taking place. For large segments of those societies, the liquidation of the Czechoslovak reform movement had ended all hopes for the self-regeneration of Soviet-style socialism. The resulting disillusionment was felt most keenly in Czechoslovakia, of course, where the euphoria of the Prague Spring gave way to pessimism and apolitical resignation, but it was present to one degree or another throughout Eastern Europe. Ideological disaffection was variously manifested in apathy, enervation, alienation, corruption (both official and unofficial), and overt dissent, the last being largely confined to human rights or "Helsinki watch" groups who pressed demands on the authorities, generally on specific and limited humanitarian issues. In Poland, however, the seeds were planted of a genuine Democratic Opposition, which grew and flourished in the fertile soil of Gierek's misrule.

As early as 1970, the conviction was growing among Polish dissident circles that the only hope for fundamental political change lay outside the ruling establishment, through social self-organization. The suppression of the Radom and Ursus strikes in 1976 sealed their conviction: they (or their political forebears) had trusted Gomulka in 1956 and had been betrayed; they had trusted Gierek in 1970 and were betrayed; they would not trust or be betrayed again. Emboldened by the conspicuous weakness of the Gierek leadership after 1976, dissidents, Catholic intellectuals, and disaffected Party members coalesced within a nascent Democratic Opposition, which began to acquire organization and purpose and gather mass support among industrial workers and even the rural peasantry. Perhaps most important, the election of Cardinal Karol Wojtyla as Pope John Paul II in 1978, and the massive outpouring of public affection accorded him on his visit to his native land a year later, served to galvanize a disillusioned Poland around an alternative, but as yet not fully defined, vision of its national future.

It was against this background that the price increases of July 1980—themselves a reflection of the failure of the Gierek leadership's economic strategy and a violation of its fragile "social contract" with a disillusioned population—touched off a wave of strikes and protest demonstrations. Within weeks, the protest had grown to a full-scale, organized assault on established methods of Party rule and a challenge to the entire interstate system in Eastern Europe, and neither martial law in Poland nor countermeasures elsewhere could erase its legacy.

Since the Second World War, the Soviet Union has seen Eastern Europe as a buffer, military and ideological, against the West, as a base for the projection of Soviet power and influence over all of Europe, and as a laboratory for the vindication of Soviet ideological and internationalist aspirations. The relative weight assigned to these factors undoubtedly has changed over time—military security considerations have perhaps receded, while ideological concerns are greater than ever—but the importance of the East European interstate system remains undiminished in Soviet perceptions. And the Soviet Union has sought to make this arrangement durable, stable, viable, organic; to establish a permanent Pax Sovietica over the entire region. This latter aim has proved elusive.

In Stalin's time, unity and stability in Eastern Europe was achieved through a rigidly controlled empire imposed by Moscow and brutally administered by East European leaderships thoroughly subordinate to the Soviet Union. It was a unified, seemingly monolithic system but a brittle one, whose surface stability concealed an underlying unviability. After Stalin's death in 1953 and the Hungarian and Polish upheavals in 1956, the Khrushchev leadership in the USSR sought to reshape the legacy of the Stalinist interstate system by eliminating the more glaring manifestations of Soviet hegemony in Eastern Europe and by trying to weld a new, more resilient alliance system, whose chief pillars were to be Comecon and the Warsaw Pact. More than that, Khrushchev encouraged his East European counterparts to overcome their Stalinist excesses and attempt to bridge the gap between rulers and ruled in Eastern Europe under a more attractive and conciliatory pattern of domestic authority. In so doing, however, Khrushchev failed to grasp the fundamental bankruptcy of Soviet-style socialism. His inconsistency and experimentation served to introduce a period of drift and disarray in Eastern Europe, whose most obvious manifestations were Romania's semi-autonomous foreign policy and Czechoslovakia's experiment in "socialism with a human face."

It was not until the Prague Spring and its forcible liquidation, nearly four years after Khrushchev's ouster, that the new Soviet leadership under Brezhnev undertook to restore unity and cohesion in Eastern Europe through a comprehensive drive toward "socialist integration." This effort demanded a rather more creative application of Soviet power and authority than in the past: aware that unity could no longer be imposed by fiat from the Kremlin, the Soviet leaders sought instead to promote cohesion by constructing new multilateral forums and integrative links susceptible to Soviet control or manipulation. Described by one Soviet commentator as the "creation of thousands of unbreakable bonds" within the region, this Soviet-led integrationist drive aimed toward the creation of a system of consultation so pervasive and an interdependence so thorough that independent action by the East Europeans would be severely circumscribed.

The nature and scope of Soviet integrationist policies after 1968 have been described at some length in the chapters above. If these aspects of Soviet integrationist efforts are more or less readily discernible, their results and significance are far less so. Indeed, no question of interest to observers of Soviet–East European relations is more slippery than that of "integration" in the region. In some respects, the interstate system in Eastern Europe is almost totally integrated, yet on closer inspection the notion of an integrated interstate system seems inappropriate. Nor does the concept of integration as a process hold much promise, for the pattern of interaction in Soviet–East European relations seems to move in an altogether different direction.

Militarily, the countries of the Warsaw Pact share common (i.e., Soviet) doctrine, organizational structure, regulations, and even uniforms; they employ standardized equipment and weaponry (down to ammunition of the smallest caliber); and they engage in joint training exercises purportedly designed to foster "combat solidarity." Yet military integration is largely confined to the upper echelons of the Warsaw Pact: even in large multinational exercises there is little contact among national forces except at the staff level, and East European units customarily maneuver side-by-side or in proximity with their allied counterparts rather than as an integrated operational force. The Warsaw Pact possesses neither a standing army nor a central body with decisionmaking authority, and recommendations issued by any pact organ must be submitted to the national governments concerned for approval. It does not even have an operational command in the usual sense of the term, for the functions of the Joint Command have been limited to matters of administration, training, and organization.

As to economic relations, CMEA has been divided for years between "plan" and "market" conceptions of socialist economic integration—between a conception which would create central planning bodies and invest them with supranational authority and one which would free "market" forces in intra-CMEA trade by facilitating direct contacts between firms and reducing trade barriers. Out of this conflict emerged the hybrid "Comprehensive Program" of 1971 and a pattern of interaction which links the CMEA economies in various ways but which lacks a clear vision of the economic (as opposed to organizational or procedural) prerequisites for integration. Thus for all the efforts toward multilateral cooperation in CMEA, Soviet–East European trade relations can best be characterized as "multiple bilateralism," a pattern in which an elaborate multilateral superstructure has been erected over an essentially unaltered system of bilateral economic relations in the region. As in the Warsaw Pact, CMEA possesses no central body with decisionmaking power; indeed, so restrictive were the procedural rules governing CMEA bodies that they had to be hastily amended just to permit the opening of collective dialogue with the EEC. Domestic economic decisions are partially based on regionwide considerations, it is true, but such limited interdependence and foreign trade coordination can hardly be said to constitute integration in any accepted sense of the term.

The integrationist drive of the early 1970s was designed to remedy some of these deficiencies by strengthening the consultative mechanisms of the Warsaw Pact, promoting multilateral economic cooperation, especially in the energy sector, and forging new ties in the realms of ideology and culture. In every sphere of Soviet–East European relations—political, economic, military, ideological, and cultural—and at every level of activity, new multilateral forums were created and new links established. To call this process integration, however, may do some violence to the concept, for the process lacks the sense of free and independent states voluntarily relinquishing portions of their sovereignty to achieve some common purpose or shared goal. The sovereignty of the East European states was relinquished more than three decades ago, and integration in Eastern Europe has amounted chiefly to a kind of Soviet-directed ''apparat integration'' linking the several Party and state bureaucracies and facilitating consultation among them.

The cumulative effect of these measures was to improve the nominal access of the East European junior allies to the levers of decisionmaking, while at the same time strengthening Soviet control and supervision through a tighter alliance infrastructure. These improved mechanisms for consultation, in turn, facilitated the forging of a coordinated Westpolitik in the era of détente, afforded a measure of political and military consolidation in the Warsaw Pact, and permitted the elaboration of new programs for economic collaboration. But neither these measures nor their associated integrationist schemes offered any solution to the pressing challenges facing Eastern Europe in the late 1970s: severe economic deterioration, ideological erosion and political malaise, and the widening gulf between the East European regimes and their disaffected populaces.

Thus the vision of a durable and viable Pax Sovietica remained in 1980 as elusive as ever. For all its external assertiveness, the Soviet-led alliance system in Eastern Europe was still beset by the internal contradictions and fundamental instability of an empire held together by force. It had failed to submerge national aspirations beneath the façade of internationalism, and it had not won popular allegiance by ideological persuasion or political achievement. It had failed to bridge the gap between rulers and ruled or arrest the growing enervation and immobility of its ruling parties. It had not even assured law and order in its half of the continent, for the chief threats to European peace since World War II had arisen in Eastern Europe itself—Hungary in 1956, Czechoslovakia in 1968, and Poland after August 1980—in nationalist outbursts aimed directly or indirectly at Soviet hegemony in the region. After thirty-five years, Pax Sovietica remained neither stable, secure, nor peaceful.

Notes
Selected Bibliography
Index

Notes

The following abbreviations are used in the notes:

CDSP   Current Digest of the Soviet Press
FBIS   Foreign Broadcast Information Service
RFER   Radio Free Europe Research

English translations of quotations from foreign-language sources are derived from the works cited in parentheses following reference to the original source.

INTRODUCTION

1 George Modelski, *The Communist International System,* Research Monograph no. 9 (Princeton: Center of International Studies, Princeton University, 1960), p. 15. The term gained wide currency with the publication of Zbigniew K. Brzezinski's *The Soviet Bloc: Unity and Conflict* (Cambridge: Harvard University Press, 1960; rev. ed., 1967).
2 Raymond Aron, *Peace and War: A Theory of International Relations* (Garden City, N.Y.: Anchor Books, 1973), p. 122; Quincy Wright, *A Study of War,* abridged ed. (Chicago: University of Chicago Press, 1964), pp. 132–35; Morton A. Kaplan, *System and Process in International Politics* (New York: John Wiley and Sons, 1957), pp. 36–37; K. J. Holsti, *International Politics: A Framework for Analysis* (Englewood Cliffs, N.J.: Prentice Hall, 1967), pp. 110 and 115; Louis J. Cantori and Steven L. Spiegel, *The International Politics of Regions* (Englewood Cliffs, N.J.: Prentice Hall, 1970), p. 18; and Roger D. Masters, "A Multi-Bloc Model of the International System," *American Political Science Review* 55, no. 4 (December 1970): 780.
3 Roman Kolkowicz, "The Warsaw Pact: Entangling Alliance," *Survey* 70/71 (Winter/Spring 1969): 86.

239

4 For an analysis of vertical and horizontal integration, see William A. Welsh, "Regional Integration in Eastern Europe: Toward a Propositional Inventory," *Journal of International Affairs* 26, no. 4 (October 1974): 243–48.

5 Speech in Moscow on the occasion of the fifty-seventh anniversary of the Bolshevik revolution, as translated in the *New York Times,* November 7, 1974, p. 8.

6 Malcolm Mackintosh, *The Evolution of the Warsaw Pact,* Adelphi Papers no. 58, International Institute for Strategic Studies (London, 1969), p. 18; and A. Ross Johnson, *Soviet–East European Military Relations: An Overview,* Rand Corporation Memorandum P-5383-1 (Santa Monica, Calif., August 1977), p. 23.

7 William Zimmerman, "Hierarchical Regional Systems and the Politics of System Boundaries," *International Organization,* no. 1 (1972).

8 Andrzej Korbonski, "Theory and Practice of Regional Integration: The Case of Comecon," in *Regional Integration: Theory and Practice,* ed. L. N. Lindberg and S. A. Scheingold (Cambridge: Harvard University Press, 1970), pp. 338–73; and Roger E. Kanet, "Integration Theory and the Study of Eastern Europe," *International Studies Quarterly* 18, no. 3 (September 1974): 368–92. See also Ernst B. Haas, "The Study of Regional Integration: Reflections on the Joy and Anguish of Pretheorizing," *International Organization* 24, no. 4 (Autumn 1970): 607–46.

9 Michael P. Gehlen, "Models of Regional Integration and the Study of Comecon" (unpublished), as cited in Kanet, "Integration Theory and the Study of Eastern Europe," p. 384.

For a quite different assessment by the same author, see Gehlen's "The Integrative Process in East Europe: A Theoretical Framework," *Journal of Politics,* no. 30 (February 1968), pp. 90–113.

10 V. I. Kuznetsov, *Economic Integration: Two Approaches* (Moscow: Progress Publishers, 1976), pp. 30, 34.

11. I. I. Iakubovskii, *Boevoe sodruzhestvo bratskikh narodov i armii* (Moscow: Voenizdat, 1975), pp. 107, 120.

12 I. F. Katushev, "V interesakh razvitiia sotsializma i ukrepleniia mira," *Kommunist* 12 (1973): 27.

13 B. Kozin, "The Drawing Together of the Socialist Countries—An Objective Regularity," *International Affairs* (Moscow), October 1976, p. 15.

14 See, for example, G. I. Tunkin, "Socialist Internationalism and International Law," *New Times* (Moscow), October–December 1957, p. 10.

15 For a fuller treatment of the relationship between proletarian and socialist internationalism, see M. S. Junusov, M. M. Skibitsky, and I. P. Tsameryan, eds., *The Theory and Practice of Proletarian Internationalism* (Moscow: Progress Publishers, 1976), pp. 247–72.

16 Ibid., esp. pp. 11–19.

17 Ibid., pp. 170–90; and E. Troitsky, "A New Study on the Nationality Question" (review of *Leninism and the Nationality Question in Present-Day Conditions*), *International Affairs,* January 1973, pp. 91–93.

18 See, e.g., L. I. Brezhnev, *Report of the CPSU Central Committee on the Immediate Tasks of the Party in Home and Foreign Policy* [25th CPSU Congress] (Moscow: Novosti Press Agency Publishing House, 1976), pp. 8–15. See also Kozin, "The Drawing Together of the Socialist Countries," pp. 14–21.

19 B. Kozin, "Socialist Countries: Unity and Cohesion," *International Affairs* (Moscow), March 1974, p. 5. Emphasis added.

20 B. Ladygin, "Socialist Internationalism: Fraternity and Cooperation," *International Affairs* (Moscow), June 1973, p. 10.

21 For the first elaboration of these "principles," see "Declaration of the Government of the USSR on the Principles of Development and Further Strengthening of Friendship and Cooperation Between the Soviet Union and Other Socialist States," *New Times* 45 (November 1956): 1.

22 Kozin, "The Drawing Together of the Socialist Countries," p. 18; and Junusov et al., *The Theory and Practice*, esp. pp. 260–65.

23 See Chapter 2, below, on " 'Limited Sovereignty': Doctrinal Disputes."

24 "Excerpts from the Report to the Tenth Hungarian Party Congress, Delivered 25 November 1970 by Zoltan Komocsin, Party Secretary in Charge of International Relations," in *Ruling Communist Parties and Détente: A Documentary History*, ed. Jeffrey Simon (Washington: American Enterprise Institute, 1975), pp. 182–83.

25 Junusov et al., *The Theory and Practice*, p. 252.

26 For more on this theme, see J. F. Brown, *Relations between the Soviet Union and Its Eastern European Allies: A Survey*, Rand Corporation Memorandum R–1742–PR (Santa Monica, Calif., November 1975), pp. 2 ff., 16, and 21.

CHAPTER 1: FROM BUDAPEST TO PRAGUE

1 Nikita S. Khrushchev, *Khrushchev Remembers: The Last Testament*, trans. and ed. Strobe Talbott (Boston: Little, Brown & Co., 1974), p. 222.

2 All of the treaties have since been renewed, some more than once; and several, most notably the ones to which Romania is party, entered the five-year extension period before renewal. (See Chapter 5, below.)

3 For more on this early round of treaty-making, see Charles D. Cary, "Patterns of Soviet Treaty-Making Behavior with Other Communist Party-States," in *Communist Party-States: Comparative and International Studies*, ed. Jan F. Triska (New York: Bobbs-Merrill Co., 1969), pp. 135–59; Boris Meissner, "The Soviet Union's Bilateral Pact System in Eastern Europe," in *Eastern Europe in Transition*, ed. Kurt London (Baltimore: Johns Hopkins Press, 1966), pp. 237–57; and Robert M. Slusser and Jan F. Triska, eds., *A Calendar of Soviet Treaties, 1917–1957* (Stanford: Stanford University Press, 1959).

4 The definitive study of the formative years of the bloc remains Zbigniew K. Brzezinski, *The Soviet Bloc: Unity and Conflict* (Cambridge: Harvard University Press, 1960; rev. ed., 1967), esp. pp. 67–151.

5 The speech was subsequently leaked to the West. A reliable version, annotated by Boris Nicolaevsky, was published by *The New Leader* (1956) as "The Crimes of the Stalin Era: Special Report to the 20th Congress of the Communist Party of the Soviet Union, by Nikita S. Khrushchev."

6 Khrushchev, *Khrushchev Remembers*, pp. 207–30.

7 Ibid., p. 221.

8 See also the account in Imre Nagy, *On Communism* (New York: Praeger Publishers, 1967).

9 "Treaty of Friendship, Cooperation, and Mutual Assistance between the People's Republic of Albania, the People's Republic of Bulgaria, the Hungarian People's Republic, the German Democratic Republic, the Polish People's Republic, the Rumanian People's Republic, the Union of Soviet Socialist Republics and the Czechoslovak Republic" [The Warsaw Treaty], *New Times* (Moscow) 21 (May 21, 1955).

10 Cf. the account in Khrushchev, *Khrushchev Remembers*, pp. 196–207.

11 "Declaration by the Soviet Government on 'Principles of Development and Further Strengthening of Friendship between the Soviet Union and Other Socialist States,' October 30, 1956," *New Times* 45 (November 1956): 1.

12 "Togliatti's Speech on 'Polycentrism' to the Central Committee of the Italian Communist Party, June 24, 1956," in *International Relations among Communists*, ed. Robert H. McNeal (Englewood Cliffs, N.J.: Prentice-Hall Publishing Co., 1967), pp. 87–90.

13 Soviet status of forces treaties were signed with Poland on December 18, 1956; the German Democratic Republic, March 12, 1957; Romania, April 15, 1957; and Hungary, May 27, 1957.

14 Khrushchev, *Khrushchev Remembers*, pp. 225–27.

15 According to Yugoslav Communist Milovan Djilas (*Conversations with Stalin* [New York: Harcourt, Brace and World, 1962], p. 129), the name of the organ was suggested by Stalin himself, in the hope that the Western press would be obliged to repeat the slogan each time the journal was cited.

16 " 'Declaration of the Conference of Representatives of Communist and Workers' Parties of Socialist Countries,' Moscow, November 22, 1957," in McNeal, *International Relations among Communists*, pp. 98–101.

17 The Warsaw Treaty. For a comparison of the texts of the Warsaw Treaty and the North Atlantic Treaty, see *The Warsaw Pact: Its Role in Soviet Bloc Affairs*, A Study Submitted by the Sub-committee on National Security and International Operations to the Committee on Government Operations, 89th Cong., 2nd sess. (Washington, D.C.: Government Printing Office, 1966), Appendix B.

18 Bela K. Kiraly, "Why the Soviets Need the Warsaw Pact," *East Europe* 18, no. 4 (April 1969): 11.

19 A Polish-born Soviet military leader in World War II, Marshal Rokossovsky was appointed minister of defense in Poland in 1949 and also became a full member of the Politburo.

20 The "units assigned" are mostly Soviet in composition; they include Soviet forces stationed in Eastern Europe, all East German forces, and limited contingents specifically assigned to the WTO by other East European countries.

21 For details of the 1969 reorganization, see Chapter 3, below.

22 Representation at the PCC has varied considerably: in its early years, sessions were attended by heads of state and defense ministers; more recently, Party first secretaries and other officials have attended as well.

23 *Voenno-morskoi mezhdunarodno-pravovoi spravochnik* (Moscow: Voenizdat,

1967). See also I. I. Iakubovskii, *Boevoe sodruzhestvo bratskikh narodov i armii* (Moscow: Voenizdat, 1975), pp. 98–100.

24 *Izvestia*, January 29, 1956.

25 Raymond L. Gartoff, "The Military Establishment," *East Europe* 14, no. 9 (September 1965): 14–15.

26 For an analysis of motivations underlying the changes, see Thomas W. Wolfe, *Soviet Power and Europe, 1945–1970* (Baltimore: Johns Hopkins Press, 1970), pp. 144–59.

27 *Izvestia*, March 31, 1961.

28 Wolfe, *Soviet Power and Europe*, pp. 150–51; and A. Ross Johnson, *Soviet–East European Military Relations: An Overview*, Rand Corporation Memorandum P–5383–1 (Santa Monica, Calif., August 1977), p. 8.

29 Whereas in 1956 PCC delegations were headed by the chief or deputy chief of government, by 1960 they were led by Party first secretaries, and by 1966 some delegations included other Politburo members, foreign ministers, members of the joint chiefs-of-staff, and other high officials. See Iakubovskii, *Boevoe sodruzhestvo*, p. 98.

30 *Pravda*, September 16, 1965.

31 See Chapter 3, below.

32 On the negative motivations for the formation of CMEA, see Nagy, *On Communism*, p. 189.

33 Khrushchev (*Khrushchev Remembers*, p. 218), describing his efforts to improve economic relations in the bloc, recounted this unlikely exchange with the head of Romania's State Planning Commission on the topic of terms of delivery:

"Please, Comrade Khrushchev, don't insist on such a system. It would cost Romania dearly."

"All right," I said, "we'll keep doing it the old way."

34 *Izvestia* (Sofia), February 23, 1960 (*East Europe* 10, no. 8 [August 1960]: 42–45). The signatories to the original charter were Albania, Bulgaria, Czechoslovakia, East Germany, Poland, Hungary, Romania, and the USSR. Albania ceased to participate in CMEA activities in 1961; Mongolia, Cuba, and Vietnam became members in 1962, 1972, and 1978, respectively. Yugoslavia is a "limited participant," and a number of states have been accorded "observer" status.

The charter was amended twice in 1962 and a third time in 1974. For a detailed examination of the changes, see J. L. Kerr, "A Revised Comecon Charter," RAD Background Report/124, *RFER*, August 6, 1975.

35 This stipulation, which Romania was able to exploit during the 1960s, was replaced in the 1974 amendment by the "interested party" principle. For details, see Chapter 6, below.

36 N. S. Khrushchev, *Kommunist* 12 (August 1962).

37 Nikita S. Khrushchev, "Vital Questions of the Development of the Socialist World System," *World Marxist Review* 5 (September 1962): 9.

38 "Statement on the Stand of the Rumanian Workers' Party concerning the Problems of the World Communist and Working Class Movement, April 12, 1964," in McNeal, *International Relations among Communists*, p. 128.

39 S. Jedrychowski, "The Economic Effects of the International Socialist Division of Labor," *World Marxist Review* 6 (March 1963): 4.

40 Tibor Kiss, *International Division of Labour in Open Economies* (Budapest: Akademiai Kiado, 1971), p. 167.

41 See also the comparison of CMEA, OECD, and EEC in Kiss, p. 173.

42 For an analysis of the "Comprehensive Program" of 1971, see Chapter 3, below.

43 "Concerning the Creation of the People's Communes in the Village," *Jen Min Jih Pao*, September 10, 1958.

44 See W. E. Griffith, *Albania and the Sino-Soviet Rift* (Cambridge: The MIT Press, 1963).

45 See Enver Hoxha's *The Khrushchevites: Memoirs* (Tirana: "8 Nentori" Publishing House, 1980). Hoxha strongly implies, but does not directly charge, that the Soviet leaders tried to "eliminate" the Albanian leaders, and offers his own account of Soviet-Albanian relations in the period 1953–1961, along with some entertaining character sketches of Soviet leaders.

46 Albania formally withdrew from the Warsaw Pact in 1968 and continues to be a nonparticipating member of CMEA.

47 For an analysis of this early period, see Stephen Fischer-Galati, *The New Rumania: From People's Democracy to Socialist Republic* (Cambridge: The MIT Press, 1967), pp. 44–77.

48 "Sino-Rumanian Joint Statement," April 14, 1958, as cited by Robin Alison Remington, *The Warsaw Pact: Case Studies in Communist Conflict Resolution* (Cambridge: The MIT Press, 1971), p. 62.

49 Cf. Khrushchev's account in *Khrushchev Remembers*, pp. 227–30.

50 This was the time of the publication of the twenty-five "propositions" outlining Chinese grievances against the Soviet Union.

51 *Pravda*, October 16, 1964. For analyses of the circumstances surrounding Khrushchev's fall, see Carl A. Linden, *Khrushchev and the Soviet Leadership, 1957–1964* (Baltimore: Johns Hopkins Press, 1966), pp. 174–208; and Michel Tatu, *Power in the Kremlin: From Khrushchev to Kosygin* (New York: The Viking Press, 1968), pp. 364–423.

52 On policy changes in the last years of Khrushchev's reign, see Wolfe, *Soviet Power and Europe*, pp. 100–127.

53 For an analysis of Yugoslav, Polish, Romanian, and Hungarian relations with GATT, see Henry Schaefer, "East European Relations with GATT," RAD Background Report/5 (Economics), *RFER*, November 18, 1971.

54 *Pravda*, January 22, 1965.

55 *Pravda*, March 30, 1966.

56 *New York Times*, June 12, 1966.

57 *Pravda*, July 9, 1966.

58 Tass, September 29, 1965; *Pravda*, September 16, 1965.

59 Although later denied by the Romanian Foreign Ministry, the proposals were circulated in the Western wire services and the *New York Times* and the *Times* (London) on May 16, 1966.

60 *Mezinarodní politika*, no. 7 (1966).

61 For an analysis of the 1969 Budapest reforms, see Chapter 3, below.
62 The treaties are summarized in *Keesing's Contemporary Archives, 1967* (London: Keesing's Publications, 1968), p. 21981.
63 *Pravda*, March 28, 1967.
64 For a discussion of the Romanian treaties of 1970 and 1972, see Chapter 3, below.
65 For an English translation of one of Liberman's most influential articles, see *Foreign Affairs* 46, no. 1 (October 1967): 54–63.
66 For an analysis of the formative years of the NEM, see William F. Robinson, *The Patterns of Reform in Hungary: A Political, Economic, and Cultural Analysis* (New York: Praeger Special Studies Series, 1973).
67 On Šik's reform ideas, see, e.g., Ota Šik, *Plan and Market under Socialism* (New York: IASP, 1968). For a listing of Šik's major publications, see Z. Hejzlar and V. Kusin, comps., *Czechoslovakia, 1968–1969* (New York: Garland Publishing Co., 1975), pp. 305–6.
68 The immediate cause for Novotný's reprisals against the Writers' Union was the debate at its 4th Congress, held in June just after the outbreak of the Arab-Israeli war. Many writers took the floor to denounce the anti-Semitic invective of the official media and the pro-Arab posture of the Novotný regime.
69 The coup attempt was launched by Novotný protégé General Jan Šejna, who in February 1968 fled to the West and some years later (1974) went public with a controversial account of secret Warsaw Pact contingency plans, including several for the invasion of Austria.
70 Among the best of the many studies of the Prague Spring are Galia Golan, *The Czechoslovak Reform Movement: Communism in Crisis, 1962–1968* (Cambridge: Cambridge University Press, 1971); Journalist M [Josef Maxa], *A Year is Eight Months* (Garden City, N.Y.: Doubleday and Co., 1971); Zdeněk Mlynář, *Nightfrost in Prague: The End of Humane Socialism* (London: C. Hurst and Co., 1980); and H. Gordon Skilling, *Czechoslovakia's Interrupted Revolution* (Princeton: Princeton University Press, 1976).
71 An English translation of the Action Program is contained in Robin Alison Remington, ed., *Winter in Prague: Documents on Czechoslovak Communism in Crisis* (Cambridge: The MIT Press, 1969), pp. 88–137.
72 For useful insights into Soviet behavior and that of the Czechoslovak leaders during the period, see Jiří Valenta, *Soviet Intervention in Czechoslovakia, 1968: Anatomy of a Decision* (Baltimore: Johns Hopkins University Press, 1979).
73 Parallels with Poland in 1980 and 1981 naturally spring to mind. For analysis, see Bruce Porter, "Warsaw Pact Maneuvers and Poland: The Political Implications," RL 118/81, *Radio Liberty Research*, March 17, 1981; and Vladimir V. Kusin, "The Moscow Summit on Poland: A Look Back to 1968," RAD Background Report/294 (Czechoslovakia), *RFER*, December 10, 1980.
74 For an assessment of developments immediately following the invasion, see Chapter 2, below.
75 *Zeri i Popullit*, December 10, 1965.
76 For details of the Prchlík interview, see Chapter 3, below, under "The Budapest Reforms."

77 Oleg Bogomolev, in *Pravda*, January 13, 1968.

78 Proposed as early as 1963, the conference finally convened in Moscow in June 1969 after several postponements.

79 On the rumors of a new ideological organization, see R. Waring Herrick, "Moscow Conference Rules Out Any New Comintern or Cominform," *Radio Liberty Research*, CRD 219/69, June 25, 1969, and the discussion in Chapter 3, below, under "Directions of Change."

CHAPTER 2: THE POLITICS OF NORMALIZATION

1 Immediately following the invasion, the Yugoslav and Romanian leaders activated their people's militias and took other steps to strengthen their defenses against possible Soviet intervention. For its part, the United States government officially warned the Soviet Union against intervention in Romania or Yugoslavia (*New York Times*, August 31, 1968).

2 Jiří Hochman, "What is 'National Reconciliation'?" *Reportér* (Prague) (*East Europe* 18, no. 1 [January 1969]: 29).

3 These included Vasil Bilak, then first secretary of the Slovak Communist party; Drahomír Kolder, leading hard-line member of the Party Presidium; Oldřich Pavlovský, former Czechoslovak ambassador to Moscow; as well as Švestka, Jakeš, and perhaps Lenárt.

4 *Sedm pražských dnů, 21–27: Srpen 1968* (Prague, 1968), p. 51 (cited by H. Gordon Skilling, *Czechoslovakia's Interrupted Revolution* [Princeton: Princeton University Press, 1976], p. 760). See also the remarkable first-hand account of Josef Smrkovský in "Mluví Josef Smrkovský," *Listy*, no. 2 (1975), pp. 4–25.

5 *Pravda*, August 22, 1968. The other kidnapped members of the Party Presidium were Oldřich Černík, the prime minister; Josef Smrkovský, a prewar Communist who served as chairman of the National Assembly; František Kriegel, chairman of the National Front; Josef Špaček, Brno Party first secretary; and Bohumil Šimon (candidate member of the Presidium), Party first secretary in Prague.

6 According to the terms of the Moscow Protocol, the "Extraordinary" 14th Congress was declared illegal, and the next Congress, held in May 1971, became the legal 14th.

7 Although the fourteenth point obliged the parties to hold the talks "strictly confidential," a number of versions of varying authenticity have been published. See Robin Alison Remington, ed., *Winter in Prague: Documents on Czechoslovak Communism in Crisis* (Cambridge: The MIT Press, 1969), pp. 379–82.

8 See, for example, " 'Declaration of the Conference of Representatives of Communist and Workers' Parties of Socialist Countries,' Moscow, November 22, 1957," in *International Relations among Communists*, ed. Robert H. McNeal (Englewood Cliffs, N.J.: Prentice-Hall Publishing Co., 1967), pp. 98–101.

9 See, for example, the resolution of the plenary session of the Central Committee of the CPSU, April 10, 1968; the report of Andrei Gromyko to the Supreme Soviet of the USSR, June 27, 1968; and the Warsaw Letter to the Czechoslovak Communist party, July 15, 1968, all in Boris Meissner, *The Brezhnev Doctrine*, East European

Monographs, no. 2 (Kansas City: Governmental Research Bureau, 1970), pp. 39–45.

10 *Pravda*, August 22, 1968.

11 *Pravda*, August 24, 1968.

12 S. Kovalev, "On 'Peaceful' and Nonpeaceful Counterrevolution," *Pravda*, September 11, 1968. All these charges were to be resurrected twelve years later by Soviet and East European commentators in characterizing the putative "counterrevolutionary" forces at work in Poland after August 1980.

13 S. Kovalev, "Sovereignty and the Internationalist Obligations of Socialist Countries," *Pravda*, September 26, 1968. In private conversations later, Kovalev reportedly expressed astonishment that his articles had generated such wide discussion in the West and denied that he felt himself to be breaking new ideological ground.

14 *Pravda*, November 13, 1968 (*CDSP* 20, no. 46 [December 4, 1968]: 3–5).

15 Cf. Brezhnev's speech to the International Conference of Communist and Workers' Parties in June 1969, as discussed in Chapter 3, below.

16 See, for example, the wording of the bilateral treaties signed since 1968, as discussed in Chapter 5, below.

17 For more on the theoretical development of "socialist internationalism," see Teresa Rakowska-Harmstone, " 'Socialist Internationalism' and Eastern Europe: A New Stage," *Survey* 22, no. 1 (Winter 1976): 38–54.

18 Malcolm Mackintosh, "The Warsaw Pact Today," *Survival*, May–June 1974, pp. 122–23.

19 Todor Zhivkov, "Communism is the Main Force in Human Progress Today," speech delivered on August 25, 1968, in *Todor Zhivkov: Unity on the Basis of Marxism-Leninism (Speeches, Reports, and Articles)*, ed. A. Rizov (Sofia: Sofia Press, 1969), p. 353.

20 Todor Zhivkov, "Unity is Our Chief Force," speech to the Fifth Congress of the Polish United Workers' Party, November 12, 1968, ibid., p. 374.

21 For analyses of East German attitudes toward the Dubček government, see Skilling, *Czechoslovakia's Interrupted Revolution,* pp. 675–81 and 740–42; and Melvin Croan, "Czechoslovakia, Ulbricht, and the German Problem," *Problems of Communism*, January–February 1969, pp. 1–7.

22 Skilling (*Czechoslovakia's Interrupted Revolution,* p. 742) cites an exchange in which Gomulka reportedly stated: "In 1960 I was the 'Polish Dubček.' In 1968 I was no longer regarded as such and I simply could not risk any changes." For more on the Polish internal conflict, see Jan B. de Weydenthal, "Polish Politics and the Czechoslovak Crisis of 1968," *Canadian Slavonic Papers* 14 (Spring 1972): 31–56. See also the account of Gomulka's interpreter, Erwin Weit, in his *At the Red Summit: Interpreter behind the Iron Curtain* (London: Macmillan & Co., 1973).

23 The "Partisans" under General Mieczyslaw Moczar (then minister of the interior and head of the veterans' organization) were actually a highly complex faction which drew strength from nationalistic, anti-Soviet, and anti-Semitic sentiment within the Party and among workers.

24 *Trybuna Ludu*, November 12, 1968 (Remington, *Winter in Prague,* pp. 426–29).

25 For more on Hungarian attitudes, see Richard Lowenthal, "The Sparrow in the Cage," *Problems of Communism,* November–December 1968, pp. 21–22.

26 *Magyar Hirlap* (Budapest), October 26, 1968, as cited by Oton Ambroz, "The Doctrine of Limited Sovereignty: Its Impact on East Europe," *East Europe* 18, no. 5 (May 1969): 20.

27 Cited in Ambroz, "Doctrine of Limited Sovereignty," p. 22.

28 *Scinteia,* August 22, 1968 (Remington, *Winter in Prague,* p. 358).

29 See, for example, Nicolae Ceauşescu, *The Leading Role of the Party in the Period of Completing the Building of Socialism* (Bucharest: Meridiane Publishing House, 1967), esp. p. 51; and Nicolae Ceauşescu, *The Romanian Communist Party: Continuer of the Romanian People's Revolutionary and Democratic Struggle, of the Traditions of the Working-Class and Socialist Movement in Romania.* (Bucharest: Agerpress, 1966), esp. p. 86. For a summary of the ideological foundations of the independent Romanian position, see Robert L. Farlow, "Romanian Foreign Policy: A Case of Partial Alignment," *Problems of Communism,* November–December 1971, pp. 54–63.

30 *Borba,* March 13, 1969 (Meissner, *The Brezhnev Doctrine,* pp. 72–73).

31 "Statement by the Central Committee of the Albanian Party of Labor and the Council of Ministers of Albania," August 22, 1968, *Peking Review,* August 30, 1968 (cited by Meissner, *The Brezhnev Doctrine,* p. 79).

32 Meissner, *The Brezhnev Doctrine,* p. 78.

33 *Peking Review,* April 30, 1969 (Meissner, *The Brezhnev Doctrine,* p. 79).

34 *Granma,* August 24, 1968 (Remington, *Winter in Prague,* pp. 334–44).

35 *L'Humanité,* August 23, 1968 (Remington, *Winter in Prague,* pp. 332–34).

36 *L'Unità,* August 22, 1968 (Remington, *Winter in Prague,* pp. 331–32).

37 Četeka, August 21, 1968 (Meissner, *The Brezhnev Doctrine,* pp. 62–63).

38 Meissner, *The Brezhnev Doctrine,* pp. 63–68.

39 "Declaration of the National Assembly of the Czechoslovak Socialist Republic," August 28, 1968 (ibid., p. 69).

40 For excerpts of these speeches, see Pavel Tigrid, *Why Dubček Fell* (London: Macdonald and Co., 1971), pp. 119–23; and Skilling, *Czechoslovakia's Interrupted Revolution,* pp. 801–4.

41 See, for example, *Student,* August 27, and *Literární Listy,* August 28, 1968, as cited in Tigrid, *Why Dubček Fell,* p. 123.

42 *Rudé Právo,* September 3, 1968.

43 Tigrid, *Why Dubček Fell,* Appendix A.

44 *Pravda,* July 30, 1968.

45 Probably the key immediate factor in the Soviet decision to invade was the prospect of far more sweeping personnel changes at the Fourteenth "Extraordinary" Party Congress, scheduled initially for early September (but convened early to condemn the invasion).

46 On "normalization" in Czechoslovakia, see esp. Fred H. Eidlin, *The Logic of "Normalization"* (New York: Columbia University Press, 1980); Vladimir V. Kusin, *From Dubček to Charter 77* (New York: St. Martin's Press, 1978); and Zdeněk Mlynář, *Night Frost in Prague: The End of Humane Socialism,* trans. Paul Wilson (London: Hurst, 1980).

47 Clubs such as K-231, named after Law No. 231 of 1948 (on political crimes), and

KAN, an association of non-Party members, sprang up in early 1968 as forums for the promotion of various progressive causes..

48 For the minutes of the negotiations between Kuznetsov and Smrkovský, see Tigrid, *Why Dubček Fell,* Appendix B.

49 Tass, October 5, 1968. Dubček and Černík headed the delegation to the October 3–4 meeting; the Czechoslovak delegation to the next meeting (October 15–16) was led by Černík.

50 Treaty on the "temporary stationing of Soviet troops on Czechoslovak territory," *Pravda,* October 19, 1968.

51 *FBIS,* November 5, 1968.

52 On October 30, for example, the chief of the Main Political Administration of the Soviet Army and Navy, General Yepishev, hosted a delegation of political workers of the Czechoslovak People's Army.

53 "Czechoslovakia from January to August," *Trybuna Ludu,* November 3, 1968.

54 For an account of this period, see Tigrid, *Why Dubček Fell,* pp. 137–53.

55 The federative arrangement was enacted on October 27, 1968, signed by the president on October 30, 1968, and put into effect from January 1, 1969.

56 See, for example, the so-called strategic plan designed to secure the removal of Soviet troops, as described in Tigrid, *Why Dubček Fell,* pp. 147–48.

57 For the remarkable evolution of the official Soviet attitude toward the March events in Czechoslovakia, see Radio Moscow and *Pravda,* March 30 through April 4, as translated in *FBIS.*

58 The proposal to replace Dubček came, ironically, from Ludvík Svoboda, who as defense minister had been instrumental in the Communist coup of 1948 and as president had played such a different role in the events of 1968. The irony is compounded by the fact that his surname means "freedom."

59 Josef Smrkovský, who was dropped from the Presidium at the time of Dubček's resignation, was by this time removed from decisionmaking circles.

   A fuller citation from Ludvík Vaculík's *The Guinea Pigs* (trans. Káča Poláčková [New York: Penguin Books, 1975], pp. 117–18) is: "It gave up, it threw in the towel, it lost its will and its courage, it had exhausted all its ideas, it called it quits, it was weak and floppy, it didn't give a damn, . . . it began to tremble, its teeth chattered."

60 For brief discussions of normalization under Husák, see Tigrid, *Why Dubček Fell,* pp. 168–93; and Edward Taborsky, "Czechoslovakia: The Return to 'Normalcy,' " *Problems of Communism,* November–December 1970, pp. 31–41.

61 Kriegel's courageous speech rejecting the grounds for his removal from the Central Committee is translated in *East Europe* 18, no. 7 (July 1969): 25–27.

62 Taborsky, "Czechoslovakia," p. 32.

63 Ibid, pp. 37–39.

64 For a listing of Husák's remarkable itinerary, see *ABSEES* (Soviet and East European Abstract Series) 1 (27), July 1970, Special Section, pp. xv–xvii.

65 *Rudé Právo,* April 22, 1969.

66 See, for example, Vasil Bilak's 1969 article in *Problems of Peace and Socialism, FBIS,* March 27, 1969.

67 Radio Prague, September 28, 1969 (*FBIS* September 29, 1969).

68 *Pravda* and *Izvestia,* October 29, 1969.

69 For excerpts from the Czechoslovak press during this period, see Henry W. Schaefer, *Comecon and the Politics of Integration* (New York: Praeger Publishers, 1972), pp. 68–69.

70 For a discussion of the 1970 treaty, see Chapter 5, below.

71 Lewis S. Feuer, "The Intelligentsia in Opposition," *Problems of Communism,* November–December 1970, p. 16.

72 Grey Hodnett and Peter J. Potichnyj, *The Ukraine and the Czechoslovak Crisis* (Canberra, 1970).

73 See Natalia Gorbanevskaya, *Red Square at Noon* (London: Andre Deutsch, 1972).

74 *Pravda,* August 10, 1968.

75 L. A. D. Dellin, "Bulgarian Economic Reform: Advance and Retreat," *Problems of Communism,* September–October 1970, pp. 44–52.

76 *Neues Deutschland,* November 13, 1968.

77 One manifestation of the Party's tougher stand was the demotion in March 1969 of dissident former premier Andras Hegedus from his position in the Hungarian Academy of Sciences.

78 *East Europe* 18, no. 1 (January 1969), p. 36. Sino-Albanian relations began to cool over the course of the next year, and the proposal for a Chinese military base was apparently dropped.

79 Gabriel Fischer, "Rumania," in *The Communist States in Disarray, 1965–1971,* ed. Adam Bromke and Teresa Rakowska-Harmstone (Minneapolis: University of Minnesota Press, 1972), pp. 162–63.

80 *Zeri i Popullit,* April 5, 1970.

81 *Magyar Hirlap,* August 13, 1971. See also F. Stephen Larrabee, "Changing Perspectives in the Balkans," RAD Backround Report/31 (Bulgaria), *RFER,* December 9, 1971.

82 *New York Times,* September 27, 1968; *Christian Science Monitor,* October 5, 1968; *Daily Telegraph* (London), October 10, 1968.

83 In a communiqué sent to the Bulgarian government, the Albanians asserted they had "incontrovertible evidence" that "large concentrations" of Soviet troops had arrived in Bulgaria. The Bulgarian reply termed the charges a "concoction." See *Daily Telegraph* (London), October 10, 1968.

84 The Soviet campaign was undoubtedly intended for domestic consumption as well, with the Yugoslavs serving as convenient surrogates for "revisionists" in the Soviet and East European leaderships.

85 This was the period, it will be remembered, in which President Nixon visited Romania (August 1969) and President Ceauşescu paid a return visit to the United States (October 1971).

86 The details of the proposals, as well as the Romanian reaction to them, will be discussed in Chapter 3, below.

87 In September, the Romanians sent a delegate to the preliminary session in Budapest, where it was agreed to postpone the conference until the following year.

88 For a discussion of the build-up to the conference, see Canfield F. Smith, "The Rocky Road to Communist Unity," *East Europe* 18, no. 2 (February 1969): 3–9.

89 *Neues Deutschland,* October 24, 1968.

90 *Problemy mira i sotsializma,* May 1969.

91 See Chapter 7, below, under "Soviet–East European Ideological Relations."

92 Apparently out of deference to the Chinese, the Albanians, North Vietnamese, North Koreans, and most of the nonruling parties in Asia were likewise absent from the conference.

93 Details on the conference are drawn from Oton Ambroz, "The Moscow Summit Conference," *East Europe* 18, nos. 8–9 (August–September 1969): 15–20; and "The Summit Conference," *East Europe* 18, no. 7 (July 1969): 35–36.

94 At its September 1969 session, the Central Committee accepted Dubček's resignation from the Presidium and condemned most aspects of his reform program, but the promised "full analysis" did not come until December 1970, when the Central Committee issued the notorious "Lessons from the Crisis in the Party and in Society after the [1966] Thirteenth Party Congress." The report, later endorsed by the Fourteenth Party Congress in 1971, was cited in numerous Czechoslovak commentaries criticizing developments in Poland after August 1980.

95 For the full text of the resolution, see *Pravda,* June 18, 1969.

96 Ambroz, "The Moscow Summit Conference," p. 18.

97 Of the sixty-six parties which signed the complete resolution, five (including Romania) added verbal reservations. Four other parties signed only parts of the document, four more declared they had not been authorized by their Central Committees to sign the resolution, and one, the Dominican, simply refused to sign at all.

CHAPTER 3: ALLIANCE RESTRUCTURING

1 For a discussion of Soviet policy toward Europe in this period, see Thomas W. Wolfe, *Soviet Power and Europe, 1945–1970* (Baltimore: Johns Hopkins Press, 1970), pp. 312–85.

2 See Chapter 1, above, under "Warsaw Pact *Westpolitik.*"

3 The Social Democrats (SPD) assumed power as leader of a minor coalition with the Free Democrats (FDP).

4 *Statistical Yearbook, 1973* (New York: United Nations, 1974), Table B.

5 Fritz W. Ermarth, *Internationalism, Security, and Legitimacy: The Challenge to Soviet Interests in East Europe, 1964–1968,* Rand Corporation Memorandum Rm–5909–PR (Santa Monica, Calif., March 1969), pp. 134–49. Wolfe, *Soviet Power and Europe,* pp. 401–4 and 422–26, presented a similar series of policy alternatives facing bloc leaders in the aftermath of the Czechoslovak invasion.

6 Ermarth, *Internationalism,* p. 135. Ermarth's third and more extreme alternative, that of "systemic reform," involved a far more sweeping restructuring of bloc relations.

7 Specifically, Soviet options concerning the German question were overstated: while in the early 1960s the Soviet leaders might have been in a position to barter away the future of the East German state, by the end of that decade Soviet commitment to the preservation of a socialist East Germany, to say nothing of the commitment of the East German regime to its self-preservation, was too thorough to permit facile proposals for a unified Germany.

8 *Pravda*, March 18, 1968.
9 For a discussion of the East German position, see John Dornberg, "East Germany: The Special Case," in *East European Perspectives on European Security and Cooperation*, ed. Robert R. King and Robert W. Dean (New York: Praeger Publishers, 1974).
10 Cited by Timothy W. Stanley and Darnell M. Whitt, *Détente Diplomacy: United States and European Security in the 1970s* (New York: Dunellen Publishing Co., 1970), p. 85.
11 On the various East European positions, see King and Dean, *East European Perspectives*; Peter Bender, *East Europe in Search of Security* (Baltimore: Johns Hopkins Press, 1972); and A. Ross Johnson, *The Warsaw Pact "European Security" Campaign*, Rand Corporation Memorandum Rm–565–PR (Santa Monica, Calif., November 1970).
12 The offer came in Brandt's inaugural address on October 28. See David Binder in the *New York Times*, October 29, 1969. See also Lawrence L. Whetten, "The Role of East Germany in West German–Soviet Relations," *The World Today* 25, no. 12 (December 1969): 507–20.
13 *Pravda* and *Izvestia*, November 1, 1969.
14 *Pravda* and *Izvestia*, December 5, 1969.
15 R. Waring Herrick discusses East European policy orientations in "Moscow Summit Sanctions 'Controlled Steps toward Bilateral Détente toward Bonn,' " *Radio Liberty Research Bulletin*, December 15, 1969.
16 For an excellent analysis of Soviet–East German differences in 1969 and 1970, see Robin Alison Remington, *The Warsaw Pact: Case Studies in Communist Conflict Resolution* (Cambridge: The MIT Press, 1971), pp. 113–64.
17 J. F. Brown, *Relations between the Soviet Union and Its Eastern European Allies: A Survey*, Rand Corporation Memorandum R–1742–PR (Santa Monica, Calif., November 1975), pp. 17, 20. See also J. F. Brown, "Détente and Soviet Policy in Eastern Europe," *Survey* 20, nos. 2–3 (Spring/Summer 1974): 46–58.
18 B. Kozin, "The Drawing Together of the Socialist Countries: An Objective Regularity," *International Affairs* (Moscow), October 1976, p. 15.
19 See Chapter 2, above.
20 *Pravda*, June 18, 1969.
21 See Wolfe, *Soviet Power and Europe*, pp. 495–96; and David Binder "Soviets Seeking New Red Grouping," *New York Times*, October 31, 1968.
22 See R. Waring Herrick, "Warsaw Pact Restructuring Strengthens Principle of National Control," *Radio Liberty Research*, CRD 72/70, March 6, 1970.
23 *Trybuna Ludu*, November 17, 1968 (cited by Henry W. Schaefer, *Comecon and the Politics of Integration* [New York: Praeger Publishers, 1972], p. 16).
24 G. M. Sorokin, *Voprosy ekonomiki*, December 1968.
25 Tad Szulc, "Soviet Economic Bloc Stalled by Two Key Problems," *New York Times*, February 2, 1969.
26 For details on these early Soviet proposals and East European counterproposals, see Chapter 1, above, under "Warsaw Pact *Westpolitik*."
27 "Report on Press Conference with Lieutenant General Vaclav Prchlík, Head of the State Administrative Section of the Czechoslovak Communist Party Central Committee, July 15, 1968," Prague Domestic Radio Service, July 15, 1968, in *Winter in*

Prague: Documents on Czechoslovak Communism in Crisis, ed. Robin Alison Remington (Cambridge: The MIT Press, 1969), pp. 214–20.

28 For the immediate Soviet reaction, see "Whose Favor Is Gen. V. Prchlík Currying?" *Krasnaya zvezda*, July 23, 1968.

29 Criminal prosecution was initiated in October 1969, and General Prchlík was ultimately sentenced to three years in prison for "frustrating and jeopardizing the activity of state agencies" (see *International Herald Tribune*, March 27, 1971).

30 *English Bulletin* (Budapest) 9, no. 38 (September 1970), as cited by Malcolm Mackintosh, "The Warsaw Pact Today," *Survival*, May–June 1974, p. 123.

31 Henry Kamm, "Rumanians Resist Warsaw Pact Maneuvers," *New York Times*, August 29, 1967.

32 R. Waring Herrick, "Mediterranean Naval Maneuvers Last May by 'Warsaw Pact—Sans Rumania,' " *Radio Liberty Research*, CRD 286/69, August 21, 1969.

33 On the evolution of the "Northern Tier" concept, see Wolfe, *Soviet Power and Europe*, pp. 298 ff. and 478–79.

34 Ibid., pp. 478–80.

35 See Henry Kamm, "Rumania Resists Pact Maneuvers," *New York Times*, March 5, 1969.

36 *Times* (London), February 20, 1969.

37 The Romanians further agreed to begin negotiations toward the renewal of the Soviet-Romanian Treaty of Friendship, Cooperation, and Mutual Assistance, which had entered the automatic five-year extension period in February 1968.

38 See, for example, Četeka, March 16, 1969; Eric Bourne, "Warsaw Pact Bloc Shows Unity," *Christian Science Monitor*, March 18, 1969.

39 Miodrag Marovic, "Blitz Conference," *Nin* (Belgrade), March 23, 1969.

40 Radio Prague, March 20, 1969 (*FBIS*, March 21, 1969).

41 The clashes began on March 2; and on March 15, just two days before the Budapest conference, Soviet troops ambushed Chinese forces on a disputed island in the Ussuri River, between Manchuria and the Soviet Far East.

42 *Mladá Fronta* (Prague), March 20, 1969; *Rudé Právo*, March 17, 1969; Radio Zagreb, March 22, 1969; and Marovic, "Blitz Conference." On March 20, however, Radio Prague reported that there had been no talk in Budapest concerning deployment of Warsaw Pact troops to the Chinese border.

43 Marovic, "Blitz Conference"; and Radio Belgrade, March 24, 1969.

44 Radio Budapest, March 18, 1969 (*FBIS*, March 19, 1969).

45 Radio Moscow, March 17, 1969 (cited by Michael Boll, "Summit Meeting of the Warsaw Pact Concluded," *RFER*, USSR/45, March 18, 1969).

46 *Trybuna Ludu*, March 19, 1969; Jan Marko's speech over Radio Prague, March 20, 1969; and *Scinteia*, March 20, 1969.

47 *Rudé Právo*, March 19, 1969, and *Mladá Fronta*, March 20, 1969.

48 Radio Prague, March 20, 1969.

49 Radio Belgrade, March 24, 1969.

50 Of the many, occasionally contradictory, summaries of the Budapest reforms, see especially Lawrence T. Caldwell, "The Warsaw Pact: Directions of Change," *Problems of Communism*, September–October 1975, pp. 2–9; R. Waring Herrick, "Warsaw Pact Restructuring Strengthens Principle of National Control," *Radio Liberty Research*, CRD 72/70, March 6, 1970; A. Ross Johnson, *Soviet–East*

European Military Relations: An Overview, Rand Corporation Memorandum P–5383–1 (Santa Monica, Calif., August 1977), pp. 11–21; and Mackintosh, "The Warsaw Pact Today," pp. 122–26.

For the fullest Soviet summary of the reforms, see I. I. Iakubovskii, *Boevoe sodruzhestvo bratskikh narodov i armii* (Moscow: Voenizdat, 1975), pp. 97–100 and 141–42. (The more common transliteration of the author's name, *Yakubovsky*, is employed in the present text.)

51 Lajos Czinege, "The Further Development of the Warsaw Pact Defense Organization," *Nepszabadsag*, May 10, 1969 (cited by Herrick, "Warsaw Pact Restructuring," p. 5).

52 Before 1969, the East European defense ministers had been doubly subordinate to their Soviet counterpart, for under the Joint Command they were subordinate to the WTO commander-in-chief, who as a Soviet deputy defense minister was himself subordinate to the Soviet minister of defense.

53 Mackintosh, "The Warsaw Pact Today," p. 123.

54 S. M. Shtemenko, *Agitator*, April 1975 (cited by Johnson, *Soviet–East European Military Relations*, p. 17). This interpretation of the function of the Military Council is confirmed by Marshal Yakubovsky in "Bastion of Peace and National Security," *Voenno-istoricheskii zhurnal*, no. 3 (March 1971).

55 Mackintosh, "The Warsaw Pact Today," p. 123, argues that the council, apparently modeled on the military councils in the Soviet armed forces, includes the WTO commander-in-chief, his deputy, the WTO chief of staff (all Soviet officers) and perhaps two other Soviet officers as well.

56 Czinege, "The Warsaw Pact Defense Organization"; and M. Titov, in *Krasnaya zvezda*, January 8, 1976.

57 *A-Revue* (Prague), July 12, 1968, pp. 28–30, and May 17, 1968, pp. 32–39 (cited by Roman Kolkowicz, "The Warsaw Pact: Entangling Alliance," *Survey* 70/71 [Winter/Spring 1969]: 93–94). The Romanians, as has been seen, voiced similar concerns. See Ermarth, *Internationalism*, pp. 33–36; and Joseph J. Baritz, "The Warsaw Pact and the Kremlin's European Strategy," *Bulletin for the Study of the USSR*, May 1970, pp. 15–28.

58 Herrick ("Warsaw Pact Restructuring," pp. 6–7) suggests that with the assignment of more East European officers to the reconstituted Joint Command, East European influence in that body, too, may have been expanded.

59 *Obrana lidu* (November 22, 1969, as cited by Johnson, *Soviet–East European Military Relations*, p. 17) reported that the Joint Staff had been formed ad hoc to support individual maneuvers prior to 1969. A 1966 Soviet naval handbook on international law, however, stated that the staff had already been established "for the constant and operational solution of special questions of the joint defense of the member states" (*Voenno-morskoi mezhdunarodno-pravovoi spravochnik* [Moscow: Voenizdat, 1967].

60 Mackintosh, "The Warsaw Pact Today," p. 123; and Herrick, "Warsaw Pact Restructuring," p. 7.

61 Mackintosh, "The Warsaw Pact Today," pp. 123–24.

62 Although the Permanent Commission and a Joint Secretariat for Technical Services were created in 1956, no mention has since been made of their activities. They

continued to exist, on paper at least, until 1966, but Soviet sources ceased to include them in organizational descriptions of the Warsaw Pact until the revival of the latter body in 1976.

63 *24th Congress of the CPSU, 30 March–9 April 1971: Documents* (Moscow: Novosti Press Agency, 1971), p. 13. Emphasis in the original.

64 In 1976, the Committee of Foreign Ministers and the Joint Secretariat were added to the Warsaw Pact's formal consultative structure (see Chapter 5, below).

65 Literally ''Who whom?'' Lenin's favorite maxim can also be rendered ''Who wins?'' or ''Who gets whom?''

66 The exercises were obviously designed as a show of bloc unity, for Czechoslovakia participated in two of the maneuvers and Romania in the third.

67 The practice of placing an East European officer in nominal command of exercises had been followed fairly regularly since 1962. ''Vesna 1969'' was touted as an especially important exercise, however, presumably to underscore the symbolic significance of East European command of Warsaw Pact maneuvers.

68 *Krasnaya zvezda*, December 24, 1969.

69 General S. Shtemenko, ''Combat Fraternity,'' *Krasnaya zvezda*, January 24, 1970. For summaries of Western press reports on the Shtemenko article, see Herrick, ''Warsaw Pact Restructuring.''

70 This thesis is developed in some detail in Herrick, ''Warsaw Pact Restructuring,'' pp. 1–3. See also ''Shtemenko on the Warsaw Pact; or, Plus Ça Change, Plus C'est La Même Chose,'' *RFER*, January 27, 1970.

71 Marian Jurek and Edward Skrzypkowski, *Uklad Warszawski* (Warsaw: Ministry of National Defense, 1970), pp. 54–63.

72 *Scinteia*, February 6, 1970 (cited in Remington, *The Warsaw Pact*, p. 132). See also Paul Wohl, ''Romania Resists Warsaw Pact Tightening,'' *Christian Science Monitor*, February 17, 1970.

73 *Smena*, February 3, 1970 (cited in ''Yakubovsky on the Warsaw Pact; or, How to Straighten Out Shtemenko,'' *RFER*, February 23, 1970).

74 The Soviet-Romanian treaty and joint trade protocol were signed in July 1970, and Romanian military forces participated in maneuvers held in East Germany in October 1970.

75 *Sovremennie problemy razoruzheniya* (Moscow: Mysl Publishing House, 1970).

76 Wolfe, *Soviet Power and Europe*, p. 497.

77 Jozef M. P. van Brabant, *Essays on Planning, Trade, and Integration in Eastern Europe* (Rotterdam: Rotterdam University Press, 1974), p. 22.

78 Cestmír Konecný, ''Prospects of New Ways of Socialist Integration,'' *International Relations* (Prague), 1970, p. 50 (reprinted from *International Relations* 3 [1969]).

79 Philip E. Uren, ''Patterns of Economic Relations,'' in *The Communist States in Disarray, 1965–1971*, ed. Adam Bromke and Teresa Rakowska-Harmstone (Minneapolis: University of Minnesota Press, 1972), p. 312.

80 Nikita S. Khrushchev, ''Vital Questions of the Development of the Socialist World System,'' *World Marxist Review* 5 (September 1962): 9.

81 *Nepszabadsag* (Budapest), September 3, 1969 (*East Europe* 18, no. 10 [October 1969]: 32).

82 Seventeen of the papers presented at the conference are compiled by Tibor Kiss, ed.,

in *The Market of Socialist Economic Integration: Selected Conference Papers* (Budapest: Akademiai Kiado, 1973). See in particular the editor's introductory summary of the conference, pp. 11–27.

83 A. Lyutov, "Economic Integration and the Socialist International Market," ibid., pp. 49–55, and O. Bogomolov, "The International Market of the CMEA Countries," ibid., pp. 31–36.

84 For summaries of East European views on CMEA reform during the period, see Henry W. Schaefer, *Comecon and the Politics of Integration* (New York: Praeger Publishers, 1972), pp. 3–38.

85 In the waning months of the Dubček regime, it will be remembered, enterprise councils were still being formed and reform ideas mooted, albeit without the high hopes of the previous year.

86 Schaefer, *Comecon and the Politics of Integration*, pp. 26–30.

87 For a dissenting conclusion, see Lawrence T. Caldwell and Steven E. Miller, "East European Integration and European Politics," *International Journal* 32, no. 2 (Spring 1977): 360–70.

88 A case in point is the negative Soviet response to Hungarian initiatives in the mid-1960s toward multilateral cooperation in the Danube basin, as discussed in Charles Andras, "The Slow Drift to Danubian Cooperation," *East Europe* 17, no. 2 (February 1968).

89 Cf. Stanislaw Wasowski, "Economic Integration in the Comecon," *Orbis* 16, no. 3 (Fall 1972): 765–71.

90 For a quasi-official presentation of the Hungarian position on CMEA integration by the secretary of Hungary's Permanent Economic Committee, see Tibor Kiss, *International Division of Labor in Open Economies* (Budapest: Akademiai Kiado, 1971), esp. pp. 124–206. See also Sandor Ausch, *Theory and Practice of CMEA Cooperation* (Budapest: Akademiai Kiado, 1972).

91 Konecný, "New Ways of Socialist Integration," p. 51.

92 *Ekonomicheskaya gazeta*, March 1969 (cited by Schaefer, *Comecon and the Politics of Integration*, p. 42).

93 Ibid., April 1969 (ibid., p. 43).

94 M. V. Senin, *Socialist Integration* (Moscow: Progress Publishers, 1973), pp. 255–56. Senin served as director of CMEA's International Institute for Economic Problems of the World Socialist System, established in 1971.

95 "Communiqué on the Twenty-third Special Comecon Session," *Pravda*, April 27, 1969.

96 Konecný, "New Ways of Socialist Integration"; and the press conference granted by Frantisek Hamouz, Czechoslovakia's permanent representative to CMEA, as reported by Ceteka and Radio Prague, May 5, 1969.

97 Schaefer, *Comecon and the Politics of Integration*, p. 50.

98 On the issue of pricing in CMEA and the differing East European views on the subject, see van Brabant, *Planning, Trade, and Integration*, pp. 127–203; and Kiss, *The Market of Socialist Economic Integration*, pp. 177–234.

99 Wasowski, "Economic Integration in the Comecon," p. 769.

100 Consider, for example, the procedural changes made in Interkhim, established just

after the 23rd CMEA session, as discussed in Schaefer, *Comecon and the Politics of Integration*, p. 52.

101 For discussion of Romanian policy during the period, see ibid., pp. 53–64, and Robert R. King, "Rumania and the Bloc: The Extent of 'Normalization,' " RAD Background Report/8 (Rumania), *RFER*, March 17, 1971.

102 "Agreement on the Formation of an International Investment Bank," July 10, 1970, in *The Multilateral Economic Cooperation of Socialist States: A Collection of Documents* (Moscow: Progress Publishers, 1977), p. 325.

103 For details of the bank, and especially of Romania's participation in it, see "The Comecon Investment Bank," *Radio Liberty Research*, CRD 403/70, November 24, 1970; and "Rumania Joins Investment Bank," Rumanian Situation Report/2, *RFER*, January 19, 1971, pp. 4–6.

104 "Communiqué on the 24th Session of the Council for Mutual Economic Assistance," *Pravda*, May 15, 1970, and *Izvestia*, May 16, 1970.

105 Schaefer, *Comecon and the Politics of Integration*, esp. pp. 127–32.

106 For details of the leadership change in Poland, see A. Ross Johnson, *The Polish Riots and Gomulka's Fall*, Rand Corporation Memorandum P–4615 (Santa Monica, Calif., April 1971).

107 Upon Walter Ulbricht's resignation in May 1971, Erich Honecker assumed leadership of the East German Communist party, the SED (Socialist Unity Party). For details of policy changes after the transition, see Peter C. Ludz, "Continuity and Change since Ulbricht," *Problems of Communism*, March–April 1972, pp. 56–57.

108 The protocol was signed in September 1970, the treaty in July 1970. For details of the treaty, see Chapter 5, below.

109 I. Radulescu, *Probleme Economice*, April 1971 (cited by Schaefer, *Comecon and the Politics of Integration*, p. 112).

110 *Pravda*, August 7, 1971. The full title of the plan is the "Comprehensive Program for the Further Extension and Improvement of Co-operation and the Development of Socialist Economic Integration by the CMEA Member-Countries." For a more detailed analysis of the integration program, see Schaefer, *Comecon and the Politics of Integration*, pp. 159–73; and Henry W. Schaefer, "The 25th Comecon Council Session and the Integration Program," RAD Background Report/2 (Economics), *RFER*, September 1, 1971.

111 See Wasowski, "Economic Integration in the Comecon," p. 772.

112 Van Brabant, *Planning, Trade, and Integration*, esp. pp. 106–9, also presents a useful distinction between the "positive" and "negative" approaches to integration and their relation to the Comprehensive Program. Positive integration, in this sense, aims at the establishment of coordinated and common policies, while negative integration, the approach favored by the Hungarians, seeks removal of discrimination in trade relations.

113 A distinction is made in the Comprehensive Program between "international" and "interstate" economic organizations. International organizations, generally narrower in scope, are not expressly governed by the interested party rule and are required only to observe and protect "the interests of individual CMEA member-countries."

114 The precise rules governing these bodies are listed in the Charter of the Council for Mutual Economic Assistance and the "rules of procedure" for its constituent bodies, all of which are printed in *The Multilateral Economic Cooperation of Socialist States: A Collection of Documents* (Moscow: Progress Publishers, 1977).

115 The third Council committee, on "Cooperation in Material and Technical Supply," was established in 1974.

116 In February 1972, some seventeen additional coordination centers for scientific information were created, with many more scheduled for creation later.

117 These include the Standing Commission on Telecommunications and Post (1971); the Interstate Conferences for Ministers of Home Trade (1971), Legal Affairs (1970), and Technical Inventions and Patents (1969); and the International Institute for Economic Problems of the World Socialist System (1971).

118 For discussion of financial and other matters relating to implementation of the Comprehensive Program, see Chapter 6, below.

119 In 1970 and 1971, three new interstate economic organizations were established—Interkhim (light chemicals), Interkosmos (space research), and Intergormash (mining equipment).

120 Typically, these involve agreements between enterprises to jointly plan, research, test, design, produce, and distribute goods in a limited functional area.

121 M. Senin, *Socialist Integration* (Moscow: Progress Publishers, 1973), p. 9. See also A. Shabalin, "The Comprehensive Programme of Integration," *International Affairs* (Moscow), April 1975, pp. 14–20.

122 Istvan Gyulai, *Nemzetkozi Szemle*, October 1971 (Hungarian Background Report/6 [1972], *RFER*).

123 Paul Marer, "Economics and Integration" (Paper prepared for the conference "Eastern Europe: Stability or Recurrent Crises?" Airlie House, Warrenton, Va., November 13–15, 1975), pp. 20–21.

124 This conclusion is supported by the data presented by Richard W. Mansbach, "Bilateralism and Multilateralism in the Soviet Bloc," *International Organization* 24 (1970): 371–80.

CHAPTER 4: CONFRONTING THE SEVENTIES

1 For background, see Chapter 3, above, under "*Westpolitik*: Controlled Bilateralism."

2 See Peter Bender, *East Europe in Search of Security* (Baltimore: Johns Hopkins Press, 1972); and Robert R. King and Robert W. Dean, eds., *East European Perspectives on European Security and Cooperation* (New York: Praeger Publishers, 1974).

3 Partly because of Romanian insistence, it was agreed at the CSCE preparatory talks that the conference would take place "outside the military alliances."

4 The Moscow-Bonn treaty was signed in August 1970, the Quadripartite Agreement on Berlin in September 1971, and West Germany's treaties with Poland, East Germany, and Czechoslovakia in May 1972, December 1972, and June 1973, respectively.

5 *New York Times*, February 20, 1972.

6 The official title of the talks thus became Mutual Reductions of Forces and Armaments and Associated Measures in Central Europe (MURFAAMCE), but Western spokesmen continued to refer to them as the Mutual and Balanced Force Reductions (MBFR) talks.

7 *Conference on Security and Cooperation in Europe: Final Act* (London: Her Majesty's Stationery Office, 1975).

8 See "Balkan *Nervenkrieg*" in Chapter 2, above.

9 Ceauşescu's personal diplomacy was increasingly active after President Nixon's visit to Romania in 1969 and Ceauşescu's visits to the United States and France the following year.

10 In late July and early August 1971, Soviet, Hungarian, and Czechoslovak troops conducted maneuvers near the Romanian border. At the same time, rumors began to circulate of possible Soviet-Bulgarian exercises in Bulgaria, and fears apparently were raised that the Soviet Union was contemplating some sort of intervention in Romania. See *International Herald Tribune*, August 26, 1971; and F. Stephen Larrabee, "Changing Perspectives in the Balkans," RAD Background Report/31 (Bulgaria), *RFER*, December 9, 1971.

11 *Pravda*, August 3, 1971.

12 The fact that the conference was also attended by Pyotr Shelest, then CPSU Politburo member and Party boss of the Ukraine, further suggests that the Balkan situation was high on the agenda of the Crimea session. It is also interesting to note that the Bulgarians, presumably because of their own efforts to ease tensions with their Balkan neighbors, did not join in the anti-Romanian diatribe. For summaries of press releases elsewhere in Eastern Europe, see Larrabee, "Changing Perspectives," pp. 9–11.

13 V. Palfi, *Magyar Hirlap* (Budapest), August 13, 1971 (Hungarian Press Survey no. 2143, *RFER*, August 27, 1971).

14 On inter-Party relations in Europe during the period, see Chapter 7, below, under "Inter-Communist Conflict."

15 Similar efforts toward *rapprochement* with Albania, obviously designed further to isolate the Chinese, were quickly rejected by the Tirana government.

16 Larrabee, "Changing Perspectives," pp. 12 f.

17 Credits totalling $990 million were announced on November 2, 1972. In September 1973 Soviet Premier Kosygin visited Yugoslavia, and in November Tito met Brezhnev and Foreign Minister Gromyko in Kiev.

18 Border negotiations have been held sporadically, and with little progress, since mid-1969. The proposal for an Asian collective security system, in which the USSR would be an influential participant, has been a familiar theme in Soviet policy since the June 1969 conference of Communist and workers' parties. The January 1971 Soviet offer of a treaty on the renunciation of force was upgraded in June 1973 to a proposal for a joint nonaggression pact.

19 *Pravda*, September 4, 1971.

20 See Ceauşescu's address to a conference of the Romanian Communist party, July 19, 1972, as cited in *Yearbook on International Communist Affairs, 1973*, ed. Richard F. Staar (Stanford: Hoover Institution Press, 1973), p. 91.

21 *Pravda*, August 1, 1972.

22 The preliminary round of MBFR discussions began in January 1971; and CSCE's first stage, the conference of foreign ministers, was held in early July.

23 *Pravda*, August 1, 1973.

24 Secretaries of the Central Committee departments for international and ideological affairs convened in Moscow in December 1973; and by the end of 1973 a total of eleven bilateral ideological agreements had been signed. For details, see Chapter 7, below.

25 Richard F. Staar, ed., *Yearbook on International Communist Affairs, 1974* (Stanford: Hoover Institution Press, 1974), p. 85.

26 For more on Ceauşescu's position, which included a reiteration of the demand that the post of Warsaw Pact commander-in-chief be rotated among all the member states, see Chapter 5, below.

27 *The Soviet Union, 1974–75* (New York: Holmes and Meier, Publishers, 1976), p. 185.

28 Ibid. Czechoslovak President Husák did, however, spend his August "vacation" in the Crimea, where he met briefly with General Secretary Brezhnev.

29 Nish Jamgotch, Jr., "Alliance Management in Eastern Europe: The New Type of International Relations," *World Politics* 27, no. 3 (April 1975): 420.

30 For an excellent, detailed summary of the Crimea conferences, see Kurt Seliger, "Brezhnevs Zwiegesprache am Schwarzen Meer," *Osteuropa*, no. 7 (1980). See also J. L. Kerr, "The Crimean Calvalcade in 1978," RAD Background Report/182 (Eastern Europe), *RFER*, August 21, 1978.

31 On July 31, 1980, barely a month before his ouster, Polish Party leader Edward Gierek and Brezhnev "informed each other about the state of affairs in their respective countries" and spoke hopefully about "the universal rapprochement of the Soviet and Polish people" (Radio Moscow, August 5, 1980).

32 This discounts three major intervening conferences: a "mini-summit," without Ceauşescu, in Warsaw during the 7th PUWP Congress in December 1975; the 25th CPSU Congress in February 1976; and the June 1976 Berlin Conference of European Communist and Workers Parties, discussed in Chapter 7, below.

33 Communiqué on the Meeting of the Political Consultative Committee, Agerpress (Bucharest), November 26, 1976. Ceauşescu's remarks were carried over Radio Bucharest, November 26, 1976 (1830 hours).

   Among the concessions apparently offered Ceauşescu were the exclusion of "socialist internationalism" and reference to the Chinese in the communiqué and the inclusion in the subsequent "declaration" of such Ceauşescu-isms as a call for liquidation of military blocs.

34 For a full text of the Bucharest Declaration, see Tass in English, November 26, 1976 (from Bucharest).

35 On the resolutions of the 24th Congress of the CPSU, see below in the present chapter, under "Coexistence and Consumerism, 1971–1975."

36 See Chapter 5, below, under "Consultation in the Warsaw Pact."

37 Ceauşescu visited Poland from May 17 to 19, East Germany from June 8 to 10, and Hungary from June 15 to 16, and played host in Bucharest to East Germany's Honecker (February 4–6) and Czechoslovakia's Husák (June 22–24).

38 For the communiqué text, see *Izvestia*, May 28, 1977.
39 For a survey of assessments of Belgrade, see East-West Institute, The Hague, *The Belgrade Conference, Progress or Regression: Eastern, Western, and Nonaligned Appraisals of an Unfinished Conference* (Leiden: New Rhine Publishers, 1978).
40 For a text of the communiqué, see Tass and BTA (Bulgarian News Agency), April 26, 1978.
41 The United States and the PRC exchanged formal diplomatic recognition in December 1978.
42 Ceauşescu's Far Eastern tour in 1978 took him to five countries: China (May 15–20), North Korea (May 20–23), Vietnam (May 23–26), Laos (May 26–28), and Cambodia (May 28–30). For the first official revelation of the Romanian-Chinese arms cooperation agreement, see *New China News Agency* (Peking), September 12, 1978.
43 For discussion, see J. F. Brown, "The Balkans after Chairman Hua," RAD Background Report/191 (Eastern Europe), *RFER*, August 29, 1978.
44 The Soviet-Vietnamese Friendship Treaty was signed in November 1978.
45 Tass, November 23, 1978.
46 Tass, November 24, 1978.
47 For a detailed analysis of the aftermath of the Moscow summit, see Charles Andras, "A Summit with Consequences," RAD Background Report/271 (Eastern Europe), *RFER*, December 14, 1978.
48 These aspects of the dispute will be explored more fully in Chapter 5, below.
49 E.g., Tass, November 29, 1978; *Rudé Právo*, November 28, 1978; and Radio Warsaw, November 28, 1978.
50 Resolution of the Central Committee of the Romanian Communist Party, Agerpress, November 30, 1978.
51 Tass, December 5, 1978. The word "demagogic" was dropped from Radio Moscow's Romanian-language broadcast of the following day.
52 For summaries of key speeches at the conference, see BTA, December 15 and 16, 1978.
53 Something obviously was going on behind the scenes, for at the time of the foreign ministers' meeting, Budapest announced that Romanian forces would take part in Warsaw Pact maneuvers soon to be held in Hungary, only to withdraw the report a few days later.
54 *Pravda*, May 16, 1979.
55 The Warsaw Pact foreign ministers met from December 5 to 6, 1979; on December 12 the NATO Council meeting in Brussels took a "dual decision," authorizing U.S. production of the Euromissiles (464 cruise missiles and 108 Pershing II ballistic missiles) but making their deployment in Europe contingent upon the outcome of East-West arms control negotiations on medium-range missiles.
56 For a detailed analysis, see William F. Robinson, "Afghanistan: The East European Reaction," RAD Background Report/21 (Eastern Europe), *RFER*, January 22, 1980.
57 For months on end, the Romanian media did not so much as mention the word "Afghanistan," nor for that matter "Iran," "hostages," "Olympics boycott," or any other controversial international issue.

58 On January 14, the General Assembly voted (104 for, 18 against, with 18 abstentions) in favor of a resolution calling for the immediate and total withdrawal of foreign troops from Afghanistan. Romanian Ambassador Teodor Marinescu's speech was carried on Radio Bucharest, January 15, 1980.

59 See, e.g., Eric Bourne in the *Christian Science Monitor*, June 4, 1980. See also the question and answer session on Radio Budapest's "Radio Diary" of February 20, as described in William F. Robinson, "On the Eve of Hungary's 12th Party Congress," RAD Background Report/61 (Hungary), *RFER*, March 18, 1980, pp. 3–5.

60 The foreign ministers' visits were drawn out over two months: Poland's Emil Wojtaszek (January 14–18) and Bulgaria's Petar Mladenov (January 24–26) came first, followed by East Germany's Oskar Fischer (February 19–20), Hungary's Frigyes Puja (March 17–18), and Czechoslovakia's Bohuslav Chnoupek (March 19–24).

61 Agerpress, 2 February 1980.

62 For a summing up of the Tito years, see "The Tito Era in Yugoslavia," RAD Background Report/100 (Yugoslavia), *RFER*, May 5, 1980.

63 Tensions resulting from student demonstrations in Kosovo in early 1981, of course, underscore the fragility of Yugoslav federalism post-Tito. For an assessment of post-Tito Yugoslavia, see Slobodan Stankovic, *The End of the Tito Era: Yugoslavia's Dilemmas* (Stanford: Hoover Institution Press, 1981).

64 See Romanian Situation Report/5, *RFER*, May 13, 1980, esp. pp. 1–8.

65 Radio Bucharest, May 10, 1980.

66 One symptom of this sentiment was a statement made by no less a figure than former West German Chancellor (and afterwards SPD president) Willy Brandt, who averred that the Soviet invasion of Afghanistan demonstrated that East and West needed more détente, not less.

67 See, e.g., A. Slobodenko, "The Strategy of Nuclear Adventurism," *International Affairs* (Moscow), no. 1 (January 1981), pp. 26–33.

68 A PCC communiqué, declaration, and statement were issued separately and carried by the Polish news agency PAP, May 15, 1980, and Tass, May 15 (datelined May 16) 1980.

69 Although delivered in milder terms than the Soviet leaders might have wished, this proposal did not, of course, conflict sharply with Soviet aims, for fulfillment of the condition for cessation of "outside interference" would presumably be left to Soviet judgment.

70 These withdrawals, of course, amounted to but a tiny fraction of the roughly 400,000 Soviet troops stationed in East Germany.

71 For analyses of these complex issues, see Charles Andras, "East and West Prepare for Madrid," RAD Background Report/149 (East-West), *RFER*, June 18, 1980; idem, "Toward a New Helsinki in the Military Field?" RAD Background Report/209 (East-West), *RFER*, August 18, 1980; and C.A., "Europe in Search of a Missile Equilibrium," RAD Background Report/124 (East-West), *RFER*, May 5, 1981.

72 On the "international significance" of the CPSU 24th Congress, see V. V. Zagladin, ed., *The World Communist Movement* (Moscow: Progress Publishers, 1973), pp. 475–85.

73 Brezhnev's full report is printed in *24th Congress of the CPSU, 30 March–9 April 1971: Documents* (Moscow: Novosti Press Agency Publishing House, 1971).

74 For discussion of the "Soviet model" under Stalin, see Zbigniew K. Brzezinski, *The Soviet Bloc: Unity and Conflict* (Cambridge: Harvard University Press, 1960; rev. ed., 1967), pp. 71–77.

75 Zagladin, *The World Communist Movement*, pp. 480 f.

76 *Pravda*, March 29, 1971. See also the March 28 *Izvestia* article by Polish Premier Piotr Jaroszewicz.

77 Cited in Richard F. Staar, ed., *Yearbook on International Communist Affairs, 1972* (Stanford: Hoover Institution Press, 1972), p. 13. The complete text is printed in *Under the Banner of Internationalism* (Sofia: Sofia Press, 1971).

78 *Rabotnichesko Delo*, April 29, 1971.

79 The report by Party leader Gustáv Husák, whose title was changed from first secretary to general secretary, is contained in *14th Congress of the Communist Party of Czechoslovakia* (Prague: Orbis, 1971).

80 One further symptom of lingering conflicts was the conviction of General Vaclav Prchlík in March to a three-year prison term for his public criticism (in July 1968) of Soviet domination of the Warsaw Pact.

81 Following the Party-wide purges of 1970, the Congress further consolidated the top leadership by replacing the remaining leaders of the Prague Spring and several leading conservatives as well.

82 Ulbricht's commitment to a reformist economic policy was also a factor in his removal. For a discussion, see Hartmut Zimmermann, "The GDR in the 1970s," *Problems of Communism*, March–April 1978, esp. pp. 3–17.

83 *Neues Deutschland*, June 16, 1971. Emphasis added.

84 For a discussion of the formative years of the "New Economic System for Planning and Managing the Economy" (*Neuen Ökonomischen System der Planung und Leitung der Volkswirtschaft*) and other reform measures in Eastern Europe, see Karl C. Thalheim and Hans-Hermann Höhmann, eds., *Wirtschaftsreformen in Osteuropa* (Köln: Verlag Wissenschaft und Politik, 1968).

85 For discussion, see Zimmermann, "The GDR in the 1970s," pp. 17–32.

86 The implications of the Polish riots, which erupted in response to the precipitous increase in food prices, will be discussed in Chapter 6, below.

87 Gierek's report is printed in *Program Report of the Political Bureau for the 6th PUWP Congress* (Warsaw: Polish Interpress Agency, 1971).

88 For an exhaustive review of the guidelines, see "Analysis of Polish Economic Policies for 1971–1975 and Beyond," Poland/27, *RFER*, December 13, 1971.

89 Nicolae Ceauşescu, *Romania on the Way of Building Up the Multilaterally Developed Socialist Society, April 1969–June 1970* (Bucharest: Meridiane Publishing House, 1970), pp. 314–33.

90 See Robert R. King, "Foreign Policy Aspects of the 11th Romanian Party Congress," Romania/20, *RFER*, December 9, 1974.

91 For elaboration, see Robert R. King, "Romania and the Soviet Union: Disharmony, in a Low Key," Romania/12, *RFER*, July 31, 1974.

92 Cited in Richard F. Staar, ed., *Yearbook on International Communist Affairs, 1971* (Stanford: Hoover Institution Press, 1971), p. 48.

93   For discussion of the Soviet oil price increases announced in 1974, see Chapter 6, below.

94   Richard F. Staar, ed., *Yearbook on International Communist Affairs, 1976* (Stanford: Hoover Institution Press, 1976), p. 45.

95   Hungarian Situation Report/17, *RFER*, April 9, 1975, pp. 8–9.

96   Kádár's report is summarized in Hungarian Situation Report/11, *RFER*, March 18, 1975.

97   Hungarian Situation Report/14, *RFER*, March 21, 1975, pp. 4–5.

98   Hungary's pursuit of a "market" solution to CMEA integration has been discussed in Chapter 3, above. For more on Hungary's economic policies, see Chapter 6, below.

99   Polish Situation Report/40, *RFER*, December 10, 1975, p. 3.

100   For more on the Congress, see ibid.; Polish Situation Report/39, *RFER*, December 9, 1975; Thomas E. Heneghan, "Poland on the Eve of the Seventh Party Congress," RAD Background Report/168 (Poland), *RFER*, December 3, 1975.

     Also of note at the Congress was the elevation to full Politburo membership of Stanislaw Kania, Central Committee secretary in charge of security and military affairs, who had been credited with successfully reorganizing the security apparatus in the wake of the abortive 1971 coup attempt of General Mieczyslaw Moczar and his "Partisans."

101   *Pravda*, February 25, 1976. On the CPSU Congress, see esp. F. Stephen Larrabee, "The Twenty-Fifth Congress of the CPSU: Problems and Prospects," RL 206/76, *Radio Liberty Research*, April 14, 1976.

102   Kevin Devlin, "Discordant Voices at the Moscow Conference," RAD Background Report/57, *RFER*, March 9, 1976.

103   On the economic aspects, see Keith Bush, "Brezhnev and Kosygin on Soviet Economic Performance," RL 119/76, *Radio Liberty Research*, March 2, 1976.

104   The only other changes to the ruling Politburo were the additions of Grigorii Romanov, Party boss of the Leningrad Oblast, and Dimitrii Ustinov, long active in the defense industries and soon to take over the Defense Ministry upon Marshal Grechko's death in 1977.

105   *Rabotnichesko Delo*, September 20, 1973.

106   G. S., "The BCP Theses on the Party and Mass Organizations," RAD Background Report/51 (Bulgaria), *RFER*, February 23, 1976; R. N., "The Bulgarian Party Theses on the Standard of Living," RAD Background Report/59 (Bulgaria), *RFER*, March 11, 1976; Bulgarian Situation Report/8, *RFER*, March 30, 1976; and Robert R. King, "The Bulgarian Party on the Eve of Its 11th Congress," RAD Background Report/67, *RFER*, March 18, 1976.

107   See G. S., "Bulgarian Plenum Devoted to Ideological Activity," RAD Background Report/31 (Bulgaria), *RFER*, April 19, 1974.

108   Among the newcomers to the Central Committee was Lyudmila Zhivkova, quixotic daughter of the first secretary. For a fascinating biographical sketch, see Yordan Kerov, "Lyudmila Zhivkova: Fragments of a Portrait," RAD Background Report/253 (Bulgaria), *RFER*, October 27, 1980. On the circumstances surrounding her death in 1981, see Bulgarian Situation Report/9, *RFER*, July 29, 1981.

109   On the immobility of the CPČS leadership, see Thomas E. Heneghan, "On the Eve

of the Czechoslovak Party Congress,'' RAD Background Report/84 (Czechoslovakia), *RFER*, April 7, 1976. For details of the congress, see *RFER* Czechoslovak Situation Reports 14, 15, and 16 of April 13, 14, and 21, 1976.

110 Svoboda had continued as president after the 1968 events until relinquishing the post to Gustáv Husák in May 1975.

111 Although Strougal alluded only obliquely at the Party Congress to the deteriorating terms of Czechoslovak foreign trade, he spoke much more forcefully in other settings on the need for a thorough revamping of Comecon trading procedures to offset the precipitous rise in prices for Soviet oil and other energy sources. (See Chapter 6, below.)

112 *FBIS* Daily Report (Supplements 39, 40, and 41) of June 9, 17, and 21, 1976. For a full text of the Congress proceedings, see *Protokoll der Verhandlungen des IX. Parteitages der Sozialistischen Einheitspartei Deutschlands*, 4 vols. (East Berlin: Dietz Verlag, 1976).

113 Article 63; See *Protokoll*, 2:293.

114 For a good discussion of their roles, and of the East German political landscape more generally, see Zimmermann, "The GDR in the 1970s," pp. 1–40. See also Ilse Spittmann, "The NÖS Team Returns," *Deutschland Archiv* (Cologne), no. 11 (1976), pp. 1121 ff.

115 See also Patrick Moore, "Romania on the Eve of the 12th Party Congress," RAD Background Report/249 (Romania), *RFER*, November 15, 1979.

116 For more on the congress, see Patrick Moore, "The Romanian Communist Party's 12th Congress: A Preliminary Review," RAD Background Report/263 (Romania), *RFER*, November 28, 1979.

117 *Scinteia*, September 9, 1979, as cited by Anneli Maier, "Ideology and Culture at the 12th RCP Congress," RAD Background Report/13 (Romania), *RFER*, January 16, 1980, p. 3.

118 Ceauşescu did disclose at the congress that off-shore oil had been discovered in the Black Sea, but offered no indication as to its size or exploitability.

119 The last Romanian leader with sufficient prestige and power to constitute a potential threat to Ceauşescu was Ion Gheorghe Maurer, who retired in 1974; since then, members of the ruling elite have been replaced or transferred before being able to establish any independent power base.

120 Cited by Moore, "The Romanian Communist Party's 12th Congress," p. 4.

121 The Pirvulescu incident notwithstanding, the personality cult reached new and bizarre heights in the celebrations of Ceauşescu's sixty-second birthday two months later. See Anneli Maier, "Ceauşescu Deified on His 62nd Birthday," RAD Background Report/34 (Romania), *RFER*, February 11, 1980.

122 Occasionally this national bond is affirmed explicitly, as in Kádár's closing address to the Party Congress: "We belong together whether we like each other or not; we are sons of the same people; we have one country; we live together. Either we prosper together or we sink together. . . . The Communists are no worse as Hungarian patriots than nonparty people. We too were born Hungarians" (cited by Andreas Hegyi, "A Communist Party Congress without Superlatives," *Berichte des Bundesinstituts für ostwissenschaftliche und internationale Studien* [Cologne], 1980, p. 16).

See also the fascinating article by Rezso Nyers, director of the Hungarian Academy of Science Institute of Economics, ''Patriotism and Economics,'' *Kozgazdasagi Szemle*, no. 1 (January 1981), pp. 1–15.

123 Speaking at the 11th HSWP Congress, for example, Soviet Politburo member Andrei Kirilenko said, ''This is real socialism.'' See also *Pravda*'s most flattering account of Hungarian ''flexibility'' and ''profitability'' at the time of Premier Tikhonov's 1981 visit to Budapest (*Pravda*, December 7, 1981).

124 See, for example, the remarkable question-and-answer session chaired by Central Committee foreign affairs department head Janos Berecz, as excerpted in William F. Robinson, ''On the Eve of Hungary's 12th Party Congress,'' RAD Background Report/61 (Hungary), *RFER*, March 18, 1980.

125 Cited in Hungarian Situation Report/7, *RFER*, April 1, 1980, p. 15. On the congress proceedings, see also Hegyi, ''A Communist Party Congress.''

126 For a detailed dicussion, see William F. Robinson, ''Hungary's NEM: A New Lease on Life,'' RAD Background Report/275 (Hungary), *RFER*, December 13, 1979.

127 Cited in Hungarian Situation Report/7, *RFER*, April 1, 1980, p. 9.

128 The other changes to the Politburo were the removal of Jenő Fock, who retired as prime minister just after the 11th Congress and had been retained to avoid a Politburo change between congresses, and the addition of Lajos Mehes, first secretary of the Budapest Party Committee, and Mihaly Korom, Central Committee secretary for Party and mass organization affairs. On other Party changes, see Charles Kovats, ''The New Hungarian Party Central Committee,'' RAD Background Report/192 (Hungary), *RFER*, August 1, 1980.

129 Cited by Hegyi, ''A Communist Party Conference,'' p. 9.

130 For a good discussion of this period, see Jan B. Weydenthal, *Poland: Communism Adrift*, Washington Papers, no. 72 (Beverly Hills and London: Sage Publications, 1979).

131 Originally the Committee of Workers' Defense (KOR, in its Polish acronym), the name was changed in 1977 to Committee of Social Self-Defense (KSS), but the earlier acronym stuck.

132 For analysis, see J. B. de Weydenthal, ''The Unofficial Report on Polish Politics and Society,'' RAD Background Report/239 (Poland), *RFER*, November 2, 1979; and idem,''The Unofficial Program for Change in Poland,'' RAD Background Report/164, *RFER*, July 2, 1980. Further DiP documents were issued after August 1980, but these naturally carried less weight than the earlier reports.

133 For a detailed account of the papal visit, see Radio Free Europe Research, *The Pope in Poland*, *RFER*, 1979.

134 Radio Warsaw, February 11, 1980, as cited in J. B. de Weydenthal with Roman Stefanowski, ''The Eighth Congress of the Polish Communist Party,'' RAD Background Report/46 (Poland), *RFER*, February 29, 1980, p. 3. On the Congress, see also J. B. de Weydenthal, ''Polish Party Opens a Precongress Campaign,'' RAD Background Report/254 (Poland), *RFER*, November 21, 1979; J. B. de Weydenthal, ''Poland's Party before Its Eighth Congress,'' RAD Background Report/30 (Poland), *RFER*, February 8, 1980; and Polish Situation Report/5, *RFER*, February 29, 1980.

135 Other changes to the Politburo were the addition of four new members (Lukaszewicz, Wrzaszczyk, Karkoszka, and Werblan) and the removal of Kepa, Tejchma, and

Stefan Olszowski. In another ironical twist, both Olszowski (who went to Berlin as Polish ambassador) and Tadeusz Grabski (who lost his Central Committee seat) were banished for allegedly harboring anti-Gierek sentiments, but returned to the top leadership later in 1980 to become defenders of orthodoxy.

136 The story must be cut off here. Of the rapidly growing body of literature on events immediately after August 1980, see especially Radio Free Europe Research, *August 1980: The Strikes in Poland* (Munich: Radio Free Europe Research, 1980); Jan B. de Weydenthal, "Workers and Party in Poland," *Problems of Communism,* November–December 1980, pp. 1–22; and the continuous stream of Radio Free Europe Research reports on Polish developments.

137 Cited in Weydenthal with Stefanowski, "The Eighth Congress," pp. 10–12.

138 Under the impact of the so-called "Polish events," the 1981 round of Party congresses—those of the CPSU, BCP, CPCS, and SED—were, if anything, even more immobilized on the major issues of the day than had been the 1976 congresses. See, e.g., Czechoslovak Situation Report/7, *RFER,* April 30, 1981.

CHAPTER 5: POLITICAL AND MILITARY RELATIONS

1 Parts of this chapter are taken from two earlier studies by the author: Robert L. Hutchings, "Twenty-five Years of the Warsaw Pact," RAD Background Report/ 105 (Eastern Europe), *RFER,* May 7, 1980; and idem, "The 'Entangling' Alliance: The Warsaw Pact on its Twenty-fifth Anniversary," RAD Background Report/108 (Eastern Europe), *RFER,* May 8, 1980.

2 Roman Kolkowicz, "The Warsaw Pact: Entangling Alliance," *Survey* 70/71 (Winter/Spring 1969): 86, 101.

3 E. Shevchenko, "Fraternal Alliance" (review article), *International Affairs* (Moscow) 7 (1976): 120.

4 Gromyko's speech on the twentieth anniversary of the Warsaw Treaty Organization, *Pravda,* May 15, 1975.

5 I. I. Iakubovskii, *Boevoe sodruzhestvo bratskikh narodov i armii* (Moscow: Voenizdat, 1975), p. 107.

6 Termed "the springboard factor" by J. F. Brown, *Relations between the Soviet Union and Its Eastern European Allies: A Survey,* Rand Corporation Memorandum R-1742-PR (Santa Monica, Calif., November 1975), p. v.

7 Cf. Thomas W. Wolfe, *Role of the Warsaw Pact in Soviet Policy,* Rand Corporation Memorandum P-4973 (Santa Monica, Calif., March 1973), pp. 2–6. See also Christopher D. Jones, *Soviet Influence in Eastern Europe: Political Autonomy and the Warsaw Pact* (New York: Praeger Special Studies, 1981), which argues that the pact's chief function is to prevent the East European states from developing independent, genuinely national armed forces.

8 On the foreign policy aspects of these sessions, see Chapter 4, above, on Soviet–East European summit diplomacy.

9 For discussion, see Chapter 3, above, on "*Westpolitik*: Controlled Bilateralism."

10 *The Soviet Union, 1974–75* (New York: Holmes and Meier Publishers, 1976), pp.

184–185; and Richard Homan, "Romanians Block Unity at Warsaw," *Washington Post*, April 20, 1974.

11 See Chapter 4, above, under "The Crimea Conferences."

12 For details, see Chapter 4, above, on Soviet–East European summit diplomacy and further discussion in the present chapter.

13 See Chapter 4, above.

14 See Chapter 3, above, under "The Budapest Reforms of the Warsaw Pact."

15 *Pravda*, November 27, 1976. See also the account in *Pravda*, December 5, 1976.

16 See Chapter 1, above, under "Toward a New Cohesion," and Chapter 3, under "The Budapest Reforms."

17 See, e.g., *Pravda*, May 22, 1980.

18 John Erickson, "The Warsaw Pact: The Shape of Things to Come?" in *Soviet–East European Dilemmas: Coercion, Competition, and Consent*, ed. Karen Dawisha and Philip Hanson (London: Royal Institute of International Affairs, 1981), p. 160.

19 See Chapter 3, above, under "The Budapest Reforms."

20 The pact commander-in-chief has claimed that the creation of the Committee for Coordination of Military Technology facilitated "the outfitting of the armies of the Warsaw Pact with new types of weapons and equipment" (V. G. Kulikov, "A Quarter Century Guarding the Achievements of Socialism and Peace," *Voenno-istoricheskii zhurnal*, no. 5 [May 1980], p. 26).

21 Report of the February 1974 meeting of the CDM, Radio Bucharest, February 7, 1974 (*FBIS*, February 8, 1974).

22 I. I. Iakubovskii [also transliterated *Yakubovsky*], "Bastion of Peace and National Security," *Voenno-istoricheskii zhurnal*, no. 3 (March 1971); K. Pashuk, "Twenty Years on Guard over Peace and Socialism," *Kommunist vooruzhenykh sil*, no. 9 (April 18, 1975), pp. 27–29.

23 V. G. Kulikov, ed., *Varshavskii dogovor-soyuz vo imya mira i sotsializma* (Moscow: Voenizdat, 1980), p. 167.

24 A December 21, 1970, session of the CDM, scheduled to follow the October meeting of the Military Council, was postponed abruptly and without explanation.

25 Cf. Erickson, "The Warsaw Pact: The Shape of Things to Come?" pp. 159–60; and A. Ross Johnson, Robert W. Dean, and Alexander Alexiev, *East European Military Establishments: The Warsaw Pact Northern Tier*, Rand Corporation Memorandum R-2417/1-AF/FF (Santa Monica, Calif., December 1980), pp. 179–84.

26 Warsaw Pact military officials frequently attend sessions of the Political Consultative Committee. Marshal Yakubovsky, for example, in his capacity as commander-in-chief of the Joint Forces (and not as head of the Military Council), delivered a report to the April 1974 meeting of the PCC in Warsaw (*New York Times*, April 20, 1974).

27 For analyses of Soviet military doctrine applied to the Warsaw Pact, see John Erickson, *Soviet Military Power* (London: Royal United Services Institute for Defence Studies, 1971), esp. pp. 65–73; Trevor Cliffe, *Military Technology and the European Balance*, Adelphi Papers no. 89, International Institute for Strategic Studies (London, 1972), pp. 29–35; Thomas W. Wolfe, *Soviet Power and Europe, 1945–1970* (Baltimore: Johns Hopkins Press, 1970), pp. 195–216, 451–58; and Friedrich Wiener, *The Armies of the Warsaw Pact Nations*, trans. William J. Lewis (Vienna: Carl Ueberreuter Publishers, 1976), pp. 111–74.

28 The first strategic echelon, derived from the WTO Order of Battle, includes contingents from all Warsaw Pact nations and thus is not synonymous with the Northern Tier, though those countries (along with Soviet forces stationed in Eastern Europe) form the core of the first echelon. For a good summary of WTO doctrine and Order of Battle, see Wiener, *Armies of the Warsaw Pact Nations,* esp. pp. 111–21.

29 For elaboration, see Wolfe, *Soviet Power and Europe,* esp. 451–58; and Wolfe, *Role of the Warsaw Pact in Soviet Policy,* pp. 5–6.

30 For analysis, see Erickson, "The Warsaw Pact: The Shape of Things to Come?" esp. pp. 150–56.

31 *The Military Balance, 1971–1972* (London: International Institute for Strategic Studies, 1971), pp. 9–11. Snapper (AT-1) and Swatter (AT-2) weapons are carried on armored vehicles; Sagger (AT-3) weapons can also be carried in a "manpack."

32 SA-6's were delivered to Iraq and Syria in 1974, and Syria received SA-7's in 1973. The SA-6 and the man-carried SA-7 replace the SA-2, used by Soviet forces to shoot down Francis Gary Powers and his U-2 on May Day, 1960.

33 *The Military Balance, 1978–1979* (London: International Institute for Strategic Studies, 1978), p. 12.

34 Ibid., pp. 8–9, 12.

35 The T-54 was built in 1949 and the follow-on T-55 in 1955. Along with the PT-76 light tank, built about the same time, they constitute the vast majority of the East European tank forces.

36 The T-62 is generally considered inferior to its NATO rivals, the American M-60, British Chieftain, and West German Leopard.

37 Adopted in May 1978, the NATO Long-Term Defense Program called for a real annual increase of 3 percent in the defense budgets of NATO members. The Soviet leadership apparently sought a similar, perhaps slightly higher, increase for Warsaw Pact members.

38 Radio Bucharest, December 1, 1978. For an excellent analysis of the PCC session and its stormy aftermath, see Charles Andras, "A Summit with Consequences," RAD Background Report/271 (Eastern Europe), *RFER,* December 14, 1978.

39 Tass, December 5, 1978. The word "demagogic" was dropped in Radio Moscow's Romanian broadcast of December 6.

40 Erickson, "The Warsaw Pact: The Shape of Things to Come?" p. 160.

41 For two recent assessments of the evolution of East German military, see Johnson et al., *East European Military Establishments,* pp. 74–133; and Thomas M. Forster, *The East German Army* (London: George Allen and Unwin, 1980).

42 This line of argument remains speculative, however. For elaboration, see John Erickson, "Soviet Military Posture and Policy in Europe," in *Soviet Strategy in Europe,* ed. Richard Pipes (New York: Crane Russak and Co., 1976), pp. 202–4; and idem, "The Warsaw Pact," in *The Soviet War Machine* (London: Hamlyn Publishing Group, 1976), pp. 238–40.

43 Since the 1966 "Vltava" exercises, Hungarian units periodically have maneuvered alongside Northern Tier forces in Warsaw Pact war games.

44 See, e.g., the discusion of the "Druzhba 79" exercises, in Erickson, "The Warsaw Pact: The Shape of Things to Come?" p. 159.

45 See "The Budapest Reforms" in Chapter 3, above.

46 See Chapter 2, above.

47 Wolfe, *Soviet Power and Europe*, pp. 482–83.

48 Iakubovskii, "Bastion of Peace and National Security."

49 See Chapter 2, above, under " 'Limited Sovereignty': Doctrinal Disputes."

50 V. D. Sokolovskii, ed., *Soviet Military Strategy*, ed. and trans. Harriet Fast Scott (New York: Crane Russak and Co., 1975). This was the third and final edition of Sokolovskii's work, published in the USSR just before his death in 1968. See also A. Ross Johnson, *Soviet–East European Military Relations: An Overview*, Rand Corporation Memorandum P-5383-1 (Santa Monica, Calif., August 1977), pp. 19–20.

51 For discussion, such as it is, see Malcolm Mackintosh, "The Warsaw Pact Today," *Survival*, May–June 1974, p. 122; Erickson, "The Warsaw Pact," in *The Soviet War Machine*, p. 241; and Lawrence T. Caldwell, "The Warsaw Pact: Directions of Change," *Problems of Communism*, September–October 1975, p. 6.

52 For summaries of Soviet military doctrine applied to the Warsaw Pact, see esp. Wiener, *The Armies of the Warsaw Pact Nations*, pp. 111–74; Erickson, "The Warsaw Pact," in *The Soviet War Machine*, pp. 239–41.

53 Johnson, *Soviet–East European Military Relations*, pp. 20–21; Mackintosh, "The Warsaw Pact Today," pp. 125–26.

54 Wiener, *The Armies of the Warsaw Pact Nations*, pp. 80–87.

55 The European War Office analogy is Mackintosh's. See also his argument that the Warsaw Pact Military Council is modeled after similar organs in the Soviet military establishment (Mackintosh, "The Warsaw Pact Today," p. 123; and Malcolm Mackintosh, *The Evolution of the Warsaw Pact*, Adelphi Papers no. 58, International Institute for Strategic Studies, [London, 1969], p. 11).

56 The contrast with NATO is obvious: unlike the WTO, NATO possesses an elaborate and functioning command and control network throughout the European theater, and exercises are regularly held to practice transferring operational control from national to NATO commands.

57 See *Krasnaya zvezda, Volksarmee, Neues Deutschland*, and others, October 7–20, 1970, as cited by R. Waring Herrick, "East-West Politics and the Recent Warsaw Pact Military Maneuvers," *Radio Liberty Research*, CRD 408/70, December 2, 1970.

58 See "Balkan *Nervenkrieg*" in Chapter 2, above; and "The Crimea Conferences" in Chapter 4.

59 Henry Kamm, "Rumania Resists Pact Maneuvers," *New York Times*, March 5, 1969; and Robert R. King, "Rumania and the Bloc: The Extent of 'Normalization,' " RAD Background Report/8 (Rumania), *RFER*, March 17, 1971, pp. 5–6.

60 Cited by Paul Wohl, "Romania Resists Warsaw Pact Tightening," *Christian Science Monitor*, February 17, 1970.

61 "Combat Fraternity," *Krasnaya zvezda*, January 24, 1970.

62 Soviet pressure during this period was so intense that rumors began to circulate that the USSR was considering an invasion of Romania. See "Fears Grow of Soviet Intervention in Rumania," *Times* (London), August 10, 1971; and F. Stephen Larrabee, "Changing Perspectives in the Balkans," RAD Background Report/31 (Bulgaria), *RFER*, December 9, 1971, pp. 11–12.

63 *Otechestven front,* October 7, 1970, p. 1, and Ulbricht's speech of November 2, 1970 (cited by Herrick, "East-West Politics," pp. 1–2).

64 *Volksarmee,* October 27, 1970.

65 See "The Crimea Conferences" in Chapter 4, above.

66 Larrabee, "Changing Perspectives in the Balkans," p. 12; and *Times* (London), August 10, 1971.

67 For discussion, see "The Crimea Conferences" in Chapter 4, above.

68 *International Herald Tribune,* June 13, 1974. See also Johnson, *Soviet–East European Military Relations,* p. 24; and Robert R. King, "Rumania and the Soviet Union: Disharmony, in a Low Key," RAD Background Report/12 (Rumania), *RFER,* July 31, 1974, p. 4.

69 *Scinteia,* November 26, 1974. Excerpts of Ceauşescu's speech are translated in Jeffrey Simon, ed., *Ruling Communist Parties and Détente: A Documentary History* (Washington, D.C.: American Enterprise Institute, 1975), pp. 239–57.

70 The invasion of Czechoslovakia, it will be recalled, ostensibly was undertaken on the basis of an "appeal" issued by unspecified members of the Czechoslovak government and Party Central Committee. See *Pravda,* August 22, 1968.

71 *Scinteia,* December 29, 1972. Cf. Brown, *Relations between the Soviet Union and Its Eastern European Allies,* p. 42.

72 Ceauşescu's address to men of science and culture, November 25, 1978, Agerpress of the same day; resolution of the RCP Central Committee of November 30, 1978, Agerpress of the same day (both cited in Andras, "A Summit with Consequences"). The Bucharest correspondent of Tanjug, the official Yugoslav news agency, added that "what official Bucharest opposes is a further integration of the Romanian armed forces into the Warsaw Pact" and attempts to force Romania "to cede part of its sovereignty to a supernational organization." (Radio Belgrade, December 2, 1978.) For analysis, see Andras, "A Summit with Consequences," esp. pp. 3–6.

73 Iakubovskii, "Bastion of Peace and National Security."

74 Iakubovskii, *Boevoe sodruzhestvo,* pp. 107–8.

75 Wiener, *The Armies of the Warsaw Pact Nations,* pp. 114–17.

76 Similar charges resurfaced in even stronger terms in Ceauşescu's remarks at the November 1978 Moscow summit. See *Washington Post,* November 27 and 30.

77 See, e.g., Boleslaw Chocha, *Obrona Terytorium Kraju,* (Warsaw: MON, 1974).

78 *The Military Balance, 1976–77* (London: International Institute for Strategic Studies, 1976), p. 14. See also Johnson, *Soviet–East European Military Relations,* pp. 24–25, who notes that top-level Romanian military visits to nonbloc capitals now outnumber those to other Warsaw Pact states.

79 For a useful cautionary analysis, see Erickson, "The Warsaw Pact: The Shape of Things to Come?" pp. 161–65.

80 This practice was outlined by General Bela Kiraly, who, as commander-in-chief of Hungarian ground forces during the 1956 invasion, was surely in a position to know. See Bela K. Kiraly, "Why the Soviets Need the Warsaw Pact," *East Europe* 18, no. 4 (April 1969): 11.

81 See, e.g., the remarks by Jiří Hochman, as summarized in "Report on the Conference on 'Eastern Europe: Stability or Recurrent Crises?' " held at Airlie House,

Warrenton, Va., November 13–15, 1975 (Washington: Office of External Research, Department of State, 1975), p. 22.

In 1975, however, the organ of the Main Political Office of the Polish Armed Forces reported the adoption of a "new form of cooperation among the Warsaw Pact armies": an exchange of designated subgroups of East German and Polish armed forces (*Zolnierz Wolnosci,* August 8, 9, and 10, 1975 [*FBIS,* August 12, 1975]). The significance of such exchanges is probably not in any practical results, but in the fact that inter–East European, as opposed to Soviet–East European, exchanges are now being encouraged.

82 The importance of these contacts has been outlined by Col. V. Senin in "A School of Internationalism," *Krasnaya zvezda,* April 11, 1975. Since 1969, a variety of military exchanges—ranging from meetings of Soviet and East European general staffs to winter sports "Spartakiads," held yearly since 1970—have taken place with increased frequency. For analysis, see Jones, *Soviet Influence,* pp. 164–226.

83 Iakubovskii, "Bastion of Peace and National Security."

84 Mackintosh, "The Warsaw Pact Today," p. 124.

85 Cf. Erickson, "The Warsaw Pact: The Shape of Things to Come?" esp. p. 157.

86 See the discussions of Tables 1.1 and 1.7 in Chapter 1, above.

87 A new treaty between Romania and Czechoslovakia was signed on August 16, 1968, just four days before the Warsaw Pact invasion.

88 According to O. Khelstov ("New Soviet-Czechoslovak Treaty," *International Affairs* [Moscow], July 1970, pp. 12–13), "the whole content of the treaty is permeated with the principle of socialist internationalism."

89 "Treaty of Friendship, Cooperation, and Mutual Assistance between the Union of Soviet Socialist Republics and the Czechoslovak Socialist Republic," *Pravda* and *Izvestia,* May 7, 1970.

90 Aspaturian considers the bloc-wide application of mutual defense obligations to be "in patent violation of a rule of international law that treaties create neither rights nor duties for non-signatories." See Vernon V. Aspaturian, "Soviet Aims in East Europe," *Current History,* October 1970, p. 208.

91 For discussion of these terms, see the Introduction, above, under "Soviet–East European Relations in Theoretical Perspective."

92 "Treaty of Friendship, Cooperation, and Mutual Assistance between the Union of Soviet Socialist Republics and the Socialist Republic of Rumania," *Pravda,* July 8, 1970.

93 Agerpress International Service (Bucharest), November 12 and 20, 1970.

94 MTI Domestic Service (Budapest), February 24, 1972.

95 ADN International Service (East Berlin), May 13, 1972.

96 "Declaration on Strengthening Friendship and Expanding Fraternal Cooperation between the CPČS and SED and between the ČSSR and GDR," *Rudé Právo* and *Neues Deutschland,* October 19, 1974.

97 "Treaty of Friendship, Co-operation, and Mutual Assistance between the Union of Soviet Socialist Republics and the German Democratic Republic," *New Times* (Moscow), no. 41 (October 1975), pp. 12–13.

98 *Rabotnichesko Delo,* September 15, 1977.

99 With obvious reference to the Quadripartite Agreement—to which the USSR, of

course, is cosignatory—the Soviet–GDR treaty (but not the others) contains an exclusion clause acknowledging the validity of other treaties or agreements previously entered into by either party. As the West German press was quick to note, this loophole would also apply to a number of wartime and immediate postwar agreements which speak of Germany as a single entity. (See Jens Hacker in the *Frankfurter Allgemeine Zeitung,* October 17, 1975).

100 Joachim Krueger, "The GDR's New Friendship Treaties with States of the Socialist Commonwealth," *Deutsche Aussenpolitik* (East Berlin) 23, no. 1 (January 1978).

101 *Neues Deutschland,* November 26/27, 1977.

102 The supposed import of these treaties for socialist internationalism is discussed in Gerbert Kroeger and Frank Seidel, *Freundschaftsvertraege: Vertraege des Sozialismus* (East Berlin: Staatsverlag der DDR, 1979).

103 Though the precise terminology may vary, the five principles generally include "complete equality, respect for territorial integrity, state independence and sovereignty, and noninterference in one another's affairs."

104 See, e.g., Melvin Croan, "A New Afrika Korps," *Washington Quarterly,* Winter 1980, pp. 21–37.

105 Agerpress, November 25, 1978. For discussion, see Andras, "A Summit with Consequences," esp. pp. 5–8.

CHAPTER 6: ECONOMIC RELATIONS

1 I am indebted to Cam Hudson, senior economic analyst for Radio Free Europe, for his useful comments on earlier drafts of the present chapter and his help in compiling several of the charts and tables.

2 For analysis, see Chapter 3, above, under "Comecon and the Comprehensive Program."

3 This suggestive term comes from Mrs. Irene B. Jaffee of the United States Department of State.

4 For details, see "Domestic Affairs: The Party Congresses" in Chapter 4, above.

5 An excellent summary of the implications of the events in Poland is given by A. Ross Johnson, *The Polish Riots and Gomulka's Fall,* Rand Corporation Memorandum F-4615 (Santa Monica, Calif., April 1971).

6 Cf. Philip Hanson, "Soviet Trade with Eastern Europe," in *Soviet–East European Dilemmas: Coercion, Competition, and Consent,* ed. Karen Dawisha and Philip Hanson (London: Royal Institute of International Affairs, 1981), pp. 97–100; and Paul Marer and John Michael Montias, "Theory and Measurement of East European Integration," in *East European Integration and East-West Trade,* ed. Paul Marer and John Michael Montias (Bloomington: Indiana University Press, 1980), pp. 21–25.

7 Jiří Štěpánek, "Further Development of Co-operation in the Council of Mutual Economic Assistance," *International Relations* (Prague), 1972, p. 35.

8 Ibid., pp. 34–39.

9 Statement at the July plenum of the Central Committee of the Czechoslovak Communist Party, as cited by Jiří Štěpánek, "On [the] 27th Session of the Council of Mutual Economic Assistance," *International Relations* (Prague), 1973, p. 9.

10 Sandor Ausch, *Theory and Practice of CMEA Cooperation* (Budapest: Akademiai Kiado, 1972), p. 217.

11 *Sovetskaya Belorussia,* November 15, 1973 (cited by Harry Trend, "Multilateral Comecon Five-Year Integration Plan Being Prepared," RAD Background Report/ 19 [Eastern Europe], *RFER,* December 12, 1973).

12 Radio Prague, June 18, 1973, and *Scinteia,* November 2, 1973 (cited by Trend, "Multilateral Comecon Plan," pp. 2–3).

13 A. Shabalin, "The Comprehensive Programme of Integration," *International Affairs* (Moscow), April 1975, pp. 14–15; and P. Alampiev, O. Bogomolev, and Y. Shiryaev, *A New Approach to Economic Integration* (Moscow: Progress Publishers, 1974), pp. 63–64 and 82–83. Various Soviet economic spokesmen have argued that the "first stage of socialist economic integration," which commenced with the signing of the Comprehensive Program in 1971, will last approximately three five-year planning periods. See, for example, Alampiev et al., p. 82.

14 C. Moisuc, "Socialist Economic Co-operation and Integration," *Era Socialista,* no. 9 (May 1974) (*RFER,* Romanian Press Survey no. 974, June 4, 1974, p. 11).

15 C. Murgescu, "The Principles of Socialist International Relations: The Basis for Improving Comecon Cooperation," *Scinteia,* June 4, 1974 (*RFER,* Romanian Press Survey no. 977, June 18, 1974, p. 2).

16 Bulgarian news agency (BTA), June 18, 1974, and Radio Sofia, June 20, 1974 (cited by Harry Trend, "The Comecon Session in Sofia: An Initial Appraisal," RAD Background Report/4 [Eastern Europe], *RFER,* June 26, 1974).

17 Trend, "The Comecon Session in Sofia," pp. 3–7.

18 "Charter of the Council for Mutual Economic Assistance," in *The Multilateral Economic Cooperation of Socialist States: A Collection of Documents* (Moscow: Progress Publishers, 1977), pp. 28–29. See also J. L. Kerr, "A Revised Comecon Charter," RAD Background Report/124 (Eastern Europe), *RFER,* August 6, 1975; and the original Comecon charter, as translated in *East Europe* 10, no. 8 (August 1960): 42–45.

    Interestingly, at least one Soviet economic analyst has interpreted these vague formulations on joint planning to mean that CMEA countries have "a statutory obligation" to coordinate economic plans (V. I. Kuznetsov, *Economic Integration: Two Approaches* [Moscow: Progress Publishers, 1976], p. 106).

19 Tass, April 22, 1975.

20 E. Hutira and I. Erhan, "The Principles of Marxism-Leninism: Permanent and Objectively Necessary Basis of Co-operation among the Socialist Countries," *Scinteia,* May 20, 1975 (cited in "Rumanian Media Call for Comecon Aid to Less Developed Members and Oppose Supranational Schemes," RAD Background Report/92, *RFER,* June 5, 1975, pp. 2–4).

21 See, for example, "Statement on the Stand of the Rumanian Workers' Party Concerning the Problems of the World Communist and Working Class Movement," April 12, 1964, in *International Relations Among Communists,* ed. Robert H. McNeal (Englewood Cliffs, N.J.: Prentice-Hall Publishing Co., 1967), p. 128.

22 G. Cretoiu, "Economic and Technical-Scientific Co-operation among Comecon Member-Countries," *Era Socialista,* no. 10 (May 1975) (cited in RAD Background Report/92, *RFER,* June 5, 1975, pp. 5–10).

23 See, for example, the interview granted by Professor Yuri Shiryaev, director of the Economic Institute of the World Socialist System, USSR Academy of Sciences, to *Zycie Warszawy,* June 1, 1975; and I. Pushkarov, "Problems of Improving the Management of Socialist Integration Process," *Mezhdunarodni Otnosheniya* (Sofia), no. 1 (1975) (cited by Harry Trend, "Backdrop for the 29th Comecon Council Session," RAD Background Report/105 [Eastern Europe], *RFER,* June 16, 1975).

24 The Hungarians and Poles, as will be seen below, were arguing for a more equitable form of integration, involving the development of full currency convertibility, facilitation of direct contacts between enterprises, and devolution of decisionmaking in CMEA. The East Germans and Czechoslovaks apparently supported the specific projects being proposed but nevertheless refrained from endorsing the broader objectives envisioned by the Soviet and Bulgarian leaders. See Trend, "Backdrop for the 29th Comecon Council Session," pp. 12–14; and idem, "Comecon Council Session Ends in Budapest," RAD Background Report/113 (Eastern Europe), *RFER,* July 3, 1975.

25 Nikita S. Khrushchev, "Vital Questions of the Development of the Socialist World System," *World Marxist Review* 5 (September 1962): 9.

26 Radio Hvezda, June 25, 1975.

27 See, for example, the terms of the September 1975 Hungarian-Soviet agreement on plan coordination for 1976–1980, as summarized in Hungarian Situation Report/39, *RFER,* September 16, 1975, pp. 4–5.

28 Baibakov's draft of the Coordinated Plan, presented before the powerful Council Committee on Coordination in Planning, is analyzed in Edward A. Hewett, "Recent Developments in East-West European Economic Relations and Their Implications for U.S.–East European Economic Relations," in U.S. Congress, Joint Economic Committee, *East European Economies Post-Helsinki* (Washington, D.C.: Government Printing Office, 1977), pp. 188–91.

29 These are fuel, energy, and primary products; machine-building; agriculture and food supply; consumer products; and transportation.

30 Hewett, "Recent Developments," pp. 188–90; and Trend,"Comecon Council Session," pp. 2–3.

31 Hewett, "Recent Developments," p. 190. The figure of 9 billion transferable rubles is based only on the eight projects for which funds already had been allocated.

32 *Rudé Právo,* July 9, 1976.

33 BTA in English, July 9, 1976.

34 *Scinteia,* July 10, 1976.

35 The text was published in *Izvestia,* July 10, 1976. For a detailed analysis of the session, see Harry Trend, "An Assessment of the Comecon Council 30th Session," RAD Background Report/183 (Eastern Europe), *RFER,* August 23, 1976.

36 *Scinteia,* July 10, 1976.

37 Communiqué of the 31st CMEA Council session, Tass in English, June 24, 1977.

38 Četeka in English, June 22, 1977.

39 PAP in English, June 14, 1977.

40 For a summary assessment, See Harry Trend, "The 31st Comecon Council Session," RAD Background Report/130 (Eastern Europe), *RFER,* June 29, 1977.

41 Tanjug, June 12, 1978.

42 The activities of these organizations are described below in the present chapter.

43 *Scinteia*, June 23, 1978. For more on the controversy, see H. G. Trend, "Disagreement within Comecon Council Anticipated," RAD Background Report/123 (Eastern Europe), *RFER*, June 15, 1978; and idem, "An Interesting Comecon Council Meeting Anticipated," RAD Background Report/134 (Eastern Europe), *RFER*, June 22, 1978.

44 Cited by J. L. Kerr, "The 32nd Session of the Comecon Council," RAD Background Report/154 (Eastern Europe), *RFER*, July 7, 1978, p. 10.

45 Tass, June 27, 1978.

46 Reuters, June 29, 1978.

47 The changes were not explained, but according to Comecon Secretary-General Fadeyev, they did not concern matters "of principle." (Radio Prague, June 29, 1979).

48 Harry G. Trend, "Communiqué of the 33rd Comecon Council Session," RAD Background Report/150 (Eastern Europe), *RFER*, July 3, 1979. The text was carried by Tass in Russian on June 29, 1979.

49 In the event, the 35th Council session formally approved the "Coordinated Plan for Multilateral Integration Measures of 1981–1985," but Romanian planning chief Emilian Dobrescu reportedly revealed that only a general framework had been set, with details still to be worked out (AP and Reuters, July 3, 1981). For analysis of the session, see Cam Hudson, "The Inconclusive 35th CMEA Council Session in Sofia," RAD Background Report/201 (Eastern Europe), *RFER*, July 15, 1981.

50 Ceteka, June 19, 1980; Radio Bucharest, June 19, 1980. For analysis, see Cam Hudson, "The 34th Comecon Council Ends," RAD Background Report/151 (Eastern Europe), *RFER*, June 20, 1980.

51 A lengthy, but probably not full, version of the speech was printed in *Scinteia*, June 19, 1980.

52 Chapter 3, above.

53 For discussion, see Harry Trend, "Comecon's 'Interested Party' Principle Extended to Permanent Commission Membership," RAD Background Report/9 (Eastern Europe), *RFER*, December 16, 1974. Between 1971 and 1975, the CMEA Council established four new permanent standing commissions: Telecommunications and Post (1971), Environmental Protection (1973), Civil Aviation (1975), and Health Affairs (1975).

54 In late 1973, CMEA leaders began to move cautiously toward a dialogue with the EEC, and in February 1975 an official CMEA-EEC meeting was convened in Moscow.

55 "Charter of the Council for Mutual Economic Assistance" (as amended in 1974), in *The Multilateral Economic Cooperation of Socialist States,* p. 34.

56 O. Chukanov, "Along the Path of Socialist Integration," *Pravda*, June 19, 1974. For analysis, see Trend, "Multilateral Comecon Plan."

57 "Ordinance on the Committee for Co-operative Planning of the Council for Mutual Economic Assistance," in *The Multilateral Economic Cooperation of Socialist States,* pp. 166–67.

58 For discussion of these committees, see Harry Trend, "Comecon's Organizational

Structure, Part II,'' RAD Background Report/138 (Eastern Europe), *RFER*, October 7, 1975, pp. 2–11.

59 R. Constantinescu, "Improving the Forms and Methods of Economic and Technical-Scientific Co-operation among Comecon Member Countries," *Era Socialista*, no. 8 (April 1974) (Romanian Press Survey no. 974, *RFER*, June 4, 1974, pp. 5–8).

60 "Comprehensive Programme for the Further Extension and Improvement of Co-operation and the Development of Socialist Economic Integration by the CMEA Member-Countries," in *The Multilateral Economic Cooperation of Socialist States*, pp. 96–98.

The principle of "voluntarism," which means that no member can be compelled to participate in any given venture, also applies to the interstate organizations, but its precise application varies somewhat. See, for example, the differences in the procedures governing Intermetal and Interkhim, in ibid., pp. 362–67 and 372–80.

61 Kuznetsov, *Economic Integration*, p. 63.

62 "Comprehensive Programme," pp. 98–100. The "interested party" principle, of course, applies to the international economic organizations as well as to other CMEA bodies.

63 A. Shabalin, "The Comprehensive Programme of Integration," *International Affairs* (Moscow), April 1975, pp. 17–18; and P. Alampiev, O. Bogomolev, and Y. Shiryaev, *A New Approach to Economic Integration* (Moscow: Progress Publishers, 1974), pp. 32–33.

64 Arthur J. Smith, for example, lists Interelektro among the international economic organizations, while Harry Trend does not (cf. Smith, "The Council for Mutual Economic Assistance in 1977: New Economic Power, New Political Perspectives, and Some Old and New Problems," in *East European Economies Post-Helsinki*, pp. 160–61; and Trend, "Comecon's Organizational Structure," RAD Background Report/114 [Eastern Europe], *RFER*, July 3, 1975, p. 10). Part of the problem, compounded by presumed Soviet experts on the subject, is that the functional areas and operating procedures of the interstate and international economic organizations overlap.

65 Smith, "The Council for Mutual Economic Assistance in 1977," p. 160; and Kuznetsov, *Economic Integration*, pp. 64–66.

66 C. Moisuc, "Socialist Economic Co-operation and Integration," *Era Socialista*, no. 9 (May 1974) (Romanian Press Survey no. 974, *RFER*, June 4, 1974, pp. 10–14).

67 *Vilaggazdasag*, February 10, 1976 (cited by Harry Trend, "Comecon International Economic Associations Unable to Function Effectively," RAD Background Report/81 [Eastern Europe], *RFER*, April 6, 1976).

68 G. Grabig (GDR), "Planned Use of Commodity and Money Relations," in *The Market of Socialist Economic Integration*, ed. Tibor Kiss (Budapest: Akademiai Kiado, 1973), p. 201. For Polish and Czechoslovak views on the subject, see the articles by Weslowski and Chalupski in the same volume. This collection of conference papers by economic experts from all the CMEA countries presents an especially clear contrast between opposing views of CMEA integration.

69 Smith, "The Council for Mutual Economic Assistance in 1977," p. 162; and Peter Marsh, "The Integration Process in Eastern Europe, 1968 to 1975," *Journal of Common Market Studies* 14, no. 4 (June 1976): 324–29.

70 *Einheit* (East Berlin), June 1975.

71 Domestic factors and considerations related to East-West trade also contributed to the creation of the production associations, but the timing of the move suggests that concern for intra-CMEA trade weighed heavily in the decision.

72 E. Honecker, "Report to the 9th Central Committee of the S.E.D.," *Neues Deutschland*, June 16, 1973.

73 Marsh, "The Integration Process in Eastern Europe," p. 329.

74 As was seen in the preceding section, the preliminary draft of the plan apparently was prepared by N. K. Baibakov, chairman of the USSR State Planning Committee (Gosplan).

75 Hewett, "Recent Developments," pp. 190–91; and Smith, "The Council for Mutual Economic Assistance in 1977," pp. 156–57.

76 John Hannigan and Carl McMillan, "Joint Investment in Resource Development: Sectoral Approaches to Socialist Integration," in U.S. Congress, Joint Economic Committee, *East European Economic Assessment* (Washington, D.C.: Government Printing Office, 1981), part 2, pp. 259–95; Harry Trend, "The Orenburg Gas Project," RAD Background Report/165 (Eastern Europe), *RFER*, December 2, 1975.

For details on the Ust Ilimsk and Kiyembaev projects, see Harry Trend, "First Joint Investment Project within Comecon's Comprehensive Program," RAD Background Report/58 (Eastern Europe), *RFER*, March 9, 1976; and idem, "Comecon Joint Investments Develop Soviet Asbestos Deposits," RAD Background Report/79 (Eastern Europe), *RFER*, April 6, 1976.

77 For discussion, see *The Soviet Union, 1974–75* (New York: Holmes and Meier Publishers, 1976), pp. 150–51.

78 Cretoiu, "Economic and Technical-Scientific Co-operation among Comecon Member-Countries" (RAD Background Report/92, *RFER*, June 5, 1975, p. 6).

79 Ibid.; and Hutira and Erhan, "The Principles of Marxism-Leninism" (RAD Background Report/92, *RFER*, June 5, 1975, p. 4).

80 This pattern, as has been seen, was followed in Romania's policy toward the International Investment Bank, Interkhim, and Intermetal. (See Chapter 3, above, under "Comecon and the Comprehensive Program.") More recently, Romania initially abstained from joining the Ust Ilimsk cellulose project but eventually agreed to supply materials (though not investment funds) for the project.

81 K. Botos, "Co-ordination of Investment Policies within Comecon," *Kulgazdasag*, no. 12 (December 1974) (cited by Harry Trend, "New Comecon Joint Investments —But Some Old Problems Remain," RAD Background Report/46 [Eastern Europe], *RFER*, March 12, 1975).

82 *Rudé Právo*, July 9, 1976.

83 Trend, "The Orenburg Gas Project," pp. 11–12; Hannigan and McMillan, "Joint Investment in Resource Development," pp. 274–86.

84 Cam Hudson, "CMEA Joint Investments in Soviet Nuclear Power Stations," RAD Background Report/11 (Eastern Europe), *RFER*, January 20, 1981.

85 Although the exact extent of Romanian, Bulgarian, and East German participation is not yet clear, it appears that all have entered into contractual agreements involving at least some investment obligations.

86 For discussion, see Hannigan and McMillan, "Joint Investments in Resource Development," pp. 290–92.
87 Similar, if less acute, imbalances existed for Soviet deliveries of other raw materials and energy sources to Eastern Europe.
88 The opportunity cost to the USSR—that is, the cost in revenues which might have been earned from selling oil on the world market—are revealed in one study which estimates that Soviet terms of trade in the period 1971–1974 might have improved by 30 to 40 percent if CMEA prices had been on a par with prevailing world market rates. See Martin J. Kohn, "Developments in Soviet–East European Terms of Trade, 1971–75," in U.S. Congress, Joint Economic Committee, *Soviet Economy in a New Perspective* (Washington, D.C.: Government Printing Office, 1976), p. 76.
89 For background to the Soviet oil price increases, see Paul Marer, "Has Eastern Europe Become a Liability to the Soviet Union?—The Economic Aspect," in *The International Politics of Eastern Europe,* ed. Charles Gati (New York: Praeger Publishers, 1976), pp. 59–74.
90 For details of the new pricing formula, see Harry Trend, "Some Effects of Comecon's Revised Price System," RAD Background Report/27 (Eastern Europe), *RFER,* February 20, 1975; idem, "Pieces of Intra-Comecon Price Puzzle Falling into Place," RAD Background Report/34 (Eastern Europe), *RFER,* February 28, 1975; and Martin J. Kohn and Nicholas R. Lang, "The Intra-CEMA Foreign Trade System: Major Price Changes, Little Reform," in *East European Economies Post-Helsinki,* pp. 139–44.
91 I. Semyonov, in the Czechoslovak daily *Svoboda,* September 13, 1972 (cited by Marer, "Has Eastern Europe Become a Liability?" p. 74).
92 J. L. Kerr, "East European Imports of Crude Oil," RAD Background Report/12 (Eastern Europe), *RFER,* January 31, 1975; and Kohn and Lang, "The Intra-CEMA Foreign Trade System," p. 141, n. 15.
93 József Bíró, "The Fundamental Principles of Our Foreign Trade," *Nepszava,* July 11, 1976, and idem, in *Esti Hirlap,* July 2, 1976 (cited in "Hungary's Economic Relations with East and West," RAD Background Report/163 [Eastern Europe], *RFER,* July 20, 1976, pp. 3–5).
94 See the section on "The Party Congresses" in Chapter 4, above.
95 Cited by Dusko Doder, "Hungary Reports Economic Setbacks," *Washington Post,* March 18, 1975.
96 Kohn and Lang, "The Intra-CEMA Foreign Trade System," p. 142.
97 Andrzej Korbonski, "Détente, East-West Trade, and the Future of Economic Integration in Eastern Europe," *World Politics* 28, no. 4 (July 1976): 578.
98 Marer and Montias, "Theory and Measurement of East European Integration," p. 26. See also Cam Hudson, "Whither Joint Equity Ventures in Eastern Europe?" RAD Background Report/240 (Eastern Europe), *RFER,* November 2, 1979.
99 Paul Marer, "Economic Performance and Prospects in Eastern Europe," in *East European Economic Assessment,* part 2, p. 36.
100 The Common Agricultural Policy (CAP) provides support measures for agricultural prices within the European Economic Community (EEC) and a tariff wall without, to insure that foreign agricultural products cannot effectively intrude on EEC markets.
    According to the Common Commercial Policy (CCP), bilateral agreements be-

tween CMEA countries and individual members of the EEC were terminated in 1974 (or in some cases 1975), after which time CMEA countries were required to negotiate trade agreements bilaterally through the EEC commissioner. Its implementation led to a prolonged, and so far fruitless, dialogue between CMEA and the EEC toward some sort of institutional understanding between the two organizations.

101 Marer, "Economic Performance and Prospects," p. 56.

102 The extremely high Bulgarian debt/export ratio in 1975 is explained by the sharp drop in Bulgarian exports to the West at mid-decade (see Table 6.6, above).

103 For discussion, see Joan Parpart Zoeter, "Eastern Europe: The Hard Currency Debt," in East European Economic Assessment, part 2, pp. 716–31.

104 Marer, "Economic Performance and Prospects," pp. 36–43 and 60–62. See also Gregor Lazarcik, "Comparative Growth, Structure, and Levels of Agricultural Output, Inputs, and Productivity in Eastern Europe, 1965–79," in East European Economic Assessment, part 2, pp. 587–633.

105 Marer, "Economic Performance and Prospects," p. 61.

106 See, e.g., Gierek's speech to the 8th PUWP (Polish United Workers' Party) Congress in February 1980, as described in Chapter 4, above.

107 For an excellent analysis of East European energy dilemmas, see Cam Hudson, "Eastern Europe and the Energy Crisis: An Overview," RAD Background Report/136 (Eastern Europe), RFER, June 10, 1980.

108 Ibid., p. 10 (table 6).

109 Kohn and Lang, "The Intra-CEMA Foreign Trade System," esp. p. 144.

110 For analysis, see Cam Hudson, "Renewed Pressure for Reform in the CMEA?" RAD Background Report/137 (Eastern Europe), RFER, May 15, 1981.

111 To decrease East European energy dependence, the Soviet Union directed the East European states to seek oil from Middle Eastern sources and began to charge world market rates for some oil (perhaps 10–15 percent) supplied to Eastern Europe above plan requirements.

112 Antoni Marszalek, "Prices in Trade Exchange Among Comecon Countries," Przegled Techniczy: Innowacje, July 6, 1975, pp. 27–29.

113 The significance of this trend was first analyzed in Cam Hudson, "Renewed Pressure for Reform in the CMEA?" See also Cam Hudson, "The 35th CMEA Council Session Meeting at a Time of Uncertainty," RAD Background Report/182 (Eastern Europe), RFER, June 29, 1981.

114 Cf. Marer and Montias, "Theory and Measurement of East European Integration," pp. 31–33.

115 B. Gorizontov, "A Unified Transport System," Gudok (Moscow), October 19, 1971, and Rynki zagraniczne, October 9, 1971, as cited in J. Wilczynski, Technology in Comecon (New York: Praeger Publishers, 1974), p. 277.

116 For further examples of production specialization in CMEA, see Wilczynski, Technology in Comecon, esp. pp. 273–80.

117 Kohn and Lang, "The Intra-CEMA Foreign Trade System," pp. 137–38.

118 Tibor Kiss, "International Cooperation in Planning within Comecon," Kozgazdasagi szemle, no. 6 (1975) (Eastern European Economics 14, no. 4 [Summer 1976]: 14–15 and 28).

119 For an excellent discussion of the linkages between economic reformism and East-

West trade, see Korbonski, ''Détente, East-West trade, and the Future of Economic Integration in Eastern Europe,'' esp. pp. 575–83.

CHAPTER 7: ON THE IDEOLOGICAL FRONT

1 B. Kozin, ''Socialist Countries: Unity and Cohesion,'' *International Affairs* (Moscow), March 1974, p. 8.
2 *Pravda*, June 18, 1969.
3 For details, see Chapter 2, above, under ''The Moscow Conference and the Quest for Stability.''
4 For more on this theme, see Jiří Valenta, ''Eurocommunism and Eastern Europe,'' *Problems of Communism*, March–April 1978, pp. 41–54.
5 Santiago Carrillo, *Eurocommunism and the State* (Westport, Conn.: Lawrence Hill and Co., 1978, p. 132. (This was first published in Spanish in 1977 by Editorial Critica, Barcelona, as *Eurocommunismo y Estado*.)
6 For a brief but authoritative summary, see Antonio Rubbi (Italian CP Central Committee secretary for foreign affairs), ''The New Internationalism,'' *World Marxist Review*, January 1977.
7 See Chapter 2, above, under ''Balkan *Nervenkrieg*'' and Chapter 4 under ''The Crimea Conferences.''
8 Carrillo visited Bucharest for talks with Ceauşescu in August 1971, two months after Ceauşescu's visit to Peking and two months before Carrillo's.
9 The first Conference of European Communist and Workers' Parties convened (*sans* Romania and Yugoslavia) in Karlovy Vary, Czechoslovakia, in 1967; the three world Communist conferences were held in Moscow in 1957, 1960, and 1969.
10 On the talks surrounding the conference proposals, see Kevin Devlin, ''The Inter-Party Drama,'' *Problems of Communism*, July–August 1975, pp. 18–34.
11 Azcárate's report to the Central Committee of the PCE was published in *Nuestra Bandera*, no. 72 (1973), pp. 15–29.
12 *L'Espresso* (Rome), February 3, 1974 (as cited by Devlin, ''The Inter-Party Drama,'' p. 26).
13 Tass, October 18, 1974.
14 For analysis, see Devlin, ''The Inter-Party Drama,'' pp. 28–32.
15 This orientation already had been affirmed at a regional conference of eighteen West European parties, held in Brussels in January 1974.
16 Texts of the November 1975 PCI-PCF communiqué were carried in *L'Unità* and *L'Humanité* on November 18, 1975. This was preceded by a PCI-PCE statement in July 1975 and followed by a PCF-PCE communiqué later in November.
17 For discussion, see Chapter 4, above, under ''Foreign Relations: Soviet–East European Summit Diplomacy.''
18 For discussion, see Kevin Devlin, ''Brezhnev's Unimpressive Summit,'' RAD Background Report/147, *RFER*, June 28, 1976.
19 See, e.g., Frane Barbieri's account of Soviet–Yugoslav negotiations in *Il Giornale*, June 20, 1976.
20 Tanjug, 6 June 1976.

21 *L'Unità*, June 30, 1976 and July 1, 1976. For analysis, see Kevin Devlin, "The Challenge of Eurocommunism," *Problems of Communism*, January–February 1977, pp. 14–18.

22 *Pravda*, June 30, 1976. For more on the speech, see F. Stephen Larrabee, "Brezhnev's Speech to the Pan-European Conference of Communist Parties," RL 340/76, *Radio Liberty Research*, July 7, 1976.

23 The text was published in *New Times* (Moscow), no. 28 (July 1976), pp. 17–32.

24 For a thoughtful assessment of the East Berlin conference, see Heinz Timmermann, *Die Konferenz der europäischen Kommunisten in Ost-Berlin: Ergebnisse und Perspektiven*, Berichte des Bundesinstituts für ostwissenschaftliche und internationale Studien, no. 28 (Cologne, 1976).

25 *L'Humanité*, July 1, 1976.

26 See J. L. Kerr, "The Media and the European CP Conference: A Study in Selective Reporting," RAD Background Report/171, *RFER*, August 11, 1976.

27 *Borba*, August 14, 1976.

28 Agence France Presse (from Madrid), March 3, 1977.

29 This process culminated in the Moncloa agreement of October 1977. For discussion, see Eusebio Mujal-Leon, "Eurocommunism 1978: The PCE in Spanish Politics," *Problems of Communism*, July–August 1978, esp. p. 27.

30 For a brief analysis, see Kevin Devlin, "Berlinguer and Carrillo Plan 'European Left' Initiative," RAD Background Report/220, *RFER*, October 11, 1979.

31 For discussion, see Kevin Devlin, "Berlinguer and the Chinese Comrades," RAD Background Report/96, *RFER*, April 25, 1980; Elizabeth Teague, "The 'New Internationalism' of the PCI in Practice," RAD Background Report/230, *RFER*, October 2, 1980; and Kevin Devlin, "A Eurocommunist in Beijing: Carrillo's 'New Internationalism,' " RAD Background Report/283, *RFER*, November 28, 1980.

32 For elaboration, see Valenta, "Eurocommunism and Eastern Europe."

33 *Svenska Dagbladet*, November 13, 1977 (cited by ibid., p. 49).

34 For more on official East European positions on Eurocommunism, see C.A., "The Critic of the Critics," RAD Background Report/20, *RFER*, January 26, 1979.

35 For discussion, see Kevin Devlin, "Sofia vs. Madrid? A Tale of Two Meetings," RAD Background Report/85, *RFER*, April 26, 1977.

36 Cf. C.A., "The Critic of the Critics," and C.A., "Soviet Loyalists Reaffirm the Validity of Their Concept of Socialism," RAD Background Report/249, *RFER*, November 16, 1978.

37 See esp. *L'Unità*, January 19 and 22, 1980. See also the roundtable discussion published in *La Repubblica*, February 13, 1980.

38 On the Romanian position, see Chapter 4, above, under "Foreign Relations: Soviet–East European Summit Diplomacy."

39 This was the time, it will be remembered, of the NATO Euromissiles decision and the Warsaw Pact's counteroffensive. (See Chapter 4, above, under "Foreign Relations: Soviet–East European Summit Diplomacy.")

40 *Rinascita*, April 11, 1980.

41 The Romanian position was expressed in a letter to the Polish co-sponsors of the Paris conference (Agerpress, April 23, 1980).

42 In addition to the Yugoslavs and Romanians, the defectors from Paris included the

Communist parties of Italy, Spain, Great Britain, the Netherlands, San Marino, Sweden, and Iceland, with the Belgian and Swiss parties participating only as observers.

43 See Kevin Devlin, "European Communism's Conference of Disunity," RAD Background Report/99, *RFER*, May 2, 1980.

44 Already in July 1980, the CPSU through the pro-Soviet Greek Communist party (KKE) was putting out feelers for another world conference (Rizospastis [Athens], July 6, 1980), but periodic echoes over the next year and a half were abruptly ended with the declaration of martial law in Poland on December 13, 1981. For discussion, see Kevin Devlin, "New Calls for World Communist Conference," RAD Background Report/335, *RFER*, December 3, 1981.

45 Radio Moscow, August 15, 1973 (cited by Charles Andras, "European Cooperation and Ideological Conflict," in *East European Perspectives on European Security and Cooperation*, ed. Robert R. King and Robert W. Dean [New York: Praeger Publishers, 1974], p. 28).

46 *Rudé Právo*, August 25, 1973.

47 For discussion, see Chapter 4, above, under "Domestic Affairs: The Party Congresses."

48 *Abgrenzung*, literally "delineation" or "demarcation," refers to the policy of strictly limiting contacts with the West, particularly the FRG.

49 Y. Solodukhin, "Ideological Cooperation among the Socialist Countries," *International Affairs* (Moscow), August 1980, p. 78.

50 "Central Committee Secretaries' Prague Meeting," RAD Background Report/56, *RFER*, March 26, 1975, p. 2.

51 I. Hlivka, "United in Ideological Work," *Život Strany*, no. 7 (April 1, 1974).

52 Following the initial December 1973 meeting in Moscow, the Central Committee secretaries met in March 1975 (in Prague), January 1976 (Warsaw), March 1977 (Sofia), February–March 1978 (Budapest), and July 1979 (East Berlin), with a follow-up meeting of deputy heads in Sofia in December 1979.

53 MTI (Budapest) and Radio Bucharest, March 1, 1978.

54 The signing of the "Agreement on the Development of Cooperation between the SED [Socialist Unity Party of East Germany] and the CPSU in the Realm of Ideology for the Years 1974 and 1975" brought the total number of bilateral ideological agreements to eleven as of December 1973.

55 PAP (Warsaw), May 31, 1973.

56 PAP, May 19, 1976, and *The Soviet Union, 1973* (New York: Holmes and Meier, Publishers, 1974), p. 130.

57 A. Loshchakov and V. Tsapanov, "Socialist Countries' Ideological Cooperation," *International Affairs* (Moscow), February 1975, p. 31.

58 The March 1977 conference in Tihany, Hungary, focused on preparations for the sixtieth anniversary of the "Great October Socialist Revolution," for example, while the June 1976 session in Moscow had been devoted the role of the mass media with respect to socialist economic integration.

59 It is also worth noting that the news agency chiefs met on 7 December 1981, just one week before the declaration of martial law in Poland, perhaps to coordinate their propaganda efforts in anticipation of widespread international reaction.

60 "The Warsaw Conference of Editors of Party History Periodicals on Tasks in the Struggle against anti-Communism," *Párttörténeti Közlemények*, September 1974 (Hungarian Press Survey no. 2355, *RFER*, January 23, 1975, p. 4).

61 At least two such meetings have been held: on November 16, 1976, and July 3, 1978, both in Moscow, and attended by representatives from all the East European countries except Romania.

62 Radio Moscow, October 31, 1975.

63 *The Soviet Union, 1974–75* (New York: Holmes and Meier, Publishers, 1976), p. 188.

64 In 1975, 1976, 1978, and 1980, respectively, *Problems of Peace and Socialism* conferences were cosponsored by the Czechoslovak Party in Prague, the Hungarian Party in Budapest, the Bulgarian Party in Sofia, and the East German Party in Berlin.

65 See. e.g., Vasil Bilak's rebuttal, in *Rudé Právo*, December 28, 1978.

66 Radio Moscow in Romanian, May 16, 1976.

67 See, e.g., the *Komsomalskaya Pravda* (March 26, 1977) account of the March 1977 conference of Central Committee secretaries responsible for youth organization and the report in *Neues Deutschland* (November 1–2, 1975) of a youth conference arranged by the East German Central Institute for Youth Research.

68 For a partial listing of these contacts, see V. G. Kulikov, ed., *Varshavskii dogovor: soyuz vo imya mira i sotsializma* (Moscow: Voenizdat, 1980), pp. 272–92. See also Col. V. Senin, "A School of Internationalism," *Krasnaya zvezda*, April 11, 1975.

69 These contacts include regular meetings at all levels, as well as collaborative efforts such as joint theoretical conferences and theoretical textbooks jointly published by Soviet and East European higher Party schools. See Loshchakov and Tsapanov, "Socialist Countries' Ideological Cooperation," pp. 30–31.

70 Solodukhin, "Ideological Cooperation," p. 79.

71 "Urgent Problems of the Social Sciences," *Kommunist*, no. 5, (1975), pp. 28–39.

72 Árpád Pullai, "The Eleventh Congress of the Hungarian Socialist Workers' Party," *Kommunist*, no. 11. (1975), pp. 83–91.

73 K. Katushev, "Ukreplenie edinstva sotsialisticheskikh stran: zakonomernost' razvitiia mirovogo sotsializma," *Kommunist*, no. 16 (1973), p. 27.
      See also Teresa Rakowska-Harmstone, " 'Socialist Internationalism' and Eastern Europe: A New Stage," *Survey* 22, no. 1 (Winter 1976): 50.

74 A. Arnoldov, *On the Path of Cultural Progress* (Moscow: Progress Publishers, 1974), pp. 128–29.

75 A. Arnoldov, *Culture and the Contemporary World: The Dialectics of the Cultural Consolidation of the Socialist Countries* (Moscow: Mysl Publishers, 1973), p. 69.

76 Arnoldov, *On the Path of Cultural Progress*, p. 137; Y. Kashlev, "Cultural Cooperation for Mutual Understanding and Détente," *International Affairs*, July 1977, p. 87.

77 For reports on some of these gatherings, see BTA (Sofia), September 28, 1975; PAP (Warsaw), October 12, 1975; Agerpress (Bucharest), October 18, 1979.

78 Arnoldov, *On the Path of Cultural Progress*, p. 137; idem, *Sotsialisticheskii obraz zhizni i kul'tura* (Moscow: Mysl Publishers, 1976), p. 133.

79 Arnoldov, *Sotsialisticheskii obraz zhizni*, p. 128.

80 N. Lunkov, "Soviet Union's Cultural Ties," *International Affairs*, September 1971, p. 37.

81 Ibid., p. 38.

82 Address to the Sixth General Conference of the International Association of Universities, *Izvestia*, August 22, 1975.

83 Arnoldov, *Sotsialisticheskii obraz zhizni*, p. 132.

84 Kashlev, "Cultural Cooperation," p. 87; Katushev, "Ukreplenie edinstva," pp. 26–27.

85 Radio Moscow in Romanian, March 20, 1976.

86 Arnoldov, *Sotsialisticheskii obraz zhizni*, p. 127.

87 D. I. Prokhorov, "Stanovlenie sotsialisticheskoi integratsii v sfere sporta," *Teoria i praktika fizicheskoi kul'tury*, September 1974, p. 4, and A. O. Romanov, *Mezhdunarodnoe sportivnoe dvizhenie* (Moscow, 1973), p. 177, as cited in James Riordan, "Soviet Sport and Soviet Foreign Policy," *Soviet Studies* 26, no. 3 (July 1974): 337.

88 *Sport v SSSR*, no. 9 (1972), p. 2, as cited in Riordan, "Soviet Sport," p. 338.

89 "Russianization" is the process of imposing Russian culture, tradition, and language on non-Russian peoples, while "Russification" refers to the more ambitious process of creating non-Russian cadres who think, feel, and act Russian.

90 A. K. Azizian, *Leninskaia natsional'naia politika v razvitii i deistvii* (Moscow, 1972), p. 363 (cited by Rakowska-Harmstone, " 'Socialist Internationalism,' " p. 50, n. 40).

91 M. S. Junusov, M. M. Skibitsky, and I. P. Tsameryan, eds., *The Theory and Practice of Proletarian Internationalism* (Moscow: Progress Publishers, 1976), esp. pp. 247–50. See also *Leninism and the Nationality Question in Present-Day Conditions* (Moscow: Politizdat, 1972).

92 E. Troitsky, "A New Study on the Nationality Question," *International Affairs*, January 1973, p. 92.

93 *Programme of the Communist Party of the Soviet Union*, (Moscow, 1961), p. 23.

94 For more on this doctrine, and the East European reactions to it, see Rakowska-Harmstone, " 'Socialist Internationalism,' " esp. pp. 38–45 and 51–54.

95 B. Kozin, "The Drawing Together of the Socialist Countries: An Objective Regularity," *International Affairs* (Moscow), October 1976, p. 15.

96 L. I. Brezhnev, *Report of the CPSU Central Committee, XXV Congress of the CPSU* (Moscow: Novosti Press Agency Publishing House, 1976), p. 9.

97 Robert C. Tucker, "The Deradicalization of Marxist Movements," *American Political Science Review*, no. 61 (June 1967), p. 358.

98 This new orientation was affirmed to varying degrees at the Soviet and East European Party congresses, as described in Chapter 4, above.

Selected Bibliography

WESTERN SOURCES

Alliance Theory and Regional Integration

Boulding, Kenneth. *Conflict and Defense: A General Theory*. New York: Harper & Row, 1962.

Cantori, Louis J., and Spiegel, Steven L. *The International Politics of Regions*. Englewood Cliffs, N.J.: Prentice Hall, 1970.

Clark, Cal. "Foreign Trade as an Indicator of Political Integration in the Soviet Bloc." *International Studies Quarterly* 15 (1971): 259–96.

Darnall, Joe Barton. "The Council of Mutual Economic Assistance as an Instrument of Transformation in the East European Communist Subsystem." Ph.D. dissertation, University of Kentucky, 1971.

Deutsch, Karl W., et al. *Political Community in the North Atlantic Area*. Princeton: Princeton University Press, 1957.

Dinerstein, Herbert S. "The Future of Ideology in Alliance Systems." *Journal of International Affairs* 25, no.2 (1971): 238–65.

Dinerstein, Herbert S. "The Transformation of Alliance Systems." *American Political Science Review* 59 (September 1965): 589–601.

Etzioni, Amitai. *Political Unification*. New York: Holt, Rinehart and Winston, 1965.

Feld, Werner. "National-International Linkage Theory: The East European Communist System and the EEC." *Journal of International Studies* 22 (1968): 107–20.

Feld, Werner. "The Utility of the EEC Experience for Eastern Europe." *Journal of Common Market Studies* 8 (1970): 236–61.

Gehlen, Michael P. "The Integrative Process in East Europe: A Theoretical Framework." *Journal of Politics* 30 (1968): 90–113.

Goldman, Kjell. "East-West Tension in Europe, 1946–1970: A Conception Analysis and a Quantitative Description." *World Politics* 23 (October 1973): 106–25.

Gray, Richard B., ed. *International Security Systems*. Itasca, Ill.: F. E. Peacock Publishers, 1969.

Groom, A.J.R. "The Functionalist Approach and East/West Cooperation in Europe." *Journal of Common Market Studies* 13, nos. 1–2 (1975): 21–60.

Haas, Ernst B. *Beyond the Nation-State*. Stanford, Calif.: Stanford University Press, 1964.

Haas, Ernst B. "The Challenge of Regionalism." *International Organization* 12 (Autumn 1958): 440–58.

Haas, Michael. *International Systems*. New York: Chandler Publishing Co., 1974.

Harle, V. "Actional Distances between the Socialist Countries in the 1960's." *Cooperation and Conflict* 6, nos. 3–4 (1971): 201–22.

Holsti, Ole R.; Hopmann, P. Terrence; and Sullivan, John D. *Unity and Disintegration in International Alliances: Comparative Studies*. New York: John Wiley and Sons, 1973.

Hopmann, P. Terrence. "The Effects of International Conflict and Détente on Cohesion in the Communist System." In *The Behavioral Revolution and Communist Studies*, edited by Roger E. Kanet, pp. 301–38. New York: Free Press, 1971.

Hughes, B., and Volgy, T. "Distance in Foreign Policy Behavior: A Comparative Study of Eastern Europe." *Midwest Journal of Political Science* 14, no. 3 (August 1970): 459–92.

Huntington, Samuel J. "The Change to Change: Modernization, Development, and Politics." *Comparative Politics* 3 (April 1971): 283–322.

International Political Communities: An Anthology. Garden City, N.Y.: Anchor Books, 1966.

Ionescu, Ghita. *The New Politics of European Integration*. London: Macmillan & Co., 1972.

Jacob, Philip E., and Toscano, James V., eds. *The Integration of Political Communities*. Philadelphia: J. B. Lippincott Co., 1964.

Kaiser, Karl. "The Interaction of Regional Subsystems: Some Preliminary Notes on Recurrent Patterns and the Role of the Superpowers." *World Politics* 21 (1968): 84–107.

Kanet, Roger E. "Integration Theory and the Study of Eastern Europe." *International Studies Quarterly* 28, no. 3 (September 1974): 368–92.

Kaplan, Morton A. *System and Process in International Politics*. New York: John Wiley and Sons, 1957.

Knorr, Klaus, and Verba, Sidney, eds. *The International System*. Princeton: Princeton University Press, 1961.

Korbonski, Andrzej. "Theory and Practice of Regional Integration: The Case of Comecon." In *Regional Integration: Theory and Practice*, edited by L. N. Lindberg and S. A. Scheingold, pp. 338–73. Cambridge: Harvard University Press, 1970.

Lindberg, Leon N. *The Political Dynamics of European Economic Integration*. Stanford, Calif.: Stanford University Press, 1963.

Lindberg, L. N., and Scheingold, S. A., eds. *Regional Integration: Theory and Practice*. Cambridge: Harvard University Press, 1970.

Liska, George. *Nations in Alliance*. Baltimore: Johns Hopkins Press, 1962.

Mansbach, R. W. "Bilateralism and Multilateralism in the Soviet Bloc." *International Organization* 24, no. 2 (1970): 371–80.

Marer, Paul. "The Political Economy of Soviet Relations with Eastern Europe." In *Testing Theories of Economic Imperialism*, edited by Steven J. Rosen and James R. Kurth, pp. 231–60. Lexington, Mass.: Lexington Books, 1974.

Masters, Roger D. "A Multi-Bloc Model of the International System." *American Political Science Review* 55, no. 4 (December 1961): 780–98.

Mitrany, David. "The Functional Approach to World Organization." *International Affairs* 24 (July 1948): 350–63.

Modelski, George. "Communism and the Globalization of Politics." *International Studies Quarterly* 12 (1968): 380–93.

Modelski, George. *The Communist International System*. Princeton: Princeton University Press, 1961.

Robinson, Thomas W. "Systems Theory and the Communist System." *International Studies Quarterly* 13 (1969): 398–420.

Rosenau, James N. *Linkage Politics: Essays on the Convergence of National and International Systems*. New York: Free Press, 1969.

Russett, Bruce M. *International Relations and the International System*. Chicago: Rand McNally and Co., 1967.

Shoup, Paul. "Eastern Europe and the Soviet Union: Convergence and Divergence in Historical Perspective." In *Soviet Politics and Society in the 1970s*, edited by Henry W. Morton and Rudolph L. Tokes, pp. 340–68. New York: Free Press, 1974.

Welsh, William A. "Regional Integration in Eastern Europe: Toward a Propositional Inventory." *Journal of International Affairs* 26, no. 4 (October 1974): 242–49.

Zimmerman, William. "The Transformation of the Modern Multistate System: The Exhaustion of Communist Alternatives." *Journal of Conflict Resolution* 16 (September 1972): 303–17.

Soviet–East European Relations: General

Aspaturian, Vernon V. "Has Eastern Europe Become a Liability to the Soviet Union? (I) The Political-Ideological Aspects." In *The International Politics of Eastern Europe*, edited by Charles Gati, pp. 17–36. New York: Praeger Publishers, 1976.

Aspaturian, Vernon V. *The Soviet Union and the International Communist System*. Stanford, Calif.: Hoover Institution Press, 1966.

August 1980: The Strikes in Poland. Munich: Radio Free Europe Research, 1980.

Bender, Peter. *East Europe in Search of Security*. Baltimore: Johns Hopkins University Press, 1972.

Bornstein, Morris; Gitelman, Zvi; and Zimmerman, William, eds. *East-West Relations and the Future of Eastern Europe*. London: George Allen and Unwin, 1981.

Bromke, Adam, and Rakowska-Harmstone, Teresa, eds. *The Communist States in Disarray, 1965–1971*. Minneapolis: University of Minnesota Press, 1972.

Brown, J. F. "Détente and Soviet Policy in Eastern Europe." *Survey* 20 (Spring/Summer 1974): 46–58.

Brown, J. F. *Relations between the Soviet Union and Its Eastern European Allies: A Survey*. Rand Corporation Memorandum R–1742–PR. Santa Monica, Calif., November, 1975.

Brzezinski, Zbigniew K. "Communist State Relations: The Effect on Ideology." *East Europe* 16, no. 3 (1967): 2–7.

Brzezinski, Zbigniew K. *The Soviet Bloc: Unity and Conflict*. Rev. ed. Cambridge: Harvard University Press, 1967.

Brzezinski, Zbigniew K., et al. *The Atlantic Community and Eastern Europe: Perspectives and Policy*. New York: Dunnellen Co., 1970.

Burks, R. V. "The Decline of Communism in Czechoslovakia." *Studies in Comparative Communism* 2, no. 1 (January 1969): 21–49.

Byrnes, Robert F. "Russia in Eastern Europe: Hegemony without Security." *Foreign Affairs* 49 (1971): 682–97.

Caldwell, Lawrence J., and Miller, Steven E. "East European Integration and European Politics." *International Journal* 32, no. 2 (Spring 1977): 352–85.

Conference on Security and Cooperation in Europe: Final Act. London: Her Majesty's Printing Office, 1975.

Czerwinski, E. J., and Piekalkiewicz, Jaroslaw. *The Soviet Invasion of Czechoslovakia: Its Effects on Eastern Europe*. New York: Praeger Publishers, 1972.

Dawisha, Karen, and Hanson, Philip, eds. *Soviet–East European Dilemmas: Coercion, Competition, and Consent*. London: Royal Institute of International Affairs, 1981.

Devlin, Kevin. "The Challenge of Eurocommunism." *Problems of Communism*, January–February 1977, pp. 1–20.

Devlin, Kevin. "The Inter-Party Drama." *Problems of Communism*, July–August 1975, pp. 18–34.

Devlin, Kevin. "Interparty Relations: The Limits of 'Normalization.' " *Problems of Communism*, July–August 1971, pp. 22–35.

Djilas, Milovan. *Conversations with Stalin*. New York: Harcourt, Brace, and World, 1962.

Eidlin, Fred H. *The Logic of "Normalization."* New York: Columbia University Press, 1980.

Ermarth, Fritz W. *Internationalism, Security, and Legitimacy: The Challenge to Soviet Interests in East Europe, 1964–1968*. Rand Corporation Memorandum Rm–5909–PR. Santa Monica, Calif., March 1969.

Farlow, Robert L. "Romanian Foreign Policy: A Case of Partial Alignment." *Problems of Communism*, November–December 1971, pp. 54–63.

Gati, Charles, ed. *The International Politics of Eastern Europe*. New York: Praeger Publishers, 1976.

Ginsburgs, George. "The Constitutional Foundations of the 'Socialist Commonwealth': Some Theoretical and Organizational Principles." *Yearbook of World Affairs* 27 (1973): 173–210.

Golan, Galia. *The Czechoslovak Reform Movement: Communism in Crisis, 1962–1968*. Cambridge: Cambridge University Press, 1971.

Griffith, William E. "The Soviet Counter-Revolution in Czechoslovakia in 1968: Causes, Course, and Aftermath." *Studies on the Soviet Union* 11 (1971): 559–72.

Griffith, William E., ed. *The Soviet Empire: Expansion and Détente*. Lexington, Mass.: Lexington Books, 1976.

Grzybowski, Kazimierz. *The Socialist Commonwealth of Nations: Organizations and Institutions*. New Haven: Yale University Press, 1964.

Hejzlar, Z., and Kusin, V., comps. *Czechoslovakia 1968–1969.* New York: Garland Publishing Co., 1975.

Hodnett, Grey, and Potichnyj, Peter J. *The Ukraine and the Czechoslovak Crisis.* Canberra, 1970.

Jacobs, Dan N., ed. *The New Communisms.* New York: Harper & Row, 1969.

Jamgotch, Nish, Jr. "Alliance Management in Eastern Europe." *World Politics* 27 (April 1975): 405–29.

Jamgotch, Nish, Jr. *Soviet–East European Dialogue: International Relations of a New Type?* Stanford, Calif.: Stanford University Press, 1968.

Johnson, A. Ross. *The Polish Riots and Gomulka's Fall.* Rand Corporation Memorandum F–4615. Santa Monica, Calif., April 1971.

Jones, C. D. "Autonomy and Intervention: The CPSU and the Struggle for the Czechoslovak Communist Party, 1968." *Orbis* 19, no. 2 (Summer 1975): 591–625.

Journalist M [Josef Maxa]. *A Year Is Eight Months.* Garden City, N.Y.: Doubleday and Co., 1971.

Jowitt, Kenneth. "Political Innovation in Rumania." *Survey* 20, no. 4 (Autumn 1974): 132–51.

Jowitt, Kenneth. "The Romanian Communist Party and the World Socialist System." *World Politics* 23 (1970): 38–60.

King, Robert R., and Dean, Robert W., eds. *East European Perspectives on European Security and Cooperation.* New York: Praeger Publishers, 1974.

Kintner, William R., and Klaiber, Wolfgang. *Eastern Europe and European Security.* New York: Dunnellen Publishing Co., 1971.

Kobal, Daniel Andrew. "COMECON and the Warsaw Treaty Organization: Their Political Role since 1953." Ph.D. dissertation, American University, 1974.

Korbel, Josef. *Détente in Europe.* Princeton: Princeton University Press, 1972.

Kusin, Vladimir V. *From Dubček to Charter 77.* New York: St. Martin's Press, 1978.

Kusin, Vladimir V. "Husak's Czechoslovakia and Economic Stagnation." *Problems of Communism*, May–June 1982, pp. 24–37.

LaPenna, I. "The Soviet Concept of 'Socialist' International Law." *Yearbook of World Affairs* 29 (1975): 242–64.

Lendvai, Paul. *Eagles in Cobwebs: Nationalism and Communism in the Balkans.* New York: Doubleday and Co., 1969.

London, Kurt, ed. *Eastern Europe in Transition.* Baltimore: Johns Hopkins Press, 1966.

Lowenthal, Richard. "The Sparrow in the Cage." *Problems of Communism*, November–December 1968, pp. 2–28.

McNeal, Robert H., ed., *International Relations among Communists.* Englewood Cliffs, N.J.: Prentice-Hall Publishing Co., 1967.

Marantz, P. "Prelude to Détente: Doctrinal Change under Khrushchev." *International Studies Quarterly* 19, no. 4 (December 1975): 501–28.

Meissner, Boris. *The Brezhnev Doctrine.* East European Monographs/2. Kansas City, Mo.: Governmental Research Bureau, 1970.

Meissner, Boris. "The Soviet Union's Bilateral Pact System in Eastern Europe." In *Eastern Europe in Transition*, edited by Kurt London, pp. 237–57. Baltimore: Johns Hopkins Press, 1966.

Mensonides, Louis J., and Kuhlman, James A., eds. *The Future of Inter-Bloc Relations in Europe*. New York: Praeger Publishers, 1974.

Mićunović, Veljko. *Moscow Diary*. New York: Doubleday and Co., 1980.

Mitchell, R. W. "The Brezhnev Doctrine and Communist Ideology." *Review of Politics* 34 (April 1972): 190–209.

Mlynár, Zdenek. *Nightfrost in Prague: The End of Humane Socialism*. London: C. Hurst and Co., 1980.

Nagy, Imre. *On Communism*. New York: Praeger Publishers, 1967.

Oren, Nissan. *Revolution Administered: Agrarianism and Communism in Bulgaria*. Baltimore: Johns Hopkins University Press, 1973.

Paul, David W. "Soviet Foreign Policy and the Invasions of Czechoslovakia: A Theory and a Case Study." *International Studies Quarterly* 15 (1971): 159–202.

Pipes, Richard, ed. *Soviet Strategy in Europe*. New York: Crane Russak and Co., 1976.

The Pope in Poland. Munich: Radio Free Europe Research, 1979.

Povolny, Mojmir. "The Soviet Union and the European Security Conference." *Orbis* 18 (Spring 1974): 201–30.

Prybyla, Jan S., ed. *Communism at the Crossroads*. University Park, Pa.: Pennsylvania State University Press, 1968.

Radványi, János. *Hungary and the Superpowers*. Stanford, Calif.: Hoover Institution Press, 1972.

Rakowska-Harmstone, Teresa. " 'Socialist Internationalism' and Eastern Europe: A New Stage." *Survey* 22, no. 1 (Winter 1976): 38–54.

Remington, Robin Alison. "Czechoslovakia and the Warsaw Pact." *East European Quarterly* 3 (1970): 315–36.

Remington, Robin Alison, ed. *Winter in Prague: Documents on Czechoslovak Communism in Crisis*. Cambridge, Mass.: MIT Press, 1969.

Robinson, William F. *The Patterns of Reform in Hungary: A Political, Economic, and Cultural Analysis*. New York: Praeger Special Studies Series, 1973.

Seliger, Kurt. "Breschnews Zwiegespräche am Schwarzen Meer." *Osteuropa*, no. 7 (1980).

Šik, Ota. "Prague's Spring—Roots and Reasons: The Economic Impact of Stalinism." *Problems of Communism*, May–June 1971, pp. 1–10.

Simon, Jeffrey, ed. *Ruling Communist Parties and Détente: A Documentary History*. Washington: American Enterprise Institute, 1975.

Skilling, H. Gordon. *Czechoslovakia's Interrupted Revolution*. Princeton: Princeton University Press, 1976.

Skilling, H. Gordon. "Reform Aborted: Czechoslovakia in Retrospect." *International Journal* 28, no. 3 (Summer 1973): 431–45.

Slusser, Robert M., and Triska, Jan F., eds. *A Calendar of Soviet Treaties, 1917–1957*. Stanford, Calif.: Stanford University Press, 1959.

Stankovic, Slobodan. *The End of the Tito Era: Yugoslavia's Dilemmas*. Stanford, Calif.: Hoover Institution Press, 1981.

Svitak, I. *The Czechoslovak Experiment of 1968–1969*. New York: Columbia University Press, 1971.

Szulc, Tad. *Czechoslovakia since World War II*. New York: Viking Press, 1971.

Taborsky, Edward. "Czechoslovakia: Return to 'Normalcy.' " *Problems of Communism*, November–December 1970, pp. 31–41.

Tigrid, Pavel. *Why Dubček Fell*. London: MacDonald and Co., 1971.

Timmermann, Heinz. *Die Konferenz der europäischen Kommunisten in Ost-Berlin: Ergebnisse und Perspektiven*. Berichte des Bundesinstituts für ostwissenschaftliche und internationale Studien, no. 28. Cologne, 1976.

Toma, Peter A., ed. *The Changing Face of Communism in Eastern Europe*. Tucson: University of Arizona Press, 1970.

Triska, Jan F., ed. *Communist Party-States: Comparative and International Studies*. Indianapolis: Bobbs-Merrill, 1969.

Triska, Jan F., series editor. *Integration and Community Building in Eastern Europe*. Baltimore: Johns Hopkins Press, various years.

Tucker, Robert C. "The Deradicalization of Marxist Movements." *American Political Science Review* 61 (June 1967): 343–58.

Ulam, Adam B. "The Destiny of Eastern Europe." *Problems of Communism*, January–February 1974, pp. 1–12.

U.S. Senate, Committee on the Judiciary. *World Communism, 1967–69: Soviet Efforts to Re-establish Control*. Washington, D.C.: Government Printing Office, 1970.

Valenta, Jiří. "Eurocommunism and Eastern Europe." *Problems of Communism*, March–April 1978, pp. 41–54.

Valenta, Jiří. *Soviet Intervention in Czechoslovakia, 1968: Anatomy of a Decision*. Baltimore: Johns Hopkins University Press, 1979.

Weit, Erwin. *At the Red Summit: Interpreter behind the Iron Curtain*. London: Macmillan & Co., 1973.

Weydenthal, Jan B. de. *Poland: Communism Adrift*. Washington Papers, no. 72. Beverly Hills and London: Sage Publications, 1979.

Weydenthal, Jan B. de. "Workers and Party in Poland." *Problems of Communism*, November–December 1980, pp. 1–22.

Whetten, Lawrence L. *Germany's Ostpolitik: Relations between the Federal Republic and the Warsaw Pact Countries*. New York: Oxford University Press, 1971.

Wolfe, Thomas W. *Soviet Power and Europe, 1945–1970*. Baltimore: Johns Hopkins Press, 1970.

Zartmann, I. William. *Czechoslovakia: Intervention and Impact*. New York: New York University Press, 1970.

Zimmerman, Hartmut. "The GDR in the 1970s." *Problems of Communism*, March–April 1978, pp. 1–40.

Soviet–East European Economic Relations

Brabant, Josef M. P. van. *Bilateralism and Structural Bilateralism in Intra-CMEA Trade*. Rotterdam: Rotterdam University Press, 1973.

Brabant, Josef M. P. van. *Essays on Planning, Trade, and Integration in Eastern Europe*. Rotterdam: Rotterdam University Press, 1974.

Brzeski, Andrzej. "Nationalism and the COMECON: A Reconsideration." *Canadian Review of Studies in Nationalism* 1, no. 2 (Spring 1974): 191–201.

Fallenbuchl, Z. M. "COMECON Integration." *Problems of Communism*, March–April 1973, pp. 25–39.

Freedman, Robert D. "The Soviet Union's Utilization of Economic Pressure as an Instrument of Its Foreign Policy toward Other Communist Nations." Ph.D. dissertation, Columbia University, 1969.

Hannigan, John, and McMillan, Carl. "Joint Investment in Resource Development: Sectoral Approaches to Socialist Integration." In U.S. Congress, Joint Economic Committee, *East European Economic Assessment*, part 2, pp. 259–95. Washington, D.C.: Government Printing Office, 1981.

Hewett, Edward A. "Recent Developments in East-West European Economic Relations and Their Implications for U.S.–East European Economic Relations." In U.S. Congress, Joint Economic Committee, *East European Economies Post-Helsinki*, pp. 174–98. Washington, D.C.: Government Printing Office, 1977.

Kaser, Michael. "COMECON and the New Multilateralism." *World Today* 20, no. 4 (April 1972): 162–69.

Kaser, Michael. *COMECON: Integration Problems of the Planned Economies*. London: Oxford University Press, 1965.

Kohn, Martin J., and Lang, Nicholas R. "The Intra-CEMA Foreign Trade System: Major Price Changes, Little Reform." In U.S. Congress, Joint Economic Committee, *East European Economies Post-Helsinki*, pp. 135–51. Washington, D.C.: Government Printing Office, 1977.

Korbonski, Andrzej. "Détente, East-West Trade, and the Future of Economic Integration in Eastern Europe." *World Politics* 28, no. 4 (July 1976): 568–89.

Korbonski, Andrzej. "The Evolution of COMECON." In *International Political Communities*. Garden City, N.Y.: Anchor Books, 1966.

Korbonski, Andrzej. "Theory and Practice of Regional Integration: The Case of COMECON." *International Organization* 14 (1970): 942–77.

Marer, Paul. "Economic Performance and Prospects in Eastern Europe." In U.S. Congress, Joint Economic Committee, *East European Economic Assessment*, part 2, pp. 19–95. Washington, D.C.: Government Printing Office, 1981.

Marer, Paul. "Has Eastern Europe Become a Liability to the Soviet Union? (III) The Economic Aspect." In *The International Politics of Eastern Europe*, edited by Charles Gati, pp. 59–81. New York: Praeger Publishers, 1976.

Marer, Paul. *Soviet and East European Foreign Trade, 1946–1969: Statistical Compendium and Guide*. Bloomington: Indiana University Press, 1972.

Marer, Paul, and Montias, John Michael. "Theory and Measurement of East European Integration." In *East European Integration and East-West Trade*, edited by Paul Marer and John Michael Montias, pp. 3–38. Bloomington: Indiana University Press, 1980.

Marer, Paul, and Montias, John Michael, eds. *East European Integration and East-West Trade*. Bloomington: Indiana University Press, 1980.

Marsh, Peter. "The Integration Process in Eastern Europe, 1968 to 1975." *Journal of Common Market Studies* 14, no. 4 (June 1976): 311–35.

Mellor, R. E. H. *COMECON: Challenge to the West*. New York: Van Nostrand, 1971.

Montias, J. M. "Obstacles to the Economic Integration of Eastern Europe." *Studies in Comparative Communism* 2, nos. 3–4 (July/October 1969): 38–60.

Nagorski, Zygmunt, Jr. *The Psychology of East-West Trade.* New York: Mason and Lipscomb Publishers, 1974.

Schaefer, Henry W. *Comecon and the Politics of Integration.* New York: Praeger Publishers, 1972.

Sirc, Ljubo. *Economic Devolution in Eastern Europe.* New York: Praeger Publishers, 1969.

Smith, Arthur J. "The Council for Mutual Economic Assistance in 1977: New Economic Power, New Political Perspectives, and Some Old and New Problems." In U.S. Congress, Joint Economic Committee, *East European Economies Post-Helsinki*, pp. 152–73. Washington, D.C.: Government Printing Office, 1977.

Szalowski, R. "The International Economic Organizations of the Communist Countries." *Canadian Slavonic Papers* 10, no. 3 (1968): 254–77; 11, no. 1 (1969): 82–107.

Thalheim, Karl C., and Höhmann, Hans-Hermann, eds. *Wirtschaftsreformen in Osteuropa.* Cologne: Verlag Wissenschaft und Politik, 1968.

U.S. Congress, Joint Economic Committee. *East European Economic Assessment.* Washington, D.C.: Government Printing Office, 1981.

U.S. Congress, Joint Economic Committee. *East European Economies Post-Helsinki.* Washington, D.C.: Government Printing Office, 1977.

U.S. Congress, Joint Economic Committee. *Reorientation and Commercial Relations of the Economies of Eastern Europe.* Washington, D.C.: Government Printing Office, 1974.

U.S. Congress, Joint Economic Committee. *Soviet Economy in A New Perspective.* Washington, D.C.: Government Printing Office, 1976.

Wasowski, S. "Economic Integration in the Comecon." *Orbis* 16, no. 3 (1972): 760–79.

Wilczynski, J. *Technology in Comecon.* New York: Praeger Publishers, 1974.

Soviet–East European Military Relations

Baritz, Joseph J. "The Warsaw Pact and the Kremlin's European Strategy." *Bulletin, Institute for the Study of the USSR* 17, no. 5 (1970): 15–28.

Bender, Peter. "Inside the Warsaw Pact." *Survey* 74–75 (1970): 254–69.

Boll, Michael. "The Dilemma of the Warsaw Pact." *Military Review* 49, no. 7 (1969): 89–98.

Braun, Aurel. "The Evolution of the Warsaw Pact." *Canadian Defence Quarterly* 3, no. 4 (Winter 1974): 27–36.

Caldwell, Lawrence J. "The Warsaw Pact: Directions of Change." *Problems of Communism*, September–October 1975, pp. 1–19.

Clemens, Walter C. "The Future of the Warsaw Pact." *Orbis* 11 (1968): 996–1033.

Erickson, John. "Soviet Military Posture and Policy in Europe." In *Soviet Strategy in Europe*, edited by Richard Pipes, pp. 169–209. New York: Crane Russak and Co., 1976.

Erickson, John. *Soviet Military Power.* London: Royal United Services Institute for Defence Studies, 1971.

Erickson, John. "The Warsaw Pact." In *The Soviet War Machine*, pp. 232–41. London: Hamlyn Publishing Group, 1976.

Erickson, John. "The Warsaw Pact: The Shape of Things to Come?" In *Soviet–East European Dilemmas: Coercion, Competition, and Consent*, edited by Karen Dawisha and Philip Hanson, pp. 148–71. London: Royal Institute of International Affairs, 1981.

Forster, Thomas M. *The East German Army*. London: George Allen and Unwin, 1980.

Gallant, George W., Jr. "Limited Sovereignty: The Political Doctrine of the Warsaw Treaty Organization." Ph.D. dissertation, Fordham University, 1971.

Gartoff, Raymond L. "The Military Establishment." *East Europe* 14, no. 9 (September 1965): 2–16.

Herspring, Dale. "The Warsaw Pact at Twenty-five." *Problems of Communism*, September–October 1980, pp. 1–15.

Johnson, A. Ross. "Has Eastern Europe Become a Liability to the Soviet Union? (II) The Military Aspect." In *The International Politics of Eastern Europe*, edited by Charles Gati, pp. 37–58. New York: Praeger Publishers, 1976.

Johnson, A. Ross. *Soviet–East European Military Relations: An Overview*. Rand Corporation Memorandum P–5383–1. Santa Monica, Calif., August 1977.

Johnson, A. Ross; Dean, Robert W.; and Alexiev, Alexander. *East European Military Establishments: The Warsaw Pact Northern Tier*. Rand Corporation Memorandum R–2417/1–AF/FF. Santa Monica, Calif., December 1980.

Jones, Christopher D. *Soviet Influence in Eastern Europe: Political Autonomy and the Warsaw Pact*. New York: Praeger Special Studies, 1981.

Kiraly, Bela K. "Why the Soviets Need the Warsaw Pact." *East Europe* 18, no. 4 (1969): 8–18.

Kolkowicz, Roman. "The Warsaw Pact: Entangling Alliance." *Survey* 70/71 (1969): 86–101.

Kolkowicz, Roman, ed. *The Warsaw Pact: Report on a Conference on the Warsaw Treaty Organization, Held at the Institute for Defense Analysis, May 17–19, 1967*. Research Paper P–496. Arlington, Virginia: Institute for Defense Analysis, International and Social Studies Division, 1969.

Korbonski, Andrzej. "The Warsaw Pact." *International Conciliation*, no. 573 (May 1969).

Krannals, H. V. "Command Integration within the Warsaw Pact." *Military Review* 41 (May 1961): 40–52.

Mackintosh, Malcolm. *The Evolution of the Warsaw Pact*. Adelphi Papers no. 58, International Institute for Strategic Studies. London, 1969.

Mackintosh, Malcolm. "The Warsaw Pact Today." *Survival*, May–June 1974, pp. 122–26.

The Military Balance. London: International Institute for Strategic Studies, published annually.

Rattinger, H. "Arms, Détente, and Bureacracy." *Journal of Conflict Resolution* 19, no. 4 (December 1975): 571–95.

Remington, Robin Alison. *The Warsaw Pact: Case Studies in Communist Conflict Resolution*. Cambridge: MIT Press, 1971.

Remington, Robin Alison. "The Warsaw Pact: Communist Coalition Politics in Action." *Yearbook of World Affairs* 27 (1973): 153–72.

Staar, Harvey. "A Collective Goods Analysis of the Warsaw Pact after Czechoslovakia." *International Organization* 28, no. 3 (Summer 1974): 521–32.

Warsaw Pact, Its Role in Soviet Bloc Affairs. Study Submitted by Subcommittee on National Security and International Operations, pursuant to S. Res. 181, 89th Congress, 1966.

Wiener, Friedrich. *The Armies of the Warsaw Pact Nations*. Translated by William J. Lewis. Vienna: Carl Ueberreuter Publishers, 1976.

Wolfe, Thomas W. *Role of the Warsaw Pact in Soviet Policy*. Rand Corporation Memorandum P–4973. Santa Monica, Calif., March 1973.

Wolfe, Thomas W. "Soviet Military Capabilities and Intentions in Europe." In *Soviet Strategy in Europe*, edited by Richard Pipes, pp. 129–67. New York: Crane Russak and Co., 1976.

SOVIET AND EAST EUROPEAN SOURCES

Alampiev, P.; Bogomolov, O.; and Shiryaev, Y. *A New Approach to Economic Integration*. Moscow: Progress Publishers, 1974.

Appatov, S. J. *Novyi tip mezhdunarodnykh otnoshenii (vneshnepoliticheskaia deiatel' nost' stran sotsializma)* [A new type of international relations (the foreign policy activity of the socialist countries)]. Kiev: Znanie, 1971.

Apro, Antal. "A New Type of Inter-state Economic Relations." *World Marxist Review* 2 (1968): 53–58.

Apro, Antal. *Sotrudnichestvo stran chlenov SEV v ekonomicheskykh organizatsiiakh sotsialisticheskykh stran* [Cooperation of the member countries of CMEA in the economic organization of the socialist countries]. Moscow: Ekonomika, 1969.

Arnoldov, A. *Culture and the Contemporary World: The Dialectics of the Cultural Consolidation of the Socialist Countries*. Moscow: Mysl Publishers, 1973.

Arnoldov, A. *On the Path of Cultural Progress*. Moscow: Progress Publishers, 1974.

Arnoldov, A. *Sotsialisticheskii obraz zhizni i kul' tura*. [Socialist way of life and culture]. Moscow: Mysl Publishers, 1976.

Ausch, Sandor. *Theory and Practice of CMEA Cooperation*. Budapest: Akademiai Kiado, 1972.

Beliaev, Iu. N. *CMEA Countries' Economic Cooperation*. Moscow: Novosti, 1970.

Brezhnev, Leonid I. "Fresh Upsurge of the Communist Movement." *World Marxist Review* 12 (1969): 3–12.

Ceaușescu, Nicolae. *The Leading Role of the Party in the Period of Completing the Building of Socialism*. Bucharest: Meridiane Publishing House, 1967.

Ceaușescu, Nicolae. *The Romanian Communist Party—Continuer of the Romanian People's Revolutionary and Democratic Struggle, of the Traditions of the Working-Class and Socialist Movement in Romania*. Bucharest: Agerpress, 1966.

Ceaușescu, Nicolae. *Romania on the Way of Building Up the Multilaterally Developed Socialist Society*. Bucharest: Meridiane Publishing House, 1970.

Československo-sovětské vztahy 1961–1971 [Czechoslovak-Soviet relations, 1961–1971]. Prague: Svoboda, 1975.

Chocha, Boleslaw. *Obrona Terytorium Kraju* [National territorial defense]. Warsaw: MON, 1974.

Comprehensive Programme for the Further Extension and Improvement of Co-operation and the Development of Socialist Integration by the CMEA Member-Countries. Moscow: Progress Publishers, 1971.

Dokumenty 1969 [Documents, 1969]. Ústí nad Labem: KV, KSČ, 1969.

Dokumenty o Národním shromáždění ve dnech 21–28/8/68 [Documents of the National Assembly in the days 21–28 August 1968]. Prague: NS, 1968.

Dokumenty o okupácii ČSSR [Documents on the occupation of Czechoslovakia]. Bratislava, 1968.

Hlavní úkoly strany v nejbližším období. Rezoluce ze Zasedaní ÚV KSČ 14.–17.11.1968 [Main tasks of the people in the present era. Resolution of the Central Committee of the Communist Party of Czechoslovakia, Session of 14–17 November 1968]. Prague: ÚV KSČ, 1969.

Hoxha, Enver. *The Khrushchevites: Memoirs.* Tirana: "8 Nentori" Publishing House, 1980.

Iakubovskii, I. "Boevoe sodruzhestvo armii stran sotsializma" [The fighting collaboration of the armies of the socialist countries]. *Kommunist* 5 (1970): 90–100.

Iakubovskii, I. *Boevoe sodruzhestvo bratskikh narodov i armii* [Combat solidarity of the fraternal peoples and armies]. Moscow: Voenizdat, 1975.

Ivanov, N. I. *Mezhdunarodnye ekonomicheskie otnosheniia novogo tipa* [International economic relations of a new type]. Moscow: Ekonomika, 1968.

Jägermann, S. *Postavení KSC v socialistické společnosti* [The position of the Communist Party of Czechoslovakia in socialist cooperation]. Prague: Vysoká skola politická ÚV KSC, 1969.

Junusov, M. S.; Skibitsky, M. M.; and Tsameryan, I. P., eds. *The Theory and Practice of Proletarian Internationalism.* Moscow: Politizdat, 1970.

Katushev, K. "Ukreplenie edinstva sotsialisticheskikh stran—zakonomernost' razvitiia mirovogo sotsializma" [Strengthening of the unity of socialist countries—regularity of the development of world socialism]. *Kommunist* 16 (November 1973): 17–31.

K listopadové rezoluci ÚV KSČ o hlavních úkolech strany v nejbližším období [On the November resolution of the Central Committee of the Communist Party of Czechoslovakia on the main tasks of the Party in the present era]. Prague: ÚV KSČ, 1969.

K udólastem v Československu. Fakta, dokumenty, svedectví v tisku i ocitých svedkû [On the events in Czechoslovakia: Facts, documents, evidence in the press and eyewitness testimony]. Prague: ČTK, 1968.

Khrushchev, Nikita S. *Khrushchev Remembers: The Last Testament.* Edited and translated by Strobe Talbott. Boston: Little, Brown and Co., 1974.

Khrushchev, Nikita S. "Vital Questions of the Development of the Socialist World System." *World Marxist Review* 5 (September 1962): 3–19.

Kiss, Tibor. *International Division of Labor in Open Economies.* Budapest: Akademiai Kiado, 1971.

Kiss, Tibor. *Problemy sotsialisticheskoi integratsii stran SEV* [Problems of socialist integration of the countries of CMEA]. Moscow: Ekonomika, 1971.

Kiss, Tibor, ed. *The Market of Socialist Economic Integration: Selected Conference Papers.* Budapest: Akademiai Kiado, 1973.

Kozin, B. "The Drawing Together of Socialist Countries: An Objective Regularity." *International Affairs*, November 1976, pp. 14–21.

Kozin, B. "Socialist Countries: Unity and Cohesion." *International Affairs*, March 1974, pp. 1–11.

Kroeger, Gerbert, and Seidel, Frank. *Freundschaftsverträge: Verträge des Sozialismus.* East Berlin: Staatsverlag der DDR, 1979.

Kulikov, V. G. "A Quarter Century Guarding the Achievements of Socialism and Peace." *Voenno-istoricheskii zhurnal*, no. 5 (May 1980).

Kulikov, V. G., ed. *Varshavskii dogovor—soyuz vo imya mira i sotsializma* [The Warsaw Pact: Alliance in the name of peace and socialism]. Moscow: Voenizdat, 1980.

Kuznetsov, V. I. *Economic Integration: Two Approaches.* Moscow: Progress Publishers, 1976.

Kvĕš, V. *RHVP a ČSSR* [Comecon and Czechoslovakia]. Prague: Svoboda, 1974.

Lavrov, K. "Laws of Development of the Socialist World System." *World Marxist Review* 14 (October 1971): 3–43.

Lebin, D. A. *Nauchno-tekhnicheskaia revoliutsiia i sotsialisticheskaia integratsiia* [The scientific-technical revolution and socialist integration]. Moscow: Nauka, 1973.

Leninské učení o stranĕ a současnost [Lenin's teachings on the Party and present times]. Prague: ÚV KSČ, 1969.

The Multilateral Economic Cooperation of Socialist States: A Collection of Documents. Moscow: Progress Publishers, 1977.

Organizatsiiata na varshavskiia dogovor, 1955–1975 [Organization of the Warsaw Pact, 1955–1975]. Moscow: Politizdat, 1975.

Pashuk, K. "Twenty Years on Guard over Peace and Socialism." *Kommunist vooruzhenyk sil*, no. 9 (April 1975).

Pecka, F. *Aktuálne otázky výstavby a práce strany* [Contemporary questions of construction and work of the Party]. Bratislava: Epocha, 1970.

Polianskii, V. *Proletarian Internationalism: Guideline of the Communists.* Moscow: Novosti, 1970.

Puja, F. *Edinstvo i diskussia v mezhdunarodnom kommunisticheskom dvizhenii* [Unity and debate in the international Communist movement]. Moscow: I.M.O., 1969.

Rohan, R. *O vedoucí úloze strany v politickém systému* [On the leading role of the Party in the political system]. Prague: Svoboda, 1970.

Sanakoev, Sh. P. *Mirovaia sotsialisticheskaia sistema* [The world socialist system]. Moscow: I.M.O., 1968.

Sanakoev, Sh. P. "Proletarian Internationalism: Theory and Practice." *International Affairs*, April 1972, pp. 3–10.

Sanakoev, Sh. P. *Teoriia i praktika sotsialisticheskikh mezhdunarodnykh otnoshenii* [The theory and practice of socialist international relations]. Moscow: Politizdat, 1970.

Sborník dokumentů ke vstupu vojsk státū Varšavské smlouvy do Československa [Volume of the documents on the entry of troops of the states of the Warsaw Pact into Czechoslovakia]. 3 vols. Brno: MeV KSČ, 1968.

Sedm pražských dní: Sborník dokumentů [Seven Prague days: Volume of documents]. Prague: Historický ústav ČSAV, 1968.

Senin, M. V. *Socialist Integration.* Moscow: Progress Publishers, 1973.

Socialist Community: Problems of Development. Moscow: Novosti, 1970.

Socialistické země a události v ČSSR [Socialist countries and the events in Czechoslovakia]. Prague: UMPE, 1968.

Sokolovskii, V. D., ed. *Soviet Military Strategy*. Edited and translated by Harriet Fast Scott. New York: Crane Russak and Co., 1975.

Sotsializm i mezhdunorodnie otnosheniia [Socialism and international relations]. Moscow: Nauka, 1975.

Statisticheskii ezhegodnik stran-chlenov Soveta Ekonomicheskoi Vzaimopomoshchi [Statistical yearbook of the member countries of the Council for Mutual Economic Assistance]. Moscow: Izdatel'stvo sekretariata SEV. Published annually.

Štěpánek, J. "Twenty-five Years of the CMEA." *International Relations* (Prague), 1973, pp. 3–15.

Tůma, V. *Skripta k výkladu problematiky kádrove práce po listopadovém zasedání ÚV KSČ v roce 1968* [Text of the comments on problems of cadre work by the November session of the Central Committee of the Communist Party of Czechoslovakia in the year 1968]. Prague: VŠP ÚV KSČ, 1969.

Tunkin, G. I. "Socialist Internationalism and International Law." *New Times*, October–December 1957, pp. 1–10.

Voenno-morskoi mezhdunarodno-pravovoi spravochnik [Naval international law handbook]. Moscow: Voenizdat, 1967.

Zagladin, V. V., ed. *The World Communist Movement*. Moscow: Progress Publishers, 1973.

Zhivkov, Todor. *Unity on the Basis of Marxism-Leninism: Speeches, Reports, and Articles*. Sofia: Sofia Press, 1969.

Index